Ancient Israel

Ancient Israel

THE OLD TESTAMENT IN ITS SOCIAL CONTEXT

Edited by
PHILIP F. ESLER

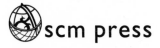
scm press

© The Contributors 2005

British Library Cataloguing in Publication data

A catalogue record for this book is available
from the British Library

0 334 04017 5

First published in 2005 by SCM Press
9–17 St Albans Place, London N1 0NX

www.scm-canterburypress.co.uk

SCM Press is a division of
SCM-Canterbury Press Ltd

Printed and bound in Great Britain by
William Clowes Ltd, Beccles, Suffolk

Contents

Part Three: Texts

Part Four: Hermeneutics

Contributors

Mario I. Aguilar is Reader in Divinity at the University of St. Andrews, Scotland. Together with Louise Lawrence he has edited *Anthropology and Biblical Studies: The Way Forward* (2004).

Marvin L. Chaney is Nathaniel Gray Professor of Hebrew Exegesis and Old Testament at San Francisco Theological Seminary, San Anselmo, and a member of the Core Doctoral Faculty of the Graduate Theological Union, Berkeley, Calif. Other publications by him pertinent to his essay in this volume include "Bitter Bounty: The Dynamics of Political Economy Critiqued by the Eighth-Century Prophets" (1989), "Whose Sour Grapes? The Addressees of Isaiah 5:1-7 in the Light of Political Economy" (1999), and "Accusing Whom of What? Hosea's Rhetoric of Promiscuity" (2004).

Robert B. Coote is Professor of Old Testament at San Francisco Theological Seminary, San Anselmo, and the Graduate Theological Union, Berkeley, California. Among other publications, he is the author of *Early Israel: A New Horizon* (1990) and Commentary and reflections on the book of Joshua in *The New Interpreter's Bible*, vol. II (1998), and he is the editor of *Elijah and Elisha in Socioliterary Perspective* (1992).

Zeba A. Crook is Assistant Professor of Religion at Carleton University, Ottawa, Ontario. He is the author *Reconceptualising Conversion: Patronage, Loyalty, and Conversion in the Religions of the Ancient Mediterranean* (2004) and "Reflections on Culture and Social-Scientific Models: A Critical Note," *Journal of Biblical Literature* (2005).

Richard E. DeMaris is Professor of New Testament at Valparaiso University in Valparaiso, Indiana. He has previously applied ritual theory to Jesus' baptism ("Possession, Good and Bad—Ritual, Effect and Side-Effects: The Baptism of Jesus and Mark 1.9-11 from a Cross-Cultural Perspective" [*Journal for the Study of the New Testament*, 2000]) and to early Christian rites in Roman Corinth ("Funerals and Baptisms, Ordinary and Otherwise: Ritual Criticism and Corinthian Rites" [*Biblical Theology Bulletin*, 1999]).

Adriana Destro is Professor of Cultural Anthropology in the Dipartimento di Studi Linguistici e Orientali in the University of Bologna.
Her publications include *Villaggio Palestinese: Mutamento sociale
in territorio occupato da Israele,* Milano (1977), *L'ultima gene-
razione: Confini materiali e simbolici di una comunità delle Alpi
Maritime* (1984), and *Antropologia e Religioni* (2004).

John H. Elliott is Professor Emeritus, Theology and Religious Studies,
University of San Francisco, San Francisco. He is author of numer-
ous publications, including *A Home for the Homeless: A Social-
Scientific Criticism of I Peter, Its Situation and Strategy* (1981/
1990), *What Is Social-Scientific Criticism?* (1993), and *I Peter: A
New Translation with Introduction and Commentary* (2000).

Philip F. Esler is Chief Executive of the U.K. Arts and Humanities
Research Council, a position he holds during a seven-year leave
from the University of St Andrews, where he is Professor of Biblical
Criticism. Among his recent publications are *Galatians* (1998),
Conflict and Identity in Romans: The Social Setting of Paul's Letter
(2003), *New Testament Theology: Communion and Community*
(2005), and, with Jane Boyd, *Visuality and Biblical Text: Interpreting Velázquez' Christ with Martha and Mary as a Test Case* (2004).
He is also editor of *The Early Christian World,* two volumes (2000).

Lester L. Grabbe is Professor of Hebrew Bible and Early Judaism at the
University of Hull, U.K. His publications include *Priests, Prophets,
Diviners, Sages: A Socio-historical Study of Religious Specialists in
Ancient Israel* (1995), *Judaic Religion in the Second Temple Period:
Belief and Practice from the Exile to Yavneh* (2000), and *A History
of the Jews and Judaism in the Second Temple Period,* vol. 1: *Yehud:
A History of the Persian Province of Judah* (2004).

Anselm C. Hagedorn has been Kennicott-Hebrew Fellow in the Univer-
sity of Oxford and is currently *wissenschaftlicher Assistent* in
Hebrew Bible/Old Testament at the Humboldt-Universität in Berlin.
His most recent work is *Between Moses and Plato: Individual and
Society in Deuteronomy and Ancient Greek Law,* FRLANT 204
(2004).

Jutta Jokiranta is a Researcher at the Department of Biblical Studies,
University of Helsinki, Finland, where she is finishing her doctoral
dissertation on reconstructing positive social identity in the Qumran
Pesharim. She is the author of "'Sectarianism' of the Qumran 'Sect':
Sociological Notes," *RdQ* 78 (2001) 223–239 and "Pesharim: A

Mirror of Self-Understanding," in *Reading the Present: Scriptural Interpretation and the Contemporary*, edited by Kristin de Troyer and Armin Lange (forthcoming).

Carolyn S. Leeb is an Instructor in the Department of Theology, Valparaiso University, Valparaiso, Ind. Recent publications by her include *Away from the Father's House: the Social Location of* Naʿar *and* Naʿarah *in Ancient Israel* (2000) and "The Widow: Homeless and Post-Menopausal," *BTB* (2002).

Bruce J. Malina is professor in the Department of Theology, Creighton University, Omaha; and research associate in the Department of New Testament Studies, University of Pretoria, South Africa. His publications include *The Social World of Jesus and the Gospels* (1996), *The New Testament World: Insights from Cultural Anthropology* (3rd revised edition, 2001), and, with co-author John J. Pilch, *Social Science Commentary on the Book of Revelation* (2000).

A. D. H. Mayes is Erasmus Smith's Professor of Hebrew in Trinity College, Dublin. He is editor and contributor to *Covenant as Context* (2003) and *Text in Context* (2000), and author of *The Old Testament in Sociological Context* (1989) and *The Story of Israel between Settlement and Exile* (1983).

Dietmar Neufeld is Associate Professor of Christian Origins in the Department of Classical, Near Eastern, and Religious Studies in the University of British Columbia. His recent publications include *Reconceiving Texts as Speech Acts: An Analysis of I John* (1994), "Clothing and Ornamentation in the Apocalypse of John," in *The Social World of the New Testament* (edited by Andreas Van Aarde, 2002), and "Christianity in Sardis and Smyrna," in *Religious Rivalries: Struggles for Success in Sardis and Smyrna* (edited by Richard Ascough, 2004/5).

Douglas E. Oakman is Dean of Humanities and Associate Professor of Religion at Pacific Lutheran University, Tacoma, Wash. He has authored *Jesus and the Economic Questions of His Day* (1986) and, with K. C. Hanson, *Palestine in the Time of Jesus: Social Structures and Social Conflicts* (1998). Recent journal articles include "The Radical Jesus: You Cannot Serve God and Mammon," *BTB* (2004), and "The Promise of Lutheran Biblical Studies," *Currents in Theology and Mission* (2004).

Mauro Pesce is Professor of History of Christianity in the Dipartimento di Discipline Storiche University of Bologna. Among his publications are *Le due fasi della predicazione di Paolo* (1994), *Antropologia delle origini cristiane* (in collaboration with A. Destro; third edition, 2004), and *Le parole dimenticate di Gesù* (2004).

John J. Pilch, is Adjunct Assistant Professor, Georgetown University, Washington, D.C.; Research Associate in the Department of New Testament Studies, University of Pretoria, South Africa; and Visiting Professor at the Studium Biblicum Franciscanum, Hong Kong, SAR, China. Among other publications, he is the author of *Visions and Healing in the Acts of the Apostles: How Early Believers Experienced God* (2004), *Healing in the New Testament: Insights from Medical and Mediterranean Anthropology* (2000), and co-author with Bruce J. Malina of *Social Science Commentary on the Book of Revelation* (2000).

Gary Stansell is Professor of Religion in the Department of Religion, St. Olaf College, Northfield, Minn. His recent publications include *Micah and Isaiah: A Form and Tradition Historical Comparison* (1998), "The Gift in Ancient Israel" (*Semeia*, 1999) and "Gifts, Tributes, and Offerings," in *The Social Setting of Jesus and the Gospels* (edited by Wolfgang Stegemann, Bruce J. Malina, and Gerd Theissen, 2002).

Preface

Apart from Chapters 1 and 2, the essays appearing in this volume are edited versions of the papers first presented at the "St Andrews Conference on Old Testament Interpretation and the Social Sciences," held in St Mary's College in the University of St Andrews, St Andrews, Scotland, from June 30 to July 4, 2004.

This conference took place almost exactly ten years after another conference held in St Andrews: "Context and Kerygma: The St Andrews Conference on New Testament Interpretation and the Social Sciences." That 1994 meeting led to the volume *Modelling Early Christianity: Social-Scientific Studies of the New Testament in Its Context* (ed. Philip F. Esler; London: Routledge, 1995) and it seemed appropriate to repeat the exercise in relation to the Old Testament. That we did so on the tenth anniversary of the former conference owes as much to sentiment as anything else. The phrase "Old Testament" was chosen for the title of the conference, rather than (say) "Hebrew Bible," because we were also interested in the Apocrypha (and indeed Qumran texts).

Participants at the 2004 Conference journeyed to St Andrews from the United States, Canada, Ireland, England, Wales, Finland, Germany, and Italy. I acknowledge with thanks financial assistance from the British Academy which facilitated the participation of some of the speakers from outside the U.K.

In both the 1994 and 2004 events many, but by no means all, of the participants were members of the "Context Group: Project for the Study of the Bible in Its Cultural Environment." I have recently published an essay setting out the history, broad intellectual orientation, and working practices of that Group (see references for Chapter 1). Whether members of the Context Group or not, all of the participants at the 2004 conference followed a methodology of the explicit application of social-scientific models or perspectives to the some aspect of the Old Testament. Chapter 1 of this volume contains a brief defense of social-scientific models in biblical interpretation against their cultured despisers.

I am most grateful to my New Testament colleague in St Mary's College, Professor Ronald Piper, currently the Vice-Principal for Teaching in the University of St Andrews, for advice he gave me at various stages during the preparations for the conference. Ms Susan Millar, of the St Mary's College office, looked after many of the administration details and I gratefully acknowledge her assistance.

Philip F. Esler
St Mary's College
St Andrews

Abbreviations

AB	Anchor Bible
ABD	*Anchor Bible Dictionary*
ABRL	Anchor Bible Reference Library
AOAT	Alter Orient und Altes Testament
ASOR	American Schools of Oriental Research
BA	*Biblical Archaeologist*
BASOR	*Bulletin of the American Schools of Oriental Research*
BDB	Brown-Driver-Briggs, *Hebrew and English Lexicon of the Old Testament*
BibInt	*Biblical Interpretation*
BibOr	Biblica et orientalia
BJS	Brown Judaic Studies
BK	*Bibel und Kirche*
BN	*Biblische Notizen*
BS	*Biblical Seminar*
BSOAS	*Bulletin of the School of Oriental and African Studies*
BTB	*Biblical Theology Bulletin*
BZAR	Beihefte zur Zeitschrift für Altorientalische und Biblische Rechtsgeschichte
BZAW	Beihefte zur *ZAW*
CAT	Commentaire de l'Ancien Testament
CBC	The Cambridge Bible Commentary
CBQ	*Catholic Biblical Quarterly*
CC	Continental Commentaries
CSSCA	Cambridge Studies in Social and Cultural Anthropology
CSRCT	Cambridge Studies in Religion and Critical Thought
CSSH	*Comparative Studies in Society and History*
ETL	*Ephemerides Theologicae Lovanienses*
FOTL	The Forms of the Old Testament Literature
FRLANT	Forschungen zur Religion und Literatur des Alten und Neuen Testaments
GKC	*Gesenius' Hebrew Grammar*, ed. E. Kautzsch, trans. A. E. Cowley

HALOT	Ludwig Köhler, *Hebrew and Aramaic Lexicon of the Old Testament*
HAT	Handbuch zum Alten Testament
HCOT	Historical Commentary on the Old Testament
HDR	Harvard Dissertations in Religion
HeyJ	*Heythrop Journal*
HSM	Harvard Semitic Monographs
HSS	Harvard Semitic Studies
HTR	*Harvard Theological Review*
HTS	*Hervormde Teologiese Studies*
HUCA	*Hebrew Union College Annual*
IB	*Interpreter's Bible*
IDB	*International Dictionary of the Bible*
IDBSup	*International Dictionary of the Bible Supplementary Volume*
IEJ	*Israel Exploration Journal*
Int	*Interpretation*
ITC	International Theological Commentary
JAAR	*Journal of the American Academy of Religion*
JAOS	*Journal of the American Oriental Society*
JB	Jerusalem Bible
JBL	*Journal of Biblical Literature*
JBQ	*Jewish Biblical Quarterly*
JJS	*Journal of Jewish Studies*
JPSV	Jewish Publication Society Version
JSJSup	Journal for the Study of Judaism Supplement Series
JSNT	*Journal for the Study of the New Testament*
JSOT	*Journal for the Study of the Old Testament*
JSOTSup	Journal for the Study of the Old Testament Supplement Series
JSS	*Journal of Semitic Studies*
JThSt	*Journal of the Theological Studies, Oxford*
LSJ	H. G. Liddell, Robert Scott, and H. S. Jones, *A Greek-English Lexicon*, 1983
LXX	The Septuagint
MT	Masoretic text of the Hebrew Bible
NCB	New Century Bible
NEB	New English Bible
NICOT	New International Commentary on the Old Testament
NJBC	*New Jerome Biblical Commentary*

NovT	Novum Testamentum
NRSV	New Revised Standard Version
NTS	New Testament Studies
OBT	Overtures to Biblical Theology
OTL	Old Testament Library
PEQ	Palestine Exploration Quarterly
RAC	Reallexikon für Antike und Christentum
RB	Revue biblique
RdQ	Revue de Qumran
RHPR	Revue d'histoire et de philosophie religieuses
RSR	Religious Studies Review
SBLDS	Society of Biblical Literature Dissertation Series
SBLSBS	Society of Biblical Literature Sources for Biblical Study
SBLSS	Society of Biblical Literature Symposium Series
SBS	Stuttgarter Bibelstudien
SJOT	Scandinavian Journal of the Old Testament
SNTSMS	Society for New Testament Studies Monograph Series
STDJ	Studies on the Texts of the Desert of Judah
SWBA	Social World of Biblical Antiquity
Targ	Targums
TDOT	Theological Dictionary of the Old Testament
TEV	Today's English Version
THAT	Theologisches Handwörterbuch zum Alten Testament
TWAT	Theologisches Wörterbuch zum Alten Testament
UF	Ugarit Forschungen
VT	Vetus Testamentum
VTSup	Vetus Testamentum, Supplements
VWGTh	Veröffentlichungen der Wissenschaftlichen Gesellschaft für Theologie
WBC	Word Bible Commentary
YES	Yale Egyptological Studies
ZAW	Zeitschrift für die alttestamentliche Wissenschaft
ZDPV	Zeitschrift des deutschen Palästina-Vereins

PART ONE

Foundations

CHAPTER ONE

Social-Scientific Models in Biblical Interpretation

Philip F. Esler

It is now some thirty years since the thriving movement to explore Old and New Testaments using social-scientific insights began, even though, as far as the Old Testament is concerned, there are precedents for this going back to the nineteenth century (as Anselm Hagedorn and I demonstrate in chapter 2 of this volume). The use of social-scientific models in biblical interpretation has already attracted considerable attention.[1] My object here is not to canvass the entirety of that discussion but to take up one central aspect of it, by explaining and defending the true nature of model use. Yet my aim is not simply to clear away misconceptions concerning model use in biblical interpretation, but also—with reference to the thought of Max Weber—to mount a positive defense of this enterprise of a kind that previously has not been essayed in detail.[2]

The Use of Models in Social-Scientific Interpretation

Social-scientific interpretation undertaken by the overwhelming majority of its practitioners is a heuristic process. It fires the social-scientific imagination to ask new questions of data, to which only the data can provide the answers.

Models are essentially simplifications, exemplifications, and systematizations of data used for comparative processes. Those who employ them in exegesis know they are merely tools available to enable comparison. It is senseless, therefore, to ask if models are "true" or "false," as one certainly could ask of some alleged social law. Rather, one must judge a model by whether or not it is helpful. All biblical critics using social-scientific models agree that if a model is not helpful, it should be modified or even replaced with one that is helpful.

Models are not used for deduction or induction, but in what one American philosopher has called "abduction"—the process of shuttling back and forth between model and data, identified by C. S. Peirce.[3] Models of phenomena such as identity, ethnicity, religion, sect, kinship, time, honor and shame, patron and client, collective memory, and so on allow us to interrogate these issues in biblical texts in helpful and socially important ways. Without models, we still deploy concepts such as these, but this presents the danger that our use of such concepts will be influenced by unexamined prejudgments and presuppositions that may (not must) reflect an ethnocentric embedding in our culture.

Models that are employed heuristically in this way cannot reasonably be tarred with the brush of social nomism or deductivism, as some have tried to do. Nevertheless, most users of models, including the members of the Context Group, of which I am a member,[4] do accept the existence of certain regularities in social life, even though these regularities fall far short of "social laws." The work of Max Weber can be employed in support of our position.

Max Weber on Social-Scientific Modeling

Talcott Parsons has pointed to important features in the intellectual context of Weber's methodology of the social sciences, which run counter to the work of Auguste Comte (1798–1857), the inventor of the word "sociology." Comte had advocated "positive philosophy" or "positivism." By this he meant a science of society that could explain the past of humankind and predict its future course by using the same methods of inquiry, especially observation, experimentation, and comparison, that had proved so successful in the natural sciences. As explained in his *Course of Positivist Philosophy* (1830–42), Comte argued that we had arrived at a scientific or positive stage in the development of the human spirit where our understanding of the causation of facts of social life involved establishing their "laws," that is, the "invariable relations of succession and resemblance" that connect them.[5] While a definition of this sort is necessary if "law" is to be used in this context, it is very difficult to find social theorists in the last one hundred years who have shared Comte's confidence in the existence of "social laws."[6] There are thousands of them, however, who use other aspects of scientific method in their research. Today an increasing number of *natural,* let alone *social,* scientists no longer hold to the theories of causation and "law" that underpinned Comte's views.[7]

Whereas in France Comte had developed a positivist program of "social laws," in nineteenth-century Germany there was strong adherence to the view that human knowledge fell into two radically different categories, the natural sciences and the studies of culture and behavior. Weber's whole project entailed building a bridge between these two intellectual traditions. On the one hand, he went along with German criticism of the attempt to assimilate the study of human behavior to the natural sciences. He recognized that this meant squeezing out the most distinctive aspect of the treatment of human problems, notably the use of subjective categories.[8] This can be seen and amplified in relation to his views on Marxism.

Alan Swingewood has observed that Weber objected to Marxism because it was a form of economic determinism in which society was seen as a system dominated entirely by its mode of production and laws of development, with human beings regarded as passive objects of an historically evolving whole. Weber objected that laws of the Marxist or positivist type "eliminated the active and conscious elements of a culture transforming all ideas to the status of automatic reflexes of external, material forces." In his early methodological essays Weber sought to demonstrate that "the fundamental task of social science lies in analysing society as a structure of meaning-endowing actions centred on the human subject."[9]

On the other hand, as far as history was concerned, there was a tendency among nineteenth-century German thinkers to regard chronological sequences of human phenomena as unique and incapable of comparison with one another and associated with this was the radical denial of the relevance of generalized theoretical categories.[10] But Weber attacked such a position, as Parsons noted: "His basic thesis in this connexion is that generalized theoretical categories are as essential to the proof of causal relationships in the human and cultural field as they are in the natural sciences."[11]

Weber did not think that because human action was subjective it was unpredictable. He defined sociology as "a science which attempts the interpretive understanding of social action in order thereby to arrive at a causal explanation of its course and effects."[12] Social action depends on human subjects selecting means to realize social ends and this purposive component separates it from natural processes. Social action is thus governed by norms relating to the means-ends continuum and this aspect allows the sociologist to undertake causal analysis.[13]

This brings us back to Weber on social generalizations:

> It is customary to designate various sociological generalizations, as for example "Gresham's Law" [which states that bad money drives good money out of circulation, since those with superior currency will horde it and the inferior currency will thus come to dominate the circulation], as scientific "laws." These are in fact typical probabilities confirmed by observation to the effect that under certain given conditions an expected course of social action will occur, which is understandable in terms of the typical motives and typical subjective intentions of the actors.[14]

In his footnote to this section of the Weber's text, Talcott Parsons notes:

> These generalizations are, however, not methodologically equivalent to most of the laws of physics, especially of analytical mechanics. The latter do not generally formulate a concrete course of events, but rather a uniform relationship between the values of two or more variables. *Weber does not even consider the possibility of formulating laws of this latter type*, essentially because he does not develop social theory explicitly in the direction of setting up a system of inter-dependent variables but confines it to the ideal type level.[15]

Thus, there is no room in Weber's theory of social causation for the "invariable relations of succession and resemblance" between phenomena that characterized the views of Auguste Comte.

A sense of what Weber had in mind can be observed in his understanding of social action. By "social action" he meant human behavior to which the human agent attaches subjective meaning that takes account of the behavior of others and is thereby directed in its course.[16] He considered it possible to observe certain empirical uniformities in the field of social action. That is to say:

> Certain types, that is, of action which correspond to a typically appropriate subjective meaning attributable to the same actors, are found to be widespread, being frequently repeated by the

same individual or simultaneously performed by many different ones. Sociological investigation is concerned with these typical modes of action.[17]

Weber's theoretical focus lay in the development of "ideal types," not social laws.[18] Elsewhere he defined an ideal type as follows:

An ideal type is formed by the one-sided *accentuation* of one or more points of view and by the synthesis of a great many diffuse, discrete, more or less present and occasionally absent *concrete individual* phenomena, which are arranged according to those one-sidedly emphasized viewpoints into a unified *analytical* construct (*Gedankenbild*). In its conceptual purity, this mental construct (*Gedankenbild*) cannot be found empirically any-where in reality. It is a *utopia*. Historical research faces the task of determining in each individual case, the extent to which this ideal construct approximates to or diverges from reality. . . .[19]

These types are used in comparison with empirical cases, as are models, which are closely related to types.[20] Some writers have sug-gested renaming Weber's "ideal" type a "constructed" type to remove any confusing suggestion that they are "ideal" in the Platonic sense.[21]

Unfortunately, Weber never attempted to analyze the structure of a total social system, but merely fixed upon certain components of such an analysis.[22] Especially notable was his classification of four types of action: (*a*) rational action oriented to the attainment of an absolute value (*Wertrationalität*); (*b*) rational goal-oriented action in which the goal and means are rationally selected (*Zweckrationalität*); (*c*) affectual action that is determined by the emotional impact on the actor; and (*d*) traditional action that is guided by custom and habit.[23]

Those who do interest themselves in social actions of the sort Weber identified, but on a broader scale, locating and documenting patterns of behavior that are widespread and frequently repeated where the actors involved attribute to them the same subjective meaning, are clearly fol-lowing in his footsteps. Such investigators are not appealing to the "social laws" of Auguste Comte, but, as Weber explained, to "typical probabilities confirmed by observation to the effect that under certain given conditions an expected course of social action will occur, which is understandable in terms of the typical motives and typical subjective intentions of the actors."[24]

The long ethnographic tradition of describing discrete cultures in the world can be related to Weber's position in that each culture tends to be characterized by a distinctive ensemble of social actions. In recent years significant steps have been taken toward isolating the key variables relevant to developing a taxonomy of cultures. In 1980 Dutch social scientist Geert Hofstede published *Culture's Consequences: International Differences in Work-Related Values,* in which he proposed five such variables, the chief among them being whether cultures were "individualistic" (with ties between individuals being comparatively weak, where individual self-assertion is a key value) or "collectivistic" (with individuals being bound together into strong in-groups, where loyalty was a key value). Thus, in the individualistic United States, a wayward teenager is often (though not always—this is a probability, not a "social law") punished by being "grounded" by his or her parents, whereas in collectivistic Japan parents may punish their teenage child by temporarily locking him or her out of the family home. Hofstede's individualism/collectivism spectrum has proved immensely useful in recent research, for example, in the hands of Harry Triandis.[25]

Bruce Malina and The New Testament World

In his important work *The New Testament World: Insights from Cultural Anthropology,* first published in 1981, Bruce Malina attempts two things. First, he seeks—at a fairly high level of abstraction that must necessarily exclude local detail—to map the "typical probabilities" of social action in the modern Mediterranean cultural zone where traditional patterns of life have not been too disrupted by modernization and Westernization. Here Malina stands squarely in Weber's footsteps. I will give two examples of these social actions.

First, in many parts of the Mediterranean people believe in the evil eye, which is a force of evil activated by envy, especially an envious stare. Children are thought to be particularly susceptible. Accordingly, a foreigner who compliments a Turkish farming couple on how beautiful their baby is will likely receive a hostile response, since they will probably (not inevitably, this is a probability, not a law) interpret the compliment as a false one, motivated by envy and damaging to their child. Second, in some parts of the region women who leave their family to run off with a young man (rather than to marry someone approved by her parents, for example, a first cousin) will shame the family to such an extent that one of her male relatives, her father or a brother most commonly, will try to kill her. Neither of these cases illustrate social laws; Comte has no place here. It will not inevitably happen that a couple will react with anger to a remark about their child, or that a family will kill their daughter who has eloped. But in both cases there is a probability that this will happen, that here we have commonly repeated actions that are understandable "in terms of the typical motives and typical subjective intentions of the actors." These probabilities can be used predictively, as in both of the cases just mentioned. Indeed, to deny the reality or the importance of social actions such as these could, in some circumstances in the Middle East, be dangerously irresponsible. But there are still those who proceed as if these regularities did not exist. For instance, anyone having even a passing familiarity with Mediterranean culture could have foreseen that for the Bush administration to offer Turkey a hefty aid package in order to secure its consent to a U.S. attack from Turkey against Iraq in the second Gulf War would be interpreted by Turks as a slight against their honor—as if their assistance could be bought! So it turned out, and the Turkish Parliament refused the United States permission to open a front against Saddam Hussein from their country.

The second thing Malina sought to do in *The New Testament World* was to bring these social actions characteristic of the modern Mediterranean into heuristic comparison with historical data in the New Testament (and the same exercise can be undertaken in relation to Old Testament data). Here again the move is quintessentially Weberian. The whole point of Weber's formulating ideal types of social action was to allow comparison with empirical data, including that from historical sources. Thus, at one point Weber described one function of sociology as follows:

> Among the various bases on which its concepts are formulated and its generalizations worked out, is an attempt to justify its important claim to be able to make a casual explanation of some historically and culturally important phenomenon.[26]

In this spirit, Weber himself investigated the rise of capitalism in the West.[27]

The Mediterranean anthropology utilized by Malina is only one among a wide range of social-scientific traditions from which models can be drawn for understanding biblical data. Other sources are sociology and, in my own work in the last decade, that branch of social psychology known as social-identity theory.

Critique of the Use of Social Sciences in Biblical Interpretation

Back in the 1970s much of the action in the area of social-scientific exegesis occurred in relation to the New Testament. In 1972 Wayne Meeks published a superlative article entitled "The Man from Heaven in Johannine Sectarianism," which sought to explain a dominant theme in the Fourth Gospel using—seemingly for the first time in biblical research—insights drawn from a sociological work that has since proved immensely helpful to numerous biblical critics: *The Social Construction of Reality: A Treatise in the Sociology of Knowledge* by Peter Berger and Thomas Luckmann. In 1974 Gerd Theissen published *Soziologie der Jesusbewegung,* in which he presented the early Jesus-movement as a balance between wandering charismatics and settled communities of sympathizers (with the English translation, *The First Followers of Jesus*, appearing in 1978), while in 1975 John G. Gager published his influential work, *Kingdom and Community: The Social World of Early Christianity.* From its inauguration in 1973 the Working Group on the Social World of Early Christianity of the Society of Biblical Literature and the American Academy of Religion attracted participants such as Meeks, Leander Keck, Abraham Malherbe, and Robert Wilken. One fruit of these meetings was the publication in 1978 of a book by Meeks and Wilken entitled *Jews and Christians in Antioch in the First Four Centuries of the Common Era*. This book was, however, almost entirely untouched by social-scientific ideas.

Wayne Meeks and The First Urban Christians

During those exciting 1970s Meeks had been working on a monograph that he published in 1983 with the title *The First Urban Christians: The Social World of the Apostle Paul*. In his preface and elsewhere in the book Meeks described this as a work of "social history." In the introduction Meeks interpreted "social history" in a manner open to the use of social sciences, yet he did so in a very qualified sense:

> In this study the use of theory will be suggestive, rather than generative in the manner of the experimental sciences. As Max Weber long ago pointed out, historical hypotheses do not admit of verification in the manner of scientific laws, and the controlled experiment is inevitably a misleading model for historical inquiry.[28]

The point that Meeks detects at this place in Weber's work[29] is not to be found there, however. In fact, Weber was making precisely the opposite point, that the generalization in economics known as "Gresham's law" had been empirically confirmed to a high degree of accuracy. Weber accepted, however, that in many other cases of historical interpretation it was not possible to produce the degree of verification "which was feasible in this case."[30] For Weber, while he certainly believed in forms of social causation, did not subscribe to a belief in social laws and a little later in this text explained the status of generalizations such as "Gresham's law," as mentioned above.

Meeks continued on from the quotation immediately above as follows:

> In asking about the social context and social forms of early Christianity, we are not undertaking to discover or validate laws about human behavior in general. We are seeking rather to understand a particular set of phenomena in the second half of the first century, although *understand* need not be taken in the special sense that Weber used.[31]

Numerous problems cluster around Meeks's position as expressed here and continue to beset his more recent views. First, Meeks neglected to say what he meant by "laws about human behavior," or to point to any social theorist in connection with them. Almost certainly, however, he had in mind the work of Auguste Comte. Second, it is noteworthy that Meeks did not cite a single biblical critic who had fallen prey to the temptation to try to discover or validate general laws of human behavior. Whether he thought some biblical interpreters were doing this, but he simply refrained from naming them, or whether he was merely raising a theoretical possibility, was left opaque.

In the introduction to *The First Urban Christians* Meeks explained what he had in mind as appropriate method by referring to Clifford Geertz's view of ethnography as an interpretive description of culture. Geertz himself described his project in his 1973 work *The Interpretation of Cultures* as "thick description," meaning the process in which there was a layering of all sorts of interpretations: those of the ethnographer, the informant, and the people themselves.[32] For Meeks, following Geertz, theory was necessary, but it had to stay closer to the ground than was the case with other sciences. Meeks advocated an eclectic use of social theory that seemed to set Comte and Geertz at the extremes but virtually ignored the huge middle ground between those extremes—occupied, for example, by the towering figure of Max Weber.

A very different approach to the appropriation of the social sciences appeared in John Elliott's and Bruce Malina's reviews of *The First Urban Christians*.[33] They criticized Meeks for not using social-scientific insights where they were available and for not having gone far enough in his use of social-scientific ideas that he did employ. Thus, these reviewers criticized him for his use of concepts such as "city," "conflict," and "ritual" without giving them any or enough theoretical attention when there was (and is) a huge and relevant social-scientific literature available.

The Work of Susan Garrett

In 1992, Susan Garrett, who had been one of Meeks's brilliant crop of doctoral students at Yale, published an entry in the *Anchor Bible Dictionary* entitled "Sociology of Early Christianity." The title was a misnomer (presumably the editors' fault, not hers), since she dealt with anthropology as much as sociology.[34] This was a fair-minded but flawed treatment of the subject. Here she adopted a line similar to that of Meeks in the introduction to *First Urban Christians* (although argued with much greater detail and nuance) by defending "sociological" (by which I suggest she meant "social-scientific") interpretation, but only on the basis that it be "interpretive" and characterized by "thick description" (as in Geertz's ethnography) and not model-oriented in nature. She was attracted to Geertz's advocacy of the total immersion by the ethnographer in a culture that enabled his or her interpretive analysis of its symbols. She saw model use as "nomothetic"—that is, as tied up with the promulgation of social "laws"—as too scientific, and as "positivist." While, like Meeks, she did not explain precisely what form of positivism she had in mind or the social theorists who were advocating it, she too was possibly haunted by the ghost of Auguste Comte.[35] Unlike Meeks, however, she did name biblical critics who typified the approach she decried (while also pointing out the strengths of their work), such as John Elliott, Bruce Malina, and Jerome Neyrey. Once again the choice was "thick description" of the Geertzian type *or* model use allegedly based on appeal to social laws; the virtuous "induction" of the interpretivists *or* the alleged "deduction" of the model users. She, too, ignored the middle ground between these extremes. She noted the social-scientific critics' complaint "that works of social history description are typically intuitive and ethnocentric, and they are rendered obscure by their authors' failure to make theoretical presuppositions explicit and open to inspection,"[36] but without acknowledging the inescapable truth and significance of this charge.

By way of critique of Garrett's view, I will make three points.[37] First, in reply to her misplaced claim that the interpretive method facilitates intercultural translation of meaning in a way that model use does not,[38] I will briefly recall my support for the suggestion of Philippe Descola. According to Descola, excessive concentration on particularity of the sort espoused by Geertz, and advocated by Meeks and Garrett, results in the failure to produce an interpretative framework that is necessary for the discussion of cultural differences, which results in a kind of "cultural apartheid."[39]

Second, there is the practical problem that the total immersion by a trained observer in another culture necessary to generate a "thick description" of it is impossible for anything other than a contemporary culture. Of all social-scientific methodologies, this is probably the least suited for work with historical evidence. Apart from a handful of works meriting notice with their soft glaze of Geertz, such as Meeks's *First Urban Christians* and Garrett's own accomplished 1989 monograph *The Demise of the Devil*,[40] appeal to the Geertzian method of thick description has not been particularly fruitful in generating significant new exegesis of biblical texts. It has, indeed, proved something of a dead end. Moreover, whereas in 1983 Meeks proposed a form of social history tinged with Geertzian "interpretive description" as its social-scientific component, the predictable failure of the Geertzian method to be of long-term benefit has left social history bereft of social-scientific support. Social history has become, in effect, a form of empiricism, whose practitioners regularly employ concepts such as "kinship," "identity," "ethnicity," and so on without subjecting these ideas to the social-scientific modeling they require for clarity of application. On the other hand, the use of social-scientific models in biblical interpretation permits intercultural communication, does not require in-depth exposure to living informants, and is a flourishing field of biblical interpretation today.

Finally, as I stated in my response to Garrett in 1995:

> The main problem with Garrett's analysis is that its image of "positivist" model-using is a stalking-horse having no resemblance to social-scientific interpretation as it is actually practised. New Testament critics who employ this method . . .

certainly do not claim that there are social laws, or that their
results are "objectively valid" (although since they certainly
reject the view that one historical opinion is as good as another,
they may well claim that their views are more plausible than
some). No ontological status is accorded to the models; they are
seen merely as heuristic tools. Either they throw up a set of new
and interesting questions, which the texts themselves must
answer, or they do not. Models which do not have this result
will be discarded and replaced with others.[41]

In Defense of Model Use

To my knowledge, no biblical critic using social-scientific models
appeals to or believes in "social laws." Indeed, as long ago as 1981 John
Elliott had stated in his *Home for the Homeless* that social-scientific
exegesis was not concerned with "social laws."[42] I have been denying
that there were "social laws" since my first academic publication, which
heavily utilized social-scientific models, in 1987.[43] In none of my dealings with the Context Group since its formation in 1990 have I seen any
sign that any of them appealed to or believed in "social laws." Along
with Max Weber, we do subscribe to a belief in social regularities, something John Elliott made clear as long ago as 1981,[44] but these, as I will
explain below, are certainly not "social laws."

The phrase "social law" is not language employed by those using
social-scientific models; it is not insider language. Rather, it is inaccurate
discourse, like the charge of "positivism," mobilized by outsiders hostile
to the enterprise. I am drawn to the conclusion that such views are triggered by a perhaps understandable unhappiness with work where there
is arguably too much model and too little data,[45] or where models are
being utilized way beyond their use-by date.

Perhaps it is really a question of taste. Some exegetes are comfortable with theory and some are not. Some of us like to subject the dominant concepts and frameworks we use to social-scientific clarification
and enrichment and some do not. Model users—like the authors of the
essays that follow in this volume—belong in the former camp, but we
certainly do not see the arguments as equally balanced: if the unexamined life is not worth living, the unexamined concept is not worth using.

Social-Scientific Analysis of the Old Testament

A BRIEF HISTORY AND OVERVIEW

Philip F. Esler and Anselm C. Hagedorn

Chapter 1 of this volume made a case—in relation to the social-scientific methodology of the Max Weber—for the intellectual integrity and value of seeking to interpret the Old Testament using models drawn from the social sciences. In chapters 3 to 17 the contributors bring various social-scientific models and perspectives to bear upon a variety of Old Testament issues and texts, while the last three chapters address certain hermeneutical questions that arise in relation to such investigation.

Yet the application of the social sciences to understanding phenomena from ancient Israel is hardly new. Indeed, it traces its lineage back to the nineteenth century. The purpose of this chapter is to provide a scholarly context for the essays in this volume, both as to the history of the exercise and as to the main ideas that have pushed it on. We hope at the same time to cover most of the bibliographic milestones in social-scientific interpretation of the Old Testament, although for complete coverage there are a number of texts that survey various parts of the field.[1]

The Late Nineteenth- and Twentieth-Century Pioneers

Anthropology

Writing in 1951, E. E. Evans-Pritchard divided the history of anthropology into three periods.[2] The first ran roughly from the eighteenth

15

century to the middle of the nineteenth century. It was characterized by writers like David Hume and Adam Smith who used facts to illustrate their theories but who did not know much about the "primitive" societies of their day. The second period lasted from the mid-nineteenth to the early twentieth century and featured great interest in gathering facts from a wide range of societies to be used for comparative purposes, especially to show that societies had evolved through similar stages. A problem with the approach was the comparison of fragments of data torn from their original contexts, rather than the comparison of systems. Evans-Pritchard's third period ran from early in the twentieth century onwards and was characterized by fieldwork and functionalism. If Evans-Pritchard were alive today he would probably introduce a fourth period, that of the postmodernist turn to an interest in the processes and subjective experience of carrying out anthropological research.[3]

The enterprise of applying social sciences to the Old Testament got off to a notably robust start in this second period with the work of Scottish academic William Robertson Smith (1846–94). Having been appointed to a chair in Old Testament exegesis and Oriental languages in 1870, Smith (a fluent speaker of Arabic) spent 1880 in Saudi Arabia and other Middle Eastern countries, observing their customs. In 1885 he published *Kinship and Marriage in Early Arabia*, and thus became one of the founders of ethnography and cultural anthropology.[4] With this fieldwork behind him, in 1888 and 1889 he delivered the first of three series of Burnett lectures in Aberdeen, which were published in 1889 as *Lectures on the Religion of the Semites: The Fundamental Institutions*.[5] These were of notable importance in establishing the comparative method as an important tool in the understanding of biblical texts.[6]

Although many of Smith's ideas now seem dated (especially because of his habit, characteristic of the time, of plucking data for comparison from their context),[7] others have had a lasting significance. Particularly influential has been his stress on ritual, especially sacrifice. Smith saw animal sacrifice as entailing "an act of communion, in which the god and his worshippers unite by partaking together of the flesh and blood of a sacred victim."[8] Whatever the fate of details of his understanding of sacrifice, his emphasis on its social function has been of abiding significance.[9] He also adopted an evolutionary theory of social development, arguing that societies passed through primitive, matrilineal and totemic stages.[10] These ideas influenced Durkheim, Freud, and many others.

In spite of the obvious anthropological concern of the research of William Robertson Smith, one cannot fully evaluate his contribution to the field of Hebrew Bible without mentioning the influence of German scholarship on his work and, in turn, the influence his anthropological interests had on German scholars. Smith undertook several trips to Germany, studying in Bonn, Heidelberg, and Göttingen.[11] It is no exaggeration to say that "Smith's theology was forged in Germany because only German theology... could offer an approach to the Bible that saw biblical criticism as the necessary handmaid of a Christianity that was deeply committed to a personal relationship with God through Christ, and evangelistic in its wish to bring all knowledge under Christ's lordship."[12] Despite his close relationship with Albrecht Ritschl (1822–89) and Paul Anton de Lagarde (1827–91), who convinced him of the importance of text criticism, it was Julius Wellhausen (1844–1918) who had the greatest influence on Smith's theological and exegetical development.[13] In turn, Wellhausen himself was particularly proud that his *Prolegomena* gained him the friendship of Abraham Kuenen and Robertson Smith.[14] Smith and Wellhausen first met in Göttingen in 1872[15] and Wellhausen became "one of the privileged persons on Smith's list . . . of those to whom he sent information from Arabia."[16] In turn, Wellhausen carefully studied Smith's *Kinship and Marriage in Early Arabia* and was quite enthusiastic about the work,[17] as well as *Lectures on the Religion of the Semites*. Smith even helped Wellhausen to overcome financial difficulties by commissioning articles from him for the *Encyclopaedia Britannica*, which Smith edited for a time, thus helping Wellhausen to make his ideas wider known in Britain. Generally speaking, Smith endorsed all of Wellhausen's results as far as Pentateuchal criticism was concerned (and had even reached similar conclusions before having read Wellhausen),[18] but continued to show that "there was nothing in this sort of criticism which was incompatible with Evangelical Christianity."[19] The relationship between the two men was one of the most fruitful and significant in the long and happy annals of Anglo-German biblical cooperation.

Another Scottish anthropologist whose work is typical of this second phase of anthropological research (even if he lived into the third) was Sir James Frazer (1854–1941), a friend of Robertson Smith. Relying not on fieldwork, but on questionnaires sent to people abroad, Frazer garnered a vast amount of material from around the world on religion and myth. Much of this appeared in *The Golden Bough*, with the first of an eventual fifteen volumes appearing in 1890. Frazer first suggested the connection between ritual and myth. He argued for a progression from magic to religion to science.[20] Although his understanding of magic has largely been rejected by modern anthropologists, it exerted a huge influence on Old Testament scholarship, even on the part of scholars who did not think it necessary to cite him as the source of their views.[21] In 1918 Frazer published a further work entitled *Folk-Lore in the Old Testament,* which contained narratives from all over the world having similarities with certain aspects of Old Testament narratives.[22] This book also displayed the problem of fragments of material ripped from their original contexts for comparative use typical of the second period of anthropological research.

The Sociological Dimension

At about the same time sociology also began to find its way into Old Testament research. Sociologists, beginning with the great figures from the formative period of sociology in the late nineteenth and early twentieth centuries—Ferdinand Tönnies (1855–1936), Emile Durkheim (1858–1917), and Max Weber (1864–1920), and moving on to more recent figures such as Bryan Wilson (1926–2004) and Gerhard (b. 1924) and Jean Lenski (1928–1994)—have proved extremely helpful in assisting scholars to come to terms with the social dimensions of Old Testament texts. This area has been helpfully charted by Andrew Mayes, one of the contributors to this volume.[23]

In his highly influential 1887 work, *Gemeinschaft und Gesellschaft,* Tönnies sought to find the core of the social history of Western Europe from the medieval to modern periods in the transition from *Gemeinschaft* to *Gesellschaft.*[24] By *Gemeinschaft* he meant a close-knit and unified group, a community, often characterized by face-to-face interaction (paradigmatically in the family), that had been common in European rural areas before industrialization. Unity of this sort could be based on kinship, locality, or even on common intellectual interests. By *Gesellschaft* he meant a form of association where individuals were essentially isolated and really came together not by reason of some underlying unity but in response to commercial or legal pressures. The factors that united them were far less important than those that kept them apart, even if they were living in proximity to one another. The masses of people who abandoned village life to crowd into European cities in the nineteenth century to gain work in the new factories represent one illustration of *Gesellschaft.*

Yet, as Mayes rightly notes, by *Gemeinschaft* and *Gesellschaft* Tönnies meant theoretical types of social structure abstracted from empirical data used to classify and explain that data, not descriptions of empirical realities.[25] This represented an assertion of a fundamentally important aspect of sociological method that Max Weber later articulated in his notion of the "ideal type," an analytical construct used for comparative purposes which was explained in chapter 1 of this volume.

Mayes has commented upon the influence of Tönnies's distinction between *Gemeinschaft* and *Gesellschaft* in the work of Louis Wallis in the first half of the twentieth century, and G. E. Mendenhall, Walter Brueggemann, Paul D. Hanson, Walter Dietrich, and Gary A. Herion in the second half.[26] Mayes has also pointed out certain problems that affect these writings to a greater or lesser degree: the failure to remember that a type is a theoretical construct and not a description of empirical reality, inordinate idealization of early Israelite society as a *Gemeinschaft* divorced from the surrounding sociopolitical milieu and an excessive readiness to read social context out of Old Testament literary forms.[27]

Emile Durkheim was determined to define the object of sociology and the methods appropriate to it. Central to this exercise was his desire to distinguish the objective reality of social facts from psychology, which he regarded as the study of individual consciousness. For Durkheim, sociological explanation dealt with collective and not individual forces.[28] A dominant theme in his work was that society had a reality over and against the individuals who comprised it, typically expressed in the form of common beliefs and values. In *The Elementary Forms of the Religious Life* (1912), for example, he argued that religion was entirely a product of society. He regarded the religious life as the concentrated expression of the collective life of a particular group. Religion was a society's idealized vision of itself.[29] Unlike Auguste Comte, Durkheim did not regard religion as a primitive science to be outgrown but as essential to society and its continued functioning.[30] Yet Durkheim's was a strongly reductionist view, since he thought he was offering a complete explanation for religion.

Durkheim regarded society as an organic whole and analyzed social processes and institutions in relation to their functions for the needs of the system.[31] He was thus one of the founders of that type of sociological theory known as "functionalism." In the 1930s and 1940s Durkheimian functionalism was a major influence on the U.S. sociologist Talcott Parsons, who fused to it a concern with social structures, hence leading to an approach known as the "structural-functionalist" tradition.[32] Among anthropologists, the term was associated with A. R.

Radcliffe-Brown in the United Kingdom. On this approach, society is cohesive and held together by shared meanings, values, and norms. It is in equilibrium, proper balance, and such a social system tends to persist over time.[33]

The structural-functionalist tradition has had more impact via the writings of social scientists influenced by Durkheim than by Durkheim himself. One such was philosopher-sociologist Lucien Lévy-Bruhl (1857–1939). Especially significant were his views on "primitive" human societies and the "primitive" mentalities to be found in them. In 1937 Antonin Causse published *Du groupe ethnique à la communauté religieuse: le problème sociologique de la religion d'Israel*, dedicated to Lévy-Bruhl and illustrating a structural-functionalist approach to ancient Israel.[34] Important themes in this work, still worthy of consideration for its bold use of social-scientific ideas, were Durkheim's notions of socially produced group mentality and Lévy-Bruhl's idea of a development from a collective prelogical mentality, to an empirical-logical mentality, and lastly to a logical mentality characterized by individualism.[35]

Max Weber generated many of the most influential ideas in sociology and this legacy lives on.[36] As noted in the introduction of this volume, central to his work was the notion of sociology as a comprehensive investigation of social action and his main theoretical focus was on the subjective meanings that individuals attach to their actions and interactions in various social settings. Here he differed decisively from Durkheim. His main empirical interest lay in the problems of institutional change.[37] This interest emerged in his concern with the historical development and structural peculiarities of Western society, but he also ranged far more widely, with studies of Chinese religion[38] and *Ancient Judaism*.[39] The latter has had the most influence on biblical scholarship of all of Weber's sociological work. Weber's study of "Judaism" unfortunately took its point of departure from his view that the "Jews" were a pariah people,[40] which anachronistically projected back onto the ancient Israelites a status that the Jews only acquired later. Nevertheless, Weber stimulated thinking about Israelite society and tradition in numerous respects. Using his methodology of ideal types, Weber identified a number of types of use in the analysis of data concerning Israel: the desert bedouin, the semi-nomadic stock breeder, the peasant and the city dweller. Israel embraced phenomena comparable with these, especially the last three. The struggles between groups within Israel were, to an extent, overcome by the development of covenants and law codes.

The hostility that existed between groups like these and the evolution of Israelite society over time in response to their interactions means that Weber's was a conflict-oriented approach. Weber also developed many other ideas of great significance: the social setting of the Levites, the nature, function, and social context of Israelite prophets (in his view, bearers of an individual charisma who were characterized by their concern with ethics), the routinization of such prophecy, and the development of an Israelite confederacy.[41]

Mayes has noted that even in the work of Old Testament critics who were not consciously sociological in their methods, many of Weber's key ideas were taken up and developed. Mayes points, for example, to the way in which Albrecht Alt developed the notions of charisma and its bearers, and of Israel in relation to the ideal-type city-state, while Martin Noth portrayed Israel as an oath or covenant community. Under Weber's influence, Noth greatly developed an existing idea of Israel as having had an amphictyonic structure.[42]

Developments Since the 1960s

Stimulus from Anthropology

Thus far we have only spoken about biblical scholars, or someone like Robertson Smith who was primarily interested in the Bible, using models and methods from social and cultural anthropology to enhance their knowledge of the Bible or to supplement more traditional historical methods of exegesis. However, in the 1960s some anthropologists began explicitly to apply their methods to the Bible. Here especially we have to mention Mary Douglas and Edmund Leach.[43]

In her *Purity and Danger* (1966) Douglas used material from the Bible (especially Leviticus) to clarify the relationship between purity and pollution. *Purity and Danger* has achieved the status of a classic inside and outside the anthropological field. Douglas's classification system (especially her insight into "pollution," that it consisted in something being out of place, being on the wrong side of a boundary), as well as her grid and group model, have been used frequently to illuminate biblical texts.[44] For Douglas, the Bible is an interesting source of ethnographical data—thus she is able to place the texts of Leviticus in a larger anthropological context.[45] The observations first made in *Purity and Danger* are further developed in her book *Leviticus as Literature* (1999). Here she also draws on redactional conclusions for the book of Leviticus as a whole and postulates that it should be possible to read Leviticus as a separate book. She also shows that Leviticus is not simply a narrow statement of an all-controlling priesthood, but rather a powerful statement of a religion based on God's liberty. Previous to her monograph on Leviticus, Douglas had studied the doctrine of defilement in the book of Numbers (1993), putting anthropological theory on the map of Pentateuchal studies as well as asking pertinent questions about general accepted scholarly views on Numbers.[46] Douglas's contributions have had a big impact on biblical studies, and her work needs to be taken seriously by anyone working on either Leviticus or Numbers.[47] In her most recent monograph on a biblical theme, *Jacob's Tears: The Priestly Work of Reconciliation*, 2004, Douglas investigates "what motivated the priestly editors to compose the Pentateuch."[48] In a way, this study brings together the insights gained from her earlier reading of Leviticus and Numbers by asking what were the political motivations of the authors behind the priestly document. On the basis of her previous anthropological fieldwork, she is able to argue that the authors formulated a subtle critique of the current status quo of the Persian period.

Edmund Leach's interest in the Bible was triggered by his reading of Claude Lévi-Strauss, even though he seems to reject all of Lévi-Strauss's conclusions.[49] Similar to Douglas, Leach develops his theory of sacrifice by looking at the biblical material.[50] He is able to use the material presented in Exodus and Leviticus because these texts provide "a detailed account of sacrificial procedures of a kind that can still be observed at first hand in all sorts of different ethnographic contexts throughout the world."[51] This, however, does not mean—according to Leach—that the texts describe a historical reality. This view leads to the second focus of Leach's work regarding the Bible: the role of myth. Leach follows Bronislaw Malinowski's insights on the role of myth in society but lifts it to a structuralist interpretation by shifting the focus from an individual society to a cross-cultural enterprise.[52]

Leach's interest in a structuralist approach, if not in the way that Lévi-Strauss practiced structuralism, is evident in his essay "The Legitimacy of Solomon."[53] Here he showed that the Old Testament account of the succession of Solomon was a myth that mediated a major contradiction between the Israelite injunction in favor of endogamy, to preserve the identity of the Israelite people amidst numerous other ethnic groups in the region, and the fact that exogamy was often necessary between Israelite kings and foreign women as a way to forge political alliances.

Ritual

> "The conclusion is, that in the study of ancient religions we must begin, not with myth, but with ritual and traditional usage." (W. Robertson Smith)[54]

In 1889, William Robertson Smith published his lectures on *The Religion of the Semites*. In the first lecture, he departs from the then-current anthropological trend to investigate the role of ritual as being derived from myth and claims instead that we have to look at the ritual first before we study myth, since "ritual originally provided its own explanation, but that explanation was eventually forgotten, and myth was invented to explain the ritual."[55]

> Belief in a certain series of myths was neither obligatory as a part of true religion, nor was it supposed that, by believing, a man acquired religious merit and conciliated the favour of the gods. What was obligatory or meritorious was the exact performance of certain sacred acts prescribed by religious tradition. This being so, it follows that mythology ought not to take the prominent place that is too often assigned to it in the scientific study of ancient faiths. So far as myths consist of explanations of ritual their value is altogether secondary, and it may be affirmed with confidence that in almost every case myth was derived from Ritual, and not the ritual from the myth. . . . [56]

For quite some time, however, anthropologists of religion did not follow Smith's call to investigate ritual independently from myth, placing—in the Frazerian manner—their main focus on the comparative study of myth and mythology.

Under the influence of Emile Durkheim, Arnold van Gennep, A. R. Radcliffe Brown, and Clifford Geertz,[57] twentieth-century anthropology rediscovered the study of ritual and sometimes even aimed at replacing religion with ritual.[58] In the works of Victor Turner, however, ritual remains—as in Smith—closely connected to religion, when he defines ritual as "prescribed formal behavior for occasions not given over to technological routine, having reference to belief in mystical being or powers."[59]

Limited space does not allow a detailed discussion of the scholarly debate on ritual and ritual theory,[60] but we can name certain elements that seem to constitute ritual:[61]

1. Ritual has to be performed.[62]
2. Rites are always repetitive.[63]
3. Ritual is part of the language of society.[64]
4. Rituals are symbolic acts.[65]

It becomes apparent that ritual forms an integral part of society, but has to be analyzed in its social and historical context if we want to decode its social meaning.[66] At the same time we need to be aware that ritual as a form of rhetoric tends to promote a certain good within society and thus has to be seen as a tool of the discourse of power[67] (and anthropologists such as Roy Rappaport can even claim that ritual creates belief). Ritual, however, is much more than simply an expression of already existing social reality,[68] and it is certainly misleading—as far as the study of the biblical world is concerned—to equate ritual with sacrifice.[69] Saul M. Olyan, for example, has shown convincingly that "mourning practices provide a ritual setting for the realization, affirmation, re-negotiation, or termination of social bonds between individuals, groups, and even political entities such as states."[70] Here, mourning functions in a way similar to other rites.

We have to note further that rituals, by being part of the performative aspect of language that shapes society, are encoded in every member of that particular society from a very early stage on. Learning the language and learning rituals go hand in hand, so that every time one speaks (or listens) social identity is shaped.[71] Accordingly, ritual helps to structure society and the decisions of its individual members since ritual tends to eliminate unclear issues and helps to reach a (moral) decision. "Ritual attempts to ritualize memory, so that when the moral system of competing social groups clash, the members of its society will not have to think twice about what to do."[72]

Ritual theory of this sort has attracted considerable attention from scholars working in the traditions of ancient Israel. Olyan has brought the theory to bear in relation to rites of shaving, of hierarchy, and of mourning.[73] David Janzen has examined purity and witchcraft in 4 Ezra and sacrifice in the Hebrew Bible.[74] Mark McVann has edited a useful collection of texts in this area.[75]

Israel's Origins and Social and Political Organization

George Mendenhall's brief yet significant essay "The Hebrew Conquest of Palestine," published in 1962, did much to stimulate the social-scientific investigation of Israel's origins and forms of social and political organization. Mendenhall was critical of the view, propagated by William Albright, Albrecht Alt, and others, that twelve Israelite tribes had entered the land of Canaan from another area and were distinct from the existing inhabitants of Canaan. He argued that disciplined social thought should be applied to the concept of "tribe," that transhuman nomadism characterized by seasonal migration had been an important feature of Israel's origins. Mendenhall made a vital advance by arguing for the centrality of conflict between village peasants and urban elites rather than between pastoral and agrarian societies.

The Impact of Norman K. Gottwald

Probably the most influential (and easily most detailed and extensive) social-scientific study of the Hebrew Bible is Norman K. Gottwald's *The Tribes of Yahweh*, first published in 1979 and recently reissued (1999). Gottwald was influenced by Mendenhall but used sociology and anthropology in a highly explicit fashion. Ever since the first reviews *The Tribes of Yahweh* has been regarded as a one of the main achievements in Old Testament study, breaking new ground and challenging conventional scholarship.[76] Thus, it is probably right to label it as belonging "to that rare collection of critical texts that have not been superseded or fallen by the wayside of criticism."[77]

To be sure, Gottwald's work is not the first modern social-scientific study on the Hebrew Bible, but it is certainly the first full-blown attempt since Max Weber's work on ancient Judaism to elucidate the earliest history of Israel by explicitly using methods and models derived from the social sciences. As such, the work inaugurated what Frank S. Frick rightly calls "a 'second wave' of socially-enlightened studies of ancient Israel."[78] In addition, the book's distinctive Marxist perspective made it especially appealing to readers from the so-called third world or persons engaged in liberation theology. Thus, the work achieved a much wider recognition than most Hebrew Bible studies.

As with most groundbreaking studies in the field, most of its arguments and major claims have not survived critical scrutiny over the past twenty-five years. The author himself admits that "any attempt to actually revise *Tribes* is unthinkable since such a project, if done properly, would necessarily produce an entirely new book. This is so, because virtually every one of the book's major claims, and much of its detailed argumentation, would today require reformulation and fresh substantiation."[79] However, many of the once revolutionary claims now seem to be part of the scholarly mainstream, since archaeological excavations and the continuing application of social theory to the biblical texts have provided us with a much thicker description of Israel's earliest stages.

The strength of the work certainly lies in the wide variety of social-science models used (Marxism, structural-functionalism, cultural-materialism, etc.), even though this "cafeteria of ideas"[80] makes reading and using the book sometimes difficult.[81] The main aim of the work is a reconstruction of the society of Israel before the monarchy. This reconstruction is done in two parts: a synchronic and diachronic reading of the texts and their social structure (here, the book moves beyond many other studies that claim to reconstruct the realities of Israel understood in a social-scientific way but neglect the literary growth of the material studied). Gottwald takes up ideas by George Mendenhall and regards early Israel as a peasant society that strives at liberation from political and economic domination. In contrast to other contemporary scholarship he abandons the idea of an "ethnic" conflict between Israel and Canaan and is thus able to integrate the Canaanite element of Israel by shifting the focus from ethnicity to social structure.[82] He sees the change as the result of indigenous conflict. He explains this shift by postulating a process of retribalization of the marginalized groups. From here, theories of tribal structure and segmentary societies are evaluated and developed in regard to early Israel. Gottwald's work remains the starting point for any reconstruction of Israelite society, since it teaches its reader that no single model or social theory will suffice to explain a society as complex as ancient Israel.

Political and Sociological Approaches

Sectarianism is one area of sociology that has had a long history in New Testament research. In addition to the seminal ideas of Max Weber, the writings of British sociologist Bryan Wilson have been especially influential.[83] The publication in 2006 of *Sectarianism in Early Judaism*, ed. David Chalcraft, will bring the sociology of sectarianism into the study of ancient Israel.

A more recent branch of sociology, the macrosociology of Gerhard and Jean Lenski, has been extremely influential in relation to the Old and New Testaments. In *Human Societies: An Introduction to Macrosociology*, which has gone into numerous editions, they trace the development of human societies from hunter-gatherer, to horticulturist (where people use digging sticks for cultivation), to the advanced agrarian phase involving agriculture using a plough (at first of wood and then with an iron tip) and beyond. The advanced agrarian stage sees peasant families producing more food than they need and the rise of elites living in cities with armies who secure the surplus, taxing and tithing the peasantry to the maximum degree. This type of approach has proved its worth in understanding the rise of the city-states in Mesopotamia and Egypt and, indeed, in the Mediterranean region generally. In relation to ancient Israel it has been used in relation to prophetic protest against socio-religious oppression in eighth-century B.C.E. Israel and to grasp the land-use systems of the Hellenistic and Roman periods.[84]

Lenski himself, in a review of Gottwald's *The Tribes of Yahweh*, proposed the importance of earliest Israel as a frontier society, as a way of describing the balance between tendencies to tribalization and monarchy in Israel.[85] Marvin Chaney developed Lenski's ideas and applied social-scientific ideas to the question of peasant unrest in Israel.[86] Robert Coote and Keith Whitelam isolated a number of factors that they argued accounted for Israel's political development, including population pressure, more intensive forms of agricultural development, and increasing social stratification leading to new political structures.[87]

Prophecy

The pioneer of the movement to apply recent ethnographic research into contemporary or near-contemporary prophetic phenomena to the Old Testament is Thomas Overholt. True to the ethnographic interest that had been a feature of the work of Robertson Smith, he began to investigate examples of prophecy from other cultures. Although a cross-cultural interest was not new in itself, Overholt was innovative in two respects.[88] First, he rejected the study of prophetic movements in other cultures not so much in themselves, but merely for the light they might throw on Israelite prophets. Second, he insisted that the prophecy in question, whether from ancient Israel or elsewhere, should be studied for its own sake and not merely as an adjunct to some other interest— as, for example, when Israelite prophecy was considered as a trailer to some larger performance focused, for example, on the relationship between Yahweh and his people. He called for and practiced a comparative methodology where both the cross-cultural and biblical prophetic phenomena were examined properly in themselves prior to comparison being attempted. He began with a study of the Ghost Dance of 1890 among the Paiute and later extended his research to the Iroquois Handsome Lake and his Gaiwiio ("Good Message") of the early 1800s and to other prophetic movements or events in the Arctic, Africa, India, and the Pacific.[89]

On the basis of his comparative work, Overholt developed a useful model of the prophetic process that integrates the prophet, the deity, and the people to whom the prophet speaks. First, a person (the "prophet") receives (essentially private) revelations from a god, which constitute the primary source of his authority. These revelations are culturally conditioned, "since both his perception and later articulation of them will be affected by the cultural and historical context in which he stands." Second, he then proclaims his message. Third, he makes this proclamation to the people who are its target audience and they react in various ways. Again, their reactions, or "feedback," are conditioned by the cultural context. Only if they recognize the point of what he is saying in their shared social setting will he have authority (or "charisma," to use Weber's word). Some will accept him and some will reject. If he encounters difficulty, the prophet may turn to his god for succor or guidance and this may elicit further revelations, followed by new proclamations and so on.[90]

In the 1970s Robert Wilson also became interested in cross-cultural approaches to Israelite prophecy. Two aspects of his work merit particular attention here. First, while insisting (like Overholt) that a prophet's social location be taken into account, he helpfully distinguished between "peripheral intermediaries," who were active in groups within a society and tended to advance the interests of those groups and the spirits who bestowed the message on the intermediaries and "central intermediaries," who were concerned with maintaining the established social order and with regulating the pace of change. Second, Wilson used the extensive social-scientific research into trances and ectstatic states ("altered states of consciousness") to shed light on similar phenomena among Israelite prophets, from 1 Samuel 10 onward.[91] It is worth noting, however, that interest in the ecstatic dimensions of prophecy goes back to a monograph by Gustav Hölscher in 1914, admittedly from a history-of-religions, and not a social-scientific, approach.

At about the same time, but in Scotland and away from the methodological hubbub of the United States, Robert Carroll was applying a different set of social-scientific theories to a different aspect of Israelite prophecy. In a brilliant leap of social-scientific imagination, Carroll introduced the theory of cognitive dissonance, first developed in the 1950s by psychologist Leon Festinger to understand what happened when a prophesied event failed to occur.[92] Dissonance refers to the gap between expectation and belief; yet dissonance does not necessarily mean the dropping of the belief, but quite often simply drives its (often powerful) reformulation. One of Carroll's important findings was that the disconfirmation of a prophecy (for example, as to the return of a Davidic king) led to a reinterpretation of traditions to sidestep the problem. "The accumulated growth of the prophetic traditions incorporated numerous responses to problems of failure and seriously modified motifs that had become obsolete."[93]

More recently, Lester Grabbe has usefully sought to compare findings by social anthropologists into contemporary or recent prophetic phenomena with ancient Near Eastern prophecy.[94] While this an area where recently re-presented and edited prophetic texts from Mari and Neo-Assyria offer considerable material for comparison with Israelite prophecy,[95] Grabbe is right to examine it from a social-scientific perspective on its own terms. Grabbe is well aware that social-scientific models are heuristic tools, allowing us to interrogate data in new ways, not to serve as a substitute for data.[96]

Law

The purpose of law in society is generally understood "either as ensuring compliance with mutually agreed rules, or as a means through which a few members of society manage to exercise power over the rest."[97] Therefore, every analysis of legal stipulations needs to evaluate the social background of those stipulations, regardless of whether the main aim is a source-critical analysis of legal corpora,[98] an ethical reading of biblical law,[99] or an analysis of whether the laws in the Hebrew Bible were ever used to enforce law and justice (cf. Anne Fitzpatrick-McKinley, who argues that "[l]egal development does not reflect social development").[100] The same applies (especially in ancient law) for the role of religious beliefs that underline the laws of a society. All this is necessary because law participates as the integrative framework in politics, economics, religion, and science;[101] thus it is hardly surprising that law codes were used as textbooks for achieving literacy and education.

Traditionally, the main concern of biblical legal scholarship has been the comparative analysis with other ancient Near Eastern law codes and the redaction-critical study of the literary origin of the different law codes in the Hebrew Bible.[102] Recently, however, closer attention has been paid to the socioeconomic development of Israelite society and how developments within a society affect the laws of that particular society.[103] This is mostly done by references to archaeological evidence or by reversion to basic social-historical insights; however, we must note that the influence of Max Weber's sociology is currently making a comeback in the study of biblical law and ethics.[104] In contrast, Harold V. Bennett's recent study[105] explicitly uses insights from critical (legal) theory to explain the societal concepts behind the legislations found in Deut 14:22-29; 16:9-12, 13-15; 24:17-18, 19-22 and 26:12-15. Additionally, he uses insights gained by Gottwald and Gerhard Lenski on social stratification and agrarian societies to determine the social setting of each law. Rather surprisingly, Bennett reaches the conclusion that the laws under scrutiny were not formulated to emphasize the humanitarian nature of Deuteronomic law but rather serve to legalize social injustice and oppression. Bennett's arguments cannot be addressed here in detail but few will be entirely convinced; nevertheless, his work is a first step towards a social interpretation of the legal material based on critical theory.

Furthermore, the rediscovery of the Greek world has opened up new avenues of research in the social analysis of biblical law. On the basis of models derived from Mediterranean anthropology it is possible to establish what anthropologists have called "small-scale comparison" (Michael Herzfeld, João de Pina-Cabral) of neighboring societies within the same geographical environment and thus conduct a comparative analysis of two legal systems without having to postulate any influence of one society on the other.[106]

A similar utilization of anthropological insights—but derived from different models—can be found in the work of Timothy Willis on the elder laws in Deuteronomy (Deut 19:1-13; 21:1-9; 21:18-21; 22:13-21; 25:5-10).[107] He combines a solid historical-critical analysis of selected texts from Deuteronomy with insights gained from cross-cultural analysis of kinship-based societies in Africa and the Middle East. Such a definition allows the other to move beyond the descriptive level and to address questions such as the understanding of social values, etc. Willis shows that the local elders of Deuteronomy function in a variety of ways in the different laws and that their role is quite similar to that of the elders encountered in anthropological field studies. Thus, he finds judicial, notarial, representative, and cultic roles played by the elders. Despite the fact that Willis's anthropology is sometimes out of date, his study has opened new avenues of research that scholars working on the social institutions of Deuteronomy cannot afford to overlook.

The application of gender theory also needs to be mentioned,[108] since it has become increasingly clear that the issues of women are intrinsically linked to the social construction of reality within any legal corpus.[109]

Looking Forward

Where might the use of social sciences in understanding the texts and phenomena of the Old Testament take us in the future? We must not underestimate the obstacles to progress. Scholars committed to a heavily empiricist historical enterprise, such as the comparative-philological approach that has long been in a powerful position in North American biblical scholarship, or to the literary-critical agenda popular in Germany, are often hard to budge from a view that social-scientific interpretation is not for them. Moreover, the growing popularity of holistic theological readings of the Old Testament is also often accompanied by a disinterest in the social-scientific approach.

There is little doubt, however, that use of social-scientific ideas and perspectives is preferable to unarticulated and often unrecognized pre-judgments and assumptions based on modern views on how cultures function that seriously impede our understanding ancient Israel, a point made in chapter 1 of this volume. The truth of this can be seen in the ease with which a heuristic, yet disciplined, application of ideas from the social sciences can be helpfully integrated into the approaches just mentioned, as well as into many other significant modes of investigating the Old Testament. In the balance of this chapter we will indicate likely growth points in the social-scientific interpretation of the Old Testament, many of them represented by the essays in this volume, as we will indicate.

There is an important and ongoing debate as to the usefulness of the Old Testament as a reliable source for the early history of Israel. Some scholars, such as Kenneth Kitchen and William G. Dever, take a high view of its historicity, often with reference to archaeological discoveries. Others, such as Phillip R. Davies, Niels Peter Lemche, and many Old Testament scholars in Germany, are very skeptical, treating it as (good historical) fiction. While the truth probably lies somewhere between these two camps, this is an area where knowledge of ethnicity developed by social scientists can make a significant contribution to interpreting archaeological discoveries that bear upon this debate,[110] as well as allowing us to situate the final forms of biblical texts and the underlying strata in relation to their social contexts in a way not easily achieved hitherto. Anselm Hagedorn's essay on ethnicity and Nahum lies in this field.

Investigations of virtually any period of Israel's history can only profit from social-scientific models that highlight the socioeconomic dimensions and social structures of agrarian societies. The essays by Marvin Chaney on political economy and Micah 6:9-11, Robert Coote on tribalism, Carolyn Leeb on polygyny, Adriana Destro and Mauro Pesce on sacrifice, Zeba Crook on exchange, and Gary Stansell on wealth all contribute to our understanding of these issues.

Similarly, it is plainly desirable that we seek to interpret the ecstatic states that are so prominent in the Old Testament (often in connection with prophecy) armed with heuristic agendas derived from the burgeoning contemporary research into comparable phenomena. The essays by Lester Grabbe, Dietmar Neufeld, and John Pilch reveal the potential here. Much of the purity system (brought into prominence by Mary Douglas) evident in the Old Testament and the honor/shame value system evident on every page still remain to be explored, as can be seen in the rich lode John Elliott opens up in relation to a mere two verses in Deuteronomy. Mario Aguilar's essay alerts us to the potential for interpretation that brings into play social-scientific research into the practice of war.

The study of intergroup relations in various periods remains a ripe field for exploration using social-identity theory that has emerged from European social psychology. While Jutta Jokiranta's essay on the Teacher of Righteousness inaugurates this approach for the study of the Qumran scrolls, there are ample possibilities for such an approach in relation to any of the abundant data in the Old Testament that relate to the development of group identity in a situation of intergroup tension and conflict.

Finally, there is the new approach to the study of Old Testament narrative that proceeds by a close analysis of the literary qualities of particular books or passages, but within an ancient context understood by use of social-scientific ideas and insights. Here the aim is to understand what meanings such narratives would have conveyed to their original, ancient audience. This manner of interpretation, fusing a social-scientific with a literary-critical agenda in the interests of discovering historical meaning, is represented in the essays by Richard DeMaris and Carolyn Leeb on the Jephthah story and by Philip Esler on 2 Samuel 10–12.

PART TWO

Themes

CHAPTER THREE

Tribalism

SOCIAL ORGANIZATION IN THE BIBLICAL ISRAELS

Robert B. Coote

The recent occupation of Iraq by U.S. and British forces and the subsequent difficulties in restoring peace have brought the continuing importance of tribes within that country to a wide audience. In his look at tribalism in Ancient Palestine and the Hebrew Bible, Robert Coote argues from the view that historical, anthropological, and sociological sources make it possible to generalize by analogy about the nature of tribalism in the ancient Near East. Tribal relations took shape in the interface of tribe and monarchic court, and neither sphere, insofar as they were separate, could speak about tribes without dealing with the other. An understanding of tribalism informed by social research into modern and recent tribal phenomena is essential for understanding the ideologies and rhetoric of tribalism in the Bible.

The extraordinary nature of the Bible notwithstanding, we have reached the point where we can view the history of Israel in comparative terms and expect to find little or nothing out of the ordinary. In all probability, Israel emerged in the late Bronze Age as a tribal coalition near or on the border between the great powers Hatti and Egypt. The Merneptah Stele suggests that Israel was the main, if not sole, rural power in this region.[1] The strength and effect of this coalition are made clear by the spread of highland villages in Palestine in the early Iron Age. These villages were located mostly on virgin sites not associated with new urban growth sites. In one sense this settlement was an extraordinary geographical development; in another sense it was just one more of the shifts in settlement that have been common to the region, and the reasons for it were probably ordinary. These new villages were, if not all then nearly so, Israelite villages, coming under what must have been a tribal dominion, without which such villages would have lacked the necessary security to exist. This was newly settled territory, with respect to extensive agricultural village settlement, and the culture—in the case of early Israel, chiefly political culture—of first settlements in a previously unsettled or newly colonized region tends to persist.[2] During the same period, similar developments occurred elsewhere in the wider region. In time, strongmen, probably all claiming tribal affiliation, assumed monarchic prerogatives over these dominions. In the central highland, the result was a run of unstable tribal monarchies. The tradition of tribal Israel lived on in the courts of these highland monarchies not only to back appeals for support from their clients and subjects and assertions of autonomy in the face of meddling monarchies, but also to define the extent of their sovereignty, which was unusually wide insofar as it was conceived in terms of the also unusually wide dominion of tribal Israel. This indeed was probably the main interest of the Israelite citadel courts, and the chief significance of the Israelite name, invoking a broad sweep of self-governing Palestine settlement. Exactly how far doesn't matter, since in any case it was far more extensive than any urban-based local sovereignty in Palestine for the entire New Kingdom and Early Iron periods. Put in terms of linguistic framing as described by George Lakoff— every word is defined in use relative to a conceptual framework—the name *Israel* brought with it the idea of a large and legitimate dominion.[3] This idea depended on thinking of Israel as the sum of tribal components, and that, I suspect, is why the tribal concept of Israel persisted in the Hebrew scriptures.

The social history of Palestine in the biblical period has benefited tremendously from archaeology, comparative social history, and the ideological criticism of prevailing historical constructs. There are significant unsettled issues, including (1) the dating of the texts of the Hebrew scriptures and (2) the social organization of the subjects under the circumscribed sovereignties indicated by those texts. As for dating the scriptures, many now believe that Judah did not become a proper state until the eighth century, and that therefore Jerusalem did not develop the wherewithal even to begin to produce the great Davidic texts like J and the sources of the Deuteronomic History until the mythic founder of the dynasty had been dead at least two hundred years. Others of us—what percentage of scholars I cannot say—continue to doubt this view. Long texts could quite readily have been written early in the history of the Davidic dynasty. It might have required only one or two scribes. On the second issue, social organization in the biblical Israels, I tend to be vague. The irony is that where there is practically no direct evidence, for early Israel, we can say with some assurance that Israel was organized as a tribal alliance, and we can say quite a bit in general terms about the nature of such an alliance. But where there is much evidence, for the Israelite monarchies and Persian province Yehud, it does not produce a clear picture of how much and how long the tribal forms of the Late Bronze and early Iron Ages persisted, with intermittent exceptions. In the hands of virtuoso detectives like Baruch Halpern, the sparse data can be made to yield tiny bits and pieces of a much larger picture, but that's all.[4] The irony—little evidence much certainty, much evidence little certainty—conveys the essential point. The difference between premonarchic Israel and later monarchic Israels was the existence of Israelite states as seats of scribal activity. Biblical literature is virtually entirely state literature, and ancient state literature typically conceals as much as it reveals of the real contours of social organization under state sovereignty.

Here we must not be misled. The tendency persists to idealize Israel as a singularity and its social organization as inherent—the essentialist fallacy. Scholars continue to use expressions like "Israel's social organization," as though there were only one, often with the assumption that it was exceptional or unique. I am intentionally vague about Israelite social organization for two reasons. One is that I do not expect that social organization in "Israelite" Palestine was always of one kind or ever one of a kind. As for tribalism, to go from the twelve tribes in J to the twelve in Joshua to the twelve in Ezekiel to the *Testaments of the Twelve Patriarchs* to the twelve apostles is not to trace a single social reality. I assume instead that social organization referred to as "Israel," "the sons of Israel," or "the house of Israel" was changeable and ordinary. The other reason I am vague is that I do not read the texts from the court of David or his successors (or the ostensible two or three significant non-Davidic texts embedded in them) mainly to discern the social organization of the Israelite or Davidic subjects, since usually, as just stated, the information is not there. And when information is there, with respect to tribalism it may or may not give a clear indication of tribal social organization for any length of time. There may be no more connection between the Bible and Israelite tribalism at any given time or in any given text than between the late eighteenth- and nineteenth-century tartans and bagpipes (first adopted by the conquering British army itself) and the clan culture obliterated in the aftermath of Culloden.

But there is something the texts do tell us, to which we need to continue to pay more attention. Whatever a text says about tribes in its own time represents the conceptuality of a court. The texts tell us what writers as servants of Israelite courts thought about tribal identity and organization. (With the controversial exception of a few short poems all the biblical texts were written after the period of early or premonarchic Israel.) This is important not only for understanding the court, but for understanding the tribes as well. It is clear from the literature on tribalism that when tribes are embedded in a monarchic or state setting tribal identities form mainly in confrontation, negotiation, and compromise between tribal and state leaders. Thus, while the texts may not give us a straightforward description of social organization of Israelite tribes in village and field in any period, they do give us insight into the political intents of a participant in the forming of tribal organization. In fact, the distinction between tribalism in actuality and tribalism as court ideology is mostly irrelevant. In the biblical world, tribal organization was nearly always embedded in monarchic settings, and therefore nearly always took shape in relation to monarchic court policy and discourse. Tribal discourse within state contexts—and *all* forms of tribal organization that went by the name Israel took shape within state contexts—did not form apart from state discourse. It is indicative that at least one well-regarded textbook of Middle East anthropology introduces tribes under the chapter heading "Meaning and Society" and begins the chapter with a discussion of ideology.[5] Before anything is said about tribal forms in biblical societies, we must discern, if possible, what the relevant court's view was and why, since it is court ideology to which the texts give us most direct access. Much has been written to help us do this, and it might be useful to give an overview of some nodal points in biblical history to see what they look like from this perspective.

But the first task, beyond which we cannot go here, is to develop a set of informed generalities about tribalism. The sources are historical, anthropological, and sociological. In biblical studies Robert Wilson's work was something of a watershed for the discussion of the social construction of biblical genealogy.[6] The Middle Bronze Age Mari texts have given a particularly illuminating early example of the relationship between monarchy and tribe.[7] Most of the generalities listed here have been known for at least a generation, so Dale Eickelman's *The Middle*

East, which others have cited as well, remains a useful statement of the ones he includes. Eickelman distinguishes four ways in which people have formed tribal identities in the Middle East: (1) ethnopolitical ideologies of tribal people themselves explaining their sociopolitical organization; (2) "concepts used by state authorities for administrative purposes"; (3) implicit practical notions that are not elaborated into formal ideologies; and (4) anthropological concepts.[8] The first—what tribal members thought and did—is assumed to be the main subject of a social-scientific approach to the Bible. It is what most biblical scholars prefer to discuss under the heading "Israelite society," although as a rule such discussions have paid little or no attention to tribalism. For the Bible as court literature the second of Eickelman's ways—concepts of state authorities—is the most important of the four. For a fuller social picture, the first and second ways would have to be combined, but usually little is known about the first as distinct from the second. Perhaps the biggest flaw in studies of biblical tribalism has been the tendency to treat social organization in village and field separate from the influence of the court—in all periods.[9] Eickelman's third way—implicit notions—are by definition the least visible in biblical sources. The fourth way—anthropological concepts—in biblical studies has had mostly to do with the first, and often in an idealized way.

A further problem is that in English the terminology of tribalism is used for the whole range of societal types, from hunting and gathering (e.g., Native Americans) to horticultural and agrarian chieftainships (in Scotland "clan," Gaelic for "offspring, family," is used instead of "tribe"), so-called pastoral nomadic societies, agrarian monarchies, industrialized societies (tribalism not only in Afghanistan but also Iraq), and recently contemporary multinational or multicultural societies (as in the expression "the newly tribalized world"). "Tribes" in such varying contexts cannot all be the same, and it is a little strange to read an article like "Tribal Society" by I. M. Lewis, in which "tribal" applies to the full range of societies.[10] As a preliminary matter, for biblical studies it is perhaps advisable to limit comparisons to examples from agrarian societies and their descendants.

A tribe is basically what the dictionary calls it: "a unit of sociopolitical organization" consisting of groups defined by kinship, real or putative, who thus share a common ancestor, and "among whom leadership is typically neither formalized nor permanent."[11] Tribalism is thus nothing more than a social extension of household kinship conceptions or—and here is a huge source of ambiguity—the most, or next

to most, comprehensive of such conceptions. As for real kinship relations in the field, the experience of the extension of kinship and its
delimitation has a real basis in mainly endogamous settlement clusters.
Gunnar Lehmann has estimated that in most periods in Palestine some
80 percent of marriages were between people within ten kilometers of
the center of a settlement cluster. Because intervillage endogamy
depended in part on proximity, small kinship districts routinely developed.[12]

Twelve Generalizations on Putative Kinship Communities as Tribes

What is to be said in general about putative kinship communities as
tribes? I suggest the following twelve generalities. These contain few if
any genuine surprises, though not all these points are yet generally
heeded in biblical studies.

First, *tribal structures and identities are fluid*; and, even as specified
by members, to say nothing of non-members, they may have little relation to actual social interaction.[13] The irony is that as an identity meant
to define a social boundary, the "tribe," perhaps because it is furthest
removed from the household level whose structure it replicates, ends up
like other terms informed by dyadic relationships: the definition that is
nominally sharp shows itself over time to be blurred and variable on the
edges and even at the center. I still remember my surprise upon discovering twenty years ago that there was practically no overlap between
sixteenth-century C.E. and early twentieth-century C.E. Palestine tribal
names, and indeed less than might be expected between earlier and later
twentieth-century names.[14] Therefore, apart from the wide agreement
that the twelvefold Israelite scheme originated in the court of the house
of David, if the tradition of twelve tribes persisted, most likely it was for
some reason other than the internal integrity and permanence of the
tribes themselves. Not surprisingly, in the Bible the twelve tribes are
"arranged in twenty different orders, only one of which (Numbers 2, 7,
10:14-29) recurs."[15] In the Bible, "genealogical lists representing traditional knowledge from both the early as well as the late monarchy . . .
indicate that clans and parts of clans moved from one place to another
and consequently realigned themselves with different tribes. The major
hint of this is '*genealogical clash*' in the lists."[16] Geneticist Bryan Sykes
recently discovered that, remarkably, all five living chiefs of the Mac-

Donald clan are, as they purport to be, descended from a single male forebear, who must be the twelfth-century chieftain and Lord of the Isles Somerled. Somerled boasted an impeccable genealogy tracing back through a long line of Irish kings, the whole of which was, as Sykes shows, false: Somerled's Y chromosome fingerprint is nearly unknown in Ireland but common in Norway, indicating that Somerled's ancestors arrived not with the Irish Scots but with the Vikings.[17] The articulation of kinship relations can usually be taken to describe a present more than a past.[18]

My second generalization is that while kinship terminology—most derived, whatever the language, from notions like "us," "born," or "generated"—typically entails a structure of *kinship levels*, which can be seen treated in anthropological works, these levels *also tend to be elastic*.[19] "Israelite . . . terminology is so plastic, the lines between different levels of tribal organization often blur."[20] The story of Achan in Joshua 7 shows the three levels that now appear everywhere in handbook treatments of Israelite social organization: the extended patriarchal household (*bêt ʾāb*), clan (*mišpāḥâ*), and tribe (*šēbeṭ*). Hebrew *šēbeṭ* can refer to subgroups within tribes (Num 4:18; Judg 20:12; 1 Sam 9:21), and both *mišpāḥâ* and *ʾelep,* as the *mišpāḥâ* under arms, can refer to the tribe as a whole (Judg 17:7; 1 Sam 9:21; Jer 8:3; Amos 3:1-2; Mic 2:3).[21] Some have argued that in the postexilic period the *mišpāḥâ* was replaced by the *bêt ʾāb*.[22] Often the word for "tribe" can stand for a whole people, as with Latin *tribus* itself. The common Hebrew term for people, *ʿam*, is vaguer than most of the biblical kinship terms, referring to various levels of groupings from individual ("kinsman" in names) to societal whole.[23] This is an important point to make, because it is only a matter of naming that has us calling Israel *ʿam*, a people, rather than a tribe. Halpern has shown that villages were sometimes regarded as clan segments, though this particularity was more theoretical than real. Instead, Israelite "clan sectors"—which Halpern compares with the clans hypothesized by Norman Gottwald, Lawrence Stager, and Robert Wilson—in reality functioned at an intermediate local level between household and clan, much like the Arab village *ḥamula*. In Halpern's words, "It is a function of their identity with the large clans, and of the plasticity of kinship terminology . . . that we have no lexical reflection of the clan sectors. But the existence of such forms of kinship organization finds reflection in a wide variety of texts."[24]

Third, *the ambiguity of kinship levels relates directly to the blurring of the boundaries of kinship functions*. Since Gottwald's *The Tribes of*

Yahweh (1979), the sharpest summary of social function has belonged to the *mišpāḥâ*, which Gottwald described as "a protective association of extended families."[25] It is a measure of the incisiveness of Gottwald's concept that J. David Schloen follows it without modification: the *mišpāḥâ* is "the circle within which a man could be required to serve as a *gōʾēl* or 'kinsman-redeemer,' a role which carried the obligation of avenging the murder of a clansman, marrying the widow of a deceased clansman to provide him with a male heir, redeeming the land of an impoverished clansman, and redeeming or otherwise supporting an indebted clansman himself and his dependents."[26] The core of this concept is the protection of kin from loss of land or loss of life, through a defensive network designed to reduce the hazards of debt and make the most of blood feud, but able to fend off direct threats to property and life as well.[27] The particular requirements obviously have their equivalents at the level of household, and at the levels of tribe and tribal coalition—assuming the differentiation of such levels. At all four supposed levels, the respective social units function as "protective associations." The end of the book of Judges gives play to intertribal strife as an exception to the rule, simultaneously capping the Deuteronomistic point that in the absence of the Davidic monarchy fragmentation and discord were inevitable.

Fourth, tribal designations have often been taken to refer to territories, both by ancients and by anthropologists and historians.[28] *Though territoriality might well be a reflex of endogamy, it is not intrinsic to kinship as a political metaphor.*[29] Most "tribes" belong to or make use of territories to which other political entities—cities, states, and other tribes—make claims.[30] In Ottoman Palestine in the sixteenth century C.E., tribes of the same name could occupy territories separated from each other by considerable distances. Also, tribal territories are no more fixed than tribal identities; in the biblical world, tribal territories were competed for and negotiated for, like other significant goods, among rivals. Even the same names refer to different territories: Hebrew *har Ephraim* can refer to the tribal territory, or to "Joseph"—i.e., Ephraim and Manasseh together—or to the whole of the hills between Jerusalem and the Jezreel Valley.[31] That in the Bible tribes as social entities tend to be defined in terms of tribes as territorial entities may have more to do with the court's interest in territory than with social reality in the field. This is evident, for example, where in the book of Joshua the house of David, following the fall of Samaria, defined the tribes of Israel (most of which were probably attenuating if they existed at all) territorially, yet

gave the highland heartland tribes Manasseh and Ephraim a comparatively spare definition.[32] And perhaps most important, insofar as the
"tribe" or "tribal people" are the most comprehensive kinship designations, the matching tribal territory will tend be both extensive and inclu-
sive. Nevertheless, despite territorial references and connotations, the
term *Israel* rarely if ever referred to a territory instead of a people, and
the practice of taking it as a territory is probably an anachronism.[33]

My fifth generalization is that *tribal organization and identity tend
to be more sharply defined in the higher levels of organization.* That is,
they tend to be reshaped more from above than from below. This is not
an arbitrary denial of local initiative or popular influence, which may be
taken for granted; it is a corollary of the primary role of regional politics among the several influences that shape changing social boundaries.
Tribal identity per se was not local identity, which for most people
would of course take precedence. Tribal organization was "differently
elaborated by tribal members, depending upon their social position.
Individuals who are socially and politically dominant often elaborate
such ideologies in complex ways and use them to solidify political
alliances with members of other tribal groups and to enhance their own
position vis-à-vis state authorities."[34] This is especially true of tribal
alliances: "confederations" among [tribal] nomads "in all circumstances
. . . emerge for military-political reasons."[35]

Sixth, *tribal organization took shape not only in relation to other
tribes, but also, and especially, in relation to regional powers or states,* an
extension of the axiom that "cultural meanings are socially employed,
produced, and maintained in social action and interaction."[36] Fredrik
Barth himself called ethnic differentiation a political act, a view given further articulation by the sociologist John Sharp: ethnic differentiation proceeds "by appealing to the *idea* of ineluctable cultural difference. . . . In
fact, people can readily invent cultural differences if it is in their political
interest to do so. Ethnicity is the pursuit of political goals. . . ."[37] Substitute "kinship" for "cultural" and the same can be said of tribal differences. Ernst Knauf-Belleri goes so far as to say that as a rule
confrontation with the state was a precondition for tribalism: "Tribal
organization usually is the political response of a non-state population to
a state expanding into their territory."[38] Hence with respect to Edom,
"the formation of tribes in Edom was due to confrontation with the outside world," probably New Kingdom Egypt, as with tribal Israel, as pre-
lude to the later formation of the short-lived Edomite state in the late
eighth century, the latter the result of interaction with Assyria, just as

with the most powerful of the Israelite states under the Omrids and later Jehuids.[39] Paula McNutt singles out political identity as the basis of Iron I tribal ideologies.[40] Resistance to the state may play a role in the formation of tribes, as reflected in the ideology of the opposition of tribes and state. But besides often operating within the state, the heads of tribes almost invariably have had to deal with the state, notwithstanding the theory of opposition.[41] This situation was the same for both early Israelite tribes and monarchic Israelite tribes, such as they were. Moreover, state rationalization is inherent to the Latin term that gave us the word "tribe"—evidently first used in English to translate the Bible—as well as its Greek counterpart. Romulus is said to have divided the original three tribes into 10 *curiae* each, and each *curia* into 10 *gentes*. (Here the word used to translate biblical "people" comes at the bottom of the structure rather than the top.) This Roman system is recorded no earlier than the age of Augustus. At the earliest it pertained to a sixth-century B.C.E. monarchy, and the bulk of its early history involves a rather complex set of uses designed to preserve the influence of the rich in the middle and late republic. The Greek "tribal" terms conventionally adduced—*phylē, phratry, dēmē*—show a similar rationalization, at the hands of Cleisthenes in 508/7 B.C.E., who wished to employ the venerable notion of tribal equality to break the power of the dominant families of Athens. Having abolished existing tribal divisions, Cleisthenes defined citizenship in terms of ten new *phylai*, each consisting of three *trittyes*, "thirds," of which there were therefore thirty altogether, ten each for the coast, plain, and city. Each *trittys* contained an unequal number of specified *dēmoi*, newly defined districts, of which there were 139 in all. Thus, the villages and Athenian neighborhoods were brought into "tribal" order by the state, in a move designed to assure not only that "tribal" constituencies did *not* replicate the abolished kinship networks, but also that they severely thwarted the recrudescence of those networks. In both the Roman and Greek cases, the supposed pre-state history of tribalism is vague.[42] In most recent studies of eastern Mediterranean sociopolitical development, exemplified by David Schloen for Palestine and Catherine Morgan for Greece, the trend has been, first, to recognize that kin-based social organization was not inherently antithetical to state administration, and second, without denying the existence of class, to use phrases like "segmentary state" to indicate the underlying social congruence between "tribe" and "monarchy."[43]

That the deceptiveness of the distinction between tribe and state has perhaps become common knowledge brings me to my seventh generalization. It should also be clear that the related distinction between the genuine use of tribal designations in village and field and the ideological use of tribal designations in the court is largely invalid. *Tribal designations and relations took shape in the interface of tribe and monarchic court*, and neither sphere, insofar as they were separate, could speak about tribes without dealing with the other.[44] This point applies, I suspect, even for the highly schematic and artificial—and latest—expressions of tribalism found in the Bible, particularly in priestly conceptions and Ezekiel. When tribal bounds were defined and sanctioned by the court, the "tribal" heads of the territories involved had reason to listen up. Given the monarch's power and privileges, local leaders could be expected to re-identify themselves, if necessary, socially.

My eighth generalization is that *ethnicity does not automatically relate to tribalism in the modern period and there is no reason to think it did in antiquity*. What this observation puts in question is not the nature of tribal identity in antiquity, but the nature of ethnicity with respect to ancient Israel. The search for ancient Israel's ethnic identity is a strange one, since it almost always seems to presuppose an anachronistic form of national identity, assuming not only the congruence of a political territorial Israel and a communal social Israel, but also the persistence of such a congruence, an impossibility—to say nothing of the assumption of shared political identity between ruler and ruled.[45] Moreover, discourse on ethnicity in biblical studies continues to deal with subjects that have long been invoked to define ethnicity, like phenotypical features, language, and religion, but that are, like ethnicity itself, socially constructed, subjectively perceived, highly variable, and, for antiquity, usually anachronistic.[46] If the notion of ethnic identity applies at all to ancient Israel before the fall of Samaria, it must do so as a function of Israelite tribalism—which often is not included in discussions of Israelite ethnicity—including the fluidities and contingencies of tribalism.[47] (The use of "Israel" later in the biblical period, when most of the traditional twelve tribes as such were defunct as social realities, may be a different matter.) Israel was not an "ethnic" designation before it was a tribal designation. "Israel" did not first become prominent as an ethnonym for a culturally defined people, but as an eponym whose descendants were variable, belying the cultural delimitation and distinctiveness, as well as the social consistency, associated with the word "ethnic." Indeed, there is reason to doubt that in the biblical period "Israel" was ever used as an ethnic entity in the modern sense. A clear case of the lack of supposed ethnic homogeneity in early Israel appears in the evidence for Iron I new village settlement in the region of upper west Galilee later associated with the tribe of Asher. Rafael Frankel has observed that

> . . . the continuity in the material culture [of these Galilee sites] and the differences from the pottery of the central hill country do not correlate with the biblical narrative, neither with regard to the [supposed] common origins of the Galilean and central hill country tribes, nor with regard to some of the Galilean tribes originating in the central highlands. As to the indications in the biblical genealogical lists regarding connections between the tribe of Asher and the tribal territories of Ephraim and Benjamin, it would seem that the ceramic data make it difficult to date these connections to the early stages of Iron I.[48]

A recent study dealing with northern Moab notes that the Mesha stela, by differentiating the "men of Gad" who "had dwelt in the land of Ataroth from of old" from "the king of Israel," appears to treat Gad as an integral part of Moab rather than of Israel from a period earlier than Iron II. The same study locates similar shifts of identity in the (textually difficult) Song of Heshbon (Num 21:27-30) and the Jephthah story (Judges 10–11), and concludes that "the material culture of the Central Highlands of Transjordan during the Iron I . . . reflects a relatively uniform horizon. Thus the combined evidence appears to preclude the possibility of connecting this material culture to a particular ethnic group in the region during the Iron I."[49] In sum, Israel was a tribal eponym before it was an ethnonym, and its ethnonymic use, whatever it might have been, makes sense only in terms of the specifics—*variable* political and cultural specifics—of its use as a tribal eponym.[50]

Politics explains descent sooner than descent politics. This is my ninth generalization. Ideologies of tribal identity typically elaborate common patrilineal descent, which anthropologists typically explain in terms of segmentary lineage theory (family tree). People in tribes believe that their notions of descent explain their political activity, but observers have long known that the reverse is more likely to be the case.[51] Most important, such ideologies, to repeat Eickelman's observation, "are differentially elaborated by tribesmen, depending upon their social position," and particularly by those who are "socially and politically dominant."[52] In the unlikely event that any complex segmentary genealogical account found in the Bible was not produced by an Israelite state—i.e., under monarchic authority—it should probably be attributed to such social elite.

Tenth, *tribalism has no necessary connection with pastoralism or pastoral nomadism*: "while tribalism has remained a common denominator of local-level social organization in the rural regions of the Levantine countries for millennia, how tribal lineages and genealogies have been conceptualized has varied as groups of kin have shifted back and forth along the nomadism-sedentism continuum."[53] However, Øystein LaBianca has postulated that in the Levant increasing sedentism has tended to foster less flexible lineage definitions, whereas "a correlate of becoming more dependent on pasture animals and rangelands . . . has typically been the adoption of looser, more flexible lineages. Such lineages have facilitated the formation of cooperative networks by means of which subsistence pastoralists have been able to maintain control over widespread rangeland pastures, watering places, camping sites, storage depots, and burial grounds."[54] Already as early as the Mari texts, this oscillation has been shown to be driven more by politics than by ecology or technology.[55]

My eleventh generalization is that *evolutionary views of social development have no place in the description of social change in Palestine from the thirteenth to the fifth centuries* B.C.E.

My twelfth and last generalization is that *to adopt an instrumentalist approach to Israelite tribalism is not to deny the social reality of tribes*. But it is to recognize that to the extent any such reality persisted, it did so fully enmeshed in sociopolitical change, whether we can specify the mechanisms of that change or not.[56]

Tribal Structure and Identity in Ancient Palestine

In the light of such generalities, what is to be said about tribal structure and identity in Palestine in any period in antiquity? The main thing to say is not too much. I quote from *The New York Times* for June 6, 2004, the back page of the "Week in Review" section, under the headline "In Iraq's next act, tribes may play the lead role." Given the breakdown of structure and authority in Iraq, "Americans have been forced to turn to a centuries-old way of restoring social order. . . . The appointment of a hereditary tribal chieftain (Sheik Ghazi Ajil al-Yawar, nephew of the paramount chief of the Shamar tribe) acknowledges the ascendancy of tribes. Indeed, just like the Ottoman Turks, the British and the Baathists, the American occupiers have turned to tribal leaders as their control of Iraq has seemed to spin out of control." The *Times* sees the role of the Iraqi tribes as temporary, but for the time being they together can provide social cohesion. The highlights and main outlines of Iraqi tribal structure and identity are relatively well known: "Today there are an estimated 100 major tribes," the writer explains, "25 tribal confederations and several hundred cohesive clans in Iraq, and experts estimate that perhaps 40 percent of Iraqis still feel a close affinity to their tribes. . . . It is impossible to account for every tribe, or give an exact picture of their territorial presence." A color-coded map represents the main tribes; the source is French—the École des Hautes Études en Sciences Sociales in Paris—and it confirms that the vagueness of American knowledge of Iraqi tribalism is inherent in the nature of tribalism and not a result, for example, of defective American government intelligence. Being colorblind I asked my wife to decode the map's hues, which even she found baffling in places, as though tribal structure and identity were immune to exact definition. In Iraq, "tribal affinity is one of the few characteristics that bridge what can seem to be intractable divisions, with many tribes counting both Shiites and Sunnis, Arabs and Kurds, urbanites and villagers, among their members. . . . The tribe has historically been a sanctuary, a self-defense guild, a social safety net, an ad hoc court and an interlocutor with the state. At the same time, tribes have competed for land, privileges and status, leaving them open to manipulation. For that reason, every ruler of Iraq has played the tribal card by co-opting, expelling, undermining or promoting tribal leaders."[57] The same thing could have been written about Middle Bronze Age Mari, and the parallels with "Israel" during at least the first half of the biblical period are patent. It might be objected that tribalism in ancient agrarian societies should not be compared with tribalism in a modern industrialized society. But this is to misunderstand the ideological and political dimensions that characterize tribalism in the Near East in any period since the beginnings of agrarian societies. One of the best recent studies of tribalism in the biblical world uses an analysis of nineteenth-century tribal relations in southern Transjordan, focusing on territory, trade, and town, state, and imperial interactions, as the basis of discussing the tribal kingdoms of the Late Iron Age in the same region.[58]

For over half the history of the Israelite monarchies, traditions of tribal Israel played a major role in the struggle among the kings of Israel and the rump kingdom of the house of David to retain or regain the monarchic sovereignty of Israel. Then, with the fall of Samaria and the

Assyrian takeover of northern Palestine, the house of David under Hezekiah asserted its revanchist claim afresh against the imperial regime and its plantations in what continued to be construed as Israelite territory. When this endeavor failed, the house of David accommodated itself to Assyrian rule and the ensuing Egyptian-Assyrian condominium, for the better part of the seventh century. By the last quarter of the century, under Josiah the house of David was ready again to assert its right, this time presumably to a plantation throughout Israel. This design, too, foundered in the face of Babylonian power. Thereafter the ancient Davidic notion of twelve-tribe Israel devolved into imaginary forms only, as presumably the set of social identities composing those tribes—excepting Benjamin and Judah—attenuated into oblivion.[59] The Deuteronomistic History, whose core originated in the early years of the house of David, is a polemical account of the Davidic claims to Israelite sovereignty, in its present form incorporating at least two earlier editions serving both Hezekiah's and Josiah's irredentist programs, despite their dissimilar stances toward the empire. The finished History, from the court of Jehoiachin in Babylon, represents for a last time, again in accommodation with the empire, the Davidic right to the sovereignty of Israel, no doubt in hope of and justification for a full restoration, under Babylonian aegis, to that sovereignty. Under ensuing Persian patronage, the same hope and justification were translated into the form of Chronicles, in which the Deuteronomists' spatial elaboration of Israel gave way to a genealogical elaboration which, whatever its reality during the Persian restoration of Jerusalem, with Darius's apparent ousting of the Davidic dynasty soon became one more imaginary construct. Though the notion of a twelvefold Israel never died, by the mid-fifth century the rosters of names in Ezra and Nehemiah no longer even pretended to represent tribal families.[60]

CHAPTER FOUR

Polygyny

INSIGHTS FROM RURAL HAITI

Carolyn S. Leeb

One of the challenges for modern interpreters of the Bible is to think their way out of the cultural settings with which they are familiar into the very different social dynamics of the ancient Mediterranean region. Carolyn Leeb leads us into this very different world. When Old Testament narratives reflect a family setting, the social unit is often an agrarian polygynous household; Old Testament legal materials and wisdom writings, as well as accounts of the Israelite monarchies, likewise assume polygyny as an important social reality. Most readers of these biblical texts have little or no experience with such family systems and find the dynamics of their internal relationships difficult to understand. In the United States, for example, the practice of polygyny is illegal and confined to communities that are marginalized and secretive. Contemporary Haiti is largely agrarian, and the structure of its social world includes polygyny as an accepted practice. Leeb draws parallels between the practices of ancient Israel and of contemporary rural Haiti and applies these insights to Old Testament texts, to provide a clearer understanding of the social worlds that underlie them.

Defining Conjugal Union and Polygyny

In our world, marriage has more or less overlapping definitions in the legal and religious arenas, but these do not fit the world of ancient Israel or of Haiti. To avoid confusion, the term *conjugal union* will be used. The hallmarks of a conjugal union are:

- expression of sexuality
- cooperation in production
- cooperation in the rearing of progeny
- intended permanence
- recognition of the union as legitimate.[1]

Conspicuous by their absence from this definition are jural and religious recognition, as well as co-residence. Societies exhibit a variety of expectations about the residential arrangements of conjugal pairs, so neither the establishment of a new residential unit nor even co-residence can be assumed to be a part of the formation of a conjugal pair. A conjugal union will involve sexual relations, but not all expressions of sexuality between a man and a woman can be considered conjugal unions. In a conjugal union, both partners will contribute in some way, either directly or by support of the partner's productive activities, to the union's material prosperity. A conjugal union will not always result in the birth of offspring, but in those cases in which children are born, a conjugal union will function to provide material resources and to furnish opportunities for enculturation of those offspring. The intention of parties entering into conjugal union will be the creation of an ongoing relationship, whether or not this ideal of permanence is realized in actuality. Finally, a conjugal union will be recognized by the society of which the two partners are a part, that is, it will correspond to the *emic* definition of pairing. Polygyny, then, is the situation in which a man is simultaneously party to more than one conjugal pairing.

Factors Favoring Polygyny

Excess of Women

One situation favoring polygyny as a conjugal strategy is an excess of women in the population. Until quite recently, the deaths of women in child bearing contributed a strong counterweight to the development of an excess of women. Large losses of men in war tend to be balanced fairly quickly, either by the carrying off of women as part of the spoils of war or by an influx of men settling in the conquered region.

Two closely related situations, which small nations in the orbit of stronger, more prosperous empires may experience, can lead to gender imbalances lasting for decades or even for centuries. First, the empire may conscript large numbers of citizens for service in imperial enterprises elsewhere, whether military service or monumental projects far from their home communities. These conscriptees are invariably men, resulting in a skewing of the natural gender ratio. In their new locations these men are outsiders and their presence does not influence the effective gender ratio because of social restraints that prevent them from forming conjugal pairs. While not actual eunuchs, they are *virtually* neutered by being denied legitimated opportunities to participate in sexuality and procreation.[2]

Second, migration can lead to an imbalance in the sex ratio in a society. When opportunities for economic survival are limited, individuals may migrate to other locations in search of a means to live. Sudden drought and famine may lead to the migration of whole family units in search of food, but more gradual reduction in productive potential in a given location may lead to the dispersal of individuals, principally males. Their departure may contribute not only to their own success, but to the success of the family unit from which they depart, either by relieving the family of its obligation to provide support (i.e., fewer mouths to feed) or by resources that the migrant sends home. Population pressures or climatological disasters may lead to a high level of outmigration when a region's production can no longer support all its residents. When the empire siphons off the production of a colony to enrich the empire, similar problems are created, or natural disasters are exacerbated.

Polygyny, as a social response to an excess in numbers of women over men, can serve to protect women and their children from starvation and exploitation. Women are also a resource, however, and when a resource is in limited supply, men may move to exert control over the resource, resulting in practices that are restrictive, even oppressive, to women. Social systems change slowly, so polygyny resulting from skewed gender ratios may continue long after the original factors that created a favorable environment for it have disappeared.

Control of Access to Women by Older Men

A *virtual* excess of women can be created by those with power in a society who control access to women, excluding some men and creating a monopoly for others. The controlling group gains two benefits: First, an excess of women are available to them for conjugal pair formation; and second, a body of males is available whose energies can be harnessed toward the projects of the controlling group. Even in cultures that do not legitimate polygyny, this control of access may be operative, resulting in a large difference of age between a man and his mate(s). Patriarchal control of the lives of women has been studied more than patriarchy's effect on younger men, an effect felt especially keenly in the area of legitimated outlets for sexuality. Young men may be required to complete a "quest"—to "slay a dragon"—prior to being permitted to form a conjugal union. This "quest" may be expressed as an expectation that a man will have served in the army or in corvée on a monumental building task prior to union formation, or simply as the achievement of a certain degree of economic success, showing that he is able to support the woman "in the manner to which she is accustomed."[3] Such barriers may require deferral of union formation for most young men and place it entirely out of reach for others.

One manifestation of the strict cultural control of women is an insistence on the virginity of women at the time of first union. Frequently the acquisition of women is accompanied by the exchange of monetary resources, whether in the form of dowry, bride price, or bride wealth, or at the very least an assumption that the parents of the bride or of the groom will provide certain elements necessary for the establishment of a household or for the festivities marking union formation. The direction in which these resources flow is not related in an obvious way to the realities of the sex ratio, but rather they serve as a "buy-in" to assure that only successful men can participate. Daughters of less successful men may end up either in unions of secondary status or in non-legitimated sexual arrangements, which will stigmatize the resulting offspring.

Factors Favoring Polygyny in Israel and Judah

Factors favorable to polygyny have been present at various times during the course of the national life of ancient Israel and Judah. Israel and Judah were dominated by a series of empires, which made use of the labor of Hebrew men for work projects or as garrisons of soldiers to varying degrees. Archaeology confirms the increasing urbanization of this period as well. The Hebrew scriptures provide much less clear evidence of the practice of polygyny than one might suppose. Some of that evidence is direct, while some is by implication. Nor is it clear which periods of Israel's life witnessed the practice of polygyny. The texts we have received may tell us less about Israel's actual past than about a presumed past.

Factors Favoring Polygyny in Haiti

In rural Haiti, two strong trends help to keep the practice of polygyny alive, despite its condemnation by the influential Roman Catholic Church and by Haiti's better-educated citizens. The first is the extremely high level of out-migration due to the crushing poverty from which Haiti suffers. Although the migrants increasingly include women, many more men attempt to leave the Haitian half-island in search of jobs, formerly heading toward the cane fields of the Dominican Republic, but increasingly the United States and Canada have become a focus for the hopes of Haitian families. In addition to emigration out of the country, large numbers of Haitian men have left the countryside for Haiti's growing cities, in search of jobs there. This movement from village to city leaves the gender ratio in the rural communities out of balance.

Structure of Household

Haitian Lakou: A Definition

The *lakou* in Haiti is a social-spatial reality which influences all of rural Haitian life. Residence, kinship, social security, religion, economics, education: all are seated in the *lakou*.

In spite of the impact of her very Western, very modern neighbors, Haiti remains roughly 85 percent rural, with most of her citizens engaged in an agrarian way of life very nearly at the subsistence level.[4] Within the rural (and even "suburban") regions, a common model of residence is a traditional system called the *lakou*. *Lakou* refers to a compound in which a shared yard signifies both the physical and spiritual sharing of its members. The *lakou* is several generations of an extended family living in a cluster of individual dwellings on shared land, under the authority of a head of household. The dwellings are occupied by conjugal families, each related to the *lakou*'s head. They occupy a plot of land with which they and their ancestors have been identified over a period of time. A portion of the shared land (*demanmbre, démembré*) contains a family graveyard and a cult house. The cult house serves the purpose of the proper attention to two categories of spirits protecting the family, the *lwa* (*les loas*) and *lèmo* (*les morts*), i.e., *vodou* rituals. Although the term *lakou* is "sometimes extended to the whole undivided family property, it is usually restricted to the household grouped together in a vague circle all around the culthouse, on the '*démembré*'."[5]

The building of a house in the *lakou* signals a young man's readiness to take on a wife.[6] An individual house (*kay, caille*) might be roughly twenty-five feet by twelve feet and composed of three rooms: a center room for living and dining, and side rooms to serve as parents' bedroom and children's bedroom. The kitchen is a hut of perhaps ten by twelve feet. The yard serves as a gathering space and work space, although important visitors are received in the living room. Around the clustered houses and yards of its dwelling units are the full *lakou*'s cultivated fields, totalling perhaps three to four acres.

Origins and Naming
A *lakou* is a "named compound," and it carries the name either of its founding ancestor or current leader. "The '*lakou*' is a social unit composed of kins who are descendants of the first owner of the land on which it is located."[7] The identification of the *lakou* and its family land or patrimony is so close that a similar collection of households clustered on rented land is *not* identifed as a *lakou*.[8]

Authority
The head of houshold is generally the oldest male of the family, although *lakous* headed by and even founded by women are not unheard of. Previously, the authority of the father or grandfather is reported to have been unquestioned, although apparently practiced with some self-restraint.[9] The cult house is his responsibility, and it is he who takes charge of services of mourning as well as other cultic services. Perhaps his most important right is the power to assign tracts of undivided family land for use by *lakou* members, especially when they arrive at their majority around age 20.[10] The head of the *lakou* is asked to approve conjugal unions, whether formal or informal.

Marriage
The conjugal units that comprise a *lakou* are established under a complex polygynous system in which there is a hierarchy of types of conjugal units. The only state-sanctioned form of marriage is marriage in a ceremony of the Roman Catholic Church, which is too expensive for most peasant couples. Accordingly, a wife by *maryaj* (*mariage*), has the highest status of all, since only the most prosperous men are able to achieve it. Men who have the economic resources to afford legal marriage in the Roman Catholic Church are more able to form other sorts of conjugal unions besides. Ira Lowenthal reports, "[B]ecause it is mar-

ried men who become polygynous with greatest frequency, as opposed
to their *plase* peers; and because the overall rates of polygyny, in peasant communities at least, are low enough so that the majority of con-
sensual unions are not second unions to a primary marriage but stand
as monogamous relationships in their own right; it is not facetious to
suggest that, in point of fact, marriage might more deservedly be
thought of as 'the polygynous mating form.'"[11]

Additional "wives" of legally married men are invariably of lower
status than the legal wife, which puts the "outside" woman at a decided
disadvantage socially, economically, and legally. Although most Haitain
men are eager to "recognize" their children, born into whatever sort of
conjugal union, by registering their births and acknowledging paternity,
legally married men are forbidden by law from recognizing any children
born outside of their marriage.

Most often, conjugal pairs are formed by *plasaj (plaçage)*, an informal and less costly practice acknowledged by the community as equally
binding. A man may have several such spouses (*plases, placées*), and
each one will occupy her own dwelling, each of which he will visit at
times, although not on a strict rotation.

The woman who shares the man's principal dwelling (*fanm kay*,
femme caille, or "house" wife) has the highest status among his *plases*,
although he is understood to be "resident" in each dwelling, provided
that he entrusts the care of some of his possessions to the woman living
there. Next in rank are those who have borne him children *(mamnan
pitit)*. A woman who has borne no children ranks lower and is simply
referred to as *fanm plase (femme placée)*. Other less permanent relationships can exist between a man and a woman, although these less
formal relationships do not qualify as conjugal unions. A women in such
a relationship ranks higher than a prostitute; she is not paid but may
receive gifts, and she owes the man no exclusivity, although unlike the
prostitute she can choose her sexual partners.[12]

The peasant cultivator controls a collection of scattered land
parcels.[13] Several of the wives of a man may live in separate dwellings
within the *lakou*, although frequently a man will build houses for secondary wives on outlying parcels that he controls and on which she will
raise crops to support herself. These are the so-called "garden women."[14]

The Roles of Women
Rural Haitian mores place no particular value on virginity in women.[15]
Indeed, there is a general expectation that both partners will come to a

conjugal union with some prior sexual experience. The death of a young woman prior to sexual initiation is held to have negative spiritual ramifications, and a practitioner may be hired by the family to perform a ritual defloration prior to burial, to prevent future problems with a restless spirit.[16]

A history of forced labor and military service have led, among rural Haitians, to an expectation that all marketing will be carried out by women, allowing men to remain out of sight in the hinterlands. Women carry products to local markets for sale, and these are distributed toward the larger cities by enterprising resellers referred to as *madanm sara's (Madam Sarah's)* or "market women."[17] A woman is under the authority of her husband, and may be disciplined by him, but women's travels beyond the confines of the local community give them information which insures that they are consulted for important decisions.

Women inherit land as well as men, although frequently they inherit smaller parcels. Typically they may be set up by their husbands with the means to earn a living. With control over less land, more women may end up in the *lakou*, where the communal living arrangement allows her to leave her children in the care of other family members when she makes her trips to the villages or cities for trading.[18]

The essence of *lakou* has always been mutual assistance.[19] Although there may be disputes and rivalries within the *lakou*, the "spiritual unity" of the family is manifested in the presentation of a united harmonious front to the outside world. This unity is symboled by a custom of commensality by sharing food, and an individual household is understood to be in solidarity with all those other households which it is "eating with."[20] In practice, this entails sending a plate of food to each house in the *lakou* each time a meal is prepared. The portion of food offered is representative and noncompetitive; less prosperous houses may contribute only a token banana without loss of face.[21]

The Israelite Bêt-ʾab

The extended family, or *bêt-ʾab*, was the basic unit of production in ancient Israel, and cooperation and mutual assistance among families were imperative for the survival of communities pioneering the hill country. Since it was a residential unit as much as a kinship group, it included both biologically related individuals as well as those with affinal or other ties. The "father's house" achieved its basic configuration in the rural communities in which it functioned at the time of Israelite beginnings and probably continued throughout much of the succeeding centuries.[22]

Although the evidence indicates that each residential structure housed only a conjugal family, an individual's identity and honor were connected to the extended family (*bêt-ʾab*), which may have lived in a collection of connected or closely situated dwellings constituting the family compound.[23] In time, the *bêt-ʾab* came to indicate descent from a common ancestor (real or fictive), thus designating the patriline.

In the ancient Israelite *bêt-ʾab* (named for its current "father") and *bêt-ʾabot* (named for their founders), we have institutions with a number of points of comparison to the Hatian *lakou* (household) and lineage. Both the *bêt-ʾab* and the *lakou* are clusters of dwelling units, each of which apparently housed a conjugal pair, but associated with other domestic units by shared courtyard space. In both instances, authority was vested in a head or father, generally the senior male of the kin group occupying the cluster of buildings. The *bêt-ʾab*, like the *lakou*, was committed to an ethic of mutual assistance, and stories appear in which the failure of this ethic received divine retribution.

The marriage system, in ancient Israel as in Haiti, was polygynous, and different wives had apparently different statuses. In spite of a patriarchal system of authority, women in Israel's early villages seem to have had considerable influence and freedom of movement, compared to their apparent restriction and devaluation in later periods in Israel's history[24]. In some instances, women in the polygynous system seem to have had their own dwelling units, in ancient Israel as in Haiti, and we find references in the Hebrew Bible to *bêt-ʾem*, or mother's household.

Shedding Light on the Biblical Text

A few examples will illustrate the ways in which these snapshots of life in rural Haiti help to illuminate our picture of life in early Israel.

Separate Dwellings

Our own vision of domestic arrangements is heavily influenced by our experiences in nuclear families. When we think of polygynous arrangements, we imagine that either the husband/father lives in the home or he does not, and that if he lives with all of his "wives," then they must all live in a single dwelling. We think of his visiting the beds of different wives on different nights, and we may even cringe at the thought that the sounds of sexual activity with one wife may be overheard by another. Clearly in the case of rural Haiti this is not the case, and we should consider that it may also not have been the case in ancient Israel.

In some important ways, rural Haiti is like early Israel, before the monarchy or during the earliest period of the monarchy. The polygynous pattern in which each "wife" is installed in her own dwelling unit, and in which the husband divides his residence among those dwellings, is probably most at home in early Israel. As the monarchy became established, and then during the successive dominations by the various empires that conquered Israel and Judah, there was increasing urbanization. With the move to the cities, men may have found it more difficult to provide separate dwellings for various wives. Indeed, Haiti has seen a shift in its population toward the cities, and many Haitian social systems are in a state of flux as a result. For some Haitian emigrants in Montreal, for example, the *lakou* may be one floor of an urban apartment complex. Lila Abu-Lughod has shared the observations of women in polygynous Bedouin families: "In the old days" a man provided a tent for each woman, but with resettlement in houses in towns, several wives are expected to coexist under a single roof, which these women see as a hardship.[25]

The biblical evidence for individual dwellings is widespread. It is to his mother Sarah's tent that Isaac takes his bride Rebekah (Gen 24:67). Although Sarah has by this point died, her tent seems to be a place where her son could come for the most intimate moments of his life. Perhaps the presence of "stepsons" would be resented in another wife's tent, or even feared by their father.

Consider the story of the flight of Jacob and his family with Laban in pursuit. The narrator tells us that "Laban went into Jacob's tent, and into Leah's tent, and into the tent of the two maids, but he did not find them [the stolen gods]. And he went out of Leah's tent, and entered Rachel's" (Gen 31:33). Although they have hastily embarked on this sudden journey, each of Jacob's wives controls her own dwelling unit. That these were of substantial size is clear from the scene in which Rachel sits on a camel saddle while her father feels all around the tent. Clearly she has a realm over which she is mistress, where she has things hidden that her husband does not know about, where she makes decisions about how to address problems. The two maids, being of lower status, do not have tents of their own.

Men's Periodic Absences and Women's Independence

Our vision of a patriarchal household includes the father of the household as a more or less constant and controlling presence. The Haitian evidence depicts a wife with a dwelling of her own in which, during the absences of her husband, she is the decision maker. We tend to view polygyny as disadvantageous to women, but some clear advantages for the women involved begin to suggest themselves. Leaving aside for the moment any question of cooperation among the wives, the addition of a co-wife might offer a welcome relief from sexual activity during the period of recovery from childbirth. At other times, the husband's absence from the home might give an opportunity for the woman to function as the head of the household and decision maker, at least until her own sons grow to adulthood to be able to function as surrogates for their father.

The independence that Rebekah shows (Genesis 24) may be the product of just such a household. Bethuel, the father of Rebekah, is absent from the scenes in which her marriage to Isaac is negotiated. Some have suggested that he is dead, although Rebekah's reply to the visitor's query does not mention his death. (His sudden appearance in verse 50—in the form of "and Bethuel"—seems to be an addition.) It is to her mother's house that Rebekah takes the servant of Abraham (v. 28); perhaps Bethuel was residing in the house of another wife at this moment, which would not be surprising. Rebekah's mother has grown children at this point, and the typical pattern in polygynous arrangements is for the husband to take a new, younger wife as his first wife reaches menopause. The younger may be his favorite, but the elder wife has more power. Rebekah's mother and brother may well have felt that when Bethuel returned and saw, based on the gifts received, that they had succeeded in making a good match for Rebekah with a wealthy man, he would be well pleased.

The "Mother's House" in Other Biblical Texts

Other Hebrew Bible texts that refer to the "house of the mother" likewise give evidence of the mother's house as a place where all children are recognized and where women have more freedom of action than we expect in a patriarchal society. Ruth and Orpah are told by their mother-in-law Naomi to "[r]eturn to your mothers' house" (Ruth 1:8). We can only speculate on such issues as whether their fathers are still alive or whether they would be welcomed back by their fathers, now that they are no longer virgin daughters. Clearly, only three possibilities exist. If their fathers are no longer living, the household of their mother is the only available refuge. If their fathers are still living and have not taken additional wives, their mothers' houses would be their fathers' houses. If their fathers have taken additional wives, we can suspect that the presence of another adult woman would be a destabilizing presence in the household. By contrast, we may suspect that, notwithstanding the tensions that can exist between mothers and daughters, their mothers' dwellings are places where they would be welcome until they can find some other way in the world.

Virginity at Marriage

The pictures painted by the poetry of the Song of Songs fall far from the vision we have of the patriarchal ideal of virgin daughters, closely supervised in their father's households. The possibility that the *pater familias* is for the moment resident in the home of a younger co-wife makes it easier to understand a situation in which a young woman could bring her lover "into my mother's house, and into the chamber of her that conceived me" (Songs 3:4; cf. 8:2). Some commentators have suggested that this term "mother's house" is used when the subject is arranging marriages.[26] A mother might, in fact, see that the most effective route to arranging a marriage for her daughter could be to give her enough freedom to lead to a pregnancy. Although this is not the ideal presented in the biblical legal material, in Haiti this is not an unusual situation. Indeed, the ideal of virginity at marriage may have developed late, perhaps under Hellenistic influence, and virginity may have been less valued at other periods of ancient Israel's life.

Advice to Young Men Moving to the City

A variety of social locations have been proposed for the book of Proverbs. A possibility to consider is the period of increasing urbanization that accompanied the rise of the monarchy and later the periods of domination by various empires. Young men were drawn, either by desire or compulsion, to leave the villages and serve in various positions in the cities. Whether they served at court or as apprentices to urban craftsmen, they became members of other men's "houses." Apprenticeship at most periods of history has been rather more like adoption or being placed as a foster child than like our notions of employment. Certainly serving at court meant becoming part of the king's household, whether or not one was placed in a state of perpetual prepubescence by castration. Parts of the book of Proverbs can be understood as advice to village boys who will be moving to the city. They will be leaving both their "father's house" and their "mother's house," and so are reminded to be attentive to the advice of both father and mother. (e.g., Prov 1:8; 6:20) A young man will become part of a new *bêt-ʾab*, the king's house or the house of the craftsman whose trade he will learn, but he will not become part of a new "mother's house." Accordingly, he is urged to become part of the household of Lady Wisdom, and not of the Strange Woman. The advantages of the house built by Lady Wisdom are celebrated throughout the Proverbs (e.g., Prov 9:1; 14:1; 24:3). The newly urban young man cannot expect to be recognized as an heir within the house of the king or of his master, but Proverbs assures him that Lady Wisdom provides an inheritance for her children (Prov 8:21).

Biblical Counterpart to Haitian "Market Women"

Finally, the *ʾešet ḥayil* of Proverbs 31:10-31 sounds very much like an urban woman in a polygynous union, who chooses to advance the fortunes of her household by diligence and hard work. This picture from Proverbs 31 of a woman with considerable freedom to carry on business enterprises without male supervision or interference is certainly similar to the picture of the women of rural Haiti, acting either as "market women" or as "garden women," supporting themselves through trade activities or through agricultural activities on a piece of land that they control. (Other parts of Proverbs suggest that another way for a woman to make a little extra money while her husband is away is to seduce the "rubes" fresh in from the villages and trick them out of their little money.)

Concubinage

In Haiti, when a woman is in union with a man who is legally married, she is considered a concubine, which is to say that the union is recognized by society, but it is acknowledged as being second-rate. This is not a legal or religious distinction, but a question of the way in which the union is regarded by her neighbors. To the state or the Roman Catholic Church, both concubine and *plase* wife are equally illegitimate. In the eyes of her community, however, the woman in a *plase* relationship is a legitimate wife, whether or not her man has other *plase* wives. Since legal marriage is generally entered into only by the privileged class, these

relationships of concubinage are almost always between a man and a
woman of markedly different social standings.

Two important differences exist between the woman who is considered a *fanm plase* and the one who is a concubine. The most important
is the status of her children. The legally married man is not able to "recognize" the children he fathers by the concubine, and so they will not
inherit upon his death. He may give them gifts, just as he undoubtedly
gives gifts to their mother, but they will not inherit.

A second difference is the ease with which a man can disentangle
himself from a concubine. When he decides to terminate the arrangement, it is finished, and the woman has no ongoing right to expect support for herself and her children. By contrast, when a man terminates a
relationship with a *plase* wife, his society places considerable pressure
on him to continue to take care of his offspring, and indeed Haitian men
take some pride in providing for their children. Often, the woman will
continue to occupy the dwelling that was provided for her at the incep-
tion of the union, especially if the dwelling was an outlying one. If the
woman does leave that house, she will return to her own kin, since it is
consanguines and not affines who are considered "family" in rural
Haiti.

When we survey the accounts of concubines in the Hebrew Bible, we
look in vain for the sorts of legal or religious distinctions that would
help us to define this status. The reality is that the relationship betwen a
man and a woman is one of "marriage" when their society recognizes it
to be, and it is one of concubinage when that is the view the society has
of their union. The issue is whether the woman has a legitimated tie to
and claim on the "father's house" in which she resides, but in which she
can never be a full member, since in ancient Israel as in Haiti, it is blood
that defines family. She can be tied to the *bêt-ʾab* only by the birth of recognized children, that is to say, by the birth of children who are recognized as legitimate heirs.[27]

Sometimes in the narratives of the Hebrew Bible, a shift in terminology occurs that causes confusion. Quite apart from the problem that
a single word, *ʾišâ*, designates both woman and "wife," we find that situations can change the social perception of a union. A woman whose
social standing would preclude her from being considered a "wife" may,
in the absence of other legitimate heirs, increase in standing by bearing
the male child on which hopes for the perpetuation of the *bêt-ʾab*
depend. One can certainly understand Sarah's dismay when a woman
who was clearly "beneath her" suddenly became her social equal by

bearing a son for Abraham. Suddenly they have become not maid and mistress, but co-wives.

Dowry and Bridewealth

Naomi Steinberg suggests that the lower status of a concubine is based on whether or not the woman brought a dowry with her to the union. Accordingly, she defines the concubine as a "woman whose continued presence within the family is not dependent on economic arrangements."[28] The "legal wife" (Steinberg's term) is distinguished by community recognition of her comparative security within the household. In Haiti, which lacks an easily recognizable dowry system, a woman brings to the marriage whatever small parcels of land she has inherited from her parents, since inheritance in Haiti is fully bilateral, although characteristically women inherit smaller parcels. Early Israel, which produced little movable wealth, might likewise have seen some sort of land-dowry system. The case of Zelophehad (Num 27:1-11) may be the final regulated vestige of some larger system for land passing through daughters. Rachel's theft of the family's gods should be understood in the context of the statement in Genesis 31:14-16. Rachel and Leah's status as wives, not concubines, is dependent on their security within Jacob's household. That security depended, in part perhaps, on the direct and/or indirect dowry that they brought to the marriage. Their father's unscrupulous actions toward his son-in-law put their status at risk, and Rachel has moved to secure that status by stealing something both valuable and movable.

Unrecognized Child Not Tied to Father's Family

In Judges 9, Abimelech, son of the concubine of Gideon (Jerubbaal), returns to his *mother's* "father's house" and reminds them that he is their "flesh and bone." The term "disinherited son of Gideon" to describe Abimelech is inaccurate precisely because he never did stand in line to inherit. The genealogical announcement of Gideon's seventy sons is meant to preclude any possibility that Abimelech could ever be Gideon's legitimate heir, and his dispatch of them was a desperate bid to be the only surviving son and thereby the socially recognized heir (v. 5). The introduction of Jotham, the seventy-first son, keeps the plot moving forward. Among his mother's kin he is recognized as family by the phrase, "He is our brother," whereas in the household of his father, he is not recognized.

Conclusion

Archaeological evidence can tell us much about the homes and villages and cities of ancient cultures. To bring these long-dead venues back to life requires an imaginative recreation of the people who lived and worked and loved and died there. Cultural anthropology can give content to our re-creations and correct our tendency to draw too heavily on our own experience. We imagine our own discomfort in a polygamous relationship and perhaps overemphasize the rivalries between wives. Although the Bible does illustrate the rivalries between Rachel and Leah (Genesis 30) and between Hannah and Peninnah (1 Samuel 1–2), the real issue is not the polygynous system but rather the inability to bear a child. In truth, the Bible has far more stories of rivalry between brothers than between wives. In an attempt to better understand the ancient practice of polygyny, we often look to the polygynous systems of Islam or sectarian Mormon practice in rural Utah. Those religiously inscribed polygynous social systems have some peculiar characteristics that may not be shared by the biblical world. Rural Haiti, on the other hand, is a society whose institutions may help us to put flesh on the dry bones of the characters in some familiar texts and to suggest what life in ancient Israel may have been like.

CHAPTER FIVE

Sacrifice

THE RITUAL FOR THE LEPER
IN LEVITICUS 14

Adriana Destro and Mauro Pesce

Patterns of sacrifice that appear in the Old Testament have long attracted attention from social scientists. Adriana Destro and Mauro Pesce seek to make anthropological sense of the sacrifice in Leviticus (using Leviticus 14:1-32 as a test case) by comparison and contrast with patterns known elsewhere. The Levitical system is inclined to attribute to a unique deity the cause of the events (a deity that has already explicitly revealed the duties of the human beings by means of a law) and tends to reduce all the negative forces under the concept of impurity. For this reason, Leviticus makes the sacrificial rituals autonomous from divination, eliminating divinatory and exorcistic rituals. The analysis of the sacrifices performed in the purification of the leper shows, however, that the Levitical system could not eliminate completely divinatory and exorcistic elements.

Analysis of Levitical sacrifice has mainly been concerned with presenting an overall theory of sacrificial rites, their cultural specificity in relation to the Near Eastern antiquity, and, finally, their place within the historical evolution of Judaic sacrificial rituals.[1] Numerous studies have been performed within this perspective.[2] We ourselves have advanced a hypothesis in this regard.[3] According to this hypothesis, the essential elements of a sacrificial act, as far as Levitical sacrifice is concerned, are the following:

1. Consecration of the animal to be offered and its exclusion from any further profane use;

2. Offering of the animal's body;
3. Symbolic value of the animal's body;
4. Slaughter of the animal and the dismemberment of its body into different parts, each assuming a specific symbolic value;
5. Recomposition of the animal's body parts in a different way, by placing them on the altar in a way that symbolizes an ideal order, different from the preceding anatomic one;
6. Transformation of the offered animal into another form of life, e.g., smoke ascending to God.[4]

Here our aim is to consider the sacrifice from a different perspective. We start from the view that the Levitical text is founded upon two main preoccupations: on the one hand, Leviticus is concerned with the *vertical interaction* between Levitical man and the deity and, on the other, the *horizontal interaction* between Levitical man and impersonal or personal forces of evil (impurity, Azazel). We believe that this dual scheme of interaction corresponds to precise textual elements in Leviticus.

In the formation of this system, the Levitical legislator "encounters" preexisting elements and needs to integrate them into an utopian scheme. With this in mind, we will discuss the case of the leper, that is to say, the human condition considered most miserable in the context of Leviticus. This is a case that throws into relief the dual character of the vertical and horizontal interaction.

Second, we set out to study sacrifice as part of a *series* of ritual acts, from which it cannot be isolated and, above all, as a ritual act carrying different levels of meaning (dual or plural).[5] Comparative analysis of sacrificial rites—for example, the sacrificial rites of the Yoruba,[6] or of Near Eastern antiquity, or again, of the Chinese divinatory texts of cave 17 at Dunhuang[7]—has shown how sacrifices are often closely tied to a number of ritual forms, for example, divination,[8] prayer, and exorcism.

It is our belief that an analysis of Levitical sacrifice from the point of view of its connection or non-connection with divination, prayer, and exorcism can lead to a clarification of its meaning and cultural function. In short, it is reasonable to suppose that a model or a logical scheme of connection among the various ritual forms may be: (1) divination, (2) prayer and sacrifice, (3) exorcism or use of talismans. In this heuristic model, it is evident that sacrifice is supposed to be a ritual that has its meaning as a part of a chain of different ritual actions.

The fact that the Levitical system makes the sacrificial rituals autonomous from divinatory rituals and from prayer has been underlined many times. Mary Douglas has recently drawn attention to the structural link existing in many cultures between sacrifice and divination: "Divination is the institution that usually links sin, misfortune, and sacrifice. There is some misfortune, the oracle finds the causes and prescribes the remedy, a sacrifice."[9] Douglas notes that Levitical system, in contrast with other cultures, marks a break between sacrifice and oracles, which were forbidden at a certain point in the evolution of the Jewish religion, while Yechezkel Kaufmann and Israel Knohl[10] have discussed the question of autonomy of Levitical sacrifices from prayer. What we think necessary is a reflection on the entirety of relations between sacrifices and other ritual forms connected to them following the model that we have proposed.

Three Days of Interconnected Rites

To examine the connection between Levitical sacrificial rituals and other ritual forms, we focus upon a particular case: the rite of purification of the leper (Lev 14:1-20).[11] We should remember that this ritual process is distributed among three distinct moments (the first, seventh, and eighth day). We do not believe it useful to give an interpretation of these three phases in the light of the abused tripartite scheme of Arnold van Gennep or to repeat here what others have said about a supposed rite of passage. We begin by highlighting several peculiarities or anomalies.

First Day

First, the text opens with the statement that the healed leper must be taken to the priest (". . . it is reported to the priest"; Lev 14:2), but then goes on to affirm that the priest must leave the camp in order to meet the leper ("the priest shall go outside the camp"; v. 4). This is the only time that the priest abandons the camp. Only through an anomaly[12]—and by integrating the anomalous cases—can the Levitical system succeed in performing a rite of purification that is absolutely crucial to its survival. This means that the religious system of Leviticus is, by necessity, open to the outside. It cannot afford not to have contact with the outside. We are therefore in the presence of a religious system that, in spite of its strongly demarcated boundaries, cannot do without the infringement of its self-imposed confines. And this implies systemic anomalies that must in some way be attributed to the systemic whole by the redactors of Leviticus.

Second, the priest ascertains that the disease has been healed. Once again, this constitutes an anomaly within the Levitical system, in that the priest assumes a diagnostic function. Here too, Jacob Milgrom acknowledges the anomaly: "The Deuteronomist brings the priest out of the sanctuary only for scale disease, clear evidence that in the case of every other disease the priest has nothing to do with diagnosis and therapy."[13] However, he points out that the priest has no function at all in prescribing the cure ("above all, the priest does nothing to promote the cure"), and therefore "Israel's priest is a far cry from the pagan physician or magician."[14] The entire operation hinges upon the priest's diagnostic skills, after which he makes his decision (a "judicial" one, as defined by Milgrom), on which the future reintegration of the healed person within the community depends: if the priest sees that healing has taken place, he sets in motion the sacrificial rite.

Third, the priest next gives the order to fetch two pure, live birds, a crimson yarn, and hyssop. The first bird is slaughtered, not by the priest and not at the altar of the Tent of Meeting. Nevertheless, from the historical-religious and anthropological point of view, it is a veritable sacrifice even though it does not follow the normal Levitical rules. Indeed, the animal is killed and its blood used for ritual purposes. Milgrom asks himself several times why the Levitical legislator does not position the sacrifice of the bird in the framework of Levitical sacrifice, particularly that of *ḥaṭṭaʾt* (חטאת). Milgrom is in fact opposing a rite that he defines as "pagan" to that of *ḥaṭṭaʾt*. In reality, the historical-religious or anthropological problem is one of defining the nature of the rite, and one cannot fail to see it as sacrificial. Thus, one must attempt to understand its meaning in relation to the ritual scenario taken as a whole. For it is a true sacrifice, only "imperfectly" collocated within the Levitical scheme or system.

Fourth, there is the issue of domesticity and non-domesticity of the animal. According to Leviticus, the birds used must be live and pure. Milgrom maintains that the Levitical legislator intends that the two pure birds should not be domestic animals (like the turtledoves and pigeons that were used in Levitical sacrifices), insofar as the bird left alive and free should not return to the encampment, taking back the impurity that it has removed. He interprets the term "live" (חיות) (Lev 14:4) as meaning wild, precisely to emphasis that they do not return to the camp.

The crucial point of the rite is that the sacrifice of one of the two birds serves to obtain the blood that must be sprinkled on to the body of the healed leper and, only after the blood has been sprinkled, can the man be declared purified (v. 7). Thus, the guiding principle of the text in question is the capacity of the blood to purify, rather than the suitability of the animal as a "sacrifice for the altar."[15]

It is only by means of a non-Levitical sacrifice performed outside the camp that the reintegration of the healed leper can take place. The reason seems to be that this sacrifice allows the purification of the body by blood, something not contemplated by the Levitical system. Baruch A. Levine has dwelt upon this limit of the Levitical system, when dealing with the ritual of the Day of Atonement, noting the lack of any rite for the body purification of the members of the people.[16] Here, this major limit of the Levitical system (the absence of rites of body purification of transgressors) is resolved, albeit in a non-Levitical way. The effect of the sacrifice is to purify the former leper through the sprinkling of blood. It appears to us that, in this case, the sacrifice has a clearly exorcistic function. While constituting different ritual acts, there is a convergence between exorcism (i.e., the expulsion of a negative force from the body of the healed leper) and sacrifice (i.e., slaughter of an animal, and the ritual use of its blood).

Some Significant Factors in the Rite of the First Day

Double Result

The rite sets out to obtain two results: that of removing the evil power from the body of the former leper and that of transporting it to a distant place (according to some, by way of a gift to the evil deity from whom the evil comes). This dual outcome cannot be attained with one sacrificial animal alone, because one must be killed in order to obtain the purifying blood. A second bird, identical to the first, is therefore introduced and assimilated into the former, by immersion in its blood. It is this blood that makes it identical to the sacrificed bird, even though it has not itself been slaughtered. The second bird, insofar as it is identified with the first through blood, can therefore assume the role of the former in taking away the evil power.

To fulfill its purpose, the ritual bird must be dead and alive at the same time. This is only possible for a pair of birds conceived as a dual unity:[17] the dead one appropriates the life of the second, while the live one carries within it the death of the first.

Mixing of Water and Blood

The priest orders the slaughter of one of the birds (he does not do it himself). However, the sacrifice in question does not take place in front of, or in relation to, the Tent of Meeting. The fact that it is a sacrifice that does not follow the normal Levitical rules serves to underscore how, in this case, the sacrifice is necessary. The bird is slaughtered over a vase containing spring water. The water collects the blood. The two processes of collecting spring water and slaughtering the bird are unified, and become one. The product constitutes a single ritual instrument. The priest also puts together the cedar wood, crimson yarn, and hyssop, and dips them into the blood of the slaughtered bird. Using the live bird, the priest sprinkles the one to be purified seven times.

The idea underlying the rite of the two birds is that sickness in general, and leprosy in particular, is caused by the presence of an evil, external, supernatural power that must be cast out of the former sick man and carried away from the camp. The mere fact that the man's skin has healed does not exclude that the power continues to inhabit his body. It must be expelled: an exorcistic rite is employed. The fact that the Levitical system insists on the function of blood also in ḥaṭṭaʾt sacrifices for the purification of the Temple's holy places by means of sprinkling confirms that Levitical sacrifice also retains an essential exorcistic function, even if it is limited to the Temple, and not the bodies of Israelites who are not priests. The ritual killing of this animal is the only way of obtaining the blood. The sacrifice of the bird is therefore finalized to the production of a material not previously available (the blood for mixing with water), usable to perform the empirical exorcistic act of sprinkling.

Entrance in the Camp

On concluding the exorcistic rite, the priest declares the man pure and sets the live bird free. At this point, a further ritual phase begins. The former leper launders his clothes, washes his body, and shaves his head, after which he may return to the camp, though he cannot enter his tent.

Clearly, since the bathing comes after the sprinkling of blood, it must have a distinct and autonomous meaning. After undergoing a rite of expulsion, the body and its coverings contain something that is unacceptable and must be eliminated. It is something that may be connected to the power of the blood itself. One can hypothesize that the bathing serves to remove the sprinkled blood.

The ritual process of the first day combines elements and acts of relevance to the systemic order. Since the sprinkling has an exorcistic function, the sacrifice of one bird also possesses this function. For the exorcism, the sprinkling of the blood is done with the live bird, only after it has been dipped in the blood of the dead bird. The live bird sprinkles the body of the healed leper, just as it sprinkles all of the surrounding space when it flies away, carrying the exorcistic power of the blood in which it is dipped.

Basically then, on the first day the ritual action starts out with the diagnostic function of the priest, which therefore corresponds in broad terms to a divinatory function. There then follows an exorcistic function (sprinkling, and releasing the live bird), strictly connected to the sacrificial one. The sequence diagnosis (or divination) and exorcism highlights the meaning of the sacrifice of the first bird, which remains strictly instrumental. It is performed in order to produce the exorcistic blood.

In this first day, it is reasonably clear that the Levitical system has not completely suppressed the divinatory rite, as a rite preceding the sacrificial one. Instead, it has reduced it to a minimal role, while attributing both the diagnostic-divinatory function and the exorcistic one to the priest (rather than to a distinct class of ritual actors). In this sense, it is also reasonably clear that there is a connection between exorcism and sacrifice. Here too, the Levitical system has eliminated a separate exorcistic phase that is distinct from the sacrifice, to which is instead directly attributed the exorcistic function.

We can now reach a first conclusion. We have said at the beginning that the Levitical system eliminates divination and separates sacrifices from prayer and exorcism. On the contrary, ancient sacrifices seem to have a structural connection to these other ritual forms. Levitical legislators tried to bring the ritual of the two birds within their own system. However, (a) they did not succeeded in eliminating the oracular-divinatory or diagnostic function as starting point of the sacrificial ritual, and (b) they attributed the exorcistic function to the sacrifice itself. Divination and exorcism are removed as autonomous procedures but reappear as features of the sacrifice itself. Consequently, the systemic structure of sacrifice is in some way modified.

Seventh Day

Let us turn now to the second ritual action. After returning to the camp, the former leper must wait seven days, after which he must shave himself of all bodily hair (14:9), launder his clothes, and wash his whole body in water.[18] At this point Leviticus asserts that "then he shall be pure" (v. 9). One problem of interpretation is that the former leper has already been declared pure twice before: the first time, after being sprinkled with blood (see v. 7), the second time, after his subsequent bathing (see Lev 14:8). Thus, taken as a whole, the ritual presents different degrees of purification. This seems to correspond to a cosmological conception in which different grades of sanctity and impurity coexist.[19] There are successive boundaries or delimitations that move from the most sacred center of the Tent toward the camp, and then the outside.

In any case, on the seventh day, the purifying function is in some way exorcistic, given that the purification of the body consists of the elimination of a negative force (impurity), which is cast out of the body. The existence of an exorcistic act not connected with animal slaughter highlights how, in certain cases, purification does not require the use of blood produced by the slaughter of a living being.[20]

Eighth Day

The eighth day marks the beginning of a new rite.[21] The former leper "shall take two male lambs without blemish" (required, respectively, for sacrifices of ḥaṭṭaʾt and ʿolah); "one yearling ewe without blemish"; three tenths of an ephah of semolina mixed with oil, and one log of oil (Lev 14:10).

The first real ritual act is the presentation of the former leper and the animals in front of the Tent: "The priest who performs the purification shall place the one to be purified, together with these [offerings] before the LORD at the entrance to the Tent of Meeting" (v. 11). It is a ritual moment of major importance, often neglected in analysis. The presentation of offerings is a preliminary request for acceptance by the deity of the offerings that will subsequently be consecrated to him. That it is an acceptance rite is deduced also from the fact that both the offerer and his offerings are presented in front of "the entrance to the Tent of Meeting." Here the Levitical sacrifice reveals its divinatory function. The divination follows a mechanism of agreement by silence.

A second rite of acceptance by the deity immediately follows, the rite of "elevation" (*tenufah*): "The priest shall take one of the male lambs and offer it as *ašam* with the *log* of oil and he shall elevate them as an elevation offering (*tenufah*) before the Lord" (v. 12). The *tenufah* was performed both for the consecration of yeast and grain offerings that were not placed on the altar. The *tenufah* was originally a distinct form of sacrifice from others, which Leviticus later integrated as a ritual part and phase of other sacrifices. In the present case, the main point is that the function of *tenufah* is to gain acceptance of the sacrifice from the deity.[22] What we wish to emphasize here is that *the sacrifice reveals its divinatory function*. Also here the divination follows a mechanism of agreement by silence on the part of the deity, that starts both because the offering is introduced into an area in which the divinity is deemed to reside, and because of the action of elevation itself.

After the slaughter, the priest takes the blood of the *ašam* sacrifice and uses it to wet the lobe of the right ear of the former leper, the thumb of his right hand, and the big toe of his right foot. The sacrifice therefore *has an exorcistic function* on the body of the man. Nonetheless, an exorcistic function does remain vis-à-vis the holy places of the Tent of Meeting, because they are sprinkled with the oil, although not with the blood. Using the oil poured into the palm of his hand, the priest actually sprinkles some seven times "before the LORD" (v. 16), and puts some over the blood applied on the lobe of the right ear, on the right thumb, and right big toe (14:17). Finally, the remainder is poured onto the head of the one being purified. The last of these acts represents the attainment of the goal of the entire ritual actions of the *ašam* sacrifice, that is to say, the elimination of impurity (expressed by the verb *kipper*) through the priest's work. From the point of view of the decontamination process, the *ašam* sacrifice is certainly the "key" sacrifice of the ritual.[23]

From the point of view of the Levitical system, however, only the *ʿolah* sacrifice will obtain the final goal of the ritual process. At this juncture, in fact, two further sacrifices follow: the first a *ḥaṭṭaʾt* sacrifice, the second an *ʿolah* sacrifice. As in the ritual of the first day, also in the eighth day a couple of animals must be presented for the sacrificial rite. In both cases the offerer needs a double in order to attain two different goals. "The sin offering (*ḥaṭṭaʾt*) served to put the individual in good standing with God, and the burnt offering (*ʿolah*) symbolized his renewed acceptability as a worshipper."[24] In other words, the *ḥaṭṭaʾt* sacrifice *has a clearly divinatory function* because it has the purpose of ascertaining whether God accepts the sacrifices from the healed leper; only afterwards can he offer the ʿolah sacrifice.

Through the ʿolah the former leper can communicate with the deity and receive from it the strength that will guarantee his or her future life. The ʿolah sacrifice reveals therefore to be the most important sacrificial act of the Levitical system. "The ḥaṭṭaʾt, in removing the impurity, restored to the person the right of access to the sanctuary; . . . the ʿolah that followed immediately upon it symbolised this renewed acceptability. It served as invocation to God, the first act of worship after being restored to purity."[25] God's acceptance of the ʿolah, however, signifies not only the readmission of the individual into the religious life of the community," as Levine writes, but is the only and fundamental act of communication with God.

On the basis of our analysis, we will now offer concluding observations in three areas.

Concluding Observations

First, to draw some general lines, it is necessary to reflect briefly on the nature of the text of Leviticus. The parts of Leviticus dealing with sacrificial rites are normative texts rather than narrative ones, as is instead the case with the parts of Genesis or 1 Samuel that relate to sacrifices. All normative texts set out to transform reality, rather than to express what already exists. The normative texts of Leviticus explicitly and directly have as their goal the transformation of rites on the basis of an ideal project.

The priests of Leviticus are writing for the reality of the Temple of Jerusalem and of the land of their own era, made up of towns, villages, and settlements that were fundamentally sedentary and agrarian. The model they propose is, however, that of sacrificial rites that were celebrated in the desert. The dwelling places of the ancient itinerant Israelites are "tents" within a "camp"; the sanctuary is the "Tent of Meeting," which is located inside the camp. The camp boundaries are marked and rigid. They delineate a zone completely regulated by the Levitical normative code, one that is completely separate from the surrounding area (the external wilderness). These physical boundaries correspond to a rigid symbolic demarcation between impurity, which must be expelled from the camp, and purity, which permits habitation inside it and in proximity to the Tent, the dwelling place of the deity and, as

such, abode of the most sacred, *qadoš*. Within the Levitical religious system, the symbolic boundaries of the people of Israel are therefore
marked by two poles: impurity and sanctity. As we have remembered at
the beginning, Levitical sacrificial rites seem to be strictly functional to
these two poles: on the one hand, they must prevent impurity, and on
the other permit contact with the sanctity of God.

Since the Levitical system is founded on the two opposing principles
of the sanctity to be obtained and of the impurity to be eliminated, it has
attempted to bring any prior or concomitant rite into this systemic duality, but without entirely succeeding to harmonize the elements and internal dynamics with its goals. This explains the persistence also in the
ritual process analyzed here of contrastive anomalous instances of
apparently redundant factors, which are difficult to trace back to the
basic Levitical framework.

Second, the limits and incoherence of the Levitical system arise from
its being founded upon an imaginary distinction between inside and outside, conceived to be in radical opposition. Because of this, the system
can represent diversity and incoherence only by placing them at its limits, or immediately outside of them (as can be seen both in the ritual of
the leper's purification and in the rite of the scapegoat sent into the
desert on the Day of Atonement).

Within the Levitical system, the exorcistic function attributed to sacrificial rites is strictly confined to the purification and elimination of
impurity from the *places* of the Temple and *bodies* of the Israelites (in
whatever form the impurity takes, whether an impersonal force or
demonic presence, etc.). The divinatory function of the sacrifices—given
the total absence of an autonomous class of diviners—is much reduced.
It reappears only in the rite of acceptance by the deity, and is upheld by
a mechanism merely of agreement by silence.

Third, the ritual process that unfolds over eight days has as its ultimate goal that of allowing the former leper to perform the ʿ*olah* sacrifice. Sacrificial rites—especially ʿ*olah*—remain in the Levitical system
the chief mechanism of communication with the deity. It is actually only
through the ʿ*olah* sacrifice that one can attain reunion with the supernatural power upon whom the survival and efficacy of the entire system
depends.

Since our aim is to elucidate the nature of the Levitical sacrifice, we
must conclude that, although in the Levitical religious system the mechanism of entering into contact with God is provided solely by sacrificial
rites, the sacrifice alone is not enough to attain the purpose of reunion

with the deity. Connected ritual acts are needed. The entire sacrificial process of the leper can be undertaken only after the live bird, dipped in blood, has been released over the open country. The elevation of the smoke of the burnt offering (ʿolah) to reach the deity can only be performed after the neutralization of the space outside the camp and of the negative forces residing there. This means that union with God requires prior decontamination not only of the bodies of the Israelites, but also of all the areas of the camp and the safeguard of their boundaries. The ritual therefore calls for two opposing and interconnected movements at the same time: the removal of the impurity or negative force by means of an ultimately exorcistic process, and a movement of vertical unification with the deity. Close examination of all Levitical sacrificial acts (ašam, ḥaṭṭaʾt, ʿolah, šelamim) always reveals this duality of opposite and interconnected movements: the blood must be sprinkled on the sacred places to decontaminate them, while the fat and other parts of the animal are placed on the altar for unification with God. The religious sacrificial act is therefore intrinsically dual.

Following the model presented at the beginning, the sacrifice is a ritual action that is necessarily connected with other preceding and following ritual actions. Among them, divination and exorcism are absolutely relevant. Following this model, if "there is some misfortune, the oracle finds the causes and prescribes the remedy, a sacrifice" or a prayer, and finally an exorcist ritual is performed.

The Levitical legislators are inclined to attribute to a unique deity the cause of the events and tend to reduce all the negative forces under the concept of "impurity." For this reason, they eliminate the divinatory function. In this sense, they are inclined to criticize some features of the culture of their environment from a so-called "monotheistic" point of view. However, their religious system is entirely located within this same culture. That is the reason why it could eliminate divination and exorcism as autonomous ritual forms, but not the sacrifice, which is a paramount expression of this culture. The sacrifice is the only ritual action that makes it possible to obtain the double goal absolutely needed by the Levitical system: communication with the sanctity of God and elimination of impurity.

CHAPTER SIX

Reciprocity

COVENANTAL EXCHANGE
AS A TEST CASE

Zeba A. Crook

One of the dominant features of social-scientific modeling is that it allows, even encourages, models to be continually tested and adjusted to make them more valuable and realistic. This can be illustrated with respect to exchange in the ancient world, as Zeba Crook demonstrates. Crook first makes a proposal for how best to theorize the subject of exchange, drawing on and modifying the work of Marshall Sahlins and of Ekkehard and Wolfgang Stegemann, making it more appropriate for understanding types of exchange in a specifically Graeco-Roman/New Testament setting. But Crook rightly calls for further modification, for in earlier periods of biblical history and antiquity, such as pre-Hellenistic Israel, we encounter a type of exchange that is not accounted for in these models, namely, covenantal exchange. Crook then considers covenant in the light of the evolving model, showing how adapting the model to include covenantal exchange allows us to be more precise in our description of exchange in the biblical world.

The two strongest features of social-scientific models is that they are abstract enough to incorporate large amounts of data and malleable enough to be adaptable to new data. John H. Elliott counseled that the ultimate, and I would add crucial, stage of applying a model to an investigation "involves either a confirmation of the model as a useful heuristic tool or its modification as prompted by the data, or its rejection and the search for a more apposite theory or model."[1] Such modification has in fact happened, as when, for instance, a model of

78

"primitive" reciprocity and exchange was modified for use in a (non-primitive) Graeco-Roman context (useful for New Testament studies). Conversely, a risk of using models is that if the model is not culturally appropriate or fully developed, its use can inadvertently result in the generation of inapposite interpretations. In this essay I illustrate how further modification of a current model of exchange and reciprocity is necessary in order to account for the data of the ancient Near East, with covenantal exchange serving as a test case.

Sahlins's Model of Exchange

The work of Marshall Sahlins, particularly his essay "On the Sociology of Primitive Exchange" in *Stone Age Economics,* has been tremendously influential in his own field of economic anthropology and in other fields, including biblical studies, and has provided scholars of antiquity with a model for understanding ancient reciprocity and exchange.[2] Sahlins defined as "primitive" those cultures "lacking a political state," found most commonly in the form of hunter and gatherer tribes.[3] In this sense, he did not imagine that his model of exchange or reciprocity would be abstract enough to apply to all cultural and social situations, least of all archaic, premodern, or modern contexts. Nonetheless, Sahlins provided an excellent foundation for understanding reciprocity in general, and his model has been easily adaptable to other locales and periods.

Sahlins's model of reciprocity rests on two theoretical foundations: *social distance* (as I shall, for convenience, call it) and *timeliness of reciprocation*. Sahlins believed that exchanges within the kinship unit were the most selfless, intimate, and therefore the purest form of exchange and reciprocity; other forms of reciprocity then were defined according to their distance from the kinship unit (hence my term "social distance"). Kinship exchanges were also the most selfless because their timeline for reciprocation was the most flexible—kinship exchanges could withstand long periods without reciprocity. From these two principles Sahlins derived generalized, balanced, and negative reciprocity.

Generalized reciprocity is characterized by selfless generosity and open-ended reciprocity, such as a mother's breast feeding, hospitality, and food sharing among kinsmen within the household and village.[4] Within generalized reciprocity, material concerns are subordinated to social concerns—what matters most is not the return but the support of the social system. With *balanced reciprocity*, exchanges are both less intimate and more demanding in terms of reciprocity—imbalance between parties breaks the social contract, and exchanges may well cease because of it. Examples of balanced exchanges include gift exchange (distinct from the "pure gift"), trade, buying and selling, peace making, and marital exchange; these occur, according to Sahlins, outside of the strict kinship center, but still within the tribe. Finally, *negative reciprocity* occurs at the greatest social distance removed, that is between tribes, because it threatens kinship stability. Sahlins considered bartering, stealing, and raiding as negative reciprocity.

Modifying Sahlins's Model

Since Sahlins's model was originally derived in a primitive (non-state) and kinship-centered society, it is not surprising that the model needs to be adapted to accommodate a Graeco-Roman environment where fictive kinship institutions (slavery, patronage and clientage, and benefaction) are equally significant and where status is derived from more than kinship alone.[5] Both of these requirements are recognized by Ekkehard and Wolfgang Stegemann, who adapt the Sahlins model to reflect ancient Mediterranean forms of exchange.[6]

Rather than relying on social distance to distinguish types of exchange, as Sahlins did, the Stegemanns rely on the more culturally appropriate status distance. This allows the Stegemann model to do four things that Sahlins's model cannot do in a Graeco-Roman context. First, it reflects the "status-conscious" culture to which it is applied.[7] Second, it recognizes that Graeco-Roman status is not derived solely from kinship but also from gender, freedom, wealth, power, and education.[8] In addition, it recognizes that regardless of similarities, kinship exchange is not like other exchanges, even (or especially) those based on fictive kinship, and secondarily that kinshiplike exchanges frequently occur between non-kin parties.[9] This means that kinship exchanges need to be disentangled from fictive kinship exchanges.[10] Finally, status distance allows one to recognize the differences, despite obvious overlaps, between gift exchange and patronage, which also involves the allocation of (things like) gifts.[11]

The model of reciprocity presented by the Stegemanns for application to Graeco-Roman exchange identifies four types of reciprocity or exchange: familial reciprocity (*Familiäre Reziprozität*), balanced reciprocity (*Ausgegleichene Reziprozität*),[12] generalized reciprocity

(*Generelle Reziprozität*), and negative reciprocity (*Negative Reziproz-ität*). Since this is the most current model of exchange and, as we shall see below, since it is the one that appears to be presupposed in several Hebrew Bible studies, it warrants some detailed explanation. In the fol-lowing discussion, I shall also rename balanced and generalized exchange in a way that better reflects the issues of status that character-ize these types of exchange.[13]

Familial Reciprocity

For the Stegemanns, familial reciprocity occurs, of course, within the family and broader family network, since "family" in antiquity com-prised a larger unit than its modern counterpart. Moreover, familial exchange could occur between and among families within a single clan, and between clans within a single tribe. The social status of family rela-tive to the rest of the world would be egalitarian, a problematic term that needs to be qualified. It is clearly not the case that each member of the family had equal status.[14] Rather, the family formed a unit within which there would be equality relative to those outside the family unit. To put it another way, the giving and receiving that occurs within the family is ideally not the source of tensions nor the arena of agonistic contests. These sorts of exchanges were quite naturally different from exchanges that occurred outside of the kinship unit, despite the fact that fictive kinship exchanges can look very similar to and can use the same language as kinship exchange.

Symmetrical (Balanced) Reciprocity

The title *symmetrical reciprocity* works as a replacement for balanced reciprocity for two reasons: the interlocutors in this form of exchange are most often of an equal (symmetrical) social status, and what they exchange is must always be of balanced (symmetrical) value. In gift exchange, there is symmetry both in status (only status equals can exchange *gifts*), and in the value of what is exchanged (gifts of unequal value result in asymmetrical exchange). In other types of symmetrical exchange, such as loan allowance and repayment or marketplace buying and selling, the relative status of the interlocutors is not as important, but symmetry in value is essential. Symmetrical exchange, moreover, can occur not only between individuals (as is very common), but also occur between families, as occurs in ancient marriage exchanges involving the assessment of value in dowries.[15] In symmetrical exchange, what is exchanged *must* be of equal or greater value; if one makes a gift and receives in return something of lesser value, the relationship becomes out of balance and begins to disintegrate (in truth, it changes into a different relationship). Gifts cannot be exchanged between people of unequal status—when a "gift" is given to a person of lower status, the recipient is generally not able (nor is it advisable) to return it with something of equal or greater value. This requires us to distinguish between a "technical" understanding of gift (symmetrical exchanges between status equals) and a general understanding of a gift as "something given" or exchanged.[16]

Trade and market transactions also constitute a form of balanced reciprocity, since goods are exchanged either for other goods of equal value or for currency (which has ascribed value).[17] What makes market/trade exchange "symmetrical" in terms of status is that, for the purpose of the exchange, the status of the participants becomes "equal" (or at worst, irrelevant to the exchange). That is, the relative social status of either party does not impinge upon the value of the goods nor what is exchanged for them (when it does, we can say that the rules of the market have been usurped).[18] In symmetrical reciprocity, then, the relative social status of giver and receiver can either be the same (which it must be in gift exchange) or irrelevant to the relationship (as in market exchange).

Asymmetrical (Generalized) Reciprocity

This is not so in asymmetrical reciprocity, which requires asymmetric (unequal) social status between interlocutors and the exchange of goods or services that do not share equal economic value. Asymmetrical reciprocity requires repayment not in kind but by "homage and loyalty or political support or information."[19] In asymmetrical reciprocity, the absence of balance, at least economically speaking, results in an ongoing and open-ended relationship. This is the same quality of exchange that Sahlins was getting at with his term "generalized reciprocity," but for the Stegemanns happens outside the family (part of the rationale for a new term is that "generalized" is not as useful for describing exchange outside the kinship unit). What differentiates asymmetrical and symmetrical exchanges, despite the fact that "gifts" can be exchanged in both, is that both parties do not have equal access to goods and services (owing to their status differences). The result is a different dynamic between the players: the recipient of asymmetrical exchange enters into a relationship of subservience to the giver, where reciprocity is marked not by balanced exchange or by a return of equal or greater value but by the giving of honor, gratitude, and loyalty. Status makes all the difference in Graeco-Roman society, and it even helps to define the nature of the gift—status equals will exchange gifts (even if they are exchanged agonistically) and those of unequal status will exchange benefactions or acts of patronage for subservient behavior, even when the language of (symmetrical) "friendship" is used.[20] In many instances of first-century exchange, language obfuscates what status clarifies. According to one anthropologist, where friendship becomes imbalanced is precisely where "friendships give way to the patron-client tie."[21]

The Stegemann understanding of asymmetrical (generalized) reciprocity works in very close conjunction with theorists of patronage and clientage in Mediterranean societies during and since the Graeco-Roman period.[22] As a result, patronage and clientage has become the epitome and characteristic type of asymmetrical exchange.[23] This presents a problem in that similar but not identical forms of asymmetrical exchange are typically collapsed into a single type: patronage and clientage. This manifests itself within the Graeco-Roman period, where some have argued, quite justifiably, that patronage and clientage is not synonymous with benefaction or *euergetism*.[24] Very briefly, benefaction involves exchanges between a single benefactor and a large group with whom the benefactor has no (or little) personal interaction (such as a nation, a city, or an association). Conversely, patronage involves exchanges between a benefactor and an individual, where the relationship is more immediate.[25]

The assumption that asymmetrical exchange equals patronage and clientage (a metonymic error) becomes even more problematic when applied to ancient Near Eastern and ancient Israelite cultures. Scholars seeing asymmetrical exchange in these other cultures will naturally assume that they are seeing patronage and clientage, because they are using a model that collapses different types of asymmetrical exchange into patronage and clientage. When these scholars see patronage and clientage in the ancient Near East, they are actually seeing another form of asymmetrical exchange—namely, covenantal exchange. Unless the model is adapted to reflect the social reality of the ancient Near East, scholars will only continue to collapse all forms of asymmetrical exchange into the very culturally specific patronage and clientage.

In what follows, I shall define and illustrate why covenantal exchange should be considered a form of asymmetrical reciprocity, and also how it differs from patronage and clientage.[26] Then I shall illustrate how this more precise understanding of exchange and reciprocity might have benefited a few recent works on aspects of Israelite culture and religion.

Covenantal Exchange as Asymmetrical Reciprocity

George Mendenhall once noted the difficulties of accounting for Israelite monotheism since, in contrast to other religions of the ancient Mediterranean and Near East, Israel lacked "the *do ut des* ["I give in order that you do"] type of religion in which man and deity are business contractors in which each agrees to confer a benefit upon the other."[27] In other words, Mendenhall recognized long ago that the system of patronage and clientage that so characterizes Graeco-Roman religion (*do ut des*) does not characterize Israelite religion or social interaction. The alternative, which has proven so fruitful a framework for so many, is that Israel's relationship with God was based on a covenant.[28]

Characteristics of Covenantal Exchange

Covenantal exchanges had three central characteristics—they involved a formal and legally binding oath, they made explicit reference to obligations, and they were entered into by parties of unequal status (examples include but are not limited to the suzerain-vassal relationship and the landlord-tenant relationship). These characteristics are evident throughout the ancient sources: ancient Near Eastern and Late Bronze Age treaties, the Hebrew Bible, and landlord-tenant papyri and inscriptional contracts. Initially, the suzerain-vassal treaties of the ancient Near East are the most relevant for a discussion of Israelite covenant ideology, though it is worth stressing that comparisons can be made without being drawn into the debate concerning whether the former provided the source and inspiration for Israelite covenant ideology.[29] That is, simply pointing out the similarities and differences is sufficient for making some theoretical comments about covenantal exchanges.

The most important feature of a covenant, and the one that most distinguishes it from patronal exchange, is that it is a formal and therefore legal agreement: Mario Liverani characterizes it as a "formal treaty (ratified by an oath and sworn in the name of the gods)."[30] That is to say, binding oaths were made and explicit terms agreed to; but covenantal exchanges, like treaties, were not loose, informal, or implied, as were the vast majority of patronal exchanges. In Late Bronze Age treaties, there were clearly demarcated stipulations that would refer to the obligations of the vassal to the suzerain, and the costs of breaking the covenant. Furthermore, in covenantal exchange, these obligations were sealed with a public oath, undertaken by both parties; however, the "stipulations of the treaty are binding only upon the vassal, and only the vassal took an oath of obedience."[31] In other words, treaties might appear to have been mutually beneficial, but ultimately they were for the benefit of the more powerful party, the suzerain, and not ultimately for the benefit of the vassal.

Old Testament Examples of Covenantal Exchange

Exodus 20 depicts the delivery of the Decalogue, which stipulated in detail what people in covenant to the God who delivered them from Egypt were obligated to do and not do in return (Ex 20:3-17). For three chapters, more laws are laid out, followed by a ratification ceremony—Moses returns from God with these stipulations, and the people swear כל־הדברים אשר־דבר יהוה נעשה (kl-hdbrym ʾšr-dbr yhwh nʿśh, "All the words that the LORD has spoken we will do," Ex 24:3). Moses records in writing what has been agreed to, a sacrifice is made, the stipulations are read back to the people, and they repeat their oath a second time, this time making the added claim that ונשמע (wnšmʿ, "and we will be obedient," Ex 24:7).

Deuteronomy 26:16 represents another ratification ceremony, bracketed on both sides with lengthy stipulations, blessings, and curses. Here the oaths are implied in the claim that the Israelites secured the agreement of the LORD to be their God, and the LORD has secured their agreement to be obedient. Unlike in Exodus 20–24, both parties apparently have obligations; as was the case, however, in all suzerain-vassal treaties, only those of the vassal were truly enforceable.[32] After all, covenantal exchange had a great deal to do with the spirit of asymmetrical reciprocity, since "the vassal is obligated to perpetual gratitude toward the great king because of the benevolence, consideration, and favor which he has already received."[33] This of course, sounds very much like patronage and benefaction, but the degree of formality and legality, represented above all by the oath swearing, sets them apart.

Joshua 24 also shares many features with Late Bronze Age covenantal treaties. First, Joshua calls together the Israelites and presents the demands of the LORD: that the people revere the LORD in sincerity and faithfulness (24:14). In response, the people proclaim וּנַעֲבֹד אֶת־יהוה כִּי־הוּא אֱלֹהֵינוּ (wnʿbd ʾt-yhwh ky-hwʾ ʾlhynw, "and we will serve the LORD because he is our God," Josh 24:18, a commitment that they repeat at 24:21 and 24:24). Even when Joshua warns them that there are ramifications involved with forsaking or disobeying the LORD, they claim again their commitment to serve the LORD, and later that they serve as witnesses to their commitment (another element found in the Near Eastern treaties). Finally, the agreement is put into writing (24:25-26). That these texts are the prototypical covenantal texts is obvious; what I wish to emphasize is the degree of formality reflected in them.

Distinguishing Covenantal Exchange from Patron and Client Relationships

These covenantal texts share common features: formality, explicit promises and threats, oaths, witnesses, written permanence, unequal status, and unbalanced exchange. This all suggests that covenantal exchange is a form of asymmetrical exchange, but also that it is not exactly like patronage. That both covenantal and patronal exchange are forms of asymmetrical exchange explains why there are significant points of similarity between them. Primary among these shared features is that both types of exchange occur between parties of unequal social status.[34] Second, both the exchanges rarely involve the exchange of goods or services of equal value, but are based on a reciprocity of gratitude, loyalty, and honor. These common elements explain the tendency to confuse patronal and covenantal exchange (which I shall illustrate below). If one's perspective were limited to these two elements alone, one might very naturally conclude that suzerains and vassals were no different from patrons and clients.

There are, however, equally important distinctions between covenantal and patronal exchange. Most importantly, each involves different levels of formality. The interlocutors of covenantal exchanges were bound by oaths that were made (and re-made) in public, and that involved witnesses and ratification ceremonies in order to make the contracts legal and binding. Offending a patron also carried consequences, of course, and the loyalty of clients to patrons and benefactors was supposed to be a *fait accompli*. Nonetheless, this was never formalized. S. N. Eisenstadt and Luis Roniger, summarizing cross-cultural research on patronage societies to produce a broad definition of patronage and clientage, come to the same conclusion: "the relations established are not fully legal or contractual; they are often opposed to the official laws of the country and are based on informal—although tightly binding—understandings."[35] The patron and client relationship begins when the client accepts something from someone more powerful, knowing he or she cannot repay in kind and that their respective statuses are unequal. Patronage and clientage was no less binding than covenantal exchange, but it was much less formalized. The elements shared in common between covenantal exchange and patronage and clientage warrant thinking of both as forms of asymmetrical exchange, and the important differences justify not collapsing them into a single type of exchange.

The recent work of three fine scholars—Niels Peter Lemche, Hannes Olivier, and Ronald Simkins—illustrates how the model each of them used led them to conflate covenantal and patronal exchange. The contribution of these scholars is not gravely undermined by their use of an inappropriate model, though their use of the proper model would certainly have strengthened their arguments. My main concern with their work is that the model has been used inadvertently to shape the data, when what is needed is for the model to be modified in order to incorporate the data of the ancient Near East.

Lemche argues that patronage and clientage is the dominant form of exchange wherever people of unequal social status live in non- or partly centralized political societies.[36] For this reason, Lemche thinks it is highly unlikely that the Romans were the inventors or sole practitioners of patronage and clientage, since most societies of the ancient Near East would have been unequal and (at most) only partly centralized. Lemche argues that this intuition is confirmed by the prevalence throughout the Hebrew Bible of the terminology of חסד (ḥsd), which he understands as loyalty.[37] The central meaning of חסד (ḥsd) implies a relationship of mutual obligation, which Lemche relates directly to patronage and clientage. While it is true that loyalty is central to patronage and clientage,[38] the problem is that Lemche relates loyalty *exclusively* to patronage and clientage, when in fact loyalty (like gratitude and honor) was an important element of all forms of asymmetrical exchange, including covenantal exchange. Lemche is not troubled by this, however, because for him covenant exchange is a form of patron-client exchange—both involve the protection and generosity of a giver and the loyalty of a receiver.

Lemche's understanding of patronage and clientage leads him to the conclusion that vows and oaths were a standard part of patronal exchange.[39] It is possible that he is safe making this claim with respect to the limited practice of emperors and conquering kings setting up loyal client-states around the empire; however, the evidence for the broader practice of patronage and clientage does not attest to this level of formality. On the other hand, this level of formality is one of the central characteristics of covenantal exchange. A model of exchange that recognizes different types of asymmetrical exchange would make it difficult for him to think of covenant as a form of patronage.

Hannes Olivier combines archeological, social-scientific, and literary approaches in his reading of Isaiah's "Song of the Vineyard" (Isa 5:1-7).[40] Olivier argues that many farmers would have relied upon the ability of landholders to prepare the land and on their generosity to leave it ready to bear fruit to farmers. Both the effort and expense of preparing the land for farming and the act of leasing it to a farmer would constitute generosity. Of course, the landowner would hope to profit from the land, but leasing it would also allow the farmer to support himself and his family. Archeological and other evidence confirms that many farmers relied upon this very sort of arrangement.[41] Because of some obvious parallels with Graeco-Roman patronage and clientage, Olivier claims that "the typical Mediterranean patron-client social system" would have given this song meaning.[42] According to this interpretation, the landowner was a protector and a benefactor; the lessees were obligated to loyalty and honor. Fittingly, the "Song of the Vineyard" opens with an honoring address, as the "farmer" calls the landowner his ידיד (ydyd, "beloved").

As we saw above, however, the patron-client relationship was strong yet informal; patrons and clients did not enter into contracts with one another. The likelihood that the relationship between a landholder and a farmer was informal is profoundly unlikely, if we can take Egyptian vineyard leases, for example, as a standard. The fact that these relationships were contractual and formalized through leases eliminates the option that the landowner was a patron (in the technical sense) to the farmer.[43] Generosity and loyalty were certainly part of this relationship, but so too were they part of covenantal exchange, which was formal and contractual. The relationship between the farmer (the singer of the first two verses) and the landowner (God) was, therefore, one of formal covenantal exchange and not informal patronage and clientage.

That covenantal and not patronal exchange lies behind Isaiah's Song of the Vineyard is evident in a number of additional ways. The court imagery in 5:3 is one example: The speaker, now arguably God, asks the people to judge (שפטו־נא [šptw-nʾ, "judge"]) whether he has done all he could to encourage the fruitfulness of the vineyard. The language is judicial, and hence contractual and covenantal. Patrons and clients did not take each other to court; a dissatisfied patron simply stopped giving to a dishonoring or ungrateful client, and a dissatisfied client was more or less powerless. Since covenantal exchanges, on the other hand, were contractual, it was possible for them to come before the courts, since inaction by one party would be a breach of contract.

Second, halfway through the Song, the speaker and genre both change. God is the speaker through the prophet, and the Song becomes an allegory—we are told that the vineyard is Jerusalem, the landowner God, and the lack of an enriching harvest is the absence of righteousness and peace among the Israelites. That this is an allegory for the relationship between God and Israel indicates again that the exchange is part of the traditional depiction of the relationship between God and the Israelites; it is a depiction of a covenantal relationship. In concluding that Isaiah presents God as a "friendly Patron," Olivier draws on a model of exchange that collapses covenantal and patronal exchange.[44] It is not that he does not understand the role of covenant in ancient Israelite depictions of God; rather, it is that his model tells him, inaccurately, that a covenant maker can also be patron, since the two types of exchange are conflated.

When Ronald Simkins analyzes the structure of economic exchange in monarchic Israel, he presupposes a structure of patronage more than he argues for it; he cites the studies of Lemche and T. R. Hobbs in particular to show the legitimacy of doing so.[45] Simkins works with a perfectly accurate definition of patronage, derived from the same sources I have used. He even recognizes that the bonds that unite patron to client and vice versa are "rarely ever formalized."[46] Yet despite this he must clearly be working with a model of exchange that conflates covenantal and patronal exchange, since on the very same page he concludes that the "suzerain-vassal relationship was an expression of patronage." Simkins acknowledges that there is very little explicit material on patronage in the Hebrew Bible, but provides four examples of exchange that reflect this institution. None of these, on closer analysis, is without problems.

In every example Simkins cites, the generous giving and the reciprocal loyalty are consistent with the role of a patron and client respectively, but they are also fully consistent with the role of the suzerain and vassal. Likewise, when discussing the relationship between Saul and David as that of patron and client respectively, Simkins points to the language

of "father" (1 Sam 24:11; 26:17-25) as indicative of patron-client relations. Yet this language too, while consistent with the rhetoric of patronage,[47] is consistent with the rhetoric of covenantal exchange.[48] What is
more, David and Saul engage far more often in the explicit language of
suzerain and vassal. For instance, David refers several times to Saul as
אדני המלך (ʾdny hmlk, "my Lord, the king," 1 Sam 24:9; 26:18 MT).
Also, though Saul recognizes that David will replace him (1 Sam 24:21
MT), while he still has power he has David swear an oath (שבע [šbʿ,
"swear"]) that he will not harm Saul's family because of what Saul has
done (1 Sam 24:22 MT), which we are told David does swear to (1 Sam
24:23 MT).

Granted, there is no elaborate ceremony and treaty signing, but as
we have seen, oath swearing was not the feature of patron-client relationships that it was of covenantal or contractual relationships.[49] It is
not accurate to say, as Simkins does, that "patronage is the root
metaphor underlying the fundamental idea of covenant in the biblical
literature." It is the case, rather, that asymmetrical reciprocity encapsu-
lates the underlying social reality, and that covenant and patronage are
both forms of that reciprocity. Again, Simkins uses a model that leads
him to collapse the two kinds of exchange despite his own recognition
of their differences.

Conclusion

Whether the covenant motif can be traced to Israel's most formative
period or whether it is a later development does not affect the point
made here, that covenant exchange can be found in the Hebrew Bible,
that it comes to typify the relationship between God and Israel, and that
it is distinct from patronal exchange. Covenantal exchange is the dominant reality behind much social interaction in the ancient Near East and
Israelite culture, and it is in addition more "experience near," to use the
phrase of Clifford Geertz, to the texts of the Hebrew Bible than is
patronage and clientage. *Pace* Hobbs, patronage and clientage is not a
better model against which to interpret the social interactions depicted
throughout the Tanakh.[50]

The studies considered above reveal that when one approaches the
texts of the ancient Near East and Israel with the current model of
exchange one is forced to collapse all forms of asymmetrical exchange
into patronage and clientage. The current model of exchange works well

in a Graeco-Roman setting, but needs to be adjusted to account for the data one encounters in the ancient Near East. A more nuanced model (see Table One), one that notes the differences between patronal and covenantal forms of exchange, brings us closer to the actual experience of exchange in ancient Israel, even while it allows us to acknowledge how much they have in common as forms of asymmetrical exchange. In closing, while we should not lose sight of the fact that these categories of exchange were in reality quite fluid—categories of familial and patronal exchange overlap, as do gift exchange and patronage—it is the nature of theoretical modeling such as this to construct strict boundaries that are more heuristically workable (and not divorced from reality either).

A Model of Exchange in the Biblical Era

Familial Exchange	Symmetrical Exchange	Asymmetrical Exchange	Negative Exchange
Kinship based	Non-kin based	Non-kin based	Non-kin based
Egalitarian (relative to non-kin); open-ended reciprocity, selfless giving	Balanced social status and balanced value of exchange	Unequal social status; unequal exchange (repayment not in kind)	Social status not relevant, treatment of enemies, opponents, and strangers
E.g., Exchanges within households, between households in clans, and between clans in tribes	E.g., Gift exchange, loan and loan repayment, buying/selling, trading	E.g., Patronage (teacher/ student, patron-client), Benefaction (imperial benefactions, euergetism), covenantal exchange (treaties, oaths)	E.g., Bartering, cheating, stealing

Wealth

HOW ABRAHAM BECAME RICH

Gary Stansell

Gary Stansell takes up a limited aspect of "wealth" in the Old Testament, namely, how patriarchs, kings, and finally the nation of Israel (in the end-time especially) acquires and enjoys wealth and riches. Rather than focusing on the materiality or objectivity of wealth in the biblical world, he analyzes the topos "acquisition of wealth" in light of three models drawn from cultural anthropology: patron-client, limited wealth, and honor/shame. Stansell focuses on how we are to understand (etic) the cultural and political significance of wealth claims in ancient Israel (emic) as they span three eras of tribal (premonarchic), monarchic, and postexilic Israel.

> I freely told you all the wealth I had Ran in my Vaines; I was a
>   Gentleman.
>   William Shakespeare, *The Merchant of Venice*, III.ii.257

> The truth is that the rich are growing poorer and the poor are
> growing richer, and that land is passing from the hands of the
> few into the hands of the many.
>   Andrew Carnegie, *The Gospel of Wealth*

The Art of Wealth Getting

The acquisition of wealth is always more than an empirical and measurable phenomenon. Bassanio's words from *The Merchant of Venice* suggest the complex, symbolic meanings attached to the concept of wealth. With his considerable wealth lost through living beyond his means and now deeply in debt, Bassanio confesses to Portia that he is "rich" only by virtue of his noble status and birth, the "wealth that Ran in [his] Vaines." On the other hand, Andrew Carnegie's lament reminds us that when wealth becomes "misplaced," there is social upheaval. The rich and the poor change places, if not immediately in status, then at least in possessions and thus potentially in power. The transfer of wealth involves, therefore, the intangibles of rank and honor, power and privilege, as economic anthropology has long instructed us.

The "acquisition of wealth" is, of course, an ancient art, and the topos interested the biblical writers as well philosophers like Aristotle. In Aristotle's discussion of state and household management (*Politics* I.iii.1–2), he establishes that, while acquiring property is a part of managing the household, there is a distinction between possessing property and its management, on the on hand, and the "art of wealth getting" (χρηματιστική, *chrēmatistikē*), on the other. Indeed, he argues that the acquisition of wealth, derived from fruits and animals, which provisions the household (being necessary and useful) is natural and honorable, while trade (exchange) and usury are not. Moreover, household wealth has it limits; while trade and usury do not; the latter are "unnatural" (*Politics* I.iii.8, 9, 12).

The Hebrew Bible, of course, contains no theory of wealth getting. But its writers speak frequently enough about wealth in varying contexts, both in neutral and positive terms (Psalm 112), as well as with disapprobation (Proverbs 28) and severe prophetic censure (Amos 5:10-12; Mic 2:1-2). Scholarly studies of wealth in the Bible typically focus upon themes of rich and poor,[1] how wealth is measured,[2] or which groups possessed various amounts and kinds of wealth.[3] This essay hopes to move beyond these and similar economic issues and initiate a more culturally contextual, social-scientific approach to only one small aspect of "wealth" in the Hebrew Bible. Taking my cue from Third Isaiah's significant and recurring phrase, "wealth of nations"[4] I focus upon the question: How is it that wealth, from outside Israel, "flows" (Isa 66:12) to the people of God? More specifically, what social significance and cultural meaning—ideas, sentiments, gestures, and symbols—are conveyed by the motif of Israel's "acquisition of wealth" as expressed in the pertinent biblical texts?

I shall discuss necessarily only three groups of biblical texts. The first group, set in the premonarchic period, belongs to patriarchal narratives (Gen 12:5, 16; 13:2; 14:21-24; 20:14-16; 24:35, 53) that tell how Abraham became a rich man. The second group, episodes set in the early monarchy, concern the kings David (1 Samuel 27, 30; 2 Samuel 8) and Solomon (1 Kings 3, 10), and relate how these two worthies came into their wealth. The third stems from the postexilic poet "Third Isaiah" (Isa 60:5, 11; 61:6; 66:12), who hopes that Israel's lost wealth will be restored by the "wealth of nations," which will flow to Israel in abundance.

To guide what follows and to help avoid thinking of wealth in the biblical world from a modern economic perspective, the essay utilizes three categories. Familiar to biblical scholars engaged in social-scientific criticism, these models are borrowed from cultural anthropology: (1) the patron-client relationship; (2) the concept of limited good; and (3) the "pivotal values" of honor and shame. These models will best help us, I believe, gain some insight into the cultural understandings of wealth and its acquisition in ancient Israel. Briefly, let us recall several minimal definitions:

The Patron-Client Relationship

The patron-client relationship has to do with relations between two parties (or individuals) characterized by inequality and asymmetry in power, combined with mutual solidarity, loyalty and obligations—e.g., landlord-tenant, ruler-servants. Patrons with access to and control of production, goods, and wealth, provide aid to their clients—loans, financial support, protection, and other needs; in return, clients offer praise and other services.[5] "The patron is a 'father' to his clients, who honor him as 'sons' and faithful 'servants.'" Through generalized exchange, "patron-client relations function to regulate and mitigate the effects of economic inequalities."[6]

Limited Good

The concept of limited good is a social construct in an agrarian society that views the world as a zero-sum game. If a group acquires wealth and prestige, it must be at the loss of another group. It is the "peasants' outlook that all good things of this world—beauty, health, wealth, land, and even reputation—exist in very limited supply."[7] This limited supply must be divided among all inhabitants of the village, since the total supply will not increase; if one party gains wealth, the other loses. One maintains the wealth and status one has and avoids the perception that one has gained more, lest one be envied.[8] Life is competitive and injustices plentiful.[9]

Honor/Shame

Honor is a group value—a sentiment of worth—that one inherits (ascribed honor) or that is publicly conferred due to virtuous deeds (acquired honor). Honor claimed is defended in perpetual challenge and struggle. It is associated with blessing, strength, courage, daring, and generosity. Wealth, like clothing, is a replication of honor and evokes praise. Shame, as the opposite of honor, is denied and repudiated honor. To lose wealth, therefore, is "to be shamed." On the other hand, to seek to gain or accumulate wealth is dishonorable.[10]

Definitions of Wealth

In the Hebrew Bible, several words are customarily translated as "wealth" or "riches": שלל (*šll*)[11] and הון (*hwn*) (chiefly Wisdom literature, Prov 1:13; 10:13; Ps 112:3) mean an abundance of property, land, buildings, agricultural commodities, livestock, slaves—basics in an agrarian peasant society.[12] The root עשר (*ʿšr*)—meaning "to become rich," "riches"—occurs in parallelism with און (*ʾwn*) (II), ("strength"; Hos. 12:9 [8]), and with כבוד (*kbwd*, "honor"; 1 Kgs 3:13; Prov 3: 6). Further, the semantic field includes such terms as המון (*hmwn*, "abundance, wealth"; Ps 37:16; Eccl 5:9; Isa 60:5); רכש (*rkš*, "to gather property"; Gen 12:5; 31:18; 36:6; 46:6); and נכסים (*nksym*, "riches, treasures"; Josh 22:9; 2 Chron 1:11; Eccl 5:9).

Considered as an abstract concept, wealth is notoriously hard to define, as economists readily agree. The simplified notion that a "wealthy person is one who is in the condition of being happy and prosperous, possessing well-being," is hardly satisfactory. Generally speaking, the word is a "collective term for those things the abundant possession of which (by a person or community) constitutes riches, or 'wealth' in the popular sense."[13] J. S. Mill's definition, considered a classic, is still widely accepted:

> Money, being the instrument of a public and private purpose, is rightly regarded as wealth; but everything else which serves any human purpose, and which nature does not provide gratuitously, is wealth also . . . To an individual, anything is wealth, which, though useless in itself, enables him to claim from others a part of their stock of things useful or pleasant. . . . Wealth, then, may be defined, as all useful or agreeable things which

possess exchangeable value . . . all useful or agreeable things except those which can be obtained, in the quantity desired, without labour or sacrifice.[14]

In that neither all material objects are constitutive of wealth, nor all wealth consists in material things, a stricter meaning, according to modern economists, is that wealth

refers to the stock of economically significant items owned by an individual or a group (such as a class or a nation). For an item to be economically significant, it must satisfy two conditions: it must (a) be useful (capable of satisfying human wants) and it must (b) be actually or potentially exchangeable.[15]

Relative to the Bible, one finds definitions such as the following: Wealth: "The abundant possession of various forms of property. In the early period of Middle East culture, wealth consisted of the possession of large and small cattle and slaves, as well as silver and gold. Material goods are esteemed because they are created and ultimately owned by God. . . ." [16]

However, such definitions from political philosophers, economists, or biblical theologians are not immediately helpful to the task of studying wealth and how it functions, materially and symbolically, in the sociocultural world of the Hebrew Bible. Set in a peasant, agrarian society, within (at times) the political economy of the Israelite monarchy, the biblical world offers a "richer" and more differentiated picture of wealth, not the least because in traditional societies economics is embedded in the two chief social institutions of kinship and politics. Moreover, these definitions do not take into account what interests the anthropology of economics, such as the relation of wealth to power, or to prestige and rank.

Concerning the relation of wealth and power in an agrarian society, the principle obtains that "wealth could often be converted into political power and vice-versa,"[17] but basically "wealth tends to follow power,"[18] or rather, "wealth is a social category inseparable from power";[19] it is not freestanding, nor has it "any meaning unless convertible into honor."[20] Prestige, on the other hand, has a somewhat more complex relationship to wealth. Wealth confers authority and the ability "to direct and mobilize the activities of society," whereas prestige and the possession of prestige objects enhance repute and moral standing. They do not, however, necessarily confer political power to control social action. For example, community headmen have distinction and repute, but they are lacking in power to deny others access to goods constitutive of wealth.[21]

In traditional, aristocratic, preindustrial societies, wealth is first of all bound up in land and its productive capabilities.[22] Aristocrats or elites who desire wealth exercise their exploitative power over peasants and also compete with other elites for control over the land where peasants live. Further, "aristocrats' desire for wealth may also make them compete for opportunities to rob or tax traders by controlling markets or trade routes and particularly for opportunities to win the spoils of war, as in the form of booty or ransom payments."[23] But the drive for wealth is bound up with the drive for power—a drive that Robert Heilbroner locates in the substratum of human nature itself—whose intensity derives "from the motive of self-preservation."[24]

With these anthropological insights in mind, let us proceed to our selected biblical texts concerning the *acquisition* of wealth and its social and symbolic *functions*.

Abraham Acquires Wealth

Genesis 11:31–12:1-5

According to Hermann Gunkel, Hebrew sagas like to tell about the wealth and possessions of the patriarchs. But at the very beginning of the patriarchal narratives (Gen 11:31—12:3) the economic status of Abraham is not entirely clear. Did he, as immigrant and sojourner (without original rights) with his family members, having neither land nor children, leave Ur with no riches, a man of very little means? In any case, it is significant in the story that, after the threefold promise of land, progeny, and blessing in 12:1-3, the narrator (v. 5, picking up 11:31-32) pointedly says that, upon leaving Haran, Abraham took Sarah, Lot, "and all their possessions which they had gathered in Haran. . . ."

In terms of the narrative itself, this notice is part of the Abraham-Lot motif and prepares for their separation, necessary because they have become rich (12:6; increase in possessions and family numbers compelled pastoral nomads to separate; Gunkel et al.). The word "possessions" (root *rkš; BDB*, "to gather property," "property") is a general term for all kinds of moveable goods—cattle, flocks, and especially booty. We are not told, in this laconic notice, precisely how Abraham gained this property. Nor is it likely the narrator's purpose. It is clear, however, that Abraham enters the land of Canaan with considerable means;[25] he therefore is a man of some power, honor, and status, though lacking land and an heir.

Genesis 12:10-20

Later in the chapter, when a famine drives Abraham and Sarah into Egypt, the Yahwist tells how the beautiful woman, said to be Abraham's sister, is taken into Pharaoh's harem. This act links the foreigner, Abraham, to the Pharaoh; Abraham becomes *client* to his *patron*, and a relationship of *loyalty* is symbolized in the marriage transaction. The required negotiation must have a reciprocal exchange,[26] and Pharaoh is obligated to compensate Abraham for loss; i.e., Pharaoh gives Sarah's brother gifts (indirect dowry?) "because of her."[27] Thus, 12:16 reports that Pharaoh

> . . . dealt well with Abraham, and he possessed (ויהי־לו, *wyhy-lw*) sheep, oxen, he-asses, menservants, maidservants, she-asses, and camels.

But upon discovery that Sarah is in truth Abraham's wife (the plagues are assumed to be divine revelation), Pharaoh is presented as the injured party (v. 18). Abraham's deceptive actions are, on the one hand, an acceptable defensive strategy vis-à-vis a foreigner, especially a more powerful one; on the other, his deception is an honor challenge to Pharaoh, who must drive Abraham away.[28] But the story emphasizes that Abraham leaves with both his wife and *"all that he owned"* (ואת־כל־אשר־לו, *wʾt-kl-ʾšr-lw*; v. 20). He is now richer than before. He has not taken someone's wealth, but only received it as gift. Since wealth elevates status, he has gained in prestige. According to Hermann Gunkel, Abraham is honored to be escorted to the border, for Pharaoh now knows that Abraham is a dangerous, powerful man. Further, he remains Pharaoh's client, later a potential benefit to both parties. Abraham's acquisition of foreign (out-group) wealth has not diminished the property of his in-group; hence, according to the theory of limited good, Abraham has advanced his own property and honor rating without diminishing the wealth of his kin-group. Abraham is passive in the sense that neither greed nor direct competition has accomplished a transfer of wealth.

Genesis 13:1-6

In Genesis 13:1 the story continues with Abraham's departure from Egypt. Genesis 13:1, coming immediately after 12:20, takes up the wealth motif again:

> So Abraham went up from Egypt, he and his wife, *and all that he had*.

To emphasize the point, verse 2 reiterates,

> Now Abram was very rich (כבד מאד, *kbd m'd*) in cattle, in silver, and gold.

But in terms of the narrative in chapter 13, this description of Abraham's wealth prepares for the separation of Abraham and Lot in verses 5-6. Lot and Abraham have so much wealth that they must settle in different areas: "for their possessions were so great that they could not dwell together."

To sum up: in the brief space of twenty-six verses (12:1—13:6), the wealth of Abraham is mentioned six times, either by simple reference ("possessions they had gathered"; "all that he had" [two times], "possessions were so great") or by specific accounting ("sheep, oxen," etc.; "he was very rich in cattle, silver, and gold"). The concatenation of the motif implies that as time goes on the patriarch grows richer and richer. But he despoils no one; he cheats no kinsman. Rather, he receives wealth from a patron, on foreign soil, thus gaining and maintaining ties to political power and largesse. As a client linked to Pharaoh's power and prestige, he shares in these attributes. Indeed, the escort to the border does honor to the patriarch—a note that must have brought a smile to the narrator (Gunkel).

Genesis 20:1-20

This unit (E), a parallel or variant story to Genesis 12:10-20, expands further the "topos of wealth of the Patriarchs";[29] the gift of "sheep, oxen, he-asses," etc., enumerated in 12:16, is made more complex in chapter 20. Thus, in E's version, King Abimelech gives two different gifts;[30] first "sheep, oxen, and male and female slaves" as payment for his (almost) sin against Abraham (20:14). But the second gift to Abraham, meant to vindicate Sarah and restore her honor, ups the take, in the sum of "a thousand pieces of silver." Moreover, Abraham, client to

Abimelech's patron, is allowed to remain in the land (a third gift?). The Elohist thus heightens two things: Abraham's wealth increases not only in moveable goods but in "silver;" permission to remain in the land underscores Abraham's honor-rating at the end of the episode, in contrast to Genesis 12. Both versions emphasize the patriarch's accumulation of wealth and honor: it comes from a foreign source, from a patron who does not end the patron-client relationship, despite the slippery, tricky ways of the patriarch.

Genesis 14

The pastoral figure of Genesis 12 and 13 is presented in chapter 14 as a "general" with an army, or better, a "hero" who selflessly rescues his relatives. Moreover, here Abraham is a player on the stage of world politics—a narrative whose date and provenance is disputed.[31] One issue in this episode is pertinent for our question. Abraham has had to rescue Lot from enemy kings who have plundered Sodom and Gomorrah's wealth and provisions, including Lot's "possessions." After the rescue operation, Abraham, having brought back Lot, "all the possessions" (כל־הרכש, kl-hrkš; 14:16), and other persons, the king of Sodom approaches Abraham. He requests that Abraham return to him the persons he has rescued but retain the goods he has captured. But Abraham, refusing to enter into further entanglements, replies (vv. 23-24):

> . . . I have sworn . . . that I would not take . . . anything that is yours, lest you should say, "I have made Abram rich" (העשרתי, h‘šrty). I will take nothing. . . . [32]

Abraham thereby refuses to have his honor as "liberator" and hero undone: to accept gifts for his heroic deeds would show that he acted out of self-interest and therefore dishonorably. This is not about Abraham's generosity (Gunkel), but about his refusal to enter into a patron-client relationship to the king. As critics have often remarked, this story moves in a very different sphere of Israelite tradition than our previously discussed texts. Abraham willingly allowed Pharaoh and Abimelech to increase his wealth and honor standing, despite an implied client status. Genesis 14, however, presents Abraham as equal in rank and honor to worldly kings. His honor and prestige are at stake; he therefore must not be beholden to others, certainly not a petty Canaanite king.

Abraham acquires wealth; this means he also acquires honor. It results from his clever dealings with foreigners (Gen 12:10-20; 20), his good fortune as herdsman (12:5; 13:6), and, in terms of the Yahwist's promise in Genesis 12:1-4, divine blessings. In no instance is there lust after gain, nor greed for power and prestige. In no instance is a kinsman despoiled, his gain being their loss (theory of limited good). Indeed, if we think of the social/cultural setting of these narratives as tribal Israel, then Abraham's acquisition of wealth is presented in the context of a "communitarian mode of production." According to Norman Gottwald, this means it was an era of "tributary-free agriculture and pastoral production."[33] The tribal head, Abraham, thus pays no one tribute; instead, he ingenuously receives patronage from the Egyptian Pharaoh and Abimelech of Gerar. The narrative in Genesis 14, by contrast, presents Abraham, superior in honor and power to other kings, refusing gifts and a resulting dependent status.

Genesis 24:35, 53

But what does one do with wealth? The Abraham narratives show that his wealth, besides granting him political connections to Egypt and honor and power in Canaan, will come to serve two important purposes: besides leaving his wealth to his heir (15:2; 24:34), he acquires a wife for his heir, Isaac, with the help of "choice gifts" (Gen 24:10), namely, gold and silver jewelry and raiment (indirect dowry, 24:22, 30, 53a), and further gifts for his daughter-in-law's family (bride-wealth, vv. 53b).[34] As Moses Finley points out in his study of economy in Homer,[35] in the ancient world one possesses treasure in order to give gifts, not for the purpose of hoarding it. Finally, the display and giving of gifts (wealth) to Rebekah publicly demonstrates the honor of the patriarch.

David and Solomon

The David narrative is likewise a story that tells of the acquisition of wealth; as in the Abraham sagas, wealth is a subsidiary motif that now accompanies the events of David's rise to power. The shepherd boy who enters Saul's service is an unknown, of no repute and lacking in means; but his rise to power illustrates his ability to increase his wealth and its concomitants, power and prestige.

1 Samuel 27

After leaving Saul's service, the fugitive and desperately poor David must deceive and beg from the priest Ahimelech (1 Samuel 21). He becomes the chieftain of a band of discontents, a fitting example of a "social bandit."[36] His flawed attempt to extract food and support from the rich man, Nabal ended with his gaining, in addition to Abigail's hand, perhaps the wealth of her dead husband (1 Samuel 25). Already in chapter 23 David had raided the Philistines and "brought away their cattle" (v. 5). In 1 Samuel 27:8-28, the narrator tells how David becomes a client (cf. the phrase "if I have found favor in your eyes" in 27:5; "your servant" in 28:2) to Achish, King of Gath, who gives David "the city of Ziklag." From Ziklag David raids distant, hostile peoples, such as the Amalekites, pretending to raid his own people. It was a profitable ruse, for David

> . . . smote the land . . . taking away the sheep, the oxen, the asses, the camels, and the garments. (1 Sam 27:9)

David's deception was effective, and King Achish trusted him, believing that David's own people held him in utter contempt—a loss of honor that signals David's status as broadly and politically subordinate to Achish (27:12). But the rules of limited good and the solidarity upon which they are based prevent David from gaining wealth at the expense of his kinship group. As in the case with Abraham and Pharaoh (and Ahimelech), deceiving the foreigner and acquiring wealth at his expense are acceptable modes of defensive action, including "playing" client to the foreign patron. With his eye on the future, David must also acquire enough wealth to pay his mercenaries and distribute goods in order to become patron to his *own* clients, or rather, future chief/king to his own people.

1 Samuel 30

David and his men, devastated after the Amalekites destroyed Ziklag, avenge their losses by killing the enemy (30:17) and recovering all the Amelekites had taken (vv. 18-19), plus taking flocks and herds as David's own booty. David's personal wealth is growing,[37] as the narrator emphasizes, rounding off the unit verses 16-20 with the pointed note: "This is David's spoil."

The distribution of plunder cements networks and gains honor and power for the one who distributes it, fostering clients' support. Generous gifts build networks and increase ties of loyalty, surely the point of the report in verse 26, which tells that David

> . . . sent part of the spoils to his friends, the elders of Judah, say-
> ing, "Here is a present for you from the spoils of the enemies of
> the LORD."

The next verses carefully enumerate precisely who, in addition to the
elders, received David's largesse (vv. 27-31). It is likely payback time,
since the places named are "all the places where David and his men had
roamed." Earlier favors are thus reciprocated, yet these gifts are "challenges" that initiate further rounds of reciprocal exchange, bringing
honor to David and preparing for the next stages of his rise to power. The
use of wealth for gaining power is dramatically illustrated by the story.

2 Samuel 8

David inherited the former lands (wealth) belonging to Saul, but contributions from leading families, as well as war,[38] enriched David's honor
and strength. 2 Samuel 8 recounts how David subjects his clients (vassals) to tribute (e.g., Aram, Edom, Moab, and Ammon). The usual word
for tribute is "gift" (מנחה, *mnḥh*; also משׂא, *mśʾ*), but tribute is of course
a "forced" gift that, if withheld, is considered as revolt (2 Kgs 3:4-5).
But before David negotiates tribute he plunders the enemy: he "took
shields of gold" and "very much bronze" according to the Deuteronomistic report in 2 Samuel 8. But the image of David the plunderer is pol-
ished up by the narrator in 2 Samuel 8:11, who states that David
dedicated silver and gold from this conquest to the Lord. But was there
a difference between temple and palace treasury? Or rather, did not the
king control both? Gaining wealth grants prestige and power; verse 13
phrases this in the code of honor values: "And David won a name for
himself" (cf. 1 Sam 18:30). David was able, through "conquests and
taxation of formerly non-Israelite regions of Canaan brought under his
rule," not to tax his own Israelite populace.[39]

Solomon's acquisition of wealth stands in contrast to David's.
Unlike his father, who acquired wealth and honor, Solomon inherits
both before amassing his own riches. Yet, he never conducted "a serious
military campaign."[40] But he was a big spender: his extravagance in
building, requiring heavy taxation,[41] undid the economic balance of his
kingdom. T. F. Carney's generalization surely applies to Solomon: "The
elites of the traditional, agriculturally based societies of antiquity
engrossed an unusually large amount of their host societies wealth and
goods."[42] Solomon's wealth (and building and trade) is "dealt with in

short notes" in 1 Kings,[43] which contain descriptions of an ivory throne, horse trading, and journeys to the land of gold (Ophir), all which contribute to the magnificence of the ruler.

1 Kings 3

The theme of Solomon's riches is given a dramatic presentation in the king's dream-prayer in 1 Kings 3, where he prays for wisdom and discernment (v. 9)—not the usual petition for honor and riches found in Mesopotamia.[44] Yet God rewards Solomon with these very blessings, which will make him an incomparable king (v. 13). Significant here is that God takes the initiative, and thus legitimates Solomon and his wealth from the beginning. This *theologoumenon* prepares for the notice in 5:1 [Eng. 4:21], which claims that

> Solomon ruled over all the kingdom from the Euphrates . . . to the border of Egypt, and they brought *tribute* and served Solomon all the days of his life.

The flow of wealth to Solomon from subdued peoples—from clients to patron—partakes of courtly exaggeration. Tribute to the king underscores his power to control and thus his prestige among clients. While David hustled wealth as raider and warrior, Solomon's wealth is a "divine gift" channeled, of course, through political means. Indeed, under Solomon, scholars perceive a shift from the old communitarian mode of production to a tributary mode of political economy. Distinctive to this era and mode of production was the fact that there was, increasingly, little or no private property. The double impact of "state tax and state permitted indebtedness allowed a concentration of wealth among a small elite of state functionaries,"[45] with Solomon way out in front.

It is likely that the reorganization of the kingdom into twelve districts was to improve the administrative tasks of tax collection. Income from taxes was of course supplemented by Solomon's control of two main trade routes (the Via Maris and the King's Highway). Solomon probably profited greatly from transit duties imposed on commercial traffic through his kingdom (1 Kgs 10:15). Further, Solomon's trading in horses and chariots gave him economic advantages in his position between Egypt and Syria. Despite all exaggerated accounts of Solomon's wealth and commercial success, which were written to give him honor and prestige, there is an historical kernel in the reports of his wealth.[46]

1 Kings 10

The traditions preserved concerning Solomon's wealth give some emphasis to its coming to him from outside Israel's borders; it is foreign money, from his clients on an international scale. But with Hiram of Tyre he swaps worthless cities in Galilee for "timber and gold" (9:11), either because Solomon is particularly clever in business or because he is in economic straits. Not only did he send his men after gold (1 Kgs 9:28); his state visitors brought him lavish gifts, the most notable guest being the queen of Sheba, who came

> with a great display of wealth (בחיל כבד מאד, *bḥyl kbd mʾd*),[47] with camels bearing spices, very much gold, and precious stones. (10:2)

After her royal reception at a banquet, Sheba participates in the hospitality ritual of gift exchange and gives Solomon "a hundred and twenty talents of gold, a great quantity of spices, and precious stones" (10:10). Solomon's parting gift to her is given "according to the king's hand" (that is, "out of his royal bounty"; JPSV). Solomon is not only wise and wealthy; he is generously rich.

After the episode with Sheba,[48] chapter 10 concludes with folktale-like details about the flow of wealth to King Solomon: gold simply comes to him—in one year 666 talents of gold—over and above the gain from trade and merchants (v. 15). Further, fleets approach every three years with gold, silver, and so forth (v. 22). Indeed, all of creation sought his wisdom and brought presents of gold, spices, mules—not tribute in the sense of enforced payment, but gifts to honor the king at a state visit. The narrator, breathless after all this, simply concludes: "King Solomon excelled all the kings of the earth in riches . . ." (v. 23). Chapter 10 thus illustrates the promise from the dream-epiphany: God grants, freely, wealth to his chosen successor David. Wealth implies honor and power, and the narratives, which mean to present Solomon's excellence in all these, go far beyond what has been said of Abraham or David.

To sum up: Wealth comes to kings, but in different ways. Prior to his accession, David the social bandit gains wealth by raiding, not his own tribesmen but foreigners, which he (re)-distributes to his clients equitably (both his own men and the elders and leaders of Judah, etc.). As king, David the warrior takes spoil from his enemies; as patron he receives tribute from his clients. Solomon, too, receives tribute from his client kings and states; however, the contrast on the matter of wealth is clear: Solomon does not take, as raider and warrior, but *receives* wealth—from taxes, trade, from tribute and gifts. But the extraction of surplus and the exploitation of slave labor of his own people morally taint his acquisition of wealth. Under a "native tributary mode of production"[49] he undermines the peasant's code of "limited good." Nevertheless, the honor and prestige of David's court is not only maintained but enhanced.

Trito-Isaiah

Thus far we have examined several biblical stories about the *transfer of wealth* from one party to another: from Pharaoh (and Abimelech) to Abraham; from Philistine towns to David; from David to his clients, and so on. The one to whom wealth is transferred is said to "acquire" or "gain" wealth. Wealth, being an abstraction, of course, is never alone, but brings with it or implies other realities: goods, property, power, honor, perhaps also evoking envy or other feelings; most surely, the possession of wealth establishes rank or status. But if one person or group acquires wealth, the other must suffer loss according to the theory of limited good—even if it is only momentary.

The later kinfolk of these ancient Israelite worthies (Abraham, David, Solomon) lost wealth, whether over time as tribute to foreign powers, or when Jerusalem fell to Babylonian invasion. Would that lost wealth and national prestige ever return? Would Israel ever again play patron to client kingdoms of the "world?" The unknown postexilic poet(s) of Isaiah 56–66, living at a time of Persian rule, envisioned a time when Israel's wealth would indeed return by means of tributary economy form foreigners (as ideally under David and Solomon). In four significant passages in chapters 60, 61, and 66, the poet speaks of the "wealth of nations" which would become Israel's.

Isaiah 60:5

Addressing his words to Zion to "get up" and see the light from God's glory (כבד, *kbd*; 60:1), the poet in chapter 60 sees a new age dawning. That the darkness is to dissolve into brightness for Zion is not a mere insubstantial poetic image; rather, the poet is talking economic realities in 60:5, for he says: "the abundance (המון, *hmwn*) of the sea, the wealth of nations (חיל גוים, *ḥyl gwym*) shall come to you."

The wealth does not come alone; nations, kings, and kinsfolk will also appear (vv. 3-4); but the thrill of the heart will be in the abundance and wealth of nations, as the כי (*ky*) clause (motivation) indicates ("your heart will thrill *because* . . . abundance/wealth . . .") As we have seen before, wealth must be enumerated; the poet mentions camels, Sheba, gold, flocks—the gifts and tribute familiar from texts studied above. The passage presents the familiar, eschatological tradition known from Isaiah 2 and elsewhere as the "nations' pilgrimage to Zion," a fluid tradition that "can be actualized"[50] in different ways: the nations can stream to Jerusalem for war and their own death (e.g., Zech 14:12) or for their salvation (e.g., Isa 2:2-4). But of special interest for this essay is that the tradition is shaped here to emphasize the coming of wealth to Zion; the centerpiece is the transfer of wealth from foreigners (nations) to Zion (vv. 5b-7). Indeed, the shame of devastation and loss of temple is reversed and Zion's honorable status and great prestige among world empires is or will be once again assumed.

Just as wealth came to Abraham, signifying his dignity, power, and place among the Canaanites; just as David moved from rags to riches, from brigand to king, so also Zion/Israel. This time, according to the poet's vision, there is neither deception (Abraham, David) nor raiding and bloodshed, exacted tribute (David, Solomon) nor heavy taxation (Solomon). The *kabod* of Yahweh (play on "wealth," since *kabod* means both honor and wealth) seems, according to Isaiah 60:1-7, mysteriously to cause the wealth to appear (the arrival of ships and camels indicating commerce from west and east), but apparently directed by the *kabod* of Yahweh. The "logic" of the passage is: the *kabod* of Yahweh shines; its light is seen by Zion and it draws to Zion the nations/kings; the absent kinsfolk appear; Zion rejoices at the abundance/wealth; the wealth is named (camels [bearing], gold, frankincense). This wealth is, however, not so much Israel's as Yahweh's, for its purpose is to glorify Yahweh on "my altar" (v. 7).

Isaiah 60:11

In what James Muilenburg calls the fifth strophe of the poem, verses 10-11,[51] the motif "wealth of nations" appears again. Here, wealth is brought into the city by men, with a procession of kings not far behind. The ominous note stuck by verse 12 (whoever does not serve Yahweh will perish) is taken by commentators[52] to be a misleading insertion into the original poem. Yet, the threatening tone of verse 14 is not to be overlooked: the sons of former oppressors will not only bow to Yahweh, but they will be submissive to Zion. Once again, the patron-client relationship is expressed through the possession of wealth: transfer of wealth to

Zion means client status for the foreigners; honor and power of the patron is enhanced. For Zion to gain wealth, neither has its own productivity increased, nor has it exploited its own people (principle of limited good).

Isaiah 61:6

This chapter speaks again of the "wealth of nations" (v. 6), but what it says about the foreigners in verses 5-6[53] is quite different from 60:4-14. In Isaiah 60, the foreigners will contribute to Zion's renewal; here they are menial laborers, servants of Zion ("aliens shall feed your flock," etc.; v. 5). This is not a patron-client, but a master-slave/serf, relationship. Further, the community of Zion will "enjoy the wealth of the nations/revel in their riches" (v. 6 JPSV). The text (in its canonical form) makes clear the reason for this: Israel's shame is to be removed and instead a double portion is given by Yahweh because this God loves justice and gives recompense (v. 8). Thus, 61:6 connects the wealth of nations with an explicit subordination of foreigners to Zion (cf. Zech 14:14); that is, "Judeans will be to Gentiles as priests to laity."[54] The restoration of Zion's honor (v. 7) takes place at considerable social and economic expense to the foreigner, but this is Yahweh's justice (v. 8). The principle of limited good means that Zion's honor and empty bank account must diminish the wealth of the "other."

Isaiah 66:12

The last chapter of the book of Isaiah contains the final reference to the "wealth of nations." This time, however, the phrase is חיל גוים (ḥyl gwym, v.12) and belongs to the "conclusion to the third major segment of the book.[55] After the summons to rejoice in verse 10, in verse 12 Yahweh speaks in the first person: "I will extend prosperity (שלום, šlwm) to her like a river, and the wealth of nations like an overflowing stream." Here, for the first time in our study, we find, an explicit statement, in the form of a prophecy, that a transfer of wealth to Israel (here Zion/Jerusalem) takes place by the direct intervention of Yahweh and is bound up with the comfort and salvation of the nation.[56] In Isaiah 60:5, the wealth of nations "comes" (יבאו, ybʾw; JPSV "flows"). In 60:11 "people bring it." Here (66:12), Yahweh himself "extends" (נטה, nṭh) the prosperity and wealth, a verb also used to "extend" a favor,[57] perhaps suggesting the gracious disposition of the one who brings wealth and comfort. If so, this passage moves away from the principle of reciprocity (the nations who conquered and humiliated you must now receive their recompense; they plundered you, now you receive their wealth). Verse 12 is to be seen in its immediate literary context: the wealth of nations that comes to Zion is the material precondition of the redistribution of resources. To "suck and be satisfied" (v. 11), to be nourished and healthy (vv. 12b-14), suggest the economic use of the eschatological wealth that will flow to Jerusalem's treasure house. The gracious "extension" of wealth to Jerusalem (v. 12) means that Jerusalem in turn, as the rich power center of the new age, will distribute its wealth and thus bring satisfaction, rejoicing, and delight and health (66:10, 12-14).

Finally, the word כבוד (*kbwd*) in the expression, "wealth of nations" (v. 12) directs the attentive reader back to Abraham, with whom the study began, and the programmatic statement in Genesis 13:2: אברם כבד מאד, *ʾbrm kbd mʾd,* "Abram was very rich"). Thus, Genesis 13:2 and Isaiah 66:12 provide a kind of thematic envelope around any number of narratives and prophecies on the theme "the transfer and acquisition of wealth" in ancient Israel.

Conclusion

I have examined selected passages in the Hebrew Bible on "wealth" and how ancient worthies, Abraham, David, Solomon, as well as personified Zion, acquire wealth. As a way of limiting and defining the approach, three categories from the realm of cultural anthropology were used. By focusing on "wealth," not as material gain to be quantified and studied according to formal economic categories, but rather in terms of cultural values, my goal was to assess these various instances of the "transfer of wealth."

The results of the investigation may be briefly stated:

1. Wealth comes to "Israel" from outside itself. Foreign patrons give, for various reasons, to Abraham, who, able to prosper on his own, is presented also as a patron-warrior who scorns the gifts of another king. David enjoys the patronage of Achish, but as a chief "takes" wealth from others and redistributes it to his kin group. David the king-patron also receives tribute from political clients subordinate to him through war. Solomon's wealth is magnificent, fabulous by comparison; wealth "flows" to him

from the world outside Israel's boundaries in the form of tribute
and gifts. To be sure, the narratives state and then presuppose
that the "invisible hand" is that of Yahweh's. Yet, while Solomon
also levies taxes on his own people, the substantial part of the
wealth streaming to Solomon must have its empirical roots in
business dealings. In the Persian period, with the old foreign tributary economy of the monarchy a thing of the past, Trito-Isaiah's
vision of the new age appeals in part to the future wealth that will
endow Jerusalem. The life-endangering shortages of economic
scarcity, and the accompanying disgrace, will be turned into magnificent abundance. Where will this wealth come from? In light
of, and consonant with, the earlier narratives we have studied,
this wealth can only come from foreigners, from the "wealth of
nations." Israel grows rich not from its own productive capacities
but from the wealth of others.

2. This conceptualization of wealth represents a certain aspect of the
   cultural theories of patron-client and limited good. Abraham,
   David, Solomon, Zion, are patrons to out-group clients. Excepting Solomon's tax and debt system, they do not grow rich,
   according to the ideological construction of the biblical materials,
   by exploiting their own people. According to the perception that
   the worlds good are limited, no in-group is diminished by an
   attainment of wealth. Only the foreigners lose.

3. To acquire wealth means, of course, that one acquires honor and
   prestige, along with power. Indeed, in these narratives, wealth
   brings power (Abraham, David, Zion) and power brings wealth
   (Solomon). Abraham, David, Solomon, and Zion are presented as
   players in international politics; they are winners, generous and
   magnanimous, who acquire their wealth, whether through deception, banditry, treaties, and tribute, or pilgrim nations streaming
   to Zion with their gold, in an honorable manner. Their honor
   guarantees their status as patrons, who stand subordinate to no
   other power. When history, however, brings moments in which
   wealthy patrons (Abraham, David, Solomon) must lose status
   and wealth (exilic/postexilic times), Israel (Zion) need only wait
   patiently until the coffers are full again, as always, with the
   wealth of nations.

CHAPTER EIGHT

Prophecy

JOSEPH SMITH AND THE *GESTALT* OF THE ISRAELITE PROPHET

Lester L. Grabbe

In recent years anthropological data and social-scientific methods have often been used to better understand prophecy in ancient Israel, but there is a danger of drawing the limits too narrowly. Although the Seneca prophet Handsome Lake has often been cited, for example, his contemporary, the Mormon prophet Joseph Smith, has been neglected. Lester Grabbe seeks to redress this balance by drawing on original documents to characterize Smith as a prophet. He then compares Smith with the Israelite prophets in a number of areas where the comparison helps to clarify, illustrate, or suggest directions for further study on the Gestalt of the ancient prophet: (1) mode of revelation; (2) stereotypical language; (3) both positive and negative traditions; (4) failed prophecies; (5) call narrative; (6) gaps in knowledge; and (7) the difficulty in determining what actually happened.

It is always interesting to observe what unconscious prejudices we scholars harbor in our scientific work. These days many scholars of the Hebrew Bible pay lip service to the social sciences, and a few embrace them with enthusiasm—if not always with sense. But there are still plenty that regard the use of the social sciences with grave suspicion. Yet those who use the social sciences are not without their blind spots. To take the example that I intend to pursue in this paper, those studying prophecy in ancient Israel have been happy to call on a variety of prophetic models, all the way from the ancient Near East to the Native Americans, a particularly useful one being the Seneca prophet Handsome Lake (about 1800).

Yet another prophet from approximately the same time as Handsome Lake seems to have escaped the attention of those writing on prophecy and the social sciences. This oversight is due, I suspect, to the prejudices of Christians in the mainline denominations regarding the Church of Jesus Christ of Latter-Day Saints. For the prophet I refer to is the Mormon prophet Joseph Smith. The Seneca prophet Handsome Lake is useful because we have a fair amount of information on him, but it is nothing compared to what we have with regard to Smith. A recent collection of early Mormon documents, meaning those relating to the lifetime of Smith, amounts to five volumes. There are not many prophets in history for whom we can claim so much information.

A Précis of Joseph Smith's Prophetic Career

Joseph Smith Jr. was born in 1805 and grew up in a rather impoverished farming family in the town of Palmyra in New York State. There were many Indian earth fortresses and burial mounds in that part of the country, and a common avocation among the local people was digging for treasure. His father devoted time to treasure digging, and Joseph Smith Jr. gained something of a reputation as being able to divine the location of treasures by means of a seer stone that he had found when digging a well. "Money-diggers," as they were called, had a somewhat dubious reputation—many regarded this a disreputable preoccupation—but the practice was certainly widespread at the time in that region.[1] It is not clear that Smith ever found any actual treasure, though he apparently found lost objects; in any case, there were those who apparently swore by his gift.

A set of accounts describes what is often referred to as his "first vision." The date of this vision is variously given as age 16[2] and age 14.[3] In the later versions, it was God the Father and the Son who appeared to Smith,[4] but the earliest version mentions only "the Lord," who is evidently Jesus Christ,[5] while another just has two angels.[6] There are several problems about this vision: Joseph's family do not seem to have known anything about it at the time, the age varies across the different accounts, and the picture of the deity develops consistently with the lateness of the account. Thus, there is some doubt as to whether this "first vision" in fact occurred or, if it occurred, what form it originally took.

An event of potential significance in Smith's life is often overlooked (or sometimes even denied).[7] This is the coming of the revivalist movement to the region of Palmyra. The Smith family seems to have responded quite enthusiastically as a whole, only Joseph Smith Sr. remaining aloof because of animosity against the local Methodist minister.[8] Joseph Jr.'s mother, sister, and two brothers joined the Methodists; Joseph Jr. himself did not affiliate with any group. He later claimed that he recognized that all churches were in error but, in any event, he had been affected by the religious enthusiasm.[9] However one explains it, the visions were not completely unexpected.

Unlike his "first vision," the one experienced on 21 September 1823 was recounted much more consistently by a variety of sources. According to it, at about age 17 Smith had a vision of the angel Moroni who told him of metal plates that had been deposited on a nearby hill, called Cumorah, by one of the early inhabitants of North America. He had the same vision three times that night, which was no doubt significant. Smith found the site where the plates were preserved in a stone box, along with a set of spectacles known as the "Urim and Thummim" that he was to use in deciphering the tablets and some other paraphernalia, but he was not allowed to take them. It was another four years before he was finally permitted to collect the tablets, which he did at the vernal equinox in September 1827. These tablets were written in a script and language that Smith called "reformed Egyptian"—a writing system unheard of in the ancient Near East, much less ancient Israel. Between December 1827 and early 1828, Smith began to "translate," using the Urim and Thummim. At first he dictated to his wife, Emma, but a local farmer named Martin Harris had befriended Smith and believed that he had been chosen by God. He not only gave money for the project, but in February 1828 he came to volunteer to help by being scribe as Smith dictated the translation from the golden plates.

It was about this time in early 1828 that Harris took a transcription of a few lines of the characters to New York City to Charles Anthon, professor of Greek and Latin at Columbia College (now Columbia University). Harris returned from that journey completely convinced as to the authenticity of "the Record," as it was sometimes referred to. Yet the accounts of the meeting between Harris and Anthon differ widely. An account written by Smith in 1832 very succinctly states that a copy of some of the characters was shown to "the learned" who said he could not read them, but the unlearned (Smith) was able to read them because the Lord had prepared spectacles. In his 1839 history, Smith mentions not just a transcription of the characters but also a translation.[10] He quotes Harris, to the effect that Anthon stated the translation was correct, more so than any he had before seen translated from the Egyptian. I then shewed him those which were not yet translated, and he said that they were Egyptian, Chaldeak, Assyriac, and Arabac, and he said that they were true characters. He gave me a certificate certifying . . . that they were true characters and that the translation of such of them as had been translated was also correct.

According to Harris, Anthon then inquired where the writing had come from, and when he was told, he took back the certificate and tore it up.

Not surprisingly, Anthon gave an entirely different version—indeed, he gave two different versions. The first is in a letter of 1834 in which he states,

Upon examining the paper in question, I soon came to the con-clusion that it was all a trick, perhaps a *hoax*. . . . [Harris] had resolved to come to New York, and obtain the opinion of the learned about the meaning of the paper which he brought with him, and which had been given him as a part of the contexts of the book, although no translation had been furnished at the time by the young man with the spectacles. On hearing this odd story, I changed my opinion about the paper, and instead of viewing it any longer as a hoax upon the learned, I began to regard it as part of a scheme to cheat the farmer of his money. . . . He requested an opinion from me in writing, which of course I declined giving, and then he took his leave carrying the paper with him.[11]

In the letter just quoted, Anthon goes on to describe the writing:

This paper was in fact a singular scrawl. It consisted of all kinds of crooked characters disposed in columns, and had evidently been prepared by some person who had before him at the time a book containing various alphabets. Greek and Hebrew letters, crosses and flourishes, Roman letters inverted or placed side-ways, who[se scribe had] arranged [them] in perpendicular columns, and the whole ended in a rude delineation of a circle divided into various compartments, decked with various strange marks. . . . I am thus particular as to the contents of the paper, inasmuch as I have frequently conversed with my friends on the subject, since the Mormonite excitement began, and well remember that the paper contained any thing else but "*Egyptian Hieroglyphics.*"

The distance between Harris's account and Anthon's is patent. To add to the puzzlement, some years later in a letter of 1841 Anthon wrote:

A very brief examination of the paper convinced me that it was mere *hoax*, and a very clumsy one too. The characters were arranged in columns, like the chinese mode of writing, and presented the most singular medley that I had ever beheld. Greek, Hebrew, and all sorts of letters, more or less distorted, either through unskilfulness or from actual design, were intermingled with sundry delineations of half moons, stars, and other natural objects, and the whole ended in a rude representation of the Mexican zodiac. The conclusion was irresistible, that some cunning fellow had prepared the paper in question, for the purpose of imposing upon the countryman who brought it, and I told the man so without any hesitation. . . . On my telling the bearer of the paper that an attempt had been made to impose upon him, and defraud him of his property, he requested me to give him my opinion in writing about the paper which he had shown to me. I did so without any hesitation. . . . The import of what I wrote was, as far as I can now recollect, simply this, that the marks in the paper appeared to be merely an imitation of various alphabetic characters, and had in my opinion no meaning at all connected with them.[12]

I think we have to accept that Anthon's two accounts were self-serving. One suspects that if the entire truth were known, there might be some embarrassing aspects for him and his professional reputation. It would not surprise me if Anthon was taken in temporarily by the lines on the paper, or at least was open to their authenticity, until Harris enlightened him as to their origin. So his claim to have immediately recognized it as a hoax rings hollow. On the other hand, he surely was no fool. A slip of paper with handwritten symbols has been preserved,[13] though it is not entirely certain whether this is the sheet of paper that Harris showed to Anthon. But the symbols on it bear no resemblance to

Egyptian hieroglyphs. As for Harris's statement that Anthon affirmed the characters were "Egyptian, Chaldeak, Assyriac, and Arabac," the marks on the sheet in no way resemble these writing systems, either. Anthon's professional competence was said to be Greek and Latin, but it would not have been surprising if he had studied Hebrew and Aramaic and even other Semitic languages such as Arabic. But knowledge of the decipherment of Egyptian by Jean-François Champollion did not reach England until 1838 nor the United States until sometime later,[14] while decipherment of Akkadian cuneiform did not come along until sometime after this.

It is therefore very unlikely that Anthon would have claimed to know those languages or to pass judgment on a translation said to be from them, nor is it very probable that he would have identified the writing with Aramaic ("Chaldeak") or Arabic. The most reasonable conclusion accords with the statement by an individual who was visited by Harris in 1828, apparently right after he saw Anthon. This person claimed (in a letter of 1840, some years later) that, according to Harris, Professor Anthon "thought the characters . . . very remarkable, but he could not decide exactly what language they belonged to."[15] Nevertheless, regardless of what precisely passed between Anthon and Harris, it seems without doubt that the latter returned from the trip convinced of the authenticity of the plates and their writing.

So Smith devoted himself to translating the text for two months, with Harris as his scribe. The mode of translation has often been described, but there is still some unclarity about some of the details. It seems to be agreed that Smith began the task by using the "spectacles" found with the plates. These were not spectacles in the conventional sense, since the two stones were apparently translucent rather than transparent, and they were larger than an ordinary pair of spectacles. How Smith used them is not entirely clear. Some accounts imply that he looked through them like spectacles,[16] but the description implies they might have been too big for this.[17] Some accounts say that he would put them in his hat and then put his face into it to exclude the light.[18] The question is whether the frame in which the stones were encased would fit into a hat,[19] though it is possible that Smith took out the stones to put them into the hat.[20] But David Whitmer stated that he would put the "spectacles" on and then look into his hat or put his face in it.[21] Part of the problem is that initially a blanket separated Smith while he dictated from Harris who was writing the translation down. Sometimes they were even in different rooms.

At some point, Smith began to use his old familiar seer stone as his translation medium. This was said to be after Harris was replaced as his scribe,[22] but one incident suggests this was earlier, because Harris tells of testing Smith by substituting another stone for his seer stone.[23] Harris, Emma Smith, and David Whitmer described Smith's use of the seer stone in detail in a number of sources.[24] Smith would put the stone in the bottom of his hat and then put his face into the hat so that all light was excluded. A character or section of text would appear, along with the English translation for it. He would read the translation to the amanuensis, who would write it down and then read it back. If it was correct, the image in the hat would disappear and be replaced by the next character or bit of text. At no point, apparently, did Smith actually consult the plates in the process of translating, although they were at hand.

As will be discussed below, it seems that no one saw the plates uncovered except Smith himself. Although Harris asked Smith to see the tablets a number of times, he was always refused. However, Harris pestered Smith until he was allowed to take the first 116 pages of the translation to show his wife, who was completely hostile to Smith and thought her husband was simply being conned out of his money. The manuscript disappeared. Although it is not certain what happened to it, it is believed that Mrs. Harris burned it. As result, the plates and the Urim and Thummim were taken away for a time by the angel.[25] Eventually, however, Smith was allowed to have them back, though the sources contradict each other about the "interpreters," some saying that they were returned,[26] but others that he now used only the seer stone,[27] and the translation was begun again. The missing pages were not retranslated but instead another section of the plates, which was said to be parallel to the lost part, was translated. Although a number of reports deny it,[28] it seems that Harris may have acted as scribe for some of the new manuscript.[29] In any case, most of the work of scribe was carried out by a young schoolteacher named Oliver Cowdery, who had been lodging with Smith's parents. The translation progressed rapidly from April 1829 and was completed by July 1829.

Despite considerable local opposition, the *Book of Mormon* was printed. The plates were eventually returned to the angel Moroni.[30] The Church was officially founded on the 6 April 1830. Smith continued to have revelations, as discussed below. In 1831 the majority of members in the Palmyra area moved to Kirkland, Ohio. Later in 1839, after much persecution in various places, they set up a semi-independent colony in

Nauvoo, Illinois, with Joseph Smith Jr, not just as a spiritual head but as a civic leader. He was even considering running for president. But he and his brother were arrested in June 1844 and while they were in custody in a nearby town called Carthage, a mob descended on the jail and murdered them. Joseph Smith Jr. was 38 years old.

This has been only a brief sketch of the events surrounding Smith's career as a prophet, but I shall fill in some relevant details when making prophetic comparisons below.

Was It All a Hoax?

First, we have to deal with the question that will have occurred to many: Was it all just an elaborate hoax? This seems to be the position of the generally excellent biography by Fawn Brodie, *No Man Knows My History*. She takes as her starting point the testimony of a neighbor, Peter Ingersoll, that Smith found some fine white sand, which he brought home wrapped up in one of his garments.[31] When asked about it by his family, Smith told an elaborate story about finding a golden Bible. He was then stuck with the story and had to find a way to deal with it. Rather than confess to his deception, he boldly carried it through to it logical conclusion, the *Book of Mormon* being the final result.

One can of course read the story this way. One of the telling asides in Lucy Smith's account of her son's activities is that he regaled the family with stories about the early inhabitants of America—their dress, their mode of traveling, their cities, their warfare, their religion—before he had translated any of the *Book of Mormon*, indeed, before he had even been allowed to collect the plates.[32] A very popular theory at the time was that the Native Americans were descended from ancient Israel. The landscape of New York was dotted with fortresses and burial mounds that were ascribed to a superior pre-Indian civilization which had been destroyed by the American Indian savages that came later. Finally, there is no reason why Peter Ingersoll would lie when he claimed to tell the story that Joseph Smith had found some sand and brought it home. The account was given as part of court testimony, and although Ingersoll was hostile to Smith, he was also careful to say when he did not know something.

Yet one can explain Ingersoll's story as one that he indeed heard from Smith, but that the latter told it to draw attention away from the golden plates. Some of Smith's treasure-digging former companions took the view that they should have a share in anything valuable he had found—

there is in fact some evidence that he had actually promised them a share. They pursued him to try to find and take the plates, but he always managed to fight them off or keep the plates well hidden. Therefore, if he had run into a neighbor at an awkward time, he might well have said he had found some sand but was deceiving his family, in order to lay down a red herring. This does not mean that Smith did not use certain tactics of deception, which were apparently part of his stock in trade from his treasure-spotting days. But apparently it is not unusual for diviners in various societies to make use of conjuring tricks despite still insisting that their essential gift of divination is nevertheless genuine.

What about the plates? Although Joseph's wife, Emma, did not see the plates uncovered at any time, she testified that the plates lay on the table covered only by a cloth:

> The plates often lay on the table without any attempt at concealment, wrapped in a small linen [table] cloth, which I had given him to fold them in. I felt of the plates, as they lay on the table, tracing their outline and shape. They seemed to be pliable like thick paper, and would rustle [with a metallic sound] when the edges were moved by the thumb, as one does sometimes thumb the edges of a book.[33]

Martin Harris also testified to having hefted the plates when they were in a box covered only by a cloth, but he was able to go further. The *Book of Mormon* contains two sets of witnesses to the authenticity of the plates from which it was translated: the statements of the Three Witnesses and the Eight Witnesses affirm that the undersigned individuals had seen and handled the plates. The first set consisted of Martin Harris, Oliver Cowdery, and David Whitmer, who went with Smith into the woods one morning and prayed until they all saw the angel standing before a table with the plates, which he picked up and showed to them, turning the pages. Some days later a number of members of David Whitmer's family plus Smith's father and two brothers are said to have been shown the plates by Smith himself and to have handled them. Although a surprisingly high number of those listed later left the Church (though in some cases eventually returning), none of the witnesses ever repudiated his testimony, to the best of my knowledge. They were convinced they had seen the plates with clear writing on them.

But this is not the whole story. Both Martin Harris and David Whitmer of the Three Witnesses, while continuing to affirm their belief in the

Book of Mormon, also stated that they had seen the plates "in spirit" or with "spiritual eyes" or in vision.[34] As far as they were concerned, this was no less real than seeing them with ordinary eyes, but to non-Mormons this distinction is likely to be important, as this testimony regarding Martin Harris suggests:

> A gentleman in Palmyra, bred to the law, a professor of religion, and of undoubted veracity told me that on one occasion, he appealed to Harris and asked him directly,—"Did you *see* those plates?" Harris replied, he did. "Did you see the plates, and the engraving on them with your bodily eyes?" Harris replied, "Yes, I saw them with my eyes,—they were shown unto me by the power of God and not of man." "But did you see them with your natural,—your bodily eyes, just as you see this pencil-case in my hand? Now say *no* or *yes* to this." Harris replied,— "Why I did not see them as I do that pencil-case, yet I saw them with the eye of faith; I saw them just as distinctly as I see any thing around me,—though at the time they were covered over with a cloth.[35]

David Whitmer made a similar statement,[36] as did Oliver Cowdery.[37]

The situation with the Eight Witnesses is more complex,[38] and some continue to assert that these members of the Whitmer family and others saw and handled the plates in a purely physical context. Some of the testimony certainly gives this impression, but we have a few later interviews with most of the Eight Witnesses. There is some evidence that their experience was also "spiritual" or "visionary" or whatever one might wish to call it:

> [John] Whitmer asked, "do you hint at me?" [Turly replied], "if the cap fits you, wear it." all I know, you have published to the world that an angel did present those plates to Joseph Smith." [Whitmer replied] "I now say I handled those plates. there was fine engravings on both sides. I handled them." and he described how they were hung, "and they were shown to me by a supernatural power." he acknowledged all.[39]

Martin Harris is reported to have testified, according to an account by former Mormon Stephen Burnett in 1838:

I have reflected long and deliberately upon the history of this church & weighed the evidence for & against it—loth to give it up—but when I came to hear Martin Harris state in a public that he never saw the plates with his natural eyes only in vision or imagination, neither Oliver [Cowdery] nor David [Whitmer] & also that the eight witnesses never saw them & hesitated to sign that instrument for that reason, but were persuaded to do it, the last pedestal gave way, in my view our foundations was sapped & the entire superstructure fell a heap of ruins.[40]

Thomas Ford, a former governor of Illinois, who knew many Mormons, gave an account about the Eight Witnesses; unfortunately, he does not give his sources and he has some of the names slightly wrong:

He [Smith] set them to continual prayer, and other spiritual exercises, to acquire this lively faith by means of which the hidden things of God could be spiritually discerned; and, at last, when he could delay them no longer, he assembled them in a room, and produced a box, which he said contained the precious treasure. The lid was opened; the witnesses peeped into it, but making no discovery, for the box was empty, they said, "Brother Joseph, we do not see the plates." The prophet answered them, "O ye of little faith! how long will God bear with this wicked and perverse generation? down on your knees, brethren, every one of you, and pray God for the forgiveness of your sins, and for a holy and living faith which cometh down from heaven." The disciples dropped to their knees, and began to pray in the fervency of their spirit, supplicating God for more than two hours with fanatical earnestness, at the end of which time, looking again into the box, they were now persuaded that they saw the plates. I leave it to philosophers to determine whether the fumes of an enthusiastic and fanatical imagination are thus capable of blinding the mind and deceiving the senses by so absurd a delusion. . . .[41]

In the end it appears that the only one who saw the plates directly was Joseph Smith himself. Even this situation could be doubted. In his testimony Stephen Burnett, already quoted above, goes on to speak about the plates:

I am well satisfied for myself that if the witnesses whose names are attached to the Book of Mormon never saw the plates as Martin [Harris] admits that there can be nothing brought to prove that any such thing ever existed for it is said on the 171 page of the book of covenants [D & C 17:5] that the three [witnesses] should testify that they had seen the plates even as J[oseph] S[mith] Jr & if they saw them spiritually or in vision with their eyes shut—J[oseph] S[mith] Jr never saw them any other way & if so the plates were only visionary and I am well satisfied that the 29 & 37 Chap[ter]s of Isai[a]h & Ezekiel together with others in which we depended to prove the truth of the book of Mormon have no bearing when correctly understood but are entirely irrelevant. . . .[42]

There is no question that people such as Martin Harris and David Whitmer were utterly sincere in their belief in the plates and Smith's revelations. I think that, whatever tricks Smith might have used on the way, he also came to believe in the finding and translation of the golden plates. The elaborate and deliberate hoax hypothesized by Brodie seems intrinsically improbable but—most important—does not fit some significant facts of the time.

Points of Comparison

I now take up some issues relating to prophecy and make some suggestions about how Joseph Smith's story might help us to understand prophecy in the context of ancient Israel.

Mode of Revelation

One of the useful pieces of information we have from the Joseph Smith story is how he received his revelations. This is something we often do not have in prophetic stories. The mode of revelation that I want to focus on here is his use of a physical object, meaning his seer stones. Smith is known to have used at least three seer stones throughout his life.[43] The first of these—a white stone—he apparently found in 1819 and used in his divining ventures. The second was a brown stone found about 20 feet underground during the digging of a well in 1822. Once he had found it, this seems to have been his favored stone and was used in the translation of the *Book of Mormon*. There also appears to have been a third, a green one, acquired at some point.

Smith seems to have used the seer stone for purposes other than just to translate the *Book of Mormon*, however. We have a number of revelations, beginning in July 1829. These were originally written down into the *Book of Commandments* of 1833, later reedited into the *Book of Doctrine and Covenants*. We know from various documents that at least some of these were received by means of the seer stone, which—confusingly—began to be referred to as the Urim and Thummim.[44] It was Smith's custom, when there was a need for a revelation, to seek one by means of the seer stone. His means of doing so seems to have been the same way as he always used the seer stone: to place it in his hat and then place his face into the hat in such a way as to exclude the light.

According to David Whitmer, Smith decided to give up using the brown seer stone in 1830.[45] After that he decided that any revelations would come by means of prayer, but he still occasionally made use of the white seer stone. For example, he used it to "translate" some Egyptian papyri that he purchased in 1835.[46] (He claimed these were the *Book of Abraham*, though Egyptologists soon identified them as texts from the *Book of the Dead*.)

Now the closest biblical parallels to the seer stones were the ephod and the Urim and Thummim, whose name Smith himself appropriated. This is not the place to debate how these worked, but they seem to have been mainly a priestly form of divination.[47] However, we should be careful about making too sharp a distinction between them and prophetic activity. The first reason is that, as I have argued for a long time—though I was not the first to do so—prophecy is a form of divination, at least for the most part.[48] But, more important, in most cases we simply do not know how the prophetic message was received. Sometimes it was by a vision, but many times we have rather unspecific statements such as, "The word of YHWH came to So-and-So," or even just "Thus says YHWH." How did God's word come to the prophet? A vision? An audition? Some divinatory device, such as the seer stone? In most cases, we do not know. Yet notice that many of the revelations, as given in the *Book of Commandments*, did not say how they were received. For example, *Book of Commandments* 7:1:

> *A Revelation given to Oliver, in Harmony, Pennsylvania, April, 1829.*
>
> Oliver, verily, I say unto you, that asuredly as the Lord liveth, which is your God and your Redeemer, even so sure shall you receive a knowledge of whatever things you shall ask in faith,

with an honest heart, believing that you shall receive a knowledge concerning the engravings of old records, which are
ancient. . . .

One might think that a voice came to Oliver Cowdery, speaking the
words of the revelation. In fact, other sources show that (*a*) the revelation did not come directly to Cowdery but rather to Smith, and (*b*) it was
received via Smith's seer stone.[49] This serves as a useful analogy to suggest that the precise mode of biblical prophecies is also concealed in the
language used.

In addition to his use of the seer stone, other revelations came to
Smith by vision. We have a number of examples of these, with detailed
descriptions. It is interesting that Smith was not the only visionary
among the early Mormons. Martin Harris was also known for receiving
various communications. According to one report, while walking home
one day he was accompanied by Jesus Christ—in the form of a deer—
who conversed with him over two or three miles.

Stereotypical Language

A number of studies have pointed out that prophecy conforms to societal norms.[50] This often involves the use of stereotypical language and
phraseology. The writings we have of Joseph Smith, although often defi-
cient with regard to spelling and punctuation, are in the standard American English of the time, to the extent that there was a standardized
form. Yet the *Book of Mormon* and Smith's revelations are in a pseudo-
Elizabethan English that imitates the language of the Authorized Version, which for many people of the time no doubt meant "biblical
language." As Mark Twain wrote in 1871:

> The author labored to give his words and phrases the quaint,
> old-fashioned sound and structure of our King James's transla-
> tion of the Scriptures; and the result is a mongrel—half modern
> glibness, and half ancient simplicity and gravity. The latter is
> awkward and constrained; the former natural, but grotesque by
> the contrast. Whenever he found his speech growing too mod-
> ern—which was about every sentence or two—he ladled in a
> few such Scriptural phrases as "exceeding sore," "and it came
> to pass," etc., and made things satisfactory again. "And it came

to pass" was his pet. If he had left that out, his Bible would have been only a pamphlet.[51]

Both Positive and Negative Traditions

We are very fortunate in having among the early Mormon documents both positive and negative views of Smith and his family. We see his story from both sides, as it were. There are those who were sure he was just perpetrating a con trick but others who were absolutely convinced that it was the work of God and the restoration of true church in the endtime. In the biblical text, we normally have only one view of a particular prophet, either his evaluation as a true prophet of God or a false prophet. What we have to appreciate, especially for those who want to take a social-scientific perspective, is that there were probably both points of view for most prophets in actual society.

Failed Prophecies

Failed prophecies are not normally dwelt on in positive reports. The writer tells of how the prophecies of those he dislikes have failed but not those of his friends. So "true prophets" will have only reliable prophecies ascribed to them, but false prophecies will be placed in the mouth of false prophets. Finding the reverse is not easy, though we do know that some of the prophecies in the name of "true" prophets did not come to pass, because they have been preserved.[52]

For the most part, the Mormon tradition is monochrome, with only true prophecies alleged. Interestingly, though, we do have one false prophecy. According to David Whitmer, in order to raise money to finance the publication of the *Book of Mormon*, it was proposed that the copyright should be sold.[53] Smith sought a revelation through his seer stone and was told that they should go to Canada and sell it. In fact, they were not able to make a deal and came back without any money. When they asked Smith why this was, he inquired again through his seer stone and received the revelation: "Some revelations are of God; some revelations are of man; and some revelations are of the devil."

Call Narrative

For most prophets we know nothing about their call. It is likely that most prophets, or perhaps even all, had a call experience. Yet the call narrative is often missing from the preserved data. With Joseph Smith, however, we have abundant information about the angelic appearance in 1823.

Gaps in Knowledge

For most prophets of the Hebrew Bible and the ancient Near East we know nothing about their life before they became prophets. We seem to know quite a bit about the prophet Jeremiah, though some would query this conclusion. But Micah is only a name, with a possible indication of his hometown. We know nothing about his occupation, background, or even where—or whether—his prophecies were delivered.

Difficulty in Determining What Actually Happened

As a historian of ancient Israel, which properly includes the religion as well, I have a particular interest in how we interpret sources. I am by no means a minimalist, but what strikes me is the confidence with which some people hold up the biblical text to the point of insisting that it should be taken at face value unless we can disprove it. But when we look at the early Mormon sources, which include multiple eyewitness statements and accounts contemporary with the events they describe, we still find obscurities, discrepancies, and contradictions. If we have this much trouble with abundant primary sources only a couple of centuries old, with the original documents still available to us in many cases, how much more so with edited and reedited, and copied and recopied, material in an imperfectly understood language?

Conclusion

The seven points just listed illustrate how Joseph Smith and early Mormonism can shed light on prophecy in ancient Israel. In most cases, such comparisons can only make us go back to the biblical texts with new questions, but trying to answer these may elucidate the situation in ways not done by traditional study. The present study has also illustrated the value of the social sciences for study of the Hebrew Bible and the world of ancient Israel. If correctly used, sociology and anthropology can greatly increase our knowledge and understanding. In my view, the use of social-scientific methods and data is essential for a proper historical understanding of prophecy. Granted, the biblical prophecies can be studied as literature and theology without appeal to sociology or anthropology, but for any attempt to understand the phenomena of prophets and prophecy—and especially their place in society—the social sciences are a *sine qua non*. As biblical scholars, however, we need to be careful not to define "social-scientific" too narrowly. We need to overcome both our myopia and our religious prejudices. Sources of comparative data are not limited to ancient societies or primitive cultures. To draw on Joseph Smith and the history of early Mormonism is as legitimate and rewarding as to draw on the contemporary Seneca prophet Handsome Lake or the Delaware prophet. The value of doing so has, I think, been demonstrated in this study.

CHAPTER NINE

Barrenness

TRANCE AS A PROTEST STRATEGY

Dietmar Neufeld

Taking the stories of Sarai and Hannah as his point of departure, Dietmar Neufeld considers the issue of a barren body as a social construct. He argues that the barren body both occupies space and is itself space upon which are written the social values and religious proclivities of a polygynous household. Anthropologists have shown that barrenness is an undesired and unsolicited bodily condition, frequently the result of the intrusion of pathogenic spirits. Such unsolicited infertility was labeled an affliction whose effect was akin to possession, which women utilized in their domestic situations as an oblique protest strategy against the frequent injustices and inequities prevalent in such settings. Changes in the woman's state of consciousness became the means by which to negotiate improvements in her social lot. Both Sarai and Hannah made a special virtue of affliction by using it to gain capital in situations of power-lessness brought on by the stresses of polygynous households.

Lester Grabbe, in his article "Ancient Near Eastern Prophecy from an Anthropological Perspective," rightly points out that the social sciences can profitably be applied to the ancient Near Eastern prophetic texts and then proceeds to do so with a concentration on the Mari material.[1] Using cross-cultural comparatives, he arrives at a better understanding of Near Eastern prophecy. In similar way, this essay will seek to use the insights of anthropologists and some ethnographic studies in order to arrive at a more complete understanding of how incidences of trance or possession relate to social order.[2]

Two main foci will be pursued: one, I will consider briefly the issue of body as a social construct—body both occupies space and is itself space upon which are written the social values and religious proclivities of groups and persons. The body plays a significant role in triggering trance states but also in such things as inscribing and maintaining structures of authority, often seen in gender-rigidified societies. It is involved also in the evasion of an unpleasant moral responsibility, seen in possessed persons who become the mouthpieces of deity; in either destabilizing or conserving social order, seen in protest movements; and in authorizing innovation and change, often seen in the status quo or persons who organize themselves to achieve political, religious or social reform. Two, I will give attention to the question of the social significance of trance; how does trance relate to social order? Are certain categories of individuals in certain social positions more prone to being possessed, and what is the payoff for them?[3]

The Social Body

The literature of antiquity describes large numbers of rituals involving the body that are designed to trigger possession. Ecstatic experiences and the body are integral to each other—achieving an altered state is impossible without the body.[4] The ritualized body invested the initiate, once in a state of ecstasy, with power and opportunity usually not available to them by heightening awareness, sharpening vision, enhancing knowledge, exciting the senses, and releasing the body from the limitations of the mundane as well as the rigid social categories in which the body was locked.[5] These trance conditions have certain important social outcomes, namely, flights of fancy into the celestial realms reflect the desire for social change, innovation, protest, and the like. Ritual instructions employed spoken word, physical exertion, and frequently involved direct, unbidden, bodily affliction/illnesses to bring about changes in states of consciousness—usually to achieve some social end. Not unusual was the complete loss of bodily control—an indication of the all-consuming nature of the experience. For example, when Enoch is confronted by the mighty, tremulous agitation of the numerous forces of heaven, trembling and fear seize him, he loses control of his loins and kidneys, and he falls faint on the ground (*1 Enoch* 60:3-4). *Apocalypse of Abraham* 10 reports the bodily effects upon Abraham when confronted with an astounding vision: "And it came to pass when I heard the voice pronouncing such words to me that I looked this way and that. And behold there was not breath of man. And my spirit was amazed, and my soul fled from me. And I became like a stone and fell face down upon the earth, for there was no longer strength in me to stand upon the earth. And while I was still face down on the ground, I heard a voice speaking. . . ." Jeremiah 4:19 records the anguish of debilitating pain the prophet experienced: "My anguish, my anguish, I writhe in pain. Oh, the walls of my heart. My heart is beating wildly; I cannot keep silent." Elsewhere he says, "My heart is broken within me, all my bones shake; I am like a drunken man, like a man overcome by wine."

Bodies are used "to symbolize the social transitions of the individual in society, i.e., transitions of the individual in the social body are inscribed on the physical."[6] The life of individuals in societies is made up of a series of transitions or passages such as birth, marriage, pregnancy, or its inverse, infertility, fatherhood and motherhood, passages from age to age, from one social space to another, from occupation to occupation, one religion to another, and death.[7] Possessed bodies are permitted to transit from one threshold to another—these could be transitions into otherworldly spaces or into social spaces to which certain persons would normally not have access. Usually at the onset or during these passages, ceremony signals a change or transformation that thresholds have been crossed and that new identities have been assumed. These social processes are also physical and are often marked by eating and drinking, changing hairstyles, modifying bodily surfaces through adornment and clothing, ritual cleansing, body painting, changes in well-being, changes in states of consciousness, dramatic body performances, body mutilations (tooth removal, circumcision, clitoridectomy, subincision).[8] In marking the body "the person is made new, *either negatively or positively*, changed by a new role, and this requires a new body which in turn symbolizes, physically, society's new demands on the individual, and the individual's new rights and duties in society.[9]

Anthropologists also point out that (possessed) bodies are both conveyers of symbolic reality and unfinished entities that develop or evolve in conjunction with a range of social forces.[10] Subjected to social forces and human investment—and I would also include forces from above (divine investment)—bodies in the rough are continually being shaped and reshaped. Moreover, they are fundamental to the construction, maintenance, and deconstruction of social realities, such as inequalities found among persons, genders, and groups (elite, peasants, social bandits, patrons, clients, artisans, men and women, etc.). The body is conceptualized as having a form of physical capital; this includes such things as the interplay between the unfinished body and the social forces within society (a reciprocal exchange of influence), the management of the body to acquire status and distinction, the body laden with symbolic forms, and the body possessed as holder of power required for acquiring a range of resources (goods, services, honor, status, influence).[11] The possessed body, as a form of physical capital, is of considerable value to societies where social, economic, political, and religious exchange is dependent upon clearly delineated social networks.

It is clear that bodies in trance inhabit a *habitus*, that is, a socially constituted system of tradition, custom, evaluation, and response that shapes the symbolic selections imposed on the body. Not all possession behavior is acceptable to everyone and, depending on community, possession behavior typically follows stereotypical patterns.[12] While *habitus* contributes significantly to the development of the unfinished body, it is also located within the body and has influence on every detail of embodiment. How humans treat their bodies "reveals the deepest dispositions of the *habitus*."[13] A body dressed, for example, is one mode of *habitus* but it also includes table manners, eating habits, food, education, blowing one's nose, walking, and trance conditions.[14] Possessed bodies inhabit *habitus*. Their deportment, dress, speech, and treatment socially expose the deepest dispositions of socially constituted systems that regulate and define how bodies interact and communicate. Possessed bodies, therefore, frequently play a central role in creating and negotiating social reality. Possessed bodies as organic entities take up space but also as symbolic entities themselves are constituted as space upon which to inscribe social roles and relationships. These bodies ". . . not only move through, inhabit, exceed, imagine, and otherwise take up space, but that they are themselves space—and place—overlapping and intertwining with countless others."[15] Possessed bodies are endowed with certain social capital of considerable value to the social networks in which they are situated for purposes of innovation, transformation, and protest.

Social Significance of Ecstasy

Anthropologists have long been interested in the question of what purpose states of ecstasy serve socially. What's in it for the possessed? What does ecstasy offer the community in which it is taking place? Why in some cases sanction its expression and in others restrict it? Anthropologists have considered the social role ecstasy plays and have provided a catalog of social functions of religious ecstasy: They suggest, first, that it serves as the basis for a charismatic leader's authority; second, that in some cases it implies the desire to evade moral responsibility where difficult and dangerous decisions are made not by men and women but by God speaking through them; third, that ecstatic revelations are used to establish and preserve the existing social order; fourth, that ecstatic revelations are employed to authorize and justify innovation and change.[16] The range may be expanded to include the function of ecstasy in social order and which categories of people in that social order are prone to being possessed in some way. Why do people in certain social positions succumb to possession more readily than others? What does ecstasy offer them that they would not have ordinarily? In an agonistic society what social functions do competitions between the possessed—elite or non-elite—perform?

To get at these questions, I. M. Lewis makes a distinction between what he calls "peripheral possession" and "central possession."[17] Peripheral possession refers to what happens on the margins of a community—it is a type of ecstasy that becomes the resort of the weak, powerless, and disenfranchised. Central ecstasy is a style of trance found fully in the center of a community, exposed to the full light of day where it becomes the idiom of expression of the powerful competing for positions of influence and authority. One of its purposes, among others, is to legitimize and strengthen the power of the one vying for power. In peripheral possession, the possessing spirits are seen to have no direct moral significance—this although the spirits are full of malice, dangerous, often pathogenic—in the sense that this refers to those possessed as bearing no responsibility for what has befallen them. These spirits come upon the person unbidden, often in the form of an affliction or illness. Physical maladies are seen to be the onset of the intrusion of some spiritual power; this happens long before the person may be approaching a condition of trance.[18]

Peripheral possession tends to run in certain social grooves—it tends to be the resort of women and dispossessed, oppressed men. Anthropologists have shown that married women in particular are chiefly prone to this type of possession and that it is usually triggered by an unbidden bodily affliction. Whatever is at the root of illness, the resultant emotions of fear, troubled minds, despair, and hopelessness stimulate a trance-like state in women in this condition. Unsolicited affliction causes great physical and mental distress and, as Lewis has shown, becomes the means to the achievement of an exalted state.[19] Peripheral ecstasy is found in cultures where sexual stereotypes and sexual differentiation are dominant. In a social milieu where men fulfill a dominant role and females a subordinate one, competition between genders is often the result. In such a context, how are women to promote their interests and values? How are they to exert influence and power in a situation where both seem to be denied them? What strategies can they deploy that improve their viability in a milieu of male dominance, especially as regards their reproductive abilities?[20]

Ethnographic studies of women in the Sudan, Egypt, parts of North Africa, and the Arabian Gulf demonstrate how women use spirit possession as an opportunity to pursue their interests and demands in an environment of male supremacy. Women's possession then becomes a specialized strategy to put forward their interests at the expense of the males. The Muslim Hausa women in West Africa are regular devotees of shamanistic exercises designed to cure and control the grounds of their bodily ailments—the result of pathogenic spirits. In the setting of domestic disputes and conflict, women succumb to the influences of these pathogenic spirits. When in such a state wives are treated with a deference and respect that would otherwise not be accorded them. In the words of a Nigerian anthropologist, "wives manipulate these episodes in such a way as to reduce their husbands to social and economic straits. Hence, it becomes a real way of defying male authority and control that pervades Hausa society. In such a state, women find an escape from a world dominated by men and through it the world of women temporarily subdues and humiliates the world of men."[21] Possession of this sort in women gives them an opportunity to pursue their interests and values in an environment dominated by male values, structures, and governing principles.

Of special interest to this essay are infertile women in patrilineal households in which female fecundity and the ability to procreate is emphatically mandated.[22] In a study of the consequences of poor, infertile Egyptian women in a patriarchal setting, Marcia Claire Inhorn comments that "in a society where the patriarchal fertility mandate is emphatic, the social and psychological consequences of 'missing motherhood'—of being a woman unable to deliver a child for her husband, family, affines, community, faith, nation, and, not inconsequentially, herself—are nothing if not profound."[23] Infertile women, labeled as the "mother of the missing one," experienced emotional duress, self-doubt and alienation, ostracism and harassment by kin and neighbors, and, in a polygynous setting, the threat of remarriage or divorce, and verbal and physical violence.[24] Not only was her identity as a human in doubt but also her identity sexually. Being able to reproduce was seen as a biological necessity and when a woman was unable to do so, she was regarded as less then human. As one woman put it, "A flowerpot without flowers is not a flowerpot."[25] Another put it in this way, "Some people think a wife is no good if she doesn't have any children. It's like having a cow and feeding it, and she doesn't give you anything, milk or calves. People think that of a woman who has no children, a man is feeding her for nothing."[26] How her humanness was viewed rested precariously in her ability to produce the necessary offspring. Moreover, barrenness also cast doubt on her sexual identity as a female, especially "in a society where 'maleness' and 'femaleness' were well bounded categories and gender ambiguity was not easily tolerated. Indeed, infertility threatened to overturn the perceived differences between men and women—differences that were assumed to be natural and whose subversion was thus deeply threatening."[27] A female body that was unproductive was regarded an ambiguous body and under suspicion that it was more male than female—inherently unfeminine and challenging clearly delineated gendered boundaries. A fertile woman said, "People hurt her. They tell her, 'You don't have children. You are like the rooster that does not break the hen and doesn't have children. You are a homosexual rooster.' Lots of people say these things."[28] Another woman with seven children commented, "Some people talk and say, 'Two men are living together. She's the same as he is. She's like barren land.'"[29] A woman whose reproductive organs failed her lacked a vital component that constituted her sexual identity and hence she was called male to her face.[30] An unproductive female body was an ambiguous body and considered useless to her husband's patrimony and patrilineage.[31]

The social consequences were far more serious for women in polygynous households who were unable to reproduce.[32] In such domestic arrangements, women competed with other women, who either happened to be co-wives, concubines, or handmaids, for a fuller share of the husband's attention. Especially at risk were women who found that they could not produce the required male offspring or had other difficulties and liabilities to overcome—though fertility problems were by far the greatest contributor to a female's despair, illness, and hopelessness and source of sexual shame and consequent loss of status in a household of competing wombs.[33] In ethnographic studies of polygyny and infertility in tribal groups in Africa, Lewis found that childlessness was regarded as the result of a pathogenic spirit that came upon women unbidden and rendered them infertile. In these cultures, unsolicited infertility was labeled as "barrenness affliction" or "womb affliction." The affliction was regarded an illness whose effect was akin to possession. In such a condition, women strove for more consideration and respect from the head of the family unity or competed with each other for a greater slice of the domestic resources. Women made a special virtue of affliction and despair by using them to gain capital in situations of powerlessness brought on by the stresses of a polygynous household. When overcome by a womb affliction, which was uninvited and arbitrary, "these possessed women gain[ed] attention and consideration and, within variously defined limits, successfully maneuver[ed] their husbands and men folk."[34] Women in their domestic situations utilized possession as an oblique protest strategy against the frequent injustices and inequities prevalent in such a setting. Because their ecstatic state was treated and diagnosed as an illness, men appeared to be reluctantly willing to put up with it. Unwelcome infertility and the ensuing despair stimulated changes in the female's state of consciousness and, when in such a state, became the means by which she could negotiate improvement in her social lot.

The Greek conception of barrenness as an affliction is documented by Plato: "The womb is an animal which longs to generate children. When it remains barren too long after puberty it is distressed and sorely disturbed: and straying about in the body and cutting off the passages of breath, it impedes respiration and brings the sufferer into the extremest anguish and provokes all manner of diseases beside. Such is the nature of women and all that is female."[35] The word for womb in this passage is *hysterai* (a plural), which LSJ tells us is a play on *hystera*, meaning "the second woman." *Hystera* and the "wandering womb" theory give us the word *hysterics*—applied to women.[36]

This survey of anthropological material concerning the social implications of peripheral ecstasy and its appearance in women sheds new light on women in the Hebrew Bible who find themselves in similar difficult circumstances. While each of their conditions differs, Sarai and Hannah find themselves in challenging circumstances—each of them experiences the consequences of barrenness in a polygynous household. "Barrenness affliction" for each woman becomes the means by which to achieve an ecstatic state, which in turn is utilized to gain improvements in her domestic sphere.

The Case Of Sarai

In the case of Sarai, we are informed that Abram takes for himself a wife—perhaps traumatic enough—but that in addition, possibly after frequent attempts, she is barren. Infertility in an honor/shame-based society would have reflected negatively not only upon Abram but Sarai. She would have been deeply humiliated, perhaps scorned by her husband and his extended kin along with inquisitive tribal neighbors. Moreover, the constant reminders that from the loins of Abram would emerge an exceedingly great nation with territorial integrity must have grated upon not only Abram but also Sarai. After all, he was to have a male heir who was to bring to fruition the pledge made to him by God. In a patrilineal system, the pressure upon Sarai to produce an heir to the promise would have been intense.[37] Indeed, the weight of barrenness presses upon Sarai with such intensity that she descends into the depths of despair, cognizant that her good reputation is in jeopardy. She cannot bear the thought of disgracing her husband or endangering her standing in the household. In women, shame is positive and indicates their sexual propriety and social modesty.[38] Female fertility represents an aspect of positive female shame. Infertile wives have a negative impact upon a husband's honor—partially indicated by his ability to father many children. Sarai, however, was unable to sustain the male's ideal of a female's role—namely, to be fertile. In this state, gripped by passionate feelings of sexual shame and desperate for Abram's continued patronage, she makes him an offer that only she is in the position to proffer—she acts shamelessly. Recognizing that her good reputation has been damaged, Sarai has nothing to lose and everything to gain. But before putting the deal before Abram, as if to drive home the depth of her disgrace, the reader is once more reminded that Sarai, Abram's wife, bore him no children. Indeed, it is not surprising then that she voices her complaint, "You see that the LORD has prevented me from bearing children" (Gen 16:2).

Note the accusing tone in the voice of Sarai: "You see that the LORD has prevented me from bearing children."[39] She appears to be saying that the Lord is playing mischief with her—a pathogenic force that has disabled her reproductive organs. In a state of despair, Sarai sees herself possessed by a force that denies her the right to produce offspring. She is the unwilling victim of a God-inflicted illness whose effect is analogous to possession. It is clear that she is competing with other women for a fuller share of her husband's attentions and regard but also with the other wombs in the domicile for male offspring. In such a context of involuntarily being possessed by a power who denies her fertility, how is she to preserve the official male ideology of female fecundity and sub-ordination while also subverting it? The affliction provides Sarai with the opportunity to reverse her misfortunes—a specialized strategy designed to forward her interests at the expense of Abram. She is aware that if she were to remain passive, Abram would in the end seek to pro-vide the child of promise through another channel. Consequently, she takes charge of her situation and subverts his intentions but also maneu-vers him to do what she desires—presumably to provide a child for Abram from his union with Hagar. But that is not what she intends—the children are to be hers. As she states, "It may be that I shall obtain chil-dren by her" (Gen 16:2). The tone appears to be mocking, retorting "that I shall have children by her" and not "that you shall have children by her." She does not seem to care a whit about providing a child that suits the plans of Abram and his god. Her plan, which involves her Egyptian handmade, will compensate for her procreative deficiencies.[40] Of concern to her is to reestablish her damaged reputation in her domus—in a state of womb affliction she finds a surrogate womb upon which she puts her stamp of approval—she will provide the children that she desires but Hagar will, ironically, also restore her primary role in the household of Abram. Hagar's surrogacy would improve her sta-tus in Abram's household even though Sarai was Hagar's social, politi-cal, and economic superior; Sarai's barrenness nevertheless lessened her status as a woman.[41]

Her attempts to maneuver her husband and at the same time pursue her interests are also seen when she proactively supplies Abram with his new wife/concubine: "Go to my slave girl. . . . Sarai, Abram's wife, took Hagar the Egyptian, her slave-girl, and gave her to her husband Abram as a wife/concubine . . . and Abram listened to the voice of Sarai" (Gen 16:2-3). Here we have a clear case of domestic control in which Sarai deals with an intolerable situation. It is an indirect protest movement against Abram and designed to protect her from his exactions—his demand for male offspring. Because Sarai was unable to produce male heirs to Abram's patrimony and patrilineage, he would have regarded her useless.[42] Her barrenness also represented a direct and public chal-lenge to his virility. Yet, she manages to preserve the official male ideol-ogy of female fecundity by the offer of Hagar to Abram. It is obvious that Abram tolerates Sarai's domestic machinations and is more or less satisfied with the outcome because he will not loose face. In an interesting reversal of domestic order, Abram passively accepts the offer of Hagar from Sarai. Sarai assumes the role of a patroness, and Abram the role of a client—a recipient of Sarai's offers to him. He puts up no protest. We are informed that Abram listens to the voice of Sarai, takes Hagar as his wife, and has success with her—she conceives and produces what at first appearances is the male heir required to bring to fruition the promise of nationhood and land to Abram.

It is also clear, however, that Sarai's schemes backfire—these specialized strategies were designed to put forward her interests at the expense of Abram's. Yet, Hagar's success only served to exacerbate Sarai's failure and, moreover, heightened tensions between the two women. Sarai, however, is not about to capitulate to her abysmal situation. In her state of affliction, Sarai challenges Abram directly: "This outrage against me is your fault! I myself put my maid in your lap. But from the moment she found that she had conceived, she has been looking at me with contempt. May the Lord judge between you and me" (Gen 16:4-5).[43] Harsh words indeed. She is acting shamelessly and bringing dishonor to her husband, but if her affliction is involuntary and the trigger for a deeply troubled mind—a form of possession—then her husband would have put up with it without a counter-challenge. The displeasures are voiced through the lips of an afflicted woman and uttered with an authority that she might not have achieved on her own. She holds her husband responsible for the way in which she has been wronged—not least of which was that Hagar had arrogated equality to herself not hers to have. The Code of Hammurabi states clearly that a slave girl whose status has been elevated to that of a concubine must not claim equality with her mistress. Hagar is eventually driven out of the house by Sarai. We can only assume that the situation in the end worked itself out with amity between Abram and Sarai—Abram passively accepted the outcome of her schemes and Sarai continued proactively to promote her interests in Abram's house.

The Case Of Hannah

Similarly, in the story of Hannah, social inequities in the domicile lead to social stresses for Hannah and to questions of how best to alleviate those tensions. She is clearly described as belonging to a domestic context of co-wives in which there is considerable hostility between the two wives—no doubt, each competing for a fuller share in their husband's attention and regard. Indeed, Hannah appears to have favored status. Not only does she receive a greater portion of Elkanah's daily sacrifices but he favors her over the other—he loved her more than Peninnah despite the fact that Hannah was a serious liability. Hannah is in a state of sexual shame because of her infertility—the Lord has closed her womb. Indeed, in a similar way to that of Sarai, God disrupts normal reproductive processes in Hannah. She consequently finds herself in a state of great despair and domestic turmoil because she is unable to sustain the male ideal of females as producers of heirs to the ancestral line. The unsolicited womb affliction is highly troubling for Hannah—indeed, so much so that it becomes the means to her possession.

Peninnah's response to Hannah serves to heighten Hannah's condition of distress—Hannah is a rival and a point of undesired competition for Peninnah: "Her rival used to provoke her severely and spitefully, to irritate her, because the LORD had closed her womb" (1 Sam 1:6). It is clear that Peninnah is directly striving for more consideration and respect from Elkanah but also competing with the head of the family for a greater slice of the domestic budget. While Elkanah supplies Peninnah and her sons and daughters with a share of the sacrifice, he nevertheless gives a double portion to Hannah even though she has no children to support. Peninnah has fulfilled her sexual obligations to Elkanah and borne him the sons who make the family economically and politically viable and yet Hannah is the favored one.[44] She deliberately and spitefully uses Hannah's barrenness as the means to degrade her status—hoping thereby to upgrade hers. The provocation continues for years. Hannah is disgraced because she is cognizant of what is thought of her and shamed sexually because of her barrenness. In this state of double affliction, she seeks the solace of the religious sanctuary and while there weeps and refuses to eat.

Weeping and food abstention are well known in the world of antiquity to trigger ecstatic states. Trance states can be readily induced in most people by a wide range of stimuli, applied either separately or in combination. Lewis avers, "Time-honored techniques include the use of alcoholic spirits, hypnotic suggestion, rapid over-breathing, the inhalation of smoke and vapours, music, and dancing; and the ingestion of such drugs as mescaline or lysergic acid and other psychotropic alkaloids. Even without aids, much the same effect can be produced, although usually in the nature of things more slowly, by such self-inflicted or externally imposed mortifications and privations as food abstention, fasting, and ascetic contemplation."[45] 4 *Ezra* mentions three famous techniques—fasting, eating flowers of the field, and drinking fiery liquid; two of them, at least, are usually understood as triggering techniques. The third, drinking a fiery liquid, occurs within the vision itself for the purpose of remembering scripture—functioning as a kind of memory potion (4 Ezra 6:35; 9:24; 14:36-40). In the case of Hannah, weeping, fasting, and praying, rather than functioning as a preparatory inducement, mark activity directly related to her possessed state. Her affliction becomes the means to the achievement of an ecstatic state while her weeping, fasting, and praying become the means to maintaining the state—she is a possessed woman who seeks out the sanctuary in which to express her grievances. It is a strategy designed shamelessly to put forward her aggrieved honor before her husband, Peninnah, her female rival, the priestly establishment, and God.

Her reception by the priestly establishment is dubious at best. In her grief she prays silently, her lips trembling, and under observation. Eli, watching her mouth and noting her quivering lips, assumes the worst, probably observing her unusual/uncontrolled state of consciousness and not knowing what to make of it. Finally, he accuses her of coming to the temple in a state of drunkenness—he issues a direct, humiliating challenge: "How long will you make a drunken spectacle of yourself?" So here, yet another disgrace befalls her but one that she refuses to countenance. In an aggressive counter-challenge to Eli's mistaken observation, she retorts, "I am an unfortunate woman. I have drunk neither wine nor strong drink. I was only pouring out my soul to Yahweh. Do not think that I am a worthless woman. It is because my complaint and my vexation are so great that I tarried this long." Whatever state it was that Eli had observed in her, it had not been induced by alcohol. Hannah's altered state of mind had been triggered by her womb affliction—she was in effect, possessed. Hannah had been overcome involuntarily by an arbitrary affliction for which she could not be held responsible, and in her possessed condition she gained attention and consideration successfully to maneuver Eli.[46] As a social inferior Hannah presses home her claims on her superior and is consequently heard; in true form, Eli, an institutionalized authority, tolerates her challenge and sends her on her way. Moreover, she has also been able to improve her lot from the confining constraints of her allotted station in her residence. No longer being pestered by Peninnah, she retires to her quarters, eats and drinks with her husband—a symbol of her status reinstatement—and her body no longer wears the disconsolate expression. Not only has she been healed of her affliction but socially her good reputation has been reestablished. What began as a divinely afflicted illness ends in ecstasy: "and the pain and suffering of the initial crisis are obliterated in its subsequent re-evaluation as a uniquely efficacious sign of divine favor that has positive social outcomes."[47]

Conclusion

Though the unbidden affliction of barrenness is undesirable for women in patrilineal and polygynous households, it nevertheless triggers a trance state in them. In this exalted state they are empowered to deal with intolerable domestic situations in such a way that it has constructive social benefits for them. A barren body is a possessed body and as such serves as an aggressive, oblique strategy to rectify the injustices of a patrilineal and polygynous system.[48]

PART THREE

Texts

CHAPTER TEN

Micah—Models Matter

POLITICAL ECONOMY AND MICAH 6:9-15

Marvin L. Chaney

Recent studies illumine the political economies of Israel and Judah in the eighth century B.C.E. The intricate textual and philological problems of Micah 6:9-15 yield fresh solutions when current knowledge of these dynamics informs their analysis. Beyond the clarification of individual cruxes, the literary structure of the passage is unified in a measure-for-measure correspondence between indictment and sentence. More precise attention to the systemic dynamics castigated also enhances detection and appreciation of the frequent paronomasia that heightens the irony and sarcasm of the unit. Taken in sum, the analysis strengthens the suggestion that Micah 6:9-15 is closely associated in context and composition with most of Micah 1–3.

A t the outset, I need to acknowledge a number of assumptions I make in the study that follows. Strictures of space preclude any significant attempt justifying these assumptions, though I shall try to reference literature that argues in greater detail for what I can only presume here.

With regard to the history of composition of the so-called eighth-century prophets, I assume that the books of Amos, Hosea, Isaiah, and Micah are, in something close to their received form, products of the Persian period. All four books also evidence levels of composition congruent in detail with the language and interests of the Deuteronomistic History.[1] In my view, the most probable social matrix for the composition of this material is the royal "reforms" of the late Judahite monarchy.[2] While this strain of composition undoubtedly continued into the exile and beyond, the late monarchy has greater explanatory power as its initiating social context. Anterior to this "Deuteronomistic" level of composition in the four eighth-century prophets lies material that was recomposed according to the needs and interests of the later periods. This earlier level of composition is characterized by a relative handful of self-contained literary forms and content subjects. While I make no claim that this material gives direct access to the named prophets, its concerns and emphases comport well with what is known about the socioeconomic dynamics of eighth-century Israel and Judah.[3] Once again, these concerns are generic enough to be of interest in many later periods, but systemic changes particular to the eighth century B.C.E. seem the most likely impetus for the generation of these prophetic oracles in the first place.

The Dynamics of Eighth-Century Political Economy

I have published previously in several articles my understanding of the social world of Israel and Judah in the eighth century B.C.E., focusing especially on the dynamics of political economy.[4] Many other scholars have contributed to that interpretation and continue to do so.[5] A brief epitome of that ongoing work may be articulated in the following points:

1. Geopolitically, Israel and Judah occupied the land bridge where the regional superpowers met and clashed. As a result, stimulus for change in their political economies often came from beyond their borders. During the long and mostly concurrent reigns of Jeroboam II of Israel (*ca.* 781–745 B.C.E.) and Uzziah of Judah (*ca.* 781–747 B.C.E.), however, the two small kingdoms were relatively free from external military threat. They were in league, with the smaller Judah probably functioning as a virtual vassal of the stronger Northern Kingdom. Coupled with the lengthy tenure in office of both kings, this situation gave the elites of the two states an unusual freedom to initiate change in their political economies. By the time foreign imperial power reasserted itself upon Israel and Judah in the person of Tiglath-pileser III, it served mostly to intensify the dynamics of political economy initiated earlier in the eighth century.
2. Israelite and Judahite elites had incentive as well as opportunity to change their political economies because of their active partic-

ipation in international trade. Their import/export trade was mostly with and through the maritime city-states of Phoenicia. Luxury goods, military matériel, and the wherewithal of monumental architecture were imported. To pay for these imports, foodstuffs and fiber were exported. Wheat, olive oil, and wine, the triad of Palestinian agriculture, headed the list of exports. The costs and benefits of this trade were grossly disproportionate by class. Imports benefited the elite few, but their cost in exported foodstuffs cut deeply into the sustenance of the peasant majority.

3. Prior to this time, wine and oil amphorae varied in capacity. The storage needs of subsistence agriculture required only utility, not uniformity, in the size of these vessels. Since wine and olive oil were the preferred exports in the greatly increased import/export trade of the eighth-century B.C.E., however, incentive for uniform units to expedite that trade resulted in a royal standardization of the בת (bt, "bath").[6]

4. One way to increase production of the three preferred agricultural commodities was through a regional specialization of agriculture. 2 Chronicles 26:10 witnesses such a process for Uzziah's Judah. Archaeological surveys show a marked proliferation of rock-cut olive and grape processing installations in the hill country in the eighth century B.C.E. The למלך (lmlk, "for the king") seal impressions from Judah point to a system of royal vineyards in the uplands, while the Samaria ostraca document the flow of oil and wine to officials of the northern royal court from both private and royal vineyards and orchards.[7]

5. When integrated with comparatively normed coefficients of density, archaeological surveys of the total inhabited area evidence a marked rise in the population of Israel and Judah in the Iron II period. While absolute growth occurred in both the lowlands and the highlands, the hill country grew faster, for the first time accounting for over half the total. One need not solve the old chicken-and-egg problem in social-scientific theory to know that rapid population growth and agricultural intensification are almost always correlated in agrarian societies. Archaeology also shows that various marginal areas, tilled only during periods of greatest central control and agricultural intensification, were inhabited in the eighth century B.C.E., many for the first time.[8]

6. Agricultural specialization and intensification fostered the proliferation of technological innovations. While scantly attested in the

previous century, the beam press came into its own in the eighth century as an instrument for increasing the volume and efficiency of oil production.

7. In the eighth century, Israel and Judah increasingly developed "command economies," in which urban elites reduced or usurped villagers' power to make their own decisions regarding the priorities and techniques of agricultural production.

8. Pressure to grow ever-increasing amounts of the few preferred crops concentrated risk and effaced the risk-spreading mechanisms of the peasants' more traditional subsistence agriculture.

9. Land consolidation proceeded apace, aided and abetted by tax policy that discouraged the subsistence farming of cereals in the hill country, and thereby incentivized the raising of olives and grapes there instead.

10. Not only were agricultural labor and land ownership separated, but the various factors of production were segmented and subjected to separate rent.

11. There was a growth in absentee landlordism. With their promise of imported luxuries and greater access to political influence and social prestige, the capital cities drew landlords away from their country estates and their need for clientele support. What had previously been multistranded relations with their peasants were reduced to a single strand of economic exploitation.

12. Attenuation of risk-spreading measures rendered peasants ever more vulnerable to the vicissitudes of an erratic climate. When natural disaster struck, they were left no alternative to survival loans at *de facto* interest rates usurious by any standards. Foreclosure on family land and/or the indentured labor of family members pledged as collateral was often at the discretion of the wealthy urban creditors. Debt instruments thus served as a major means of accomplishing both land consolidation and the pauperization of the peasantry.

13. Traditional village courts had few procedural safeguards. Increased socioeconomic stratification gave urban elites the power to coerce or suborn their decisions. Thus perverted, these courts gave a façade of legality to foreclosures deemed illegal by most peasants and other members of the lower classes. Against this background, the rhetoric of the eighth-century prophets appeals these cases to YHWH's divine law court in the sky. As auditors on the proceedings in God's court, the prophets report

the vindication there of the peasants' cause, and declare that YHWH has found the urban elites guilty with regard to the matters under adjudication.

Can knowledge of these systemic dynamics inform and enhance the textual exegesis of oracles belonging to the earliest level of composition in the eighth-century prophets? Only a book-length treatment of the many oracles of these prophets whose subject is political economy could fully address that question. This far briefer venue allows only limited explication of one representative example.

Micah 6:9-15 as an Example

I have chosen to use Micah 6:9-15 for that purpose. Micah 6:9-16 is widely regarded as constituting a discrete unit.[9] Elements of both form and content demarcate it from what precedes. Verse 16, which ends the unit in its canonical form, is virtually self-contained. Its vocabulary and rhetorical vector seem to echo the Deuteronomistic Historian's appropriation of Jehuid apology in 1 and 2 Kings, and likely mark it as an addition to the older unit.[10]

Of all the materials in the book of Micah after chapter 3, moreover, the unit in 6:9-15 is that most frequently associated by historical scholars with the dynamics of the prophet's own time. The unambiguous lines of this pericope seem to evince the same processes of political economy reflected elsewhere in the eighth-century prophets—including, quite notably, Micah 1–3. The passage so bristles with textual and/or philological difficulties, however, that both its literary structure and its relation to any known set of socioeconomic dynamics have been in doubt. Proposed "solutions" to these problems have most often proceeded piecemeal, leaving both text and context in a focus decidedly blurred. The more extreme of these "solutions" have simply rewritten the text. Can insights from political economy help to illumine any of these issues?

Critically Established Text of Micah 6:9-15

9   קול יהוה לעיר יקרא[a] שמע[b] מטה[c] ומי יעדה[d]

10 האשא[e] בת[f] רשע ואיפת רזון[g] זעומה

11 האזכה במאזני רשע ובכיס אבני מרמה

12 אצרות רשע אצרו[h] עשיריה[i] מלאו חמס
     ישביה[j] דברו שקר לשונם רמיה בפיהם

גם אני החליתי הכותך^k השמם על חטאתך   13
אתה תאכל ולא תשבע^l וישחך^m בקרבך   14
תסגiⁿ ולא תפליט^o תפלט^p לחרב אתן
אתה תזרע ולא תקצור   15
אתה תדרך זית ולא תסוך שמן
ותירוש^q ולא תשתה יין^r

Translation of the Critically Established Text

The voice of YHWH calls the city (to account)—
Pay heed, O "tribe" that perverts (justice),
    for who can summon *him* (to court)?!
"Can I bear the wicked *bath* measure,
Or the accursed *ephah* of {leanness}   ?
                              {the 'potentate'}
Can I be clear with balances of wickedness,
Or with a bag of deceitful weight-stones?
Stores of wickedness they lay up,
Its [the city's] rich are full with wrong-doing.
Its lords speak lies;
As for their tongues—treachery is in their mouths!
For my part, *I* shall make sore your smiting,
Devastating (you) for your sins!
You will eat, but not be satisfied,
For you will be bent double with regard to your insides!
Should you {overtake} (something),
          {encroach upon}
          {fence}
    you will not secure (it),
Should you 'deliver' (someone),
    I shall give (them) to the sword!
You will sow, but not reap;
You will tread olives, but not pour oil (in anointing),
And (you will tread/dispossess) must, but not drink wine."

a. In view of the poetic parallel and literary structure to be discussed below, יקרא is best understood in the well-attested sense of "call to account, summon."[11]

b. Read שמע, with LXX and Syriac, for MT's שמעו. MT's plural probably reflects the influence of Micah 6:1-2. ותושיה יראה שמך is a later addition, as seen by many commentators.[12]

c. מטה probably involves paronomasia. As "tribe," it is kinship language used sarcastically of the urban elite, whose policies in Micah's time tended to efface such affiliations and their concomitants. Note a similarly sarcastic use of משפחה in Micah 2:3. But מטה is also the Hiphil participle of נטה. Used in the Hiphil, נטה often refers to "thrusting aside," "perverting," or "wresting" justice, even when the object is only implied, but not expressed.[13] Thus, מטה can mean simultaneously "tribe" and "perverter (of justice)."

d. ומי יעדה עוד, MT's much-discussed crux, has never received convincing interpretation. Many moderns since Wellhausen have followed LXX in preferring עיר (πόλιν) to MT's עוד, and then redividing and emending the resulting text to read ומועד העיר, "and assembly of the city."[14] Offered with Wellhausen's characteristic brevity and reserve— "vielleicht darf man, zum Teil nach der Septuaginta, ומועד העיר, lesen"[15]—this solution is ingenious, but suffers major liabilities. Lexicographically, מועד elsewhere means the "appointed time or place of meeting," not "assembly (of citizens)." The presumed sense of מועד in the reconstructed text of Micah 6:9 is unparalleled elsewhere, even though attestation is quite broad.[16]

Once social history and the social perspective of the remainder of the unit are invoked, moreover, this emendation becomes even less plausible. No citizen assembly is evidenced for Jerusalem in Micah's time, nor is one likely according to any credible model for his society and its dynamics. Other lines in the oracle castigate the ruling elite of the capital and their activities. Given the known parameters of change in eighth-century Judahite society, social-scientific models would predict increased social stratification and centralization of power, not citizen assemblies. On the other hand, "the city" in Micah's parlance is Jerusalem, the capital.[17] Its population had grown substantially in his lifetime, but in the rank order of cites and towns, its power had grown even more significantly, and at the expense of other sites, save, perhaps, Lachish. In that social and rhetorical context, "the city" in verse 9a refers far more probably to the few whose power is symbolized and made manifest in the monumental architecture of Jerusalem than to the city's total population, understood without differentiation.

Wide acceptance of Wellhausen's tentative emendation of verse 9c has probably obscured evidence for the line's elucidation that lies close to hand. Micah's text should probably be read in light of Jeremiah

49:19; 50:44; and Job 9:19, the certain occurrences in MT of the Hiphil of יעד. The meaning of these Hiphils is, unambiguously, "to summon" or "to arraign." Jeremiah 49:19b reads, with YHWH speaking, "For who is like me? Who can summon/arraign me (ומי יעידני)? Who is the shepherd who can stand before me?" Jeremiah 50:44b reads, again with YHWH speaking, "For who is like me? Who can summon/arraign me (ומי יועדני)? Who is the shepherd who can stand before me?" Job 9:19 reads: אם־לכח אמיץ הנה ואם־למשפט מי יועידני. In the first half of this verse, הנהו should probably be read for MT's הנה. With most moderns, I read the last word of the verse as יועידנו instead of MT's יועידני; cf. LXX and Syriac.[18] The tradition behind MT likely made the change to remove even the slightest suggestion that a human being might call God to account. The texts in Jeremiah might also have influenced this passage in Job. In any case, the slightly emended text may be translated, "If it is a matter of power, *he* is the strong one; if it is a matter of justice, who can summon/arraign *him*?" In each of these three passages, then, this use of מי with the Hiphil of יעד clearly involves a rhetorical question expressing God's incomparable power to summon any human being to arraignment. What could be more at home in a judgment oracle by a prophet named מיכה?

Since all three occurrences of מי plus the Hiphil of יעד appear to have God as the object of the rhetorical question, it is probably easiest in Micah 6:9 to read ומי יעדהו, "for who can summon/arraign *him*?" with YHWH in verse 9a taken as the antecedent of the pronominal suffix. Read thus, verse 9c is a brief and disputatious ejaculation addressed to the urban elite who are indicted and judged in the remainder of the oracle. As a class, they were accustomed to summoning others and passing judgment upon them. They were also Micah's opponents who repeatedly tried to silence him. In this impassioned parenthesis, the prophet warns them to listen up, for it is *YHWH* who is calling the city and those who rule it to account. They cannot summon him up they way they do the peasants whom they cheat and dispossess. Quite the reverse. In his call to the city, YHWH is summoning *them* for judgment. Micah's use of the rhetorical question may also be a defense of the source and authority of his judgment oracle. He does not speak in his own right, he insists, but only as an auditor on YHWH's court. No mere mortal summons YHWH to court for arraignment!

The עוד that follows יעדה in MT probably took its rise as עיר, a gloss suggesting that the suffix be read as third feminine singular rather than third masculine singular, with the city of verse 9a rather than

YHWH as the antecedent. Such a reading is witnessed by LXX's πόλιν, which does not have the article. The tradents who originated this gloss might have had the same pious concerns as those in Job 9:19—to remove any hint that a human being could call God to account. Once the tradition behind MT lost the Hiphil inflection of יעד, however, עיר was easily corrupted into עוד.

e. After the ardent interjection of verse 9c, and as promised in verse 9a, YHWH here in verse 10 begins to speak directly in the first person. Of the two minor emendations standardly proposed for the first word of verse 10,[19] I prefer האשא, "can I bear," to האשה, "can I forget," for two reasons. The loss of the א from the form seems the more likely of the two haplographies. נשא in the sense of "bear, endure, permit" seems the closer parallel to זכה (ב), "be clear (with)."

f. If אצרות רשע is understood as intrusive in verse 10—as will be argued below in the discussion of verse 12—the reading of בת for בית allows verses 10 and 11 to be read as a poetic unit, clearly integrated in structure and content, and dealing exclusively with the dishonest use of weights and measures in exchange transactions to cheat those already vulnerable.

> "Can I bear the wicked *bath* measure,
> Or the accursed *ephah* of leanness?"

> "Can I be clear with balances of wickedness,
> Or with a bag of deceitful weight-stones?"

בת and איפה also occur paired, and in the same order, in the futility curse of Isaiah 5:10:

> "For ten acres of vineyard shall produce but one *bath*,
> And a *homer* of seed shall produce only an *ephah*!"

This curse is part of a sentence issued in God's court for the crime of unscrupulous land consolidation. I have sought elsewhere to explicate its social location and rhetorical vector.

> The word translated "acre" is צמד, which means literally "yoke" or "span." By extension, it also signifies the amount of land a plowman can plow in a day with a yoked team of traction animals (BDB: 855; *HALAT*: 967). Like its counterparts in

the native languages of many other traditional agrarian societies, it is basically a unit of peasant labor, not a mathematically
exact quantity of land treated as a commercial entity. In Isaiah's
carefully crafted language, however, the futilely low yield of formerly subsistence land now planted to vineyard is expressed in
terms of a wine amphora of standardized capacity, designed to
facilitate trade in wine as a commodity. Archaeology has now
recovered several exemplars of this royally standardized eighth-
century amphora inscribed with either בת or בת למלך (Avigad;
Inge; Mittmann; Naveh). Isaiah's parallel line continues the contrast between a positive valence for vocabulary rooted in the
world of village subsistence and a negative tenor for terms that
epitomize the innovations pressed by the urban elite in their program of agricultural intensification. The חמר is an "ass-load,"
an inexact measurement pertinent to the work realities of peasants (*HALAT*: 317). The איפה, approximately one tenth of a
חמר, is the dry measure equivalent of the בת (BDB: 35; *HALAT*:
41), and like it, is a standardized unit intended to expedite commercial transactions—this time, in grain. As is so often the case
with prophetic language, Isaiah's words have both a concretely
precise denotation and emotionally charged connotations that
assist rhetorically in driving home the judgment rendered.[20]

These same connotations for בת and איפה are as likely for Micah's
usage as for Isaiah's, since both critique the same generic context.

g. Is there a sarcastic pun here between רזון, "leanness, wasting,
scantness," and רזון "potentate," a title that appears parallel to מלך in
Proverbs 14:28? Certainty is impossible, but several lines of reasoning
render such paronomasia plausible. As seen above, the איפה was the
dry-measure counterpart of the בת, which is known to have undergone
royal standardization in the eighth-century B.C.E. Because this standardized liquid measure was ceramic, numerous exemplars of the eighth-century בת have survived, several with identifying inscriptions. As a dry
measure, on the other hand, the איפה would have been constructed of
organic materials that decompose without leaving evidence for the
archaeological record. Social-scientific study of agrarian societies
regarding exchange transactions in grain may go far to make good this
lack of more concrete evidence.

The function of units of dry measure for cereals in such societies is
complex. When grain is involved in commerce among agrarian elites,

accurate, standardized units are of the essence to expedite large-scale trade between relative equals. When transactions entailing grain take place between landlord and peasant or grain merchants and the poor, however, the exact size of baskets or other devices used to measure cereals is characteristically malleable, almost always to the disadvantage of the weaker party to the transaction. Amos 8:5 famously witnesses the situation in which grain is scarce and dear, and the poor must buy it in the market for survival. The איפה is smaller than standard, the counterweight in the balances used to weigh the payment in silver is heavier than standard, and the balances themselves are rigged to exacerbate the overpayment.

When a tenant's rent is due to his landlord at harvest time in kind, however, grain measures tend to expand. James Scott analyzes a typical example from Burma and its impact within peasant culture:

> The most transparent and despised method of circumventing local traditions was to devise a "landlord's basket" that held more. The ingenuity of landowners and their agents in the design of such baskets was seemingly inexhaustible. Some baskets were constructed so as to balloon out as they received rice, others were shaped to prevent leveling and ensure a heaping basket, certain methods of pouring increased the basket's capacity, and if it were shaken vigorously several times as it was filled, it would hold more. . . . The capacity of absentee landlords to adapt a special "rent-basket" that was always larger than the "village basket" came to be a galling symbol of their power to impose their will.[21]

Couper reports that the peasants affected by such practices often named the offending instrument, blaming it for their plight.

> But the light in which the villagers regard these baskets may be seen from the names which they give to them; for example the basket of a Letpadan landlord is known as "the cart-breaker," this basket is said to equal 150 milk tins as compared with the village basket of 136.
>
> Tenants resent bitterly this right of enlarging the basket which the landlords have arrogated to themselves and many ascribe [to it] their present distress.[22]

In Micah's generic counterpart to that world, then, it is not a far reach to suggest that poor peasants would protest bitterly that "the potentate's איפה"—whether as a standard unit for the grain that was rushed from their fields into international trade, as scant measure for the poor at the grain merchant's stall, or as the enlarged landlord's unit that alienated more and more of the crop from those who produced it—was, for them, "an איפה of leanness, wasting, and scantness." The Burmese example, and those like it from virtually every agrarian society from which there is sufficient evidence, at the very least grant verisimilitude to the conjecture that the language of Micah's oracle involves a bitterly ironic play between the two meanings of רזון in biblical Hebrew.

h. The reconstruction of this half-line presumes the following history of textual transmission: אצרות רשע was first lost by haplography, the basis of which is patent. The parent of MT later added it back, perhaps from a marginal gloss, but misplaced it into verse 10. This misplacement was probably influenced by the frequent association of בית and אוצר and the occurrence of רשע in both expressions. Thus, this same process of transmission accounts for the reading of בת as בית in verse 10. This change, in turn, would have influenced the reading of האש for האשא, since without the reading of בת, האשא was no longer intelligible. Some version of the full half-line reconstructed here as verse 12a may have occurred in the Hebrew *Vorlage* of the LXX in verse 10. LXX reads θησαυρίζων θησαυροὺς ἀνόμους as a part of verse 10.

The loss of אצרות רשע in verse 12 by haplography left אצרו orphaned at the beginning of verse 12, where it was subsequently read as אשר, a particle often in evidence in the book of Micah. Possible influences include the form עשיריה, which follows immediately, and, perhaps, the smudging of the tail on the צ. If the reading of ואשר in verse 14 already existed, it, too, could have been such an influence. Alternately, the reading of a secondary אשר in verse 12 might have been the source or the pattern for the reading of ואשר in verse 14. While the reading of אשר in verse 12 was intelligible and transmittable, it is hardly poetic, as most commentators have seen. The secondary אשר, however, might have seemed to assist in bridging the gap between the עיר of verse 9 and the third feminine singular suffixes of verse 12. Such a function might have helped to solidify its place in the text.

The form אצרו, reconstructed as a part of verse 12a, bridges between the divine first-person address of verses 10 and 11 and the third-person indictment of verse 12. It is congruent with the plural perfects, מלאו and דברו that follow. The "they" that "lay up stores of wickedness" are both the unjust weights and measures that are the subject of YHWH's first-person speech in his own voice and the "rich" men and "lords" of the city who are castigated in the third-person indictment that follows immediately. Micah says that wicked and deceitful weights and measures have increased the "surplus" extracted by the urban elite from the peasants of the countryside. Thus the storehouses of the capital city lay up "stores of wickedness."

i. Content and context require that the antecedent of the third feminine singular suffixes of verse 12 be the עיר addressed in the beginning in verse 9a. This construction is bold, but it is no license to reorder the verses. The overweening supremacy of Jerusalem and its ruling elite in eighth-century Judah allowed such elliptical syntax to remain unambiguous.

j. As I have argued at length elsewhere,[23] the participle יֹשֵׁב, in this and other contexts where the urban elite are clearly the addressees, is not to be read as an undifferentiated indication of the "inhabitants, citizens, townsmen," or "people." In such contexts, the יֹשְׁבִים are those who "besit" large estates and seats of judgment and power. The יֹשֵׁב par excellence is the king who "besits" the throne.

k. גַּם־אֲנִי signals the hinge between indictment and sentence. It marks the sharpest possible disjunction between the human criminals and their divine prosecutor. YHWH, the judge who summoned the ruling elite of Jerusalem for trial in verse 9, and then prosecuted their crimes, now announces their sentence and serves as its executor. That the heavenly judge at this point personalizes the sentence by addressing each perpetrator in the second masculine singular should occasion no surprise. This rhetorical device for heightening the specificity of address is common in the prophets. The exalted social position of those so addressed had effectively placed them beyond the justice of human courts. How the worm turns when the prophet's rhetoric takes the case on appeal to the heavenly court of last resort!

l. The sentence proper now begins with this first in a series of futility curses.

m. After all the discussion,[24] MT's consonants are most easily read as a Hiphal imperfect third masculine singular from שחח or שׁחה plus the second masculine singular suffix. A literal translation would be, "For it will bend you down with respect to your insides." Most forms once thought to be Hithpalel from שׁחה are, of course, in the light of the Ugaritic evidence, Hishtaphel from חוה. But Proverbs 12:25 seems to witness a Hiphil form from שׁחה, with a use of the preposition בְּ not

unlike that here. Two forms in Isaiah 25:12 and 26:5, both parallel to
הַשְׁפִּיל, are standardly read as Hiphil from שׁחח. In our text, I read the
third masculine singular form as expressing an indefinite subject[25] and
the בְּ־ of בְּקִרְבּךָ as meaning "with regard to, respecting," much as in
Proverbs 12:25. The image thus conveyed is that the haughty rich, who
are overly full of food wrested from the starving poor, will become victims of their own gluttony. They will be humbled, bowed down, and
brought low by severe nausea and/or diarrhea. Such an understanding
of the line seems to be supported by both Syriac and Targ.

n. תֵּסַג is a second masculine singular Hiphil jussive, but from what
"root"? Wordplay seems likely among נשׂג, "overtake," as what a predator does to its prey, סוג I, which in the Hiphil usually refers to "displac-
ing" or "moving back" a boundary marker, and סוג II, which seems to
deal with "fencing about." From Micah's perspective, the urban elites of
his time were guilty of all three actions against the persons or fields of
the poor peasants. Knowledge of the systemic dynamics of the political
economies of Judah and Israel once again provides the background
against which sarcastic paronomasia can be explored.

o. In its other occurrence in the Hiphil, Isaiah 5:29, פלט is used in
figurative speech of a lion carrying off its prey to secure it. That image
works well here, too. The rapacious elite may "overtake" the persons
and fields of their peasant prey, they may gain more land by "displac-
ing" boundary markers, they may even "fence about" the land they have
taken, but they will not be able to "drag off into security" the prey upon
which they have pounced. Fields cannot be carried into exile.

p. As discussed above, וַאֲשֶׁר is probably secondary. Its occurrence at
this point may be related to the secondary אֲשֶׁר in verse 12. In a delicious
play on פלט in two different conjugations, the predator has become the
prey. The urban elite, unable to secure their kill in the first half of the
bicolon, have, by its second half, themselves become the kill!

q. As seen by Pope and Loretz,[26] among others, וְתִירוֹשׁ involves
wordplay. The form can be heard both as a noun, meaning "must, new
wine," and as a second masculine singular imperfect verb, meaning, variously, "you shall tread, take possession of, dispossess, drive out, impov-
erish." In the prophet's sarcastic paronomasia, it probably means all of
the above simultaneously and in concert.

r. As here reconstructed, the oracle proceeds in regular bicola, save
only for the single tricolon that marks its conclusion. Recognition of
such a terminating device confirms the judgment of many scholars,
noted above, that verse 16 derives from a later recomposition of the

book of Micah that is reminiscent of the language and concerns of the Deuteronomistic historian's incorporation and reorientation of Jehu's apology. This tripartite capstone of the series of futility curses, of course, reprises the triad of Palestine's agricultural economy and the terms of its production and distribution. The architects and beneficiaries of agricultural intensification will reap none of the fruits of all the labor they worked so hard to commandeer!

Conclusions

1. When combined with the textual, linguistic, and literary tools standardly in use in exegesis, attention to the dynamics of agrarian political economy facilitates fresh and intrinsic interpretation of several of the cruxes in Micah 6:9-15.

2. The results unify the oracle rhetorically and clarify its literary structure. It opens with a summons to judgment in verse 9 expressed in the prophet's voice. In verses 10 and 11, the קול יהוה (voice of YHWH) asks in the first person a dramatic series of rhetorical questions that begin the indictment. Verse 12 continues the indictment in the third person. The divine first person reappears in verse 13 to initiate the sentence. Thereafter, the judgment is personalized to each of those guilty of the crimes indicted by use of the second-person singular. A measure-for-measure correspondence between the indictment and the sentence makes the punishment fit the crime. A version of this measure-for-measure dynamic also operates within the futility curses that express most of the sentence.

3. As interpreted here, the oracle more clearly and consistently reflects systemic processes well known from numerous other passages in the eighth-century prophets, including most of Micah 1–3. This congruence strengthens the suggestion that it is closely associated in context and composition with those earlier chapters in the book.

4. When the dynamics of political economy castigated by the eighth-century prophets are brought into sharper focus, modern interpreters are better positioned to detect and appreciate the frequent paronomasia that heightens the irony and sarcasm of prophetic judgment oracles.

5. If I am correct in my assessment of one such pun in verse 10—if
   איפת רזון identifies both an "איפה of leanness" and "an איפה of
   the potentate"—the reading adds allusive witness to a growing
   body of archaeological and textual evidence for change and conflict in the configuration and function of weights and measures in
   eighth-century Israel and Judah.

6. Adding the perspectives of political economy to the exegetical
   toolbox has proved fruitful enough in the interpretation of Micah
   6:9-15 to invite similar study of other pericopes in the eighth-century prophets that presume and address the same systemic
   dynamics.

CHAPTER ELEVEN

Deuteronomy— Shameful Encroachment on Shameful Parts

DEUTERONOMY 25:11-12 AND BIBLICAL EUPHEMISM

John H. Elliott

Employing one or more euphemisms for genitals, Deuteronomy 25:11-12 proscribes the shameful encroachment of a wife on the "shameful parts" of her husband's male adversary in the course of a physical altercation and requires a unique form of punishment for this behavior. Elliott combines exegetical analysis with cross-cultural sociolinguistic research on euphemism to examine the statute's content, motivation, and rationale and to assess the social-cultural roots and implications of the euphemisms employed.

In January 2004 a California legislator attempted to introduce a bill banning from television seven notorious "dirty words." A month later the exposure (inadvertent?) of an American female singer's breast before a television Super Bowl audience of some 80 million viewers displaced news about the Iraq war from the front page. The uproar caused by these events, however, was peanuts in comparison to the level of outrage expressed over the torture of Iraqi "detainees" at Abu Ghraib prison in Baghdad that came to light later this same spring. The football incident was euphemistically labeled a "wardrobe malfunction" and the prison

torture, a process of "intelligence gathering." As Americans like me
worry about offensive language, euphemize bared boobs, and dissemble
about our sponsorship of wanton torture across the globe these days, it
seems an appropriate moment to consider an example of biblical euphemism and its social-cultural context. Deuteronomy 25:11-12 offers a
fascinating and relevant case in point.

The twenty-fifth chapter of Deuteronomy, a portion of a body of
statutory rulings extending from 12:1 to 26:15, includes reference to a
legal case and employs language that is unusual in several ways. Verses
11 and 12 of this chapter follow a statute concerning levirate marriage
(25:5-10), but in contrast to verses 5-10 they envision a case that
appears nowhere else in scripture—an Israelite wife physically interfering as her husband wrestles with another male Israelite and being punished for this action. In describing the nature of her interference, the
Hebrew text contains an expression for a portion of a male's anatomy
that never again appears in the Hebrew Bible and that seems to be
employed as a euphemism. The punishment for the action described—
amputation of a body part—is also unique, never again prescribed in
Israel's legal codes.

The text reads as follows:

כי־ינצו אנשים יחדו איש ואחיו וקרבה אשת האחד להציל את־אישה מיד
מכהו ושלחה ידה והחזיקה במבשיו: וקצתה את־כפה לא תחוס עינך:

If [two] men fight with each other, a man with his brother, and
the wife of the one draws near to rescue her husband from the
hand of him who is beating him, and puts out her hand (יד), and
seizes him (במבשו), 12. then you shall cut off her hand (כף); your
eye shall have no pity. [My intentionally literal translation]

The passage has received relatively minimal scholarly attention.
This is surprising, given the several philological, literary, social, and cultural questions it raises. Precisely what action on the part of the wife is
forbidden here? What is the female imagined to be doing with her
hand—touching, squeezing, hitting, karate chopping? What object is she
thought to attack? What is the meaning of the expression "his מבשים
(mebušîm)"? To what male body part does this refer? What is the reason and rationale for this prohibition? Did this action, whatever it might
be, occur so frequently that a law had to be passed proscribing it? Why
so severe a punishment for this act—"one of the most severe legal judgments in the Old Testament"[1] and "the only example of mutilative pun-

ishment in Israelite law"[2]? Why amputation of a *hand*, rather than, say, removal of fingers or another body part, or punishment of another kind altogether, say exclusion from the community or a heavy fine? Is this law an instance of *lex talionis*? What was the intent of the law? Why was the statute placed in *this* literary context? What is one to make of the fact that this is the only mention of this law in the entire Bible?

In addressing these questions I shall focus on the term מבשים, its referent, meaning, and euphemistic function, and its broader cultural-social implications. Exegetical studies of our text generally take the term to be a euphemism for the male adversary's genitalia.[3] But the reasons for use of a euphemism here and for this term in particular are questions rarely raised. Discussions of biblical euphemisms,[4] like studies of euphemisms in antiquity generally,[5] cite examples but offer little analysis along social-scientific lines, with the study of J. N. Adams on the Latin sexual vocabulary being a happy exception. To address these questions and to gain some clarity on the nature, motivation, function, and sociocultural moorings of this biblical euphemism, I will draw on cross-cultural sociolinguistic research on euphemism and dysphemism.[6] Since these studies, however, involve research and theory on general issues and illustrations from different periods and cultures but give little attention to biblical discourse, I shall link this work directly to our biblical text. From this research I derive a set of postulates for examining our Deuteronomic passage and biblical euphemisms generally, and for assessing their social and cultural implications. Finally, I will briefly mention translations of מבשים, beginning with the Septuagint, to consider how the euphemisms and their social contexts vary from language to language and era to era.

Modeling Euphemism and Dysphemism

Euphemism is a rhetorical device in which a "well-sounding" word is substituted for "harsh-sounding" word or word to be avoided altogether. According to the *Concise Oxford Dictionary* (1982), *euphemism* is a "substitution of a mild or vague or roundabout expression for a harsh or blunt or direct one." Euphemism has also been defined as "a polite, tactful, or less explicit term used to avoid the direct naming of an unpleasant, painful, or frightening reality" (*Webster's Third New International Dictionary*, 1961). The term derives from the Greek *euphēmos*, meaning "fair of speech" or "well-sounding." *Euphēmismos*, in turn, was the "use of an auspicious word for an inauspicious one"[7] Use of "the palliative phrase," notes Jasper Griffin, was common also in antiquity. "One very old form was essentially superstitious, arising from the reluctance to utter the real names of terrible and possibly malevolent beings."[8] A circumlocution is a long, drawn-out euphemism. Silence is the ultimate euphemism. The counterpart to the rhetorical device of the euphemism is the *dysphemism*. "A dysphemism is an expression with connotations that are offensive either about the *denotatum* or to the audience, or both, and it is substituted for a neutral or euphemistic expression for just that reason"[9]

Euphemisms are employed in all cultures, according to linguists Keith Allan and Kate Burridge, "as an alternative to a 'dispreferred' expression, in order to avoid possible loss of face: either one's own face or, through giving offense, that of the audience, or of some third party."[10] They are neutral or harmless terms substituted for words judged to be too powerful, dangerous, or offensive (for whatever reasons) to be spoken or heard. Euphemism can be prompted not only by social, moral, or even stylistic concerns but also by more basic feelings of revulsion and disgust toward certain things like blood, snot, feces, urine, vomit, and the like. In antiquity, fear and awe were among the most potent prompters of euphemism.[11]

Euphemisms can serve various ends or aims. They point, but do not name explicitly. On the whole, they veil, conceal from view, or obscure what is deemed dangerous to individuals and groups and threatening to their well-being, harmony, and social cohesion. They soften the blunt edge of truth; they buffer and protect. They act as linguistic deodorant, "verbal placebos,"[12] or conversational fig leaves. In this protective capacity they serve both personal and collective interests. They shield from potentially disturbing sights and sounds, thereby minimizing emotional disturbance while aiding good order and smooth, unruffled social communication and interaction. They assist in the maintenance of good relations among neighbors by replacing potentially insulting and disrespectful talk and providing language that honors the status and respects the sensitivities of others. On a darker note, euphemisms can also be employed to evade, conceal, mask, or distort the truth supposedly to protect the sensitivities of a vulnerable public.

The social domains of discourse where euphemisms are employed range from personal and private to the public realms of economics, social relations, politics, and religion. Chief and most extensively evidenced among these domains are actions and interactions involving the personal body: physical body parts (particularly primary and secondary sex organs), bodily evacuation and effluvia, sexual relations; disease and decay, and death.[13] Things that are taboo are seen as especially *potent*, full of power to help or to harm.[14] Therefore, they require some tactic of protection and this includes the use of euphemism. Euphemisms, like obscenities, thus indicate the persons, objects, and activities to which a culture ascribes power and that it regards with a combination of awe and aversion, fear and fascination. Describing the chief social domains of euphemism in antiquity, L. Opelt lists six areas, with examples of each: sexuality (acts, potency, organs, prostitute, eunuch, etc.); bodily functions; death; illness; acts of force and violence; politics. Others add the domain of the sacred (names of the gods and demons, holy personages, names, sites, activities).[15] Similarity and continuity in these domains over the centuries and across cultures is remarkable and worthy of further cross-cultural analysis.

Euphemisms are characterized by a broad range of evasive devices or techniques. These include the use of metaphor and figurative imagery, circumlocution, abbreviation, acronyms, ellipsis, synecdoche, metonymy; hyperbole, understatement, similar-sounding words, archaisms, foreign terms, and techno-babble[16] Euphemisms for specific items can vary not only from culture to culture but also within any given culture from subculture to subculture and from era to era. This variation is a consequence of the fact that euphemisms are reflective and expressive of cultural, class, and social sensibilities, perceptions, and values, which themselves are subject to variation over time.

The following summarizes salient features of euphemisms across cultures and presents eight postulates drawn from research on euphemism and dysphemism over the centuries that can guide the further analysis of our Deuteronomy passage and its cultural context.

1. The resort to euphemism in discourse appears common to all cultures ancient and modern.
    Postulate 1: Consequently, we can expect to find euphemisms in the biblical literature. Deuteronomy 25:11-12 is a likely instance of such euphemism.
2. Resort to euphemism generally is prompted by a felt need to shield speakers, hearers, and entire communities from words and expressions deemed to be dangerous. Euphemism thus is closely related to the phenomena of taboo, obscenity, and associated patterns of belief and avoidance behavior.[17]
    Postulate 2. The euphemisms of the Bible, like the items that are treated as taboo or obscene, are tell-tale indicators of what the biblical communities perceived as powerful and potentially

threatening to the well-being of persons and groups. The euphemisms themselves will indicate what the biblical communities regarded as safe and acceptable language that endangers no one. This, as we shall see, is illustrated by Deuteronomy 25:11-12.

3. Several of the personal and social domains where euphemism is pressed into service are common across cultures, including those of antiquity: e.g., illness and physical defects; death and dying; sexual organs and activities; excretory functions; matters of the sacred.

   Postulate 3. Consequently, it is likely that the euphemisms of the biblical communities and their surrounding cultures also are associated with these domains. It is further likely that biblical and surrounding communities will have in common many of these euphemisms. Research has demonstrated both to be the case.[18] This, as we shall see, is illustrated by Deuteronomy 25:11-12 and its extra-biblical parallels.

4. As a correlate of number 3, where euphemisms are employed, a reference to something in the sexual domain is possible and often probable. Conversely, where matters of sex are in focus, euphemism is likely to be employed. [19]

   Postulate 4. Reference to sexual matters in the Bible is likely to include euphemisms, and where euphemisms are employed, sexual matters may be under discussion.

5. Euphemism has social as well as personal significance. Uttering or hearing forbidden words is thought to endanger not only speaker and audience but the entire community, disturbing and undermining its cohesion, order, and stability. Employment of euphemism avoids this danger. Euphemisms also serve as markers of social identity (specific social and cultural sensibilities, values, norms) and demarcations of in-group from out-groups.

   Postulate 5. Euphemisms in the Bible will illustrate the group orientation of the biblical communities and point to areas where the well-being of the group is considered vulnerable. Biblical euphemisms and taboo items will be part of the means whereby the communities asserted their distinctive identity and demarcated themselves from other groups.

6. The terms forbidden and the language allowed reflect the perceptions, social institutions and structures, and cultural sensibilities of a given society at a particular time.

Postulate 6. Taboo items and employed euphemisms in the Bible will result from and reflect a constellation of social and cultural features and sensibilities of the biblical communities. This, as we shall see, is illustrated by Deuteronomy 25:11-12.

7. Correlative to number 6, changes in the taboo items and substituted euphemisms of a society reflect and point to social and cultural changes in the society generally.

Postulate 7. Changes in the taboo items and substituted euphemisms of the biblical communities will result from, and point to, changes in their social and cultural sensibilities, institutions, and other related features of these communities. This, we shall see, is illustrated by Deuteronomy 25:11-12.

8. Since societies and cultures also differ from one another in aspects of their social and cultural make-up, the items that are taboo and the euphemisms (and dysphemisms) employed tend to differ in varying degrees across cultures. There can also be differences among subcultures *within* the same society, as well as differences or cleavages between genders, generations, and classes.

Postulate 8. The euphemisms of the biblical communities can be expected to display some differences from those employed by their neighbors, especially where differing perspectives and values are concerned. Differences can also be expected between groups within Israelite society.

Guided by these postulates, we now turn to an analysis of the Deuteronomy text and its context.

Deuteronomy 25:11-12—Interpreting the Hebrew Text in Light of the Model

What is the meaning of the Hebrew term מבשׁים and to what does it refer? It occurs only here in the Hebrew Bible, so that other linguistic usage cannot settle the matter. Paronyms of its verb בושׁ and its semantic field (בשׁת, בושׁנה, בושׁה) generally have the sense of "shame," "put to shame," "be ashamed," "feel shamed." This suggests for מבשׁים the meaning "shameful things/parts," which is likely to be rooted in cultural notions of shame (and honor).[20] The Hebrew term itself is indefinite, indicating no body part in particular. Virtually all translations and commentaries, however, presume that the word refers to the male adversary's genitals or at least some part thereof. Although this is generally assumed rather than demonstrated, it is most likely correct.

For one thing, the genitals of both male and female were among those things conventionally euphemized in the Hebrew Bible, as in the ancient world generally. "There is no biblical term for genitals," notes Jacob Milgrom,[21] "only euphemisms." In the Hebrew Bible, apart from מבשים, we find the following euphemisms for male (either penis and testicles, or penis alone, or testicles/scrotum) and/or female genitalia:

- "feet/legs" (רגלים): Exod 4:25; Ruth 3:4, 7; 2 Sam 11:8; Prov 19:2; Isa 6:2; 7:20; for female *genitals*: Deut 28:57; Ezek 16:25. See also "hairs of the feet" for *pubic hair* (Isa 7:20); "water of the feet" (2 Kgs 18:27//Isa 36:12) for *urine*.[22]
- "heel" (עקב): Gen 25:26; Jer 13:22; Hos 12:3.[23]
- "knees" (ברכים): Judg 16:19, female; Ezek 7:17, 21:12, male.
- "thigh" (ירך) for *lower abdomen, loins, crotch,* and especially for *penis/phallos* as organ of vitality, procreative power: Gen 24:2, 9; 46:26; 47:29-31; Judg 15:8?; of the female genitals: Deut 28:57; Num 5:21, 22. Sons are "offspring of the thigh" (Gen 46:26; Exod 1:5; Deut 28:57; Judg 8:30).[24]
- "fluid duct," "spout"(שפכה): of male, Deut 23:2 MT [RSV 23:1]), from שפך, "pour out."[25]
- "loins" (מתנים, חלצים): Gen 35:11; Deut 33:11; Judg 8:30; 1 Kgs 8:19; 12:10; 2 Chron 6:9; Job 40:16; Prov 31:17 (female genitals?); Ezek 1:27? 8:2?; 29:7). Children are "offspring/issue/fruit of the loins" (Gen 35:11; 46:26; Exod 1:5; Deut 28:57; Judg 8:30; 1 Kgs 8:19). See also 1 Kgs 12:10 where Rehoboam is counseled to claim as a show of strength that "my little finger is thicker than my father's loins" (מתנים,1 Kgs 12:10 = 2 Chron 10:10).
- "flesh" (בשר): Gen 17:11, 14, 23-25; Exod 28:42; Lev 6:3; 15:2-18, 19; 17:13; Ezek 16:26 (LXX: μεγαλοσάρκους); 23:20 (LXX: αἱ σάρκες αὐτῶν; parallel to τὰ αἰδοῖα αὐτῶν); 44:7, 9.
- "nakedness" (ערוה) for male or female genitalia in the expression, "uncover the nakedness of": Gen 9:22-23; Exod 28:42; Lev 18:6-17 passim [contrast LXX: "uncover the *shame* of. . ."]; 20:17; Ezek 16:8, 36; 23:18; Hos 2:11; for female genitalia see also Ezek 16:37; 23:10. Compare also מער (Nahum 3:5; cf. Hab 2:15?).[26]
- "horn" (קרן) for *phallus*: Ps 92:11 MT; cf. also Ps 75:5, 6, 11 MT?
- "vessel" (כלי) for *penis*:1 Sam 21:5; 4Q416 Fg. 22,21.

- the thing "mutilated through crushing" (פְּצוּעַ־דַּכָּא), i.e., the testicle, which is unmentioned but implied: Deut 23:2 MT.
- "lying" (שְׁכָבָת) for *penis*: Lev 18:20, lit. "You shall not use your *lying* for seed."
- "hand"/"forearm" (יד), over 1600x in the MT. As a prominent symbol of power see Exod 6:1; 13:3; Ps 78:42; Heb 10:31. As a euphemism for *penis/genitals*: Isa 57:8, 10; Song of Songs 5:4; also 1QS 7.13-14 (thirty-day penalty for man who puts out his יד/*penis* from beneath his clothing or whose clothing is so torn so as to reveal his *nakedness* [עֶרְוָה]). For כף ("hand," "socket," "concavity"), occasionally interchangeable with יד (Gen 40:11, 13; Num 5:18, 25), as a related euphemism for genitals see Gen 32:26, 33; Song of Songs 5:4-5, and possibly Deut 25:12.[27]

Many euphemisms for genitals are terms for body parts proximate in area to the sexual organs, or, in the case of "hand," symbols of potency. Others are metaphors having some feature in common with the genitals in shape, or appearance, or number.

A second reason for regarding מבשים as a euphemism for genitals is the conventional association of genitals and their exposure with shame[28] This association continues in the LXX where עָרוֹה is rendered not only by "nakedness"[29] but also by "shame." [30]

Israel's use of euphemisms for the genitals is consistent with Postulates One, Three and Four. The euphemisms themselves are frequently identical to those employed by their neighbors.[31] מבשים, "shameful parts," denotes something that evokes a *feeling* of shame, thereby focusing on the *affect* associated with these organs.[32] Postulates Two and Six suggest that the euphemism may point to something considered powerful in the culture and prompt an exploration of its social-cultural roots and ramifications. Postulate Five encourages us to consider the *social* as well as personal significance of the euphemism מבשים.

Expressive of an honor and shame code prevalent throughout the ancient Near East and Circum-Mediterranean, בוש and its derivatives denote a shame felt by having one's personal and family honor and reputation reduced or sullied, being insulted and demeaned, having one's dignity removed as clothes are stripped off and one is left naked and defenseless. Accordingly, the Israelites, like their neighbors, regarded the exposure of the genitals as a stripping of one's dignity and honor and being made defenseless and impotent, with the result of feeling dishonored and shamed. Thus "nakedness," used as a euphemism for genitals and in expressions for sexual intercourse,[33] is also associated with shame.[34] The euphemistic use of "hand," a symbol of power, for genitals illustrates the association of the genitals with potency. Male honor, strength, sexual potency, courage, and virility were symbolized by his genitals.[35] The larger the size of the penis and testicles, the greater a man's virility, status, and honor. Consequently, this region of a male's body was surrounded by safeguards and was to be covered at all times. Exposure (and sight) of the genitals were condemned (Gen 9:20-27; Lev 20:17-21; 1 Sam 20:30; 2 Sam 6:20; 1QS 7.14); priests who allowed their genitals to be seen while serving at the altar were put to death (Exod 20:26; 28:42-43). Genital exposure also served as a metaphor for personal or collective punishment.[36] Where public exposure of the genitals was forbidden, the *physical touching or seizing of the genitals* was a more grievous deviation, and even more so when a female should touch a male who was not her husband. The recent outrage of Iraqis and other Arabs over the U.S. treatment of Iraqi "detainees" in Abu Ghraib prison and elsewhere in the war zones, and the horror over the sexual humiliation and shaming of nude prisoners, is a modern and gruesome illustration of this Near Eastern sensibility and its violation. For a female to violate this male genital zone was and continues to be an even greater outrage in Near Eastern culture—as the American torturers well knew.

In Deuteronomy 25:11-12, what might seizing by the genitals have entailed and what might the intention have been? Is the act a punch "below the belt"? a pulling on the penis? a squeezing of the testicles? The latter, if vigorous, would temporarily disable the opponent and would seem most likely if the wife's aim was to free her husband from the hold of his opponent. In any case, the action envisioned here is very unusual and involves a gender issue as well. While Israel's story does contain examples of women succeeding in challenging and besting men—Deborah, Jael, Esther, Judith spring to mind—this is the only recorded case in which a woman is envisioned interfering in a male *mano-a-mano* contest and coming to her husband's aid by seizing the opponent's genitals. Was such wifely interference so frequent as to require a law forbidding it?

How often, moreover, did such wifely interference take place? In the agonistic, conflict-ridden society of antiquity, stories of males fighting and scrapping in public and private are beyond number. But was the interference of a wife or woman as envisioned in this passage so frequent that it required legal proscription? P. Eddy Wilson does not think so. He claims that this was an instance of a "substantive" law that was meant only to *deter* wives from ever doing such a shameful thing, a law not enforced but only "for the books." While this might account for the unusual severity of the punishment—an amputation that then would never have been carried out in real time—and explain the later silence of the Bible concerning this law, the theory amounts to nothing more than an interesting conjecture.

The fact, on the other hand, that there is a parallel to this case in Assyrian law suggests that the action also occurred elsewhere and was regarded as serious enough by the Assyrians as to require similar proscription. The Assyrian statute states:

> If a woman should crush a man's testicle during a quarrel, they shall cut off her fingers. And even if the physician should bandage it, but the second testicle then becomes infected (?) along with it and becomes . . . or if she should crush the second testicle during the quarrel—they shall gouge out both her [. . .]-s.[37]

Despite the differences in some details,[38] the combat scene, the female interference with disabling effect, and the severe punishment are common to both laws.[39] If this Assyrian law makes it likely that the Deuteronomic statute actually was in effect some time in Israel's history, what *rationale* lay behind its prescribed punishment? The severe punishment may have been prompted by the gravity of the violation of the "sacrosanct" nature of the genitals.[40] H. D. H. Mayes suspects something more concrete. The statute of verses 11-12, he maintains, was deliberately joined by the Deuteronomic author to the case on levirate marriage immediately preceding it (vv. 5-10) because "both are concerned with the possibility of a family becoming extinct," with the term "brother" (v. 11) being a redactional addition further cementing the connection.[41] In this case, "the crime here is not immodesty on the part of the woman so much as the possibility of her damaging male sexual organs, thus destroying creative ability." The law of Deuteronomy 25:11-12 could also have been designed to protect fellow Israelite males from having their genitals damaged and thereby disqualified from the cultic assembly (see Deut 23:1). The Achilles heel of both these theories, however, is the unlikelihood of a wife possessing enough strength to actually *crush* and so permanently maim a man's genitals as to disqualify him from cultic participation or destroy his reproductive capacity.

Others consider *concern over honor and shame* to have been the chief factor prompting this law. The expression מבשׁים, "the shameful parts," already signals a concern with shame and the cultural context confirms it. In cultures like Israel's where exposure and sight of the genitals was discouraged or forbidden, the physical *touching* of the genitals was an even weightier deviation. Howard Eilberg-Schwartz imagines that the law aimed to protect male superiority and honor. "Even at the moment when her husband may need help, she may not grab the manhood of his opponent. Her husband's safety is less important than his opponent's honor."[42] That honor, male status, and public face were at stake is indeed likely, given the intensity with which honor was sought and prized in this society,[43] and given the fact that it was a male's genitals that were the chief physical symbol of his honor as well as of his virility. Lyn Bechtel[44] and P. Eddy Wilson[45] also see shame as paramount here, serving as a motivational factor meant to discourage female interference in struggles like this and functioning as a social sanction. Robert Coote[46] takes this point a step further. He sees a deliberate redactional juxtaposition of the statutes of verses 11-12 and verses 5-10, with women publicly shaming men as the common factor. Verses 11-12 were added and joined to verses 5-10, he suspects, to place limits on a wife's shaming of males in public. A widow should openly shame her brother-in-law if he refused his levirite obligation by tearing off his sandal (an act with sexual implication) and spitting in his face (vv. 5-10). But this was no license for any wife with a living husband to publicly shame him and his adversary by interfering in a fight and seizing male genitals (vv. 11-12).[47]

It is likely that both honor and shame would be at stake. As to the males, the mere fact of their fighting in public had already put the issue of honor and shame on the table. To the victor would go the plaudits of an admiring crowd (the collective "eye" of the witnessing public, v. 12). To the loser, only shame. The wife's interfering crotch-grope would have brought profound shame on *all* concerned. Shame for the *wife* because she transgressed into male space and violated the physical boundary of a male not her husband or relative. Shame for the *husband* because he allowed his wife to "help out," thereby showing that (1) he needed help and could not finish off his adversary by himself; (2) that he accepted help from a female in an exclusively male affair; and (3) that he allowed his woman to encroach on another male's "holy of holies." Shame for the *husband's adversary* for allowing an "inferior" female to get the better of him by grabbing his "family jewels," knocking him to his knees with her nutcracker grip, and violating his *sanctum sanctorum*. Given the anxiety about such socially damaging shame, the formulation of this law becomes quite plausible. The statute and its severity were designed to spare not just the struggling males and the wife from shame, but also to protect the well-being and good order of the community, a concern consistent with, and envisioned by Postulate Five.

Why amputation of the wife's *hand*? One might imagine that since it was her hand that did the dastardly deed, it was her hand that should be punished. Israel's euphemistic practice, however, suggests another possibility. Since the words for "hand" here (יד, כף, vv. 11, 12) were both used euphemistically for the genitals,[48] Deuteronomy 25:11-12 could be another case of *lex talionis* (as in Exod 21:23-24; Lev 24:17-22; Deut 19:21).[49] כף (for female genitals) would balance מבשׁים (for male genitals) and the principle informing the prescribed punishment would be that of proportionality: a *hand* for a *hand*, or a "hand for a gland," so to speak—amputation of the wife's genitals (her "hand") for her seizing the adversary's genitals (his "shameful parts," alias "hand"). This interpretation is favored by Lyle Eslinger, who notes that כף, while also denoting "the palm of the hand" or "sole of the foot," is used twice elsewhere to denote the genitals (Gen 32:26, 33 [MT] and Song of Songs 5:5). He takes כף in Deuteronomy 25:12 as a euphemism for the wife's "vulva," whose amputation would proceed something like the four stages of female circumcision in modern Egypt.[50] The fact that the concluding statement of verse 12, "your eye shall have no pity," occurs also in the clear talionic formulation of Deuteronomy 19:21 gives further weight to this theory and could represent additional evidence of redactional activity.

Although elegant, the proposal is not without problems. It would require (a) a euphemistic use of כף for *genitals* here and in Genesis 32:26, 33 MT and Song of Songs 5:5; (b) an association of מבשׁים with the genital euphemism "hand"; and (c) an ability on the part of the audience to appreciate the correspondence of מבשׁים and כף as different euphemisms for the same object (genitals), but of different-gendered persons. In addition, while the male's genitals were only seized or squeezed temporarily but left intact, the wife would suffer permanent mutilation or removal. For Wilson, this disproportionality is fatal to Eslinger's case. Like Calum Carmichael,[51] Wilson finds no *talio* here but rather a statute intended solely as deterrent and never made operative.[52] Most recently Jerome Walsh has argued that that Deuteronomy 25:12a be translated "you shall shave [the hair of] her groin." In this case, the punishment would involve a talionic public dishonoring of a female for publicly shaming a male, an action focusing on her genital area corresponding to her violation of the male's genitals, but entailing a less severe and only temporary punishment matching the assumed impermanent injury of the male. The argument requires two assumptions:[53] (1) that כף generally denotes *concave* things and in Deuteronomy 25:12 denotes not a hand but "the open concave curves of the pelvic region," thus making "groin" a conceivable translation; and (2) that the verb קצץ, which most frequently means "amputate" in the MT, here should be rendered "shave." Both assumptions, however, lack probative lexical support.

Thus, at present, no proposed explanation has gained general acceptance. The *talio* theory and the balance of euphemisms remains a plausible, if not probable, explanation, but the jury is still out. In any event, there is no doubt that shame and honor would have been at stake in this envisioned case and that a notion of shame lay behind the Hebrew euphemism used here for the male genitals.

The Septuagint Version and Other Translations

Examination of translations of our Hebrew text indicates, however, that shame was not always a feature of the euphemisms preferred by subsequent translators. This is evident already in the Greek of the Septuagint where a different euphemism for genitals was employed that points to an entirely different social frame of reference.

> 11 And if men should strive together, a man with his brother, and the wife of one of them should advance to rescue her husband out of the hand of him that strikes him, and she should stretch out her hand and take hold of *his twins* (τῶν διδύμων αὐτοῦ), 12 you shall cut off her hand; your eye shall not spare her.

Although aligned closely to the Masoretic Text on the whole, the LXX introduces a different euphemism for genitals, namely οἱ δίδυμοι ("the twins"). The expression is not so much a *rendition* of במבשו as it is a *replacement* drawn from a different semantic field related to a different cultural-social domain. As I show elsewhere, the euphemism "twins" refers not to anything concerning shame but rather to the two testicles, that, along with the "thigh" (= penis), played an essential role in ancient oath taking.[54] This function is explicitly acknowledged in the Latin where *testes/testiculi* mean "the (little) witnesses."[55] The Septuagint rendition also eliminates any correspondence between the attacked testicles of the antagonist and the "hand" of the interfering wife. The references to the LXX version of Deuteronomy 25:11-12 by Philo of Alexandria in *On Dreams* (2.68-69) and *On the Special Laws* (3.31.169-180) add an additional clarifying feature; namely, the identification of the "twins" (οἱ δίδυμοι) as "the genitals" (τὰ γεννήτικα). Philo's interest in the "twins" was not as witnesses in oath taking, however, but as organs of generation, an interest evident in his sustained comments on the topics of generation and male-female gender differences. Later biblical versions of our text[56] use the English cognate of τὰ γεννήτικα, namely "the genitals," to render מבשׁים (NEB, NRSV, TEV). The *Children's Living Bible* term, "testicles," is no nursery euphemism but rather a surprisingly "adult" term (now devoid of oath-taking implication). Other versions, reflecting cultural sensitivity to the "private" versus public sphere of sex and sexual organs prefer the translations "secrets" (KJV, JPS) or "private parts" (Goodspeed, RSV, JB). On the whole, the variety among the translations illustrates and confirms the substance of Postulates Six through Eight presented above.

Summary and Conclusions

Euphemistic practice in Israel, coupled with similar Assyrian language and legislation, make it virtually certain that מבשׁים in Deuteronomy 25:11-12 was a euphemism for the genitals and part of a statute that was actually enforced. The offense consisted not in permanent damage to the male adversary's genitals, but in a female's touching and seizing male sexual organs, which were considered powerful and sacrosanct body parts emblematic of a man's virility, generative power, strength, and honor, and evoking feelings of profound shame when uncovered and exposed. Such an action, if carried out in this society so preoccupied with the values of honor and shame, could have only profoundly shaming ramifications for all concerned. Hence the severe punishment—amputation. The punishment could be an instance of *lex talionis* requiring a "hand" for a "hand" in one of two ways: the wife's *actual* hand amputated for seizing the male adversary's euphemistic "hand" (his "shameful part"/genitals), or her euphemistic "hand" (her vulva) amputated for grasping his euphemistic "hand," thus genitals for genitals. Or the punishment might have involved only one hand, namely, the wife's actual hand wreaking all the shameful havoc. In any case, the *severity* of the offense—violation of gender and genital boundaries and the shame this brought on all concerned—required a severe punishment. Ultimately, the Masoretic Text of Deuteronomy 25:11-12 condemns shameful encroachment on shameful parts in a culture preoccupied with honor and shame.

Translations of מבשים in subsequent biblical versions vary from "awesome/shameful parts" (Vulgate, Luther, Zürcher Bibel, Bible de Jerusalem, La Sacra Biblia), to "secrets" (KJV, JPS), "private parts" (Goodspeed, RSV, New American Bible), "genitals" (NEB, NRSV, TEV), and "testicles" (Children's Living Bible). The changing translations reflect changes in cultural and social patterns and sensitivities. The shift from "shameful parts" to "secrets" and "privates" for the sex organs, for instance, signals and meshes with a characteristic general trend of modern Western culture, namely, the waning of group orientation with its pressure of shame and a growing focus on the individual, the separation of private from public, the interiorization of moral standards, and the dominance of guilt over shame. The preference for "testicles" and "genitals" in modern time points to and coincides with the general technologization of modern life, the preference for scientific medical terminology, and the separation of the sexual organs and naked body from shame (and oath taking) altogether.

Finally, a word about our subject generally. Euphemism is not simply linguistic deodorant for modesty's sake. Euphemisms also avoid, obscure, and conceal the truth; they blunt the force of ugly reality. This includes moral as well as physical ugliness—as when weapons are labeled "peacekeepers" and nuclear submarines are dubbed "Corpus Christi," when the slaughter of innocent non-combatants in war is called "collateral damage," when lying in political campaigns is called "spin," when "preemptive strike" substitutes for "starting a war," when "final solution" replaces "genocide." In such cases, and myriad more, we encounter the dark, sinister side of euphemism that reminds us that with euphemism we are never dealing only with puritanicalism, fig leaves, and shyness about sex. The fig leaf always has falsehood as its flip side.

CHAPTER TWELVE

Judges—(Dis)Honor and Ritual Enactment

THE JEPHTHAH STORY: JUDGES 10:16–12:1

Richard E. DeMaris and Carolyn S. Leeb

Richard E. DeMaris and Carolyn S. Leeb challenge current biblical scholarship that typically casts Jephthah, his vow, and the sacrifice of his daughter in negative terms. Employing ritual theory and an honor-shame interpretive framework, they analyze Judges 10:16 to 11:40 as a sequence of rites that resolves Jephthah's inconsistent honor status. If the narrative begins with a Jephthah whose status is inconsistent—a mighty warrior expelled from his father's house—the series of public promises, vows, and rites that follows eliminates any uncertainty or contradiction in his social identity. By the end of the narrative, Jephthah emerges as a figure with unambiguously high honor. Understood as an element in the ritual process, Jephthah's notorious vow appears not as superfluous and unnecessary, as scholars claim, but as a crucial step in the positive resolution of his (and his daughter's) honor status.

The Dilemma of Jephthah and His Daughter

An unusual vow, a daughter mourning her virginity, a father sacrificing a child to God—these features belong to a story that has fascinated heirs of the biblical tradition for millennia. In fact, it is fair to say that attention to the story of Jephthah, from both biblical scholars and Western culture generally, has been all out of proportion to the story's brevity. A frequent subject of medieval art, Jephthah and his daughter received regular treatment in the early modern era, and they continue to do so today. They were the subject matter of tragic plays in Tudor and Elizabethan England, many oratorios, including one by Handel, and even several operas. Jephthah and his daughter have also appeared regularly on canvas, most notably Degas's "The Daughter of Jephthah," from the mid-nineteenth century. More recently (1981) Israeli Aharon Harlap composed a piece for chorus and horn entitled "Bat Yiftach" (Jephthah's Daughter), performances of which are widely available on compact disc.

For all the artistic attention to the Jephthah story, however, this troubling tale remains puzzling and difficult to understand. Nor has scholarly interpretation produced much insight, because it has often moved too quickly to making judgments about the story or avoided dealing with the story as it is. One line of interpretation, because it insists that human sacrifice is anathema to the biblical tradition, under-stands the fulfillment of Jephthah's vow to be the consecration of his daughter to cultic service for life and her concomitant vow of celibacy—the sacrifice of her virginity, not her life.[1] A related line of argument insists that the story underwent alteration after the Deuteronomistic edi-tors finished with it: a hellenizing editor introduced human sacrifice in imitation of the Agamemnon-Iphigenia story.[2] These perspectives shy away from the story as it stands and from the likeliest meaning of it, that Jephthah offered up his daughter as a burnt offering to Yahweh.

Other scholars hold that Jephthah did indeed slaughter his daughter in fulfillment of his vow to God, but their outrage at this act skews their reading of the story. Focus falls so exclusively on one event, the father's sacrifice of the daughter, that the story as a whole is neglected. Conse-quently, some feminists and womanists label the story nightmarish and hideous.[3] It amounts to a tale about a marginalized, silenced,[4] expend-able,[5] passive, and nameless[6] daughter and little more.

When scholars do look at the whole Jephthah story, they typically treat it as a tragedy. Few have assessed the story's conformity to Aristo-tle's definition of that form; most label the story, or some aspect of it, tragic without argument. Hence, we find mention of the story's tragic vision[7] or tragic art,[8] the daughter as tragic victim,[9] and the tragic out-come or consequences of success in war.[10] Western literature has favored such a take on the story, but if one defines tragedy as a story in which a person of high status falls because of a character flaw, Jephthah does not readily fit the category.

Judgments about Jephthah's character and his vow are thick in the scholarly literature, but support for such assessments is thin. The narrative says nothing about Jephthah's personality, but that silence has not prevented scholars from demonizing him. Renita Weems finds Jephthah ambitious, impulsive, and blind;[11] Phyllis Trible insists that Jephthah's insecurity and doubt drive him to the vow, a manipulative bargain with God that is an act of unfaithfulness on his part.[12] Likewise, the narrative does not characterize his vow, but scholars have consistently stigmatized it: it is awful;[13] intemperate;[14] heedless;[15] superfluous;[16] rash and ill-considered;[17] unsolicited and vain;[18] unnecessary and stupid;[19] foolish and reckless.[20]

Is the story of Jephthah and his daughter tragic? Was his vow superfluous and unnecessary? We think not. Consequently, the task of this chapter is to account for why the vow was essential and necessary to the story. In doing so, we intend to make sense of the whole story and to determine how the various elements and episodes of the entire story cohere.

An Interpretive Framework for Making Sense of the Jephthah Story

Before we undertake a close reading of the Jephthah story, a few words about how we will approach it are in order. Jephthah's vow is a salient feature of the story, as is the rite his daughter and her companions engage in toward the end of the story, so we want to pay close attention to ritual in the story. As modern Westerners, we value rational, productive activity and therefore tend to dismiss ritual as nonrational and unproductive, hence useless or empty. Such a bias undoubtedly lies behind many of the characterizations of Jephthah's vow.

Yet the presence of vow taking and other rites in the story suggests the opposite to us—they point to something significant—for the one thing that virtually all ritual theorists agree about is that rites occur at crisis points in the life of a group or individual. One does not have to look too hard to see that society hedges social change, transition, or crisis—birth, coming of age, marriage, retirement, and death—with all manner of rites.[21] As Victor Turner notes in the opening of what is perhaps his most significant study of rites, *The Ritual Process*:

> As we became increasingly a part of the [Ndembu] village scene, we discovered that very often decisions to perform ritual were connected with crises in the social life of villages. . . . Here I

merely indicate that among the Ndembu there is a close connection between social conflict and ritual . . . and that a multiplicity of conflict situations is correlated with a high frequency
of ritual performance.[22]

Many ritual theorists, including Turner, define the relationship
between social crises and rites in terms of cause and effect. Crises
prompt or generate or attract rites, which address, solve, or negotiate
the crises.[23] According to Turner, when rules, norms, customs, or laws
are breached, society typically resorts to rites to limit the disruption and
restore social equilibrium. Hence they are what he calls adjustive or
redressive social mechanisms.[24]

What crisis prompted the flurry of ritual activity that occupies Jephthah and his family in the narrative? This question naturally follows
from the way we have introduced ritual, and accurately characterizing
that crisis constitutes the second major focus of this study. The opening
verses of the story (Judg 11:1-3) describe an incredible ambiguity or
inconsistency in Jephthah's social identity: He is a person of substance
and evidently has a reputation for excellence on the battlefield, but he is
also the offspring of a prostitute and has been disinherited and expelled
from his household. In the parlance of honor and shame, values we
regard as pivotal in the biblical world, the indicators of Jephthah's
honor ranking are contradictory or inconsistent. Honor is a claim to
worth that is socially acknowledged, and it has two aspects: Honor can
refer both to status or position and to personal excellence or achievement.[25] In Jephthah's case, we meet a terrible uncertainty, because the
honor he has gained by excellence is high, but the honor derived from
his birth—his ascribed or inherited honor status—is incredibly low.

An ambiguous or inconsistent honor rating cannot stand in a world
defined by honor and shame. As anthropologist Julian Pitt-Rivers notes,
such uncertainty must be resolved "by an appeal to some tribunal, the
'fount of honour': public opinion, the monarch, or the ordeal of judicial
combat which implied a direct appeal to God."[26] Hence, we claim that
the inconsistency in Jephthah's honor ranking introduced at the beginning of the story is the crisis that engenders the many rites of the Jephthah story. Indeed, what ties the whole narrative together is the
resolution of that ambiguity and contradiction through a series of rites.

Ritual is crucial to the process of resolution, because it is in the very
public arena of ritual where honor is won and lost, where society
acknowledges gain or loss. As anthropologists J. G. Peristiany and

Julian Pitt-Rivers note, "Rites establish consensus as to 'how things are' and thus they fix legitimacy. Hence ritual is the guarantor of the social order, conveying honor, not only in the formal distribution of dignities on ceremonial occasions, but also in the sense of making manifest the honorable status of the actors."[27]

The Jephthah Story through a Ritual and Honor/Shame Bifocal

Jephthah's story properly begins with Judges 10:17, a tale that is structured as a ritual process that includes promise, vow, and rite.

In contrast to both oath and vow, a promise is an "unsecured" statement of intention, usually a conditional statement of the form, "If you do this, then I will do that." The promissor delivers the reward upon completion of the condition by the promissee. Promises in the Hebrew Bible use ordinary declarative verbs.

In an oath, a statement of intention is "secured" or strengthened by inviting the deity to administer the negative consequences or punishment for non-completion of the stated intention. To categorize Jephthah's vow with Saul's "rash oath" is inappropriate since Jephthah uses none of the characteristic language patterns that distinguish oaths in the Hebrew Bible.[28]

In a vow, the speaker promises a reward to Yahweh, such as a sacrifice or other offering, in exchange for some blessing. Vows, which are made only to the deity, use special terminology.[29] Vows may be made privately, but are fulfilled publicly, often at an altar or other cult site.[30] Vows are a response to crisis, and the value of the promised gift must match the size or difficulty or importance of the request.[31]

Promise (Judges 10:16-18)

Verse 17 provides the setting for the story of Jephthah and his daughter, with the disclosure that the Ammonites have encamped against the Israelites, and the plot is set in motion by the announcement (v. 18) that the Gileadite commanders are searching for a leader to initiate the battle. The princes of Gilead make the first promise: the condition is the initiation of war against the Ammonites; the reward is headship over all the tribes of Gilead.

The man who will fulfill the condition of the promise is introduced in Judges 11:1. In the first half of the verse, Jephthah is introduced as a *gibbor hayil*, a "personage of substance," a "man of means," a "force to be reckoned with." This phrase is variously translated, frequently as "mighty warrior," but also by a variety of other phrases that indicate this is a person of *accomplishments*.[32]

In a social world characterized by honor and shame, a man may possess two sorts of honor: ascribed honor and acquired honor. *Ascribed honor* comes from family, name, house, the honor of the world into which a man is born. *Acquired honor* comes from those things a man accomplishes on his own. Jephthah has been successful; he is a man of *acquired* honor.

However, the description of Jephthah conveys the utter and complete absence of *ascribed* honor. Ascribed honor comes from father and father's house or *bet-ʾab*; Jephthah has neither. He is fatherless and houseless, unrecognized and illegitimate. Although we are told that Gilead sired Jephthah, Gilead is never called Jephthah's father. Jephthah is never called Gilead's son. He is son of a woman, and a prostitute at that. Jephthah suffers from "status inconsistency."

He is a man of acquired honor, but not of ascribed honor. The story will be driven by the need to resolve this inconsistency. One possible resolution would be through recognition by his genitor. Gilead could recognize Jephthah, could call him son, could embed him in the *bet-ʾab*, ending any ambiguity about his status, but this is not the way of our story. The ambiguity is resolved the other way, the way of completely cutting him off from the household of his genitor.

Ritual of Disinheritance (Judges 11:2-3)

This verse is a ritual of disinheritance, a performative ritual, which actually accomplishes the disinheritance.[33] The other sons of Gilead, the "recognized" sons, detach Jephthah from the *bet-ʾab*. Had there not been recognized sons, Jephthah might have hoped to inherit, but the half-brothers act to eliminate any ambiguity about his standing within the family. He can never aspire to the position of elder, i.e., head of household, because he no longer has a house. He is cast out, "detached" from the *bet-ʾab* by the same ritual of disinheritance with which Sarah cast out Ishmael.

After disinheritance and detachment from the *bet-ʾab*, Jephthah (like Ishmael) will be reintegrated into a lower status group. They have lost ascribed honor; their disinheritors will gain honor. Jephthah and Ishmael become sons of their mothers, without claim to father or father's house. Both will succeed in their new situations. Jephthah will join a band of "good-for-nothings" and will rise to leadership, from which position he is able to *acquire* honor by achieving wealth and military power, but he cannot recover his lost *ascribed* honor.

The Ammonites encamp against the Gileadites (vv. 4-5). Those who bear the name of Gilead (and thus the ascribed honor that inheres in that name) are made vulnerable. To be defeated in battle would result in the ultimate loss of ascribed honor. In response, they bring Jephthah from the land of Tob, where his status is unambiguous, and place him in a renewed state of transition, ambiguity, and danger.

Promise Reiterated (vv. 6-7)

The condition, to battle the Ammonites, remains the same as when the promise was initially stated in 10:17-18. The reward has subtly shifted, however; the Gileadites offer Jephthah a *generalship*, i.e., a military status but not reinstatement into the household, family, clan, or tribe. Such a military position, particularly in the book of Judges, would be understood to be *ad hoc* and temporary.[34] This revised proposal offers Jephthah the opportunity to gain additional acquired honor, but not to recover lost ascribed honor. Jephthah points out the irony of the fact that the elders of Gilead are now the ones facing danger and doubt.

Promise Renegotiated (v. 8)

The promise's condition remains the same, but the reward is now upgraded. The man who fulfills the condition will now become "chief/head to all the tribes of Gilead"; the successful meeting of the condition leads to a restoration to the kinship network and a place of leadership within it; in other words, the prize has been upgraded to include ascribed honor.

Renegotiated Promise Conditionally Accepted (v. 9)

Jephthah indicates that the promise, with its renegotiated reward, will be accepted with added conditions. If Yahweh will give the Ammonites into his presence, place them in his path, then Jephthah will meet the conditions and reap the reward. Victory over the Ammonites has not yet been presented as a condition of the reward, either by the men of Gilead or by Jephthah. They had specified that the man for whom they were looking must *initiate* the battle. Jephthah himself specifies that Yahweh must place the enemy in his path. Neither party has explicitly made victory a condition of the promise. The condition that is added by Jephthah at this point is restoration: "If you are indeed *restoring* me, i.e., if I am being dis-disinherited, then I will do your dirty work for you."

Mutual Public Affirmation of Renegotiated Promise (vv. 10-11)

In verse 10, the revised deal is agreed to, and Yahweh is invoked as witness to the promise. Verse 11 confirms that the reward is carried out and that Jephthah is granted both military and kinship status, illustrating that victory is still not part of the conditions of the promise.

As required by the original promise, Jephthah engages the enemy in battle. His first tactic is a negotiation, a battle of words (vv. 12-28). Words are powerful in this narrative; they are performative and world changing. Jephthah's long palaver with the Ammonites delays the narrative. In it he engages the Ammonites in the sort of challenge and riposte, or battle of wits and words, by which his brothers challenged and disinherited him. This battle of words is the occasion for Yahweh to "recognize" Israel as his legitimate "son." Yahweh, as father, provides Israel with an inheritance.

In verse 29, the battle of words breaks down. In a story full of speech that is effective, ritual that is performative, this is the point where words no longer hold power.

Jephthah's Vow: Condition and Reward (vv. 29-33)

This is not an unsecured promise. Jephthah makes a vow; the condition: if you (Yahweh) will "give them into my hand." Finally, the condition involves not mere initiation of the battle, not mere engagement of the enemy, but victory.

The reward, offered to Yahweh if the conditions of the vow are met, is a sacrifice, a whole burnt offering. In this case, the offering will be whatever chances to wander out of his house. In exchange for being restored to a "house," Jephthah offers the first-fruits of that house. Whatever comes forth from it will be designated for Yahweh.

Nothing in the narrative suggests that this is a "rash oath," a hasty or impulsive vow. The negotiations with the Ammonites have established Jephthah as a man who thinks carefully, who speaks rationally, who understands the power of words.

The question must be asked: What was he thinking? Did he not know that his daughter would be first out of the house? Potentially, it is precisely the *possibility* that his daughter might be the victim that gives honor to Jephthah in making this vow. The costliest sacrifice brings the highest honor.[35]

Yahweh meets the conditions of the vow: the Ammonites are engaged, and Yahweh grants decisive victory in battle—a battle fought, in part, in the vineyards.

Ritual of Return from Battle (v. 34)

Going off to war involves detachment from the community, a period of danger and ambiguity, and hopefully a reintegration into the community. In the case of a victorious return from battle, the warriors are reintegrated with more honor, higher status, than was theirs when they departed.

We assume that earlier, the warriors have been "sung off to war," just as Laban suggests that he would have sent Jacob and his daughters on their way with tambourines, if only he had known they were leaving (Genesis 31). Our drama depicts the joyous return, when the victors, the successful, the survivors are welcomed home with tambourines and dancing and singing. The danger and ambiguity are over, and those returning can be reintegrated into the fabric of the society. This was clearly a common ritual.[36] Miriam and the women celebrate the crossing of the Reed Sea with tambourine and song (Exodus 15). The women go out with tambourine and singing to celebrate the victory over the Philistines and to welcome the victors back into the community (1 Samuel 18). David dances the ark into Jerusalem after its safe journey (2 Samuel 6). Alas for Jephthah, none other than his beloved daughter—his only child—performs the ritual of singing the victorious warriors home.

Ritual of Mourning or Repentance (v. 35)

The welcoming daughter is not a welcome sight. The tearing of clothes is the ritual to mark the transition from shalom, from wholeness, to grief, to sorrow, to despair. Celebration has turned to mourning. The vow must be completed.

Confirmation/Acceptance/Acquiescence of the Reward Offered in the Vow (v. 35)

Should not Jephthah have anticipated that his daughter would be the first out of the house, the first to welcome him home, and thus become the promised sacrifice to Yahweh? And if he knew that his daughter would perform the ritual of return, why did Jephthah make the vow? Could not this have been foreseen? Could not this have been prevented?

Perhaps. But in the texts in which this ritual appears, it is not children, but women—young women, marriageable women, married women—who welcome the warriors, with singing and dancing and tambourines. How old was Jephthah's daughter when he left home? The text does not tell us. Did he leave her a child? Did he expect that someone else would come out to sing the victors home, because she was not yet ripe for such activities? We cannot know, but we may well consider what that might mean for our story.

Since she appears to know of his vow, why does she come out? Why does she acquiesce? Our analyses fail to resolve the ambiguity. Our questions remain unanswered, but the values and rituals of this ancient world suggest other possibilities. We assume that, in offering up his daughter as an offering to Yahweh, Jephthah is cutting off the future of his house. Yet in reality, his house cannot continue through his daughter. If he were to make a successful marriage for his daughter, that marriage would build up another man's house, his grandchildren would bear the name of the head of that bet-ʾab. They would not inherit Jephthah's name, even if he had a name. They would not constitute his house, even if he had a house. But in truth, without this victory he is not likely to be able to arrange a successful marriage for his daughter. Those, like Ishmael, who are without house and without father, must settle for marriage to "the other," to outsiders, foreigners, outcasts.

Without his success in battle and restoration to a legitimate place in the society, both Jephthah and his daughter remain socially dead. He can never become an elder, nor be part of an elder's household. They have become like the widow, orphan, and sojourner, who have no legal representation in Israel. He cannot negotiate a suitable marriage for his daughter, so when she reaches marriageability, her only options may be concubinage or perhaps prostitution. (Unrepresented households make poor marriage choices. The negotiation of a marriage contract is an opportunity to increase the family's ascribed honor by establishing a tie to an honorable household, basking in the reflected glow, so to speak, of a bet-ʾab that radiates honor. Without house, without honor, prospects were limited: Hagar finds an Egyptian wife for Ishmael; after Elimelech's death, Naomi finds Moabite wives for her sons.) Perhaps a noble death is better than a shameful marriage.

The objection is raised that Yahweh's spirit is already with Jephthah and so he already has what he needs, prior to his making this vow. Alas, a careful reading of the text suggests that this is not the case. Prior to Jephthah's vow, only initiation and engagement have been promised. The Gileadite leaders have promised "headship" to the one initiating the battle. Jephthah has promised that he will indeed be their head, if Yahweh places the enemy in his path. Yahweh, who controls the outcome of the battle, has promised nothing. Nor, prior to his vow, has Jephthah asked Yahweh for victory. What happens, then, if Jephthah does not make his vow? If Gilead is defeated, then Jephthah has been restored to a defeated house. Jephthah, by his restoration, gains a share in the ascribed honor of Gilead, but by its defeat, Gilead would lose honor. To ally with losers is not a noble thing; it is a dishonorable thing. Jephthah is once again re-allied with Gilead; their honor is his honor. Yahweh controls the outcome of the battle, which establishes the honor of Gilead. Far from being a faithless or superfluous gesture, Jephthah performs the ultimate act of faith—he relies not on his own strength to win the battle, but entrusts the victory to Yahweh.

Ritual of First Menstruation/End of Childhood/ Loss of Virginity (vv. 37-38)

Jephthah's daughter acquiesces; she will be complicit in her own destruction, but the *betûlâ* asks a deferral: to bewail her *betûlîm* with the other *betûlot*. Many recent commentators view *betûlâ/betûlîm* not as a state of virginity, but rather a stage of life, the point at which a young woman is ready for marriage, a stage that can be called "nubility."[37]

Jephthah's daughter asks to participate in the cotillion, the coming out party, the annual ritual in which the daughters who are ready for marriage are displayed as available.[38] That she is asking to participate in a recurring ritual is suggested by her request to wait two months. If she were simply inviting a few girlfriends from her village to go with her to mourn what has befallen her, there would be no reason to delay the fulfillment of a vow, which is always risky. She is waiting for the time of the *annual* ritual performed by the marriageable women of the village. If the spring of the year is, as 2 Samuel 11:1 suggests, the time when "kings go out to war," then the time of the Ammonite encampment against the Gileadite, the restoration of Jephthah, his negotiations with the Ammonites, and finally the two-month delay requested by Jephthah's daughter may well bring us to the time of the celebration of the harvesting of the vineyards, a traditional time for the marriageable maidens to come out to dance publicly.[39]

Why do the young women weep? The author of this account of Jephthah and his daughter understands that they weep in remembrance of her. They are, after all, about to find their fulfillment as wives and mothers within the male value system. From *their* point of view, however, there is much to weep over. By the time the next grape harvest comes, most of them will be married. For most of them, that means separation from parents and siblings, submission to a husband, perhaps submission to a senior wife or to a mother-in-law. For most it will mean the risk and pain of pregnancy, with a significant chance of losing the infant or of losing her own life.

Why does Jephthah's daughter weep? Translators and commentators have struggled with the concept that Jephthah's daughter "bewails" or "weeps over" her virginity. In a world that valued virginity, it seems a strange lament. Jephthah's daughter will be separated from her parents and siblings not by marriage but by death. But perhaps she does indeed bewail her *betûlîm*. Had she not been *betûlâ*, would she be sacrificed? If she had still been *yaldah*, girl-child, would she have gone out of the house to sing the victor home? If she had still been girl-child or if she had already been married, would she have been a suitable sacrifice? The limited evidence that we have for human sacrifice in ancient Israel and her neighbors does not suggest child-sacrifice, but rather sacrifice of adult offspring. Much of the evidence for animal sacrifice in ancient Israel suggests that firstborn but not newborn animals were sacrificed, frequently year-old calves, that is, calves who were sexually mature, but who had not yet bred. Jephthah's daughter laments her "virginity" because it is precisely her virginity that makes her eligible to pay the extreme price for her father's restoration to ascribed honor.[40]

We do not like the way this story ends, and so we try to rewrite the ending. Surely Jephthah or his daughter could have done something to bring a more comfortable conclusion to this story. We either demonize Jephthah or we blame the victim for not avoiding this awful sacrifice. Since Jephthah's daughter seems to know of her father's vow, why did she not remain inside? Why not let someone or something else make the sacrifice? But to do so would dishonor her father and denigrate his victory. Honor must be publicly acknowledged; the ritual of singing the victors home is precisely the public acclamation of that honor. That ritual is enacted by wives and maidens, and for a man's wives and adult daughters not to participate in this ritual would be a shameful thing.

The value of the sacrifice matches the weightiness of the request. Without this vow, this coming out, this sacrifice, both Jephthah and his daughter remain non-persons, socially dead. Through this vow, this coming out, this sacrifice both will live—he now as a man with honor, with house, with name. Jephthah's daughter will live on, not bearing her own name—that would be a dishonorable thing in this ancient world—but bearing the name of a now-honorable father, remembered not through the memories of the children that she bore, but through the memories of those other maidens who ritualize their own fears and losses as they memorialize her greater sacrifice.

A Conclusion to the Story

If Jephthah's social identity is fraught with uncertainty at the beginning of Judges 11, it is crystal clear by the beginning of chapter 12. Our argument has been that this is so because the rites generated by the crisis over Jephthah's social identity have been instrumental in resolving the crisis. That Jephthah is now an unambiguously honorable person is implicitly acknowledged in 12:1, where it says that the Ephraimites, in approaching Gilead, parley with him. It is beyond the scope of this essay to treat Judges 12 in any detail, but it is worth noting that when the leaders of the Ephraimites approach Jephthah, they launch an honor challenge to which Jephthah ably responds. Such challenge-riposte interaction happens only between parties of relatively equal ranking in the world of honor and shame. Hence, what happens between Jephthah and the Ephraimites verifies what we determined to be the result of the ritual process in chapter 11: the removal of ambiguity and contradiction in Jephthah's honor rating.

We do not need to know the information in Judges 12 to be sure that the ambiguity clouding Jephthah's honor ranking has been removed, however. For the report about the rite at the end of chapter 11 (vv. 37-40), though it concerns Jephthah's daughter and her companions, serves to recapitulate the main ritual action that has occurred in the chapter. In the parlance of ritual theory, the daughter's rite references or indexes the social crisis and ritual negotiation that Jephthah has gone through. By connecting Jephthah's story with a straightforward rite of passage, the narrative underscores the centrality of ritual in the logic of the story, and it reiterates what the ritual process achieves.

As our close reading of the Jephthah story indicated, we follow the scholarly consensus holding that Jephthah's daughter and her companions were away on the mountains undergoing their passage from childhood to adulthood. Theirs was a puberty or menarcheal rite that brought about the transformation of their social status. In this rite they departed from their former status as children, marked their transition through an in-between, liminal phase, when they are physically but not yet socially mature, and now emerge ready to enter their adult roles. They return from the mountains prepared to marry and establish a new identity in a new household.

The closing verses of Judges 11 underscore what ritual accomplishes, then and now: it determines social identity, it resolves social uncertainty and ambiguity by negotiating social crises, it alters social status. And that, in capsule form, is what the story of Jephthah is about.

CHAPTER THIRTEEN

2 Samuel— David and the Ammonite War

A NARRATIVE AND SOCIAL-SCIENTIFIC INTERPRETATION OF 2 SAMUEL 10–12

Philip F. Esler

In my second essay in this volume on using social-scientific ideas to understand a biblical narrative, I argue that 2 Samuel 10–12 forms a clearly circumscribed narrative unit that illustrates the social dynamic of "challenge-and-response" known from Mediterranean anthropology. David's delay in defeating the Ammonites, his "tarrying" in Jerusalem, causes him to initiate his liaison with Bathsheba and to have her husband, Uriah, killed. Uriah's own loyalty and sense of honor serve as a counterpoint to David's dishonorable behavior. At the same time, the prophet Nathan's announcement to David of how God's displeasure with his actions means the sword will never leave his house, the trigger for the evolving plot of 2 Samuel 13–24, is best explained, again within the framework of Mediterranean anthropology, in terms of patron (God), broker (Nathan), and client (David).

S ocial-scientific ideas can be brought to bear on the processes of biblical interpretation in many ways.[1] My own predilection is to call on them in aid of understanding particular texts, either complete works like Luke-Acts or a Pauline letter or smaller units, such as chunks of narrative focusing on a particular character or a series of events. Given that even within the social-scientific study of biblical narrative many approaches are possible, I wish to narrow the field to one particular interest, namely, how 2 Samuel 10–12 would have functioned as a narrative within the ancient Mediterranean culture in which it appeared. How would the first

audience of a biblical narrative, listeners rather than readers, have understood and related to it? This means paying close attention to the details
of the story in the manner of narrative criticism, as J. P. Fokkelman did
very perceptively in 1981, but doing so in a way that takes proper
account of the very distinctive cultural environment in which the narrative unfolds. While this was not Fokkelman's interest, it is worthy of note
that so perceptive an interpreter of biblical narrative as Cheryl Exum has
sought to explore the tragic dimension of several Old Testament texts in
a manner that respects their "ancient character" and "cultural assumptions" and does not wrench "them wholly or violently out of their
ancient context" to make them fit modern notions of the tragic.[2] It is possible to develop Exum's approach by noting that we are greatly helped in
situating biblical texts in their ancient cultural context through the use of
social-scientific ideas and perspectives. These alert us both to a body of
valuable comparative material from other (mostly preindustrial modern)
cultures, but also highlight the contingency of our own cultural values
and assumptions. I have elsewhere applied social-scientific insights in aid
of understanding the narratives of 1 Samuel 8–31 and the Book of Judith
in their ancient Israelite contexts.[3]

An interpretative method can only justify itself if it produces insights
into a biblical text that go beyond the yield from existing scholarship. I
submit that using social-scientific insights to investigate 2 Samuel 10–12
as a narrative embedded in the peculiar culture of the ancient Mediterranean world does lead to results of this kind, not least the fact that this
section of the text comes alive as a tight artistic unity that integrates the
war with the Ammonites and David's interactions with Bathsheba and
Uriah more strongly than in existing discussions.

I am not assuming the historicity of any element of this narrative,
nor am I denying it. My point is to explore how an ancient audience
would have perceived what was happening. When I refer to "David" or
any of the other persons mentioned, I am treating them as characters in
the narrative, whether they existed or not and whether what is described
actually happened or not. I am also concerned with the how this narrative works in its final form, not with its composition history.[4]

There is no need for present purposes to propose too precise a date
for the final form of the Masoretic text. While the text seems to contain
preexilic materials that received a final editing in exilic or postexilic
period, possibly in Deuteronomistic hands,[5] the two issues of the context
upon which I will focus are applicable across the entirety of this period;
they are in no way tied to the specific features of any particular period.

Two Social-Scientific Perspectives

In undertaking this task I rely on two perspectives that derive from anthropological research conducted into the Mediterranean region in the last four decades and are now so well known in the biblical field, since their systematization by Bruce Malina, initially in 1981,[6] that I need only briefly sketch them out here. In chapter 1 of this volume I have offered a defense for model use of this kind based on Max Weber's social-science methodology.

Challenge and Response

The first is the social dynamic of challenge and response, first analyzed by French anthropologist Pierre Bourdieu in relation to the Kabyle, an Arab people from North Africa and given prominence by Malina.[7] In a world where honor is the primary social good and exists in finite quantities, every social occasion offers one participant the chance to enhance his or her honor at the expense of someone else, so long as that someone is roughly equal in social status. This social dynamic begins with a challenge, which is a claim to enter someone's social space. Most commonly this happens in a negative way, by an insult or a physical assault. But a challenge can also be positive in nature, as when one person gives another a gift, or praises him or sends a message of goodwill. The person then challenged must consider how to respond, fully aware that there is an audience that will rapidly view a failure to respond or a weak response as a victory for the challenger, and hence award him or her honor at the challenged person's expense. There are three broad modes of response: positive rejection, usually with scorn and contempt; acceptance coupled with a counter-challenge; and the dishonorable course of no response.

In 1 Samuel 17 young David is painfully aware that the failure of a single Israelite to go out to meet Goliath has dishonored Israel. "What shall be done," he asks, "for the man who kills this Philistine and takes away the reproach from Israel?" (1 Sam 17:26 MT). Most typically a challenge is met with a strong response, which is the honorable way to act, and may in turn elicit a counter-response from the challenger. This can produce an escalating spiral of hostility such as we see between Jesus and the Judeans in John 8:31-59. If the person challenged cannot respond, and is therefore shamed, he or she will harbor a desire for vengeance that may become possible on a later occasion.

Patron/Broker/Client Relationships

The second perspective is that of the relationship between patron and client, a relationship often mediated by a broker. In the Old Testament field the importance of the patron-client relationship has been proposed by Niels Lemche in 1995 and 1996, by Raymond Hobbs in 1997, and by Ronald Simkins in 1999.[8] Zeba Crook, on the other hand, has usefully pointed out in his essay in this volume that patron and client relationships are really a subspecies of what he calls "asymmetrical reciprocity" (otherwise less helpfully known as "generalized reciprocity"). Other examples of relationships where there is a marked inequality of power and resources between the parties, such as vassal treaties, are probably best viewed as another instance of this general pattern of asymmetrical reciprocity rather than as being assimilated to the patron-client relationship (as sometimes occurs in the field at present). But in cases of vassal treaties and other covenants, as Crook notes, there is a high degree of formality, with *explicit* promises and threats, oaths, witnesses, and, above all, solemnization of the relationship in *writing*. Patron and client relationships, on the other hand, although a form of asymmetrical reciprocity, are far more informal and lack these features.

Although I follow the broad lines of Crook's proposal here, many of the ideas of Lemche, Hobbs, and Simkins remain useful. Thus Lemche is correct to argue that *ḥesed* expresses the loyalty that binds together patron and client and the parties to other relationships such as covenant and treaty (even if the latter should now not simply be regarded as particular cases of patron-client relationships).[9] We can use the notion of higher level of generalization or of abstraction to relate phenomena such as covenant and the patron-client relationship to the more general category of asymmetrical reciprocity.

A patron is a person in an elevated socioeconomic position in possession of material goods, such as land and other wealth, and immaterial goods, such as honor and power in a particular urban or rural setting. In a world of limited goods, a patron is able to share access to some of these benefits with a limited number of clients. In return the clients honor the patron with their attention and provide services when required. The relationship is an asymmetrical but mutually beneficial one. These relationships are informal, that is to say, they are not solemnized in written form, as are, for example, vassal treaties. At times a broker will mediate between a patron and a client. Often a broker will function as a client to the ultimate patron and as a patron to the clients.[10] Patron-client relations take on aspects of relationships between kin. Patron and clients are bound together by mutual commitment, solidarity and loyalty, as seen in the asymmetrical reciprocity that marks their dealings with one another.[11]

The relationship between patron and client appears well suited to interpreting a number of biblical phenomena, especially the relationship between God and God's people, as mediated by the prophets in the Old Testament and Jesus in the New. Some work along these lines already exists. In 1988 Bruce Malina published an essay entitled "Patron and Client: The Analogy behind Synoptic Theology,"[12] which suggests a model for understanding the relationship between God, Jesus the Messiah, and God's people along the lines of patron, broker, and clients, which is also applicable to the Old Testament understanding of God.

Application of the Model

Current Explanations of the Structure of 2 Samuel 10–12

Most critics, especially because they are driven by interests in source criticism or composition history, fail to discern the extent to which 2 Samuel 10–12 is a tightly integrated and unified narrative. Often the war with Ammon is seen merely as the "background" for the David-Bathsheba-Uriah story. According to A. A. Anderson, for example, it "seems that chapters 10–12 comprise *a more or less unitary* (emphasis added) account of three consecutive events during David's Ammonite-Aramean wars, namely, the defeat of the Ammonite-Aramean coalition (10:6-14), the defeat of the reinforced Aramean alliance (10:15-19), and, finally, the siege and capture of Rabbah, the Ammonite capital (11:1 + 12:26-31)." Anderson considers that the description of the Ammonite-Syrian wars was probably derived from annalistic sources and reworked. "In the present context," he adds, "it provided the *setting and background* (emphasis added) for the David-Bathsheba-Uriah story."[13] Similarly, Kyle McCarter observes that "The resolution of the Ammonite conflict is deferred in the narrative as our attention is directed away from public affairs to the private life of the king."[14] This comment makes a distinction between "public" and "private" in relation to David that we will soon see is unsustainable and generally overlooks the tight connection between the course of the Ammonite war and the king's behavior in Jerusalem. Even a scholar such as Fokkelman, who insists on what he calls the "organic unity" of this section of

2 Samuel with respect to how the war with the Ammonites and David's affair with Bathsheba are interwoven, misses the real character of their integration, which, as we will see, centers around David's culpable delay in taking vengeance on Ammon.[15] Applying the social-scientific perspectives set out above, on the other hand, will bring out the unity of 2 Samuel 10–12 within the culture of the ancient Mediterranean world. It will also allow us to discern how an audience in such a context would have appreciated this section of 2 Samuel as a coherent narrative.

Ammon's Challenge to Israel: The Casus Belli

The narrative begins with the death of the king of Ammon and the accession of his son Hanun in his stead (2 Sam 10:1). Since the deceased king Nahash had expressed *ḥesed* toward David, a word that carries the connotation of reciprocity marked by loyalty,[16] probably in this case by providing him assistance when he was being hounded by Saul,[17] David decides to extend such loyalty (here with a strong connotation of kindness) to his son. He does this by sending ambassadors to Hanun with a message of consolation concerning his father. The message probably included a rehearsal of the great deeds and high honor of Nahash, a view confirmed in verse 3. Within the dynamic of challenge and response, this initiative represented a challenge, that is, a claim to enter the social space, and indeed here the physical space, of Hanun. As far as David was concerned, it was what we are calling a positive challenge, made with friendly intentions. Nevertheless, a challenge it was and it necessitated that Hanun consider it and determine how he should respond in such a way as to preserve his self-respect. Presumably David assumed that the new king would simply take up the relationship that his father had enjoyed with David.

Yet David reckoned without the princes of the Ammonites, who are advising the new king and the possibility that they would put a different interpretation on his embassy. In a statement that brings to the surface the honor code in which the scene is being played out, they ask Hanun, "Do you think that because David has sent comforters to you, he is honoring (חמכדב, *ḥmkdb;* δοξάζειν, *doxazein*) your father?" (2 Sam 10:3). No, they insist, David's real aim is to use his ambassadors to reconnoiter the city and overthrow it. It is not clear *why* the princes offered Hanun this advice.[18] In any event, they interpret David's gesture as a negative challenge, here one that takes the form of a surreptitious threat and an attempt at fulfilling it, and persuade Hanun that their view is correct.

That David should fail to foresee this particular interpretation that the princes of Ammon would put on his actions indicates a certain naïveté on his part within the story line of 2 Samuel. On a previous occasion, after all, when he was willing to trust Abner (who wanted to be reconciled to him), Joab warned David that Abner really came to deceive him, to learn about his movements and dispositions (2 Sam 3:25).

Of the three options available in responding to a challenge noted above, only the second—acceptance and counter-challenge—was likely to satisfy Hanun and those advising him. From their perspective, David's ambassadors posed an actual threat to Ammon and a strong riposte to meet it was necessary.

The action taken by Hanun brings out once again the social script of honor and shame in which this narrative is written.[19] The king apprehends the ambassadors, shaves half their beards,[20] and cuts off their garments around their waist so that their buttocks are exposed. This particular humiliation may have been administered with mordant humor aimed at the purported basis for the embassy, since it was perhaps a parody of the shaving that accompanied conventional rites of mourning (Isa 15:2).[21] We can imagine Hanun saying, "You come to mourn my father? I'll help you mourn!"

We have evidence from other contexts of the damage done to a person's honor produced by being shaved (Isa 7:20) and having one's buttocks exposed (Isa 20:4). The text summarizes the effect of such indignities within the honor and shame code of operating in this setting when it says that David went to meet his ambassadors, because they were greatly ashamed (מאד נכלמים, m'd nklmym; ἠτιμασμένοι, ētimasmenoi; 2 Sam 10:5). Their shame prevented them traveling to Jerusalem lest their condition be exposed to public gaze. So he told them to stay at Jericho until their beards had grown.

From David's perspective, the insult that had been inflicted on his embassy by the Ammonites constituted a deadly affront. For clearly implied in the text is that by insulting his ambassadors they had also grievously insulted him and, indeed, Israel itself. Honor earned or received by one member of a group is enjoyed by all, while the shame suffered by one touches all. For we learn in the very next verse (2 Sam 10:6) that the Ammonites saw that "they had become odious to David" (נבאש בדוד, nb'š bdwd).

The expression נבאש בדוד (nb'š bdwd) deserves close attention. The qal באש (b'š) means "to stink." It is used of the Nile stinking with dead and rotting fish (Exod 7:18, 21), of stinking manna (Exod 16:20), and of fish stinking in dried-up rivers (Isa 50:2). It is thus employed of a very powerful and unpleasant smell. In the niphal (as here), occurring only three times in the Hebrew Bible (1 Sam 13:4; 2 Sam 10:6; 16:21), it means "to be/become stinking (to someone)."

Yet we need to be aware of the force of נבאש (nbʾš) and the context in which it appears. First, since the niphal carries the connotation that someone has become as offensive to another as rotting fish, it conveys that an extreme pitch of detestation has been reached. Second, *the niphal belongs exclusively to the social dynamic of challenge and response*. It refers to the condition of someone who has grievously shamed another, and who has thereby incurred the enmity of that person and expects a robust response. Consider the example in 1 Samuel 13, which bears close similarities to the incident of David's ambassadors to Hanun. For here Jonathan had defeated the Philistines and Saul then trumpeted the news throughout the land (1 Sam 13:3). So all Israel heard that Saul had destroyed the Philistine garrison (the actions of Jonathan being attributed to his king) and Israel considered that they had "become odious" to the Philistines (1 Sam 13:4). Thus, the whole collectivity of Israel, typically for this culture, incurs responsibility for the actions of some of its members. In fact, Israel's realization of this is followed immediately by Saul's summoning the people and their being threatened by the Philistine host (1 Sam 13:5).

At 2 Samuel 16:22 נבאש (nbʾš) is used to describe the consequence of one of the most heinous insults offered anyone in the Old Testament, when Absalom has sexual intercourse with his father's concubines (as Nathan had previously predicted in 2 Samuel 12:11). By so doing, Absalom "became odious" to his father, meaning that he had injured him grievously and desecrated his honor to such an extent that a severe reaction from David was to be expected. Indeed, Ahitophel had urged Absalom to do this, since the ire it would stir up in David would strengthen the resolve of Absalom's group (2 Sam 16:21).

The meaning of נבאש (nbʾš) at 2 Samuel 10:6 is essentially the same as in these two other instances. This interpretation of נבאש (nbʾš) within framework of challenge and response receives ancient confirmation in the way the Septuagint translates it—by use of καταισχύνειν (kataischynein, "put to shame") or αἰσχύνομαι (aischynomai, "be put to shame") in each case.[22]

The Ammonites not only realized the enormity of what they done in insulting David's ambassadors, but also foresaw the likely reaction—a military response from David. The model suggests that the grievous challenge offered to David's ambassadors—and hence to him—demands a response. *David needs to take decisive action to restore his honor and that of Israel.* The original audience of this text would have been itching to learn what steps David took to this end. The obvious one was for him to lead an army of Israelites out to crush the Ammonites and capture and sack their city. This is what an honorable man would have done within the social script forming the context of this narrative. We can be certain this is an accurate interpretation of the situation because this was exactly what the Ammonites themselves were expecting. The Ammonites appreciate that David has been so enraged by what they have done to his ambassadors that he will inevitably attack them in force. Accordingly, they begin to augment their own army by hiring thousands of extra soldiers, namely, the Syrians, the army of the king of Maacah and the men of Tob (2 Sam 10:6). No doubt they were expecting that David would soon appear at the head of a huge host to confront them.

David's Response: The Beginnings of the Ammonite War

Yet the original audience must have received a big shock when they learned what David did upon discovering that Ammon was mustering its own forces and those it had hired: "he sent Joab and all the host of mighty men." Joab? Why did David not lead the army himself? It had, after all, been central to the Israelites' demand of Samuel that they have a king that he would govern them and go out before them and fight their battles (1 Sam 8:20). Although Peter Ackroyd considers it "normal procedure" for David to entrust this mission to Joab,[23] that is not the message the text conveys. This will emerge clearly later, at the start of chapter 11, but even here the point is implied from the fact that it was David's ambassadors whom Hanun had insulted and he, as Israel's king, had been insulted with them. The Ammonites saw that "they stank before David" (2 Sam 10:6). So why does he delegate leadership of his army to Joab? David was, after all, the man who, at an earlier point in his career, had been the only Israelite brave enough to redeem the honor of Israel from the arrogant reproaches of Goliath (1 Sam 17:26). Thus begins a theme that will not only be prominent until the very end of this narrative in 2 Samuel 12, but will also constitute the prime factor in the plot, namely, David's inexplicable and dishonorable failure to take to the field against Ammon.

In the event, Joab and his brother Abishai are successful against both the Ammonites and the Syrians, with the Ammonites withdrawing to their city, an important element in the plot as it unfolds (2 Sam 10:9-14). Yet compounding the sense in the text that David is behaving in a way that is culturally disordered is that he does now lead Israel out to war, yet not against the Ammonites who had insulted him, but against the Syrians whom they had hired and other Syrians who came to their aid from beyond the Euphrates. David defeated them and they feared to help the Ammonites thereafter (2 Sam 10:15-19). But none of these actions constitute an appropriate response to the insult offered by the Ammonites. They have fled to the protection of their city and David himself has not taken a single step against them, being content to leave the campaign in the hands of Joab.

David, Bathsheba, and Uriah

The implicit unease with David's behavior in the text bursts to the surface at the start of the next chapter:

> And it came to pass, in the spring of the year, when kings go forth [sc. to battle], that David sent Joab and his servants with him, and all Israel, and they ravaged the Ammonites and they besieged Rabbah. But David remained in Jerusalem. (2 Sam. 11:1)

Here "kings" is read in the first line with virtually every ancient witness (including 1 Chron 20:1) except the Masoretic Text (which reads "messengers").[24] The reading in the Masoretic Text seems an obvious attempt to salvage David's reputation. This campaign against Ammon is a continuation of the previous year's war with the Ammonites, in spite of Peter Ackroyd's surprising view to the contrary.[25] The siege of Rabbah mentioned here reflects the fact that in the previous year the Ammonites had fled to the protection of their capital (2 Sam 10:14). The siege of Rabbah will be a crucial feature of the narrative as it develops.

The text offers no reason why David now repeats his failure of the previous year to lead the assault on Ammon. It merely asserts in the bluntest terms his breach of social convention applicable to kings by his remaining in Jerusalem, a breach that, in this narrative, entails his failure to respond appropriately to the shame heaped on his ambassadors by the Ammonites. David's disregard of the responsibility of kings to take to the field, especially when they have an egregious insult to avenge, proves to be the causal factor for the whole shape of his life thereafter, a life into which tragedy intrudes—beginning with his adultery with Bathsheba, the death of her husband, Uriah, and the sword that will never thereafter depart from his house, a sword most visible in the rebellion of Absalom. Put bluntly, if he had done the right thing and led his men to war, he would never have got into the trouble he did.

The account of his liaison with Bathsheba is remarkable for its brevity and its androcentric character. From his rooftop David sees a beautiful woman washing herself, he finds out that she is Bathsheba the wife of Uriah the Hittite (whom he apparently knows is off fighting the Ammonites with Joab),[26] he sends messengers to bring her, he has intercourse with her (which is possible for her, ironically, because her rooftop bathing has purified her of her monthly uncleanness), she returns to her house, she conceives, and then sends David the news that she is pregnant. All of these details are compressed into two verses. The emphasis is upon David as the agent in all this; Bathsheba is passive and speculation as to whether she counted on the possibility that David would see her while she was bathing seems wide of the mark.[27]

The main interest in this part of the narrative falls on the interaction between David and Uriah, about whose character we learn important details. Although Uriah is described as a Hittite, the "Yah" element in his name (which means "Yahweh is my light"), suggests a connection with Israel. Perhaps "Hittite" indicates his ancestry.[28] It emerges later in the text that Uriah was one of David's thirty heroes, some of whom are non-Israelite (2 Sam 23:39). David sends to Joab to have Uriah sent to him (2 Sam 11:6).

When Uriah arrives, David goes through the charade of asking him about the campaign, as if that had been the purpose for his presence (2 Sam 11:7). David then tells Uriah to go home and sends food after him (2 Sam 11:8), no doubt to encourage a festival atmosphere in Uriah's house. David wants Uriah to sleep with Bathsheba so it can be claimed the baby is his. Instead of going home, Uriah sleeps at the door of the royal palace with David's men (2 Sam 11:9). On learning of this puzzling event, David asks Uriah for an explanation (2 Sam 11:10).

Uriah's answer deserves quotation in full:

The ark and Israel and Judah dwell in booths; and my lord Joab and the servants of my lord are camping in the open field; shall I then go to my house, to eat and to drink, and to lie with my wife? As you live, and as your soul lives, I will not do this thing (2 Sam 11:11).

There is one emic expression, admittedly not used here, that describes the motivation for Uriah's actions: it is חסד (ḥsd). What Uriah manifests is loyalty—loyalty to his God, his divine patron (who is represented by the ark, which is the visible sign of his presence [1 Sam 4:3-9]); to his people (Israel and Judah), also dwelling in tents; to his commander Joab (his patron in the military sphere); and to his fellow soldiers, who are camping in the open field. For Uriah loyalty entails that, as far as possible, he shares the privations that they are experiencing. In short, Uriah exemplifies חסד (ḥsd). David exemplifies its opposite. It is sometimes suggested that Uriah sees through David and realizes he has slept with Bathsheba;[29] but this would mean he is playing games with David just as David is with him, and such a similarity would damage the stark contrast the author is drawing between the characters of two men: the dutiful Uriah and the manipulative David.

After this, David tries to soften Uriah's will by having him stay a few days in Jerusalem and plying him with food and wine. All to no avail; he does not go home (2 Sam 11:12-13). As Ackroyd nicely puts it: "Uriah drunk is more pious than David sober."[30] From David's perspective, this means that there is no alternative but to have Uriah killed. He achieves this end with Joab's help, through orders that Uriah is to be placed in the most dangerous place in the battle (2 Sam 11:14-25). When Bathsheba hears that Uriah is dead, she mourns for him, probably for seven days (1 Sam 31:13). Immediately thereafter, David sends for her to become his (latest) wife and she bears him a son, who passes unnamed in the text. Yet this section of the text ends with the ominous statement that prepares the audience for what is about to occur: "The thing which David had done was evil in the sight of the Lord" (2 Sam 11:27).

David and Nathan

This divine displeasure with David manifests itself as the next episode in the narrative, when God sends Nathan to him. The details of the account make good sense within the framework of God as patron, Nathan his prophet as broker, and David as client.

Nathan's begins with the tale of two men in one city—a rich man, with many flocks and herds, and a poor man, with only one ewe lamb, to which he was greatly attached. Having heard how the rich man spared his own flocks and took the poor man's lamb to feed a visitor, David explodes with "As the LORD lives, the man who has done this deserves to die; and he shall restore the lamb fourfold, because he did this thing, and because he had no pity" (2 Sam. 12:5-6). Then Nathan springs his trap: "You are the man (אתה האיש, *ʾth hʾyš*)" (2 Sam. 12:7). David has condemned himself by his own mouth. What David wrongly thought were the facts of a real case turn out to be a parable about his own behavior.

We should note how Nathan categorizes David's wrong. The story does not refer expressly to some provision of Israelite law, but rather focuses upon the situation of a poor man robbed of the creature he loved. Nathan responds to David in a manner that brilliantly illuminates the patron-client relationship that existed between God and the king:

> Thus says the LORD, the God of Israel, "I anointed you king over Israel, and I delivered you out of the hand of Saul; and I gave you your master's house, and your master's wives into you bosom, and gave you the house of Israel and of Judah; and if this were too little, I would add to you as much more." (2 Sam 12:7-8)

The primary function of a patron, as far as his clients are concerned, is to provide them with goods, material and immaterial, in a society where all goods are thought to exist in finite quantities. Nathan is reminding David that God has given no one as many goods as him. No one has had a more generous patron; indeed, God substituted David for Saul as king of Israel. If David had wanted more wives, God would have provided them. By taking Bathsheba in this way, David has scorned the generosity of his divine patron. He had not done what was expected of a client in his culture.

Yet there is more. "Why have you despised (בזה, *bzh*) the word (דבר, *dbr*) of the LORD,"[31] Nathan continues (2 Sam 12:9), "to do what is evil in his sight?" We should not interpret despising God's word too narrowly as meaning contravening this or that provision of his law. Despising God's word is essentially equivalent to despising God, a charge explicitly leveled against David in the next verse (2 Sam 12:10). The context here is that of a patron/client relationship, where the gifts of one should find reciprocation in the loyalty and obedience of the other. This is an honor/shame culture where to despise means to treat someone with disrespect, to dishonor him or her. Having given David so much, the implied subtext here is that all God wants in return is loyalty (*ḥesed*). Instead, David dishonors God by doing what is evil in God's sight. David has proved himself a disloyal client and his scorned patron will now act to punish him.

Although by taxing David with having despised the word of the
Lord, Nathan thus underlines the relational and honor-based nature of
the king's offense, the prophet then proceeds in the remainder of
2 Samuel 12:9 to give content to this insult in terms of David's treatment
of Uriah: "You have smitten Uriah the Hittite with the sword, and have
taken his wife to be your wife, and have slain him with the sword of the
Ammonites." This element in the narrative discloses something fundamentally important about this divine patron—he has an abiding concern
for justice.

To interpret the offense in David's liaison with Bathsheba in terms
of this or that provision of the Pentateuch applicable to all Israelites forbidding murder and adultery would not be wrong in a technical sense
but would miss the real point of David's wrong—that not only had he
breached his obligations to his patron but he had murdered a man and
stolen his wife. David's wrong is, indeed, far worse than that of the rich
man in the parable who did not, at least, have the poor man murdered
to conceal the theft of his lamb. Thus the text focuses upon the devastation David has wrought both in his personal relationship with God and
in its effect on Uriah rather than on his infringement of any specific provision of Israelite law.

With bitter irony, Nathan proceeds to announce that since David
(acting through the Ammonites of 2 Samuel 11:17) slew Uriah with a
sword

> ... now therefore the sword shall never depart from your house,
> because you have despised (בזה, *bzh*) me, and have taken the
> wife of Uriah the Hittite to be your wife. (2 Sam 12:10)

The sorry course of David's life and reign henceforward is then inti-
mated in the details Nathan next provides, which again refer to punishment for David in a form that ironically replicates upon him what he
perpetrated on Uriah:

> Thus says the LORD, "Behold, I will raise up evil against you out
> of your own house; and I will take your wives before your eyes,
> and give them to your neighbor, and he shall lie with your wives
> in the sight of the sun. For you did it secretly; but I will do this
> thing before all Israel, and before the sun. (2 Sam 12:11-12)

Sharpening the force of this penalty is the added factor that David
will be harmed in relation to the wives that he himself had inherited

from Saul as part of the blessings that God had showered upon him. God, speaking through Nathan, at least spares David the news that the "neighbor" will actually be his son Absalom (2 Sam 16:21-22). There is an ironic narrative logic to David's being punished in the same way that he had injured Uriah. Whereas Uriah exemplifies loyalty, David, in this instance, has exemplified disloyalty, so it is appropriate in narrative terms that the sword David inflicted on the loyal man he in turn should suffer as the disloyal man.

Having heard Nathan, David acknowledges that he has sinned against the Lord; in our terms, he recognizes that he has offended his patron. With some dignity, David does not ask for mercy. Nathan tells him, however, that the Lord has put away his sin and he shall not die (this is in spite of the fact that David had adjudged the rich man worthy of death). But this is not the end. Because by his deed David "has caused the enemies of the Lord to blaspheme,"[32] the child of his adulterous union with Bathsheba will die (2 Sam 12:13-14). This soon happens. After Nathan's departure, the child falls ill and David begins a period of fasting and prayers for his recovery that went on for seven days. David clearly hopes that, in spite of his sin and Nathan's prophecy that the child would die, his heavenly patron might yet extend another benefit to him in the form of the child's life (2 Sam 12:22). Yet the child dies. So David comforts Bathsheba for the death of their son and she conceives and gives birth to another son, Solomon, whom God loves (2 Sam 12:24). Then comes the curious episode in the story when God sends Nathan to give Solomon another name, Jedidiah, meaning "Beloved of the Lord," even though this name is not used of Solomon thereafter (2 Sam 12:25).

At this point in the narrative the scene has been set for the second half of 2 Samuel and the beginning of 1 Kings, especially the terrible events that will engulf David's family as the sword ravages his house (2 Samuel 13–24). Yet, at the same time, a son has been born to him who has particular favor with the Lord. Solomon will be the focus of the much happier story in 1 Kings 2–11. Yet all that lies in the future, and David still has unfinished business to attend to in the present.

The Defeat of the Ammonites and Capture of Rabbah

The last six verses of 2 Samuel 12 bring the ancient Israelite audience back to the Ammonite war. Enculturated into the honor-laden dynamics of challenge and response, they will have been waiting to hear that

David, his lesson learned, had now taken the field at the head of his army to smite the Ammonites and to avenge their treatment of his ambassadors. Yet such an audience would have been amazed to learn that even now David was not performing in accordance with local cultural values. For in spite of the Ammonites' insult and the trouble he got into when he stayed behind in Jerusalem, David has still not taken command of the campaign himself but continues to entrust that responsibility to Joab. His general is actually doing rather well, having captured part of Rabbah (2 Sam 12:26).

At this point in the narrative the ancient audience would have well understood Joab's exasperation at David's failure to take command and gasped at the threat to David's honor that Joab considered necessary to get the king out of Jerusalem:

> And Joab sent messengers to David, and said, "I have fought against Rabbah; moreover, I have taken the city of waters. Now, therefore, gather the rest of the people together and encamp against the city and take it, lest I capture the city and it be called after my name." (2 Sam 12:27-28)

This finally provokes David into action. At long last he gathers all the people, fights against Rabbah, and captures it (2 Sam 12:29). He takes their king's crown and puts it on his head. This is a personal touch that shames the Ammonites in a way that repays the shame David endured in the treatment of his embassy. After this he despoils the city (2 Sam 12:30) and sets the Ammonite population to work. So, at last, having taken due vengeance on the Ammonites for their original insult, he returns to Jerusalem with the people.

Conclusion

By undertaking an investigation of 2 Samuel 10–12 with particular attention to textual data relating to the social dynamics of challenge and response and of patron/client that were central to this ancient context, I have argued that these chapters form a tightly integrated narrative. They focus upon avenging an insult offered to Israel, but one where the execution of that vengeance is inappropriately delayed and with tragic consequences. The David of this narrative seems in part to have learned his lesson, for we see him later in life fighting with his men against the

Philistines, until his weariness, presumably a product of old age, raised the prospect of his being killed, so that the Israelites themselves begged him no more to go out to battle with them (2 Sam 21:15-17). By using social-scientific perspectives heuristically to highlight data in the text— that is, to ask questions that only the data can answer—I have been able to produce (it is hoped) significant exegetical gains.

Finally, it is easy to imagine that the original audience of this text would have wondered how, as the years rolled on, David must often have reflected upon his behavior in relation to Ammon and looked forward with foreboding to the problems he now faced. Not the least of those problems was the inevitable question from his bright young son Solomon, posed with natural but misplaced family pride: "What did you do in the Ammonite War, father?"

Ezekiel—An Altered State of Consciousness Experience

THE CALL OF EZEKIEL: EZEKIEL 1–3

John J. Pilch

John Pilch argues that by using the social-science disciplines of cultural anthropology and cognitive neuroscience to analyze God's call of Ezekiel to be a prophet (Ezekiel 1–3), a reader can better appreciate that this event, like all prophetic calls, took place in an altered state of consciousness or an alternate level of human awareness. Cultural anthropologists have demonstrated that altered states are a pan-human experience across cultures that occur and are reported in strikingly similar ways. Cognitive neuroscientists explain that, because human beings share a common human biology, this essentially neurophysiological experience can occur and be reported. These social-scientific insights thus sharpen our understanding of the nature and function of literary forms that derive from social systems. In short, Ezekiel's neurological experience, his response to it, and his report of it was shaped and interpreted by his culture.

In "One Memorable Fancy," one of many brief sections in his poem, "The Marriage of Heaven and Hell," William Blake (1772–1827) recorded his dinner conversation with Isaiah and Ezekiel. Blake wanted to know "how they dared so roundly to assert that God spoke to them; and whether they did not think at the time that they would be misunderstood, and so be the cause of imposition (deception)." The prophets talked about inspiration (which Blake called Poetic Genius) and perception. At the end of their conversation, Blake concluded: "If the doors of perception were cleansed every thing would appear to man as it is, infinite. For man has closed himself up, till he sees all things through narrow chinks of his cavern."[1]

For more than two decades now my research on the Bible and that of my colleagues in The Context Group[2] has utilized the social sciences as a tool for cleansing the doors of perception. Cultural or social anthropology and cognitive neuroscience are two disciplines that have proven to be remarkably effective cleansing agents.[3] These same disciplines applied to Ezekiel's call to be a prophet (Ezekiel 1–3) cast fresh light on this extensively researched topic.[4] Exegetes are in general agreement concerning the structure of these chapters. I adopt the outline proposed by Joseph Blenkinsopp[5] with emendations from Daniel Block:[6]

Ezekiel 1–3	God Calls Ezekiel to be a Prophet:
Ezek 1:1-3	Superscription
Ezek 1:4-28a	Inaugural Vision (the Throne)
Ezek 1:28b—3:11	Commissioning of Ezekiel
Ezek 3:12-15	Preparation of Ezekiel
Ezek 3:16-21	Ezekiel as Sentry or Watchman
Ezek 3:22-27	Initiation of Ezekiel (Loss of Speech)

Ronald Hals identifies Ezekiel 1:1—3:15 as a single unit, which he calls "a vocation account in autobiographical prose" similar to Isaiah 6:1-8 and Jeremiah 1:4-10.[7] Because his book is in the "Forms of the Old Testament Literature" series, he also distinguishes discrete subunits or literary forms within the larger unit such as the prophetic word formula, the commissioning formula, the messenger formula, and the like.

In 1965, Norman Habel published an excellent form-critical analysis of call narratives, including that of Ezekiel.[8] He isolated six elements in the call narratives of Moses, Gideon, Isaiah, Jeremiah, Ezekiel, and Second Isaiah, though not every element was found in each report. The elements as they appear in Ezekiel are as follows:

1. Divine Confrontation: Ezek 1:1-28a
2. Introductory Word: Ezek 1:28b—2:2[9]
3. Commission: Ezek 2:3-5
4. Objection: implied in Ezek 2:6, 8
5. Reassurance: Ezek 2:6-7
6. Sign: Ezek 2:8—3:11

In my analysis of Ezekiel I combine these outlines (that of Blenkinsopp and Block with Habel) and assess their interpretations as well as those of other scholars from the perspective of altered states of consciousness ("ASCs") as analyzed in cultural anthropology and cognitive neuroscience.[10]

Ezekiel's Call: An Altered State of Consciousness Experience

In describing the call of Isaiah (Isaiah 6), Habel notes: "The experience is not depicted as an ecstatic trance in the proper sense of the term, for rational reflection and dialogue are possible during the encounter."[11] He then points out that Ezekiel 1:1—3:15 was patterned upon the call of Isaiah. Habel concludes:

> In recounting their own call they [the prophets] preserve the ancient dialogue character of the experience which is typical of the mediatorial office. In this way the prophets also guard against classifying their experience as an ecstatic suspension of personality. Inasmuch as the various formal elements of the call accounts, including the opening confrontation, are so basic to an understanding of the material, it is virtually impossible to analyze the psychological dimensions of the prophetic calls. The form does not merely reflect the inner emotions of the prophet; it reflects the *Gattung* appropriate for his message.[12]

Though he does not explicitly deny that Ezekiel's experience was an ASC (as he does for Isaiah), Habel implies it when he states that Ezekiel 1:1—3:15 was patterned upon the call of Isaiah.[13] Regarding Ezekiel, Block is explicit: "the prophetic call was not an ecstatic or trancelike experience. When information is provided, the divine confrontation occurred when the person was engaged in the normal activities of life."[14] Blenkinsopp is among many, perhaps the majority of scholars, who would disagree. He is convinced that Ezekiel's experience took place in a "state of ecstasy or trance."[15] For reasons I explain below, I believe that this is the more plausible opinion and will seek to explore in this paper.

Habel and Block do not give a definition of ecstatic trance, but their skepticism is based on the fact that the various encounters with God experienced by Moses, Ezekiel, et al. occurred while they were performing routine activities and that they engaged in rational dialogue with God, who was somehow experienced with the senses. It is reasonable to conclude, therefore, that Habel and Block consider ASC experiences as unusual, or not part of routine human experience. Further, they view ASC experiences as belonging to the category of the irrational. Yet anthropologists recognize that 80 percent of a worldwide population research sample routinely and regularly had ASC experiences.[16] Indeed, ASCs were institutionalized into the social practices of 96 percent of the 486 small societies that were studied in the database of the Human Relations Area Files at Yale University.[17]

I shall therefore analyze the call of Ezekiel as his experience of God and the divine realm in an ASC. The information reported in Ezekiel 1–3 resonates with much of contemporary scientific knowledge about ASC experiences. Even though scholars admit that the biblical information is a mixture of Ezekiel's report and later elaborations by disciples, the passage at hand yields important insight into the nature of Ezekiel's experience, and how it was understood and embellished by himself and by others who shared his cultural values.

Ezekiel 1:1-3: The Superscription

The aim of these verses is to set the date of Ezekiel's inaugural vision. The thirtieth year (v. 1) should quite likely be calculated from Ezekiel's birth. He is thirty years old, the age at which priests assumed their office (see Numbers 4:30, though Numbers 8:23-25 says it could be the age of 25). If it was the fifth year of the exile (598 B.C.E., v. 2), the date would be June or July, 593 B.C.E. Ezekiel's career (593—571 B.C.E.) would thus span the twenty years prescribed by Numbers. He experienced his vision in Babylon by the Chebar Canal, which looped its way around the city of Nippur (modern Nuffar) in the plains of southern Iraq (see Psalm 137).

"The heavens were opened" and Ezekiel saw "visions of God" (RSV). I have argued elsewhere[18] that in the Bible *heaven* refers either to the physical sky above the earth or to the realm of God beyond. Ezekiel saw the physical sky open (compare Isa 63:19b [MT 64:1]: "Oh that thou would rend the heavens and come down"). It is impossible to look into the realm of God unless someone makes an opening for the visionary. The passive voice is the theological or divine passive, that is, God opened the sky so that Ezekiel could peer into the divine abode. (See Genesis 7:11 where God opens the "windows of the sky" to let the rains of the flood pour down.) What did he see? "Visions of God!" Since, however, Ezekiel normally refers to Yahweh rather than God it is appropriate to translate the genitive מראות אלהים (mr'wt 'lhym) as "divine visions" rather than "visions of God." In other words, Ezekiel could see realities in the realm of God not normally accessible to the naked human eye.[19] Clearly, Ezekiel is already in an ASC. He is enabled to see divine visions because God has made an opening in the sky for him. His alternate level of awareness is confirmed in verse 3 (see below, "hand of the LORD").

Additional information about Ezekiel's identity helps us to appreciate his experience and how he interprets it. He is a priest, son of Buzi (v. 3). As a priest, Ezekiel was a member of a very learned elite for some of whom reading and writing was normal practice. Ezekiel wrote the bulk of the book that bears his name, a book that was subsequently embellished by his disciples in the form to which it has come to us. As a priest and literate person, Ezekiel drew on many sources to interpret his visions: priestly lore, poetry (e.g., Psalm 18), and ASC experiences of earlier prophets (e.g., Micaiah ben Imlah in 1 Kings 22:19-22; Isa 6:1-8, etc.). In social-scientific terms, such sources constituted the latent discourse of a culture. This is the normal source to which visionaries have recourse in order to interpret their ASC experiences. We shall examine the details in a moment.

The editor (verses 2-3 shift to the third person singular after verse 1, which has been in the first person singular) reports that "the word of the LORD" came to Ezekiel, and "the hand of the LORD" was upon him (v. 3). In the RSV, the phrase "the word of the LORD" occurs approximately six times more often than the phrase "the voice of the LORD," yet the significance is the same. Ezekiel heard God speak, he heard an intelligible message, presumably in Hebrew. Anthropological research indicates that the content of trance experiences is vacuous. It is pictures without a soundtrack, a silent film as it were. The visionary provides the soundtrack, which in its turn originates in the latent discourse of a visionary's culture.[20] Ezekiel heard a message from God that he will unfold and unpack in subsequent chapters. At the moment, he simply notes that his vision had a soundtrack.

"The hand of the Lord" occurs in the Bible eleven times as an indication of one aspect of prophetic experience (Ezek 1:3; 3:14, 22; 8:1; 33:22; 37:1; 40:1; 1 Kgs 18:46; 2 Kgs 3:15; Isa 8:11; Jer 25:17). Though

Walther Zimmerli presents a detailed discussion of the expression,[21] J. J. M. Roberts presents a still-broader perspective.[22] According to Roberts, a majority of scholars understand this phrase as a "rather specific reference to an ecstatic or trance state, though these terms harbour their own ambiguities."[23] Perhaps because he was writing more than thirty years ago, Roberts was unable to resolve the ambiguities. At the present time, these no longer exist except in the minds of skeptics, including some exegetes. Actually, one interpretation that Roberts rejects is probably as close as one might have gotten to the contemporary understanding at the time he wrote. Roberts should not have dismissed the cross-cultural insight of Johannes Lindblom so cavalierly:

> What we read about the Israelite prophets in such passages ["hand of God"] fully corresponds to what ecstatic men and women the world over have had to say about the psycho-physical phenomena which accompany their ecstatic fits. The Finnish trance-preachers say that somebody seized them by the shoulder, that an invisible hand is put upon their forehead and their breast, etc. St. Birgitta of Sweden tells us that in the ecstasy she felt as if the hand of God were grasping her within her breast. The idea of a hand seizing or grasping one from without is a very appropriate expression indeed for the feeling of a psycho-physical convulsion or cramp so common in ecstatic experience.[24]

While Lindblom's comment ought to be nuanced or rephrased in the light of present knowledge about ASCs, his basic conclusion is correct. Research conducted by associates of The Cuyamungue Institute of Santa Fe,[25] which has been investigating ASCs since its founding in 1970, has discovered that those who practice deity-oriented ecstatic trance often feel a pressure at the top of the head when the trance begins (not a "psycho-physical convulsion or cramp"!). The ancients may well have been describing this same feeling as the "hand of God." Roberts's conclusion that "the peculiarly prophetic use of the expression 'hand of Yahweh' is dependent on a similarity between the prophetic phenomenon designated by the expression and certain symptoms of a pathological nature"[26] is simply mistaken and unfortunately casts him into the company of those—like modern psychiatrists!—who consider ASC experiences in general and those of Ezekiel in particular as aberrations rather than normal human experience.[27]

Ezekiel 1:4-28a: The Inaugural Vision (the Throne)

Block structures this section in this way:

- Introduction (v. 4);
- Living Creatures (vv. 5-15);
- Wheels (vv. 15-21);
- Platform and Throne (vv. 22-27);
- Concluding Colophon (v. 28a).[28]

Block further observes that words connoting brilliance, magnificence, and brightness permeate this section: brightness (v. 4), flashing fire (v. 4), gleaming bronze (v. 4), sparkling burnished bronze (v. 7), burning coals of fire (v. 13), bright fire (v. 13), lightning (vv. 13, 14), gleaming chrysolite (v. 16), and shining crystal (v. 22). According to cognitive neuroscience, these colors relate to neurological activity.[29] To see a bright color is a definite sign that one is in an ASC. Indeed, this color characterizes the first of three possible stages of ecstatic trance. In this first stage, the visionary sees a bright or white color and geometric patterns. Now, in the Israelite tradition, light is the manifestation of God's honor or glory (Isa 60:1; 62:1; Luke 2:9), that is, God's very self. The light takes the form of a cloud (Exod 24:15ff.) or fire (Deut 5:24) flashing brightly (Ezek 1:4, 27-28; 10:4). In this first stage of his ASC, Ezekiel is indeed experiencing "divine visions," realities in the realm of God. The bright colors he sees prove it.

Since the prevailing winds in this part of Mesopotamia are northwesterly from May to October, the north wind might not have impressed Ezekiel as much as the brightness, fire, and other indications that he is in trance (v. 4). The first thing he reports seeing are beings that have "the likeness of four living creatures" (vv. 5). These creatures have a composite form, that is, they share human and animal features (vv. 5-8). In stage two of an ASC experience, the visionary tries to make sense of the varied geometric patterns usually in bright colors perceived in stage one. In stage three, the objects a visionary sees are often transformed into unusual, sometimes bizarre, beings, and appear to be distortions of reality. Notice the words "likeness" (vv. 5, 10, 26, 27), "like" (vv. 7, 13, 14, 27, 28) and similar terms in this segment. Ezekiel says, "this is what I saw, but not exactly like that."

The living creatures of his vision would indicate he went rapidly to stage three of his ASC. While the living creatures might seem bizarre to westerners, according to Malina and Pilch,[30] they are the four Babylonian seasonal constellations in the sky, namely: Scorpioman, Leo, Taurus, and Pegasus or Thunderbird. Ezekiel has made immediate sense of his vision. He is looking into the night sky and interprets the constellations in line with Babylonian understanding. For this reason, Ezekiel is considered an astral prophet. He learns God's will from the stars in the sky. The fact that the rims of the wheels (v. 18; see vv. 15-21) on which the living creatures moved were "full of eyes" confirms this. The ancients called stars "eyes, " and thought them to be living entities. Constellated stars, called "full of eyes," were perceived as animate beings like persons or animals. Since Ezekiel sees all four constellations moving at once, his vantage point was high above the entire cosmos (vv. 4-11).[31]

According to ancient star lore, the constellations support the firmament, that solid bowl-like object that covers the earth. That is precisely what Ezekiel saw (vv. 22-23). Then he began to hear (or provide) the soundtrack of his vision. As often occurs in ASC experiences, soundtracks are neither always clear nor always verbal. They can be the sound of animals (bird calls) or music (familiar or unfamiliar melodies). Ezekiel hears these sounds: many waters, tumult as in a military encampment, the sound of *Shaddai*, a voice from above the firmament over the heads of the living creatures/constellations (vv. 24-25; cf. Ps. 18:8-16; 29:3; 104:3-4). The firmament in its turn serves as a platform for a throne above it, and on that throne is seated a humanoid figure radiating fire and brightness (vv. 26-28).

The prophet Micaiah reports this experience: "I saw the LORD sitting on his throne, and all the host of heaven standing beside him on his right hand and on his left" (1 Kings 22:19). Ezekiel's vision is similar to Micaiah's, and the throne is of special significance. It is the symbol of royal authority in a monarchic society. It symbolizes the monarch's ability effectively to control the behavior of the kingdom's subjects and to extract loyalty from these subjects. Now if these prophets see a throne, it is possible that their vision took place at night as they gazed at the sky. In ancient sky lore, a throne constellation was very well known. The famous Farnese sphere depicting the chief constellation of the second century B.C.E. places a throne with a non-visible occupant (Jupiter, the sky *deus pater*) near the North Pole over Leo and Cancer. Another familiar throne in the sky is that of Cassiopeia. The constellation Virgo-Isis is a throne occupant in Hellenistic Egyptian sky lore. In the Israelite tradition, Isaiah wrote, "Thus says the LORD: The sky is my throne" (Isa 66:1 LXX). So if Habel believes that Isaiah's vision has influenced Ezekiel's report, then both are looking at a constellation in the sky, quite likely at night. Matthew's Jesus echoes this belief: "But I say to you, Do not swear at all, either by heaven [the sky], for it is the throne of God, or by the earth, for it is his footstool . . ." (Matt 5:34-35; see also Matt 23:22).

From a form-critical perspective, Habel identifies Ezekiel 1:1-28a as the Divine Confrontation. According to him, the elements of this vision (living creatures, coals of fire, temple resonances, the throne, the royal form, and glory and the voice) are borrowed from Isaiah but translated into Ezekiel's perspective in Babylon. Yet as we know, all these elements are readily available in the latent discourse of this culture. Ezekiel might not have borrowed from Isaiah at all.

Ezekiel 1:28b–3:11: The Commissioning of Ezekiel

Blenkinsopp translates the Hebrew phrase מראה דמות כבוד־יהוה (*mrʾh dmwt kbwd-yhwh*) in verse 28b as "the appearance of the likeness of the effulgence of Yahweh."[32] He fittingly replaces the familiar word "glory" with "effulgence." Given the documented neurological features of ASC experiences appropriately reported in biblical literature with various synonyms for brightness, effulgence is a preferable term to glory. This notion was richly developed in the priestly traditions so familiar to Ezekiel (see, e.g., 1 Sam 4:21-22, the exile of the divine effulgence). In the P tradition, the mysterious effulgence was manifested in fire and storm clouds (see Exod 14:24-25) and permeated the tent-sanctuary as the Israelites meandered through their mythological exodus wanderings. Divine effulgence mediates the presence of God. Divine effulgence is, "so to speak, the recto of which the face of God is the verso."[33] In other words, what does God look like? A blinding light to which the eyes only gradually become accustomed.

The commissioning scene reports the intelligible soundtrack of Ezekiel's ASC experience. Moreover, Ezekiel is not simply reporting but interpreting as he reports.[34] Research in ASC experiences indicates that the visionary experience is not linear; it is rather jumbled (like a forward and backward, in- and out-moving, oscillating spiral). The visionary must write the experience down immediately afterward, lest he or she forget it. The visionary will also revise and reinterpret the experience with the passage of time as more details are remembered or a better interpretation suggests itself. Blenkinsopp's comment is apropos: "Here too [regarding the throne scene and visual experiences] we see how traditional motifs and ancient mythological themes associated with divine appearances have been fused in the moment of intense personal experience imperfectly recollected and even less perfectly articulated."[35]

In many ASC experiences reported in the Bible and elsewhere, the visionary is at first frightened by the experience. The one appearing usually offers a word of comfort: "Fear not," and then identifies self: "It is I" (e.g., Gen 15:1).[36] Ezekiel, however, is not afraid. God's threefold reminder not to be afraid concerns the challenge of Ezekiel's assignment rather than his response to the vision. Actually, Ezekiel's reaction to the vision is a gesture of homage ("fell upon my face," that is, prostrated). God is no stranger to Ezekiel the priest, and Ezekiel may have previously encountered God in ASCs. The divine effulgence that appears to Ezekiel here was also thought to appear at the conclusion of the ordination service of Levitical priests (see Lev 9:6). Indeed, on that occasion not only the priest but the people experienced the divine effulgence (Lev 9:23). They went into an ASC. The response was to prostrate themselves (Lev 9:24). Thus Ezekiel responds to the experience as expected, no doubt as he learned, and as he was accustomed to do when the shift in consciousness began.

God commanded Ezekiel to stand up, and the Spirit raised him to his feet (Ezek 2:1-2). Perhaps in reaction to ecstatic prophets ("the sons of the prophets"), eighth- to sixth-century B.C.E. prophets spoke very rarely of spirits. In contrast, Ezekiel does not hesitate to draw on the primitive tradition reflected in the careers of Elijah and Elisha in whom the Spirit was very active. "For Ezekiel, the spirit is an energy originating in the divine sphere which manifests itself as a force that propels (Ezek 1:12, 20-21), lifts up (Ezek 2:2; 3:12, 14, 24), transports (Ezek 8:3; 11:1, 24; 37:1), and energizes and renews both individual and community (Ezek 11:19; 18:31; 36:26-27; 37:14; 39:29)."[37]

In contemporary research by associates of The Cuyamungue Institute, the ritual that prepares for the inducement of an ASC invites the spirit world to participate. Moreover, the variety of ritual postures assumed by the visionary in an ASC experience tends to produce different effects. Some trance postures produce kinesthetic results more than visual experiences. That seems to be the case with Ezekiel in his trance. Whatever the nature of a spirit in the biblical tradition, it was always powerful. The spirit or wind of God hovered over the primordial waters and put order into the chaos (Genesis 1). When the spirit of the Lord came upon Samson, he killed a lion bare-handed (Judg 14:6) and thirty able-bodied men single-handedly (Judg 14:19). The spirit of the Lord came upon Mary, and she became pregnant (Matt 1:18). The last instance is explicitly explained as the activity of a good spirit. Ezekiel was lifted to his feet from a prone position by a mighty wind or spirit. Such experiences have been documented to occur in ASCs.

The chief contents of the soundtrack to Ezekiel's vision are two commissioning speeches: Ezekiel 2:3-7 and 3:4-11. This is entirely in accord with the main functions of ASCs: they help visionary select a new path in life, or they provide answers to puzzling questions.[38] In the first speech, God sends Ezekiel to impudent and stubborn fellow ethnics. The key word is "send" (see Ezek 2:3, 4, 3:5, 6; compare Exod 3:10; Judg 6:14; Isa 6:8). Thus, the speech reveals the name of the sender, Yahweh; the name of the messenger, Ezekiel, and the target audience, the people of Israel in exile. Ezekiel is formally commissioned as a spokesperson for God.

A vision of a scroll now separated the first from the second commissioning speech (Ezek 2:8–3:3). The papyrus is written on both sides containing "words of lamentation and mourning and woe" (Ezek 2:10). Its message is obviously bad news. God commands Ezekiel to eat the scroll (2:8; 3:1) and then sends him to speak its contents to the house of Israel. Ezekiel obeys and finds that the scroll tasted as sweet as honey. Recalling that Ezekiel is still in an ASC, his vision and action are totally comprehensible. Once again, research associates in The Cuyamungue Institute report that while some ASCs are visual and others more kinesthetic, some subjects also detect aromas or hear sounds during an ASC which are not physically present and which no one else in the group detects or hears.[39]

A question commonly asked by Western readers is, Did he eat the scroll in vision or in reality? The same question has been posed concerning the Lukan report of the Risen Jesus eating a piece of broiled fish (Luke 24:41-42). The answer to both questions, of course, is yes![40] Block makes a relevant observation. "The reader will observe a blurring of boundaries between visions and reality in all of Ezekiel's visions."[41] He further notes that this is true of other prophets such as Isaiah, Daniel, Zechariah, among the rest. Still, he rightly insists that the experience is real. Indeed it is, and to ask whether Ezekiel ate the scroll in vision or reality is to fail to appreciate that visions or ASCs are very real, an important dimension of reality. Human beings are capable of at least twenty different levels of awareness or states of consciousness.[42] They are all real. Ezekiel's experience of eating the scroll is as "real" as an erotic dream. Which part of that experience is real, and which part is only dream? That the scroll tasted sweet is very likely influenced by the latent discourse of Ezekiel's culture. The psalmist sings: "How sweet are thy words to my taste, sweeter than honey to my mouth!" (Ps 119:103; see also Ps 19:11; Jer 15:16).

The second commissioning speech (Ezek 3:4-11) assures the prophet that God has equipped him for his task. God has given him the message and the fortitude. Whereas previously the people were described as rebellious, now they are described as unresponsive. Quite in accord with ethnographic data on ASCs as noted above, the soundtrack of Ezekiel's vision provides him with new information and charts yet another dimension of his career for him.

Once again returning to the form-critical analysis, Habel restricts the commission to Ezekiel 2:3-5.[43] While he admits that there is no explicit objection to the commission in the passage, he believes it is implied in Ezekiel 2:6, 8. One can deduce from the assurance (Ezek 2:6-7) that he was indeed fearful and perhaps personally rebellious against his assignment. In other words, he was not much different from his fellow ethnics. From the perspective of ASCs as noted above (recall the reflection on "fear not"), Habel's discussion here does not seem well founded. Deducing objections where none is explicit is difficult to reconcile with the typical ASC experience. Finally, while Habel identifies Ezekiel 2:8—3:11 as the sign confirming Yahweh's intention, he claims it is best summed up in Ezekiel 3:26-27. Ezekiel's ensuing dumbness symbolizes that he will be able to speak only what and when God wants him to speak. More about this later.

Ezekiel 3:12-15: Preparation of Ezekiel: His Return to the Field of Service

As his call vision is concluding, Ezekiel takes a brief spirit journey. The RSV translation is misleading: "The Spirit lifted me up and took me away, and I went in bitterness in the heat of my spirit, the hand of the LORD being upon me" (Ezek 3:14). The problem is with "bitterness" and "heat." While some visionaries experience a surge of body temperature during an ASC, "bitterness" is difficult to explain. Brownlee offers a preferable translation: "I soared aloft in the ecstasy of my spirit, as Yahweh's hand overpowered me."[44] As already explained above, "the hand of God" or "Yahweh's hand" expresses one physiological aspect of being in an ASC. The new idea that Ezekiel introduces here is that he traveled in his ASC. Technically, anthropologists call such travel "soul-loss" or a "sky journey." Since he is already in Babylon (Ezek 1:1, 3), the wind or spirit that lifted him up (Ezek 3:12) returned him from the isolated place of his vision to the company of the exiles at Tel-abib (Ezek 3:15).[45] According to Block, six times in the book of Ezekiel does he identify the spirit as an "agent of conveyance."[46] So to repeat, this spirit journey (and the others taken by Ezekiel) are normal experiences in ASCs.[47]

At the end of his journey, he sat overwhelmed in the midst of the exiles for seven days. Blenkinsopp suggests that Ezekiel's temporary catatonic state was a psychologically plausible aftereffect of his ecstatic exultation.[48] This is certainly possible if one adds to it Block's observation that the charge to go and proclaim to an unresponsive audience, among other things, left Ezekiel in a wretched state.[49] From a cultural perspective, the scenario is that Ezekiel, a collectivistic personality who derives his identity and draws energy from the group, has been set by God against this very group! The task God assigns him is equivalent to committing social suicide. That would render any collectivistic person speechless.[50]

Ezekiel 3:16-21: Ezekiel as Sentry or Watchman

Some scholars consider these verses a secondary insertion that breaks the flow of ideas from verse 16a to verse 22,[51] but I follow Block who believes that Ezekiel 3:1-9 is an expansion and reapplication of 3:16-21. The sentry was an important person who was to warn a city or village of the approaching invasion by enemies. What is painful here is that Yahweh is the one attacking! Having reflected on his ASC experience for seven days, Ezekiel is now prepared to receive still a further charge from Yahweh. He is to summon fellow collectivistic personalities to individual responsibility. There can be no passing of the buck, no hiding behind the group. Ezekiel himself is not exempt. He will be held accountable for the way in which he fulfills his assignment just as each listener will be held accountable for his or her response.

Ezekiel 3:22-27: Initiation of Ezekiel (loss of speech)

Once again Ezekiel enters an ASC: the "hand of the LORD" was upon him, the spirit possessed him and stood him upright (after he had prostrated in homage before the "glory of the LORD" (Ezek 3:22-24). It is worth noting that ASC experiences are not necessarily continuous. This means that during an ASC experience a visionary might move through various levels of awareness and even return to "normal waking consciousness." This is surely the case with the report of Ezekiel's call vision.

Yahweh's message to him had three parts: he was to go home and isolate himself; the exiles will bind him and circumscribe his movements; Yahweh will tongue-tie him (vv. 24-27). While psychologists and psychiatrists have floated stunning speculation about Ezekiel's mental health at this point,[52] scholars on balance believe that it is best to interpret Ezekiel's muteness as both actual and metaphorical, physical and symbolic.[53] Blenkinsopp thinks it best to take the case as genuine aphasia that resulted from a relentless accumulation of jarring emotional experiences in Ezekiel's life.[54] But perhaps the larger question for Ezekiel in his social system is not *what* but rather *who* caused or allowed such an accumulation of life crisis situations: his wife's death combined with the destruction of the city and temple to which he was deeply attached; his elite group being exiled in a hostile country; living in a swampy lowland climate; the social dissonance in his loss of status as priest; the hostility of his compatriots. All these negative events were attributable to the God of Israel. The overwhelming theological dissonance alone could sufficiently account for his aphasia. According to Ezekiel 24:27, when news of the fall of Jerusalem reached Ezekiel, the same God who caused those untoward events and made him speechless now opened his mouth to speak again.

Ezekiel's hindsight interpretation of his experiences and the events of which he spoke was that his mission was to speak *only* what God wanted him to say and *only when* God wanted him to say it. He was, after all, able verbally to interpret his sign actions and deliver other oracles during this period of silence. His experience of confinement, restriction, and transient speechless were his initiation into the prophetic office. Habel's form-critical identification of Ezekiel's muteness in 3:16-17 as a symbol that he could only speak what God planted on his lips is thus confirmed by exegetical consensus.

Conclusion

Habel convincingly argued that the real-life event that gave rise to the literary form of the call narratives was Abraham's commissioning of his servant to get a wife for his son, Isaac (Genesis 24).[55] He concludes:

> If the *Gattung* arises from the practice of an ambassador publicly presenting his credentials before the appropriate audience,

then it seems logical that the goal of the prophetic formulation of the call in this *Gattung* is to announce publicly that Yahweh commissioned the prophet in question to act as His representative. Thus the word of the call narrative gives the individual's credentials as a prophet, messenger and ambassador from the heavenly council. The word summarized the ultimate commission from the Master.

What is lacking in Habel's analysis is recognition that the calls of individuals to be prophets or messengers of God took place in ASCs. Indeed, Habel denied it. That some prophets adopted this "literary form" to describe their call is easy to explain. It is not simply that they were struggling to put the ineffable into words and reached for the stereotypical. Rather, the *Gattung* that Habel and other form critics identify in literature are, in the words of Bruce Malina, "culturally specific wording patterns that derive from the social system. Genre always derives from the social system since genres are not part of language or the linguistic system." Since the social system also specifies the behavioral pattern by which ASCs are experienced and interpreted, it is quite plausible that visionaries did behave in just the way the literary pattern reports.[56] The report of Ezekiel's call vision fits the pattern of ASC experiences described by contemporary cognitive neuroscience and cultural anthropology.

Nahum—Ethnicity and Stereotypes

ANTHROPOLOGICAL INSIGHTS INTO NAHUM'S LITERARY HISTORY

Anselm C. Hagedorn

In dealing with the redaction history of Nahum 1–3, Anselm Hagedorn proposes that the original book of Nahum (which consisted of the oracles now located in chapter 3) underwent at least three redactions. He then proceeds to interpret the language used. Rather than simply using form-critical or traditio-historical approaches, he applies a model from cultural anthropology to explain some linguistic features. On the basis of recent research into ethnicity, he explains the reasons for the chronological development of the book of Nahum. He suggests that the notions of ethnicity seem to change over time and correspond to different stages in the development of the book. At the same time, the stereotypes employed to characterize the other remain stable and do not seem to be affected by the change of the reference.

τὸν ξένο καὶ τὸν ἐχθρὸ τὸν εἴδαμε στὸν καθρέφτη
—G. Seferis, Μυθιστόρημα 4 (Ἀργοναῦτες)[1]

While working on a literary-critical analysis of the book of Nahum, I realized that different attitudes to "the other" or more precisely Nineveh and Assyria seem to correspond to the different redactional layers of the book. In this essay I will look at the picture of "the other" in a little more detail, using recent anthropological research on stereotypes and ethnicity.

Literary and Historical Issues

The book of Nahum commences with a double heading, a feature that is unique in the Book of the Twelve. The first part of the heading, "An oracle concerning Nineveh" (משׂא נינוה), refers to the content of the book. The second part, however, "The book of the vision of Nahum the Elkoshite" (ספר חזון נחום האלקשׁי), attributes the literary work as a whole to the authorship of the otherwise unknown prophet Nahum the Elkoshite. Naturally, such a double heading raises some suspicion regarding the literary origin of the book and, ever since Heinrich Ewald's comments on the prophet,[2] scholars have used the superscription as a point of departure for tracing literary growth. Yet this does not mean that attempts to read the book as a unified whole cannot be successful, as the impressive studies by Klaas Spronk (1997), Peter Machinist (1997), Bob Becking (1995), and J. J. M. Roberts (1991) have shown.

Within the Book of the Twelve the only other book devoted to an announcement against one specified foreign people is Obadiah. Its twenty-one verses are directed against Edom (כה־אמר אדני יהוה לאדום) and explicitly described as a vision (חזון) of the prophet. However, we need to remind ourselves that Nahum speaks against "Nineveh" (cf. Isa 17:1 [משׂא דמשׂק] and Isa 23:1 [משׂא צר]), i.e., a concrete city, and one has to ask whether the city is used as *pars pro toto* for Assyria.[3]

Only the book of Nahum is explicitly called "book" (ספר) in the superscription. The final compiler/redactor wants to stress his "literary awareness"[4] and to provide the prophecy with a certain physical presence within society (cf. Deut 17:18). The book—or better, the scroll—then serves as "a book of remembrance" (ספר זכרון; Mal 3:16) of the destruction of Nineveh and of the acts of YHWH.

After the heading we find a theophanic hymn that (including all expansions) runs until Nahum 1:10.[5] This psalm is probably part of a tradition (*Traditionsstück*) and does not use any elements from the corpus of the book. Rather, one gets the impression that the text is concerned with the universal judgment of the world—in contrast to the latter part of the book (Nah 3:11, 13), the enemies mentioned (Nah 1:2, 8) seem to refer to their totality, i.e., to the enemies from outside as well as to enemies from the inside. This all points to a very late origin of the passage.[6] Furthermore, the feminine suffix in מקומה ("her place") in Nahum 1:8 clearly refers to Nineveh in Nahum 1:1a.[7] This implies that the psalm must be younger than the original collection under the heading מַשָּׂא נִינְוֵה.

The Oldest Stratum of the Book of Nahum

Following the insights of Klaus Seybold we are postulating that the oldest part of the book consisted of a cycle of Nineveh songs.[8] These songs are concerned with the fate of the city. It is one of the remarkable facts of this oldest kernel that all forms of religious legitimation or divine acts are missing. Hence it is hardly surprising that Nahum has been labeled a cultic prophet who simply announces doom for the enemies of Judah.[9] The original edition of the book commenced in Nahum 2:2. A complex verse with a puzzling change in suffixes:

עלה מפיץ על־פניך
נצור מצרה צפה־דרך
חזק מתנים אמץ כח מאד:

The NRSV translates like this:

A shatterer has come up against you.
Guard the ramparts; watch the road;
gird your loins; collect all your strength.

The first line is directed against a feminine entity. If one maintains the feminine suffix,[10] the only possible reference can be Nineveh from the first part of the superscription (מַשָּׂא נִינְוֵה), since the immediately preceding feminine form Judah in Nahum 2:1 can hardly be addressed here. The following three masculine imperatives (צפה, חזק, and אמץ) must refer to the ruler of the city, who is only once explicitly mentioned by name (Nah 3:18), but often referred to (cf. Nah 2:6).[11] There follows a description of the (first) attack against the city (Nah 2:2, 4-5), before the attention is turned to the defenders (Nah 2:6, 8-11) and a brief description of the status of the city is given in Nahum 2:7 (שַׁעֲרֵי הַנְּהָרוֹת נִפְתָּחוּ וְהַהֵיכָל נָמוֹג). It is a characteristic feature of this oldest edition that the language employed is very short—the reader never gets a complete report but only staccato-like impressions of the siege and conquest of Nineveh. If one assumes that the first edition has been written down before the fall of the city, it is hardly surprising that the text only employs general metaphors. Even in those verses where one could think of concrete information, the text only repeats general knowledge. Thus, for example, it was a well-known fact that several city gates of Nineveh led towards the river Tigris[12] so that Nahum 2:7 (שערי הנהרות) does not display any "local knowledge." The same can be said of the attribute פרק מלאה in Nahum 3:1bα. The only concrete historical knowledge in this stratum of the book of Nahum—and indeed in the book as a whole—is the reference to the sack of Thebes at the hand of the Assyrians in 634/3 B.C.E. However, this *terminus post quem* should not be used as an argument for accuracy, since Nahum's description of Thebes is equally vague[13] (a fact supported by the later interpretation of the text in the Targum, where No-Ammon can now refer to Alexandria).[14] All this seems to support a dating of the oldest part of the book to a period before the sack of Nineveh in 612 B.C.E.[15] This position can be upheld despite the statement "wasted is Nineveh" (שדדה נינוה)[16] in Nahum 3:7. As it stands now, Nahum 3:7aβ is introduced as a quote (ואמר) and framed by the second extensive redaction of the book that introduces several theological aspects and is close to the language and theology of Deutero-Isaiah.

In order to combine the three—probably independent—oracles of doom for Nineveh (Nah 2:2, 4-11; 3:1-7aβ; 3:8-15) to a first short flyer that was then circulated as משא נינוה, a first editor (or redactor) added a compositional layer that uses images of the powerful city of Nineveh and stresses that these symbols of power will vanish in the conquest. In contrast to the obvious poetic structure and language of the kernel, these additions are kept in prose-like language. We encounter the first compositional addition in Nahum 2:12-14, where the city and its inhabitants are likened to a family of lions in their den. The use of the relative particle אשר especially points to prose here.[17] Further additions can be found in Nahum 3:4 and 3:16-19. It is a striking feature of these additions that they all describe a condition without using any taunts or irony—a fact that caused some difficulties for later editors who the added ילק פשט ויעף in Nahum 3:16b and the final taunt "For upon whom has not come your unceasing evil" (כי על־מי לא־עברה רעתך תמיד) in Nahum 3:19bβ. Although one can only speculate why such irony is missing, the anonymous character of the prophecy and its place of origin (Jerusalem during the time of the reign of Manasseh) point to the fact that such subversive prophecy bore a certain risk for its author: therefore the doom for Nineveh is described only in the most general terms.

The Second Layer of Redaction

All this changes during the second significant redaction that reworked the "The oracle concerning Nineveh" (משא נינוה) during the Babylonian period. Prerequisite for this addition was the fact that Nineveh indeed fell in 612 B.C.E., thus providing proof for the authenticity of the prophecy. We encounter the first words of this redaction in Nahum 1:11, a problematic verse, since the feminine suffix in Nahum 1:11a (ממך יצא; "From you came out. . .") is in the need of a feminine reference word and the only feminine word encountered so far has been Nineveh in Nahum 1:1a.[18] The linguistic evidence seems to support such a view: The unusual construction מן + suffix followed by יצא is found seven times in the Hebrew Bible (Gen 17:6; Isa 49:17; Ezek 5:4; Nah 1:11; Zech 10:4; Job 28:5; Dan 8:9) and describes in the book of Nahum the going out from a place—thus it is similar to the more common construction יצא מן. In such a way, for example, the book of Micah can speak of God, saying, "For behold the LORD is coming forth out of his place" (כי־הנה יהוה יצא ממקמו; Mic 1:3a) and Deuteronomy constructs in a similar way when it refers to the Cretans in Deut 2:23 ("the Caphtorim who came forth from Caphtor"; כפתרים היצאים מכפור).

The person who comes forth from Nineveh is described as "plotting evil against the LORD" (חשב על־יהוה רעה), where the masculine participle (חשב) identifies the person as the (Assyrian) king who resides in Nineveh. In contrast to Nahum 2:1, the person in Nahum 1:11 "plotting villainy" (יעץ בליעל) is not yet personified.[19] Rather, בליעל is used in an attributive sense here, similar, for example, to the use in Proverbs 6:12 (אדם בליעל). Furthermore, YHWH is introduced, who will now bring destruction to the enemies and salvation to Judah.

This is done in the divine speech in Nahum 1:12-14. The passage is again full of changes in person. At the same time, the passage uses language well known from the Deuteronomistic parts of the Bible, when it speaks of "the graven and molten image" (פסל ומסכה; cf. Deut 27:15; Judg 17:3, 4; 18:14, 17, 18; Isa 42:17; Hab 2:8), as well as employing elements that show a certain familiarity with the treaty literature of the ancient Near East.[20] These features of the pericope make it unlikely that the text originated in preexilic times.

Furthermore, the problematic words "because you are vile" (כי קלות) in Nahum 1:14b sound like a conclusion to an oracle of doom for the (Assyrian) king.[21] We encounter the work of this redaction on two further places: Nahum 2:14 and 3:5-7*. On both occasions the addition is introduced with the same formula: "Behold I am unto you, saying of the LORD of Hosts" (הנני אליך נאם יהוה צבאות), which again stresses that the destruction of Nineveh is now seen as an act of the hand of God.[22] It is interesting that elements from the compositional layer of the book are taken up and are transformed. For example, the image of the powerful family of lions, which appears in in Nahum 2:12-13 as an image for the strength of the Assyrian army (cf. the similar use in 2 Sam 1:23; Isa 15:9; Jer 2:5; 4:7; 50:17; Ps 57:4; 58:6; 91:13) now triggers the remark, "the sword will devour your lion's whelps" (וכפיריך תאכל חרב) in Nahum 2:14. The same can be said of the image of the harlot. In Nahum 3:4 the harlot is used to describe the fascination and power that Nineveh exercises over her enemies (or better subjects). In contrast to such a view Nahum 3:5-7* takes up the female imagery and transforms it into a public shaming at the hand of YHWH. This second layer (probably from the time of the exile) makes it abundantly clear that YHWH will be responsible for the destruction of Nineveh—in accord with exilic theology and thinking, a concrete political entity is replaced by the divinity who now acts on behalf of his subjects.

The Third Layer of Editing

The Persian period prompts a third reworking of the Book of Nahum. Under the influence of Deutero-Isaianic thinking (cf. Isa 52:7 with Nah 2:1), the aspect of restoration for Judah is introduced (Nah 2:1, 3). This is done by taking up vocabulary from the previous layer: For example, בליעל is—just as at Qumran later on—now a concrete person.[23]

As already mentioned above, the latest stage of the expansion of the book of Nahum is found in the theophanic hymn in Nahum 1:2-10. As has been the case with the other expansion from the Babylonian period, the hymn is constructed with a view to the first part of the heading. This is seen most clearly in the use of "her place" (מקומה) in Nahum 1:8, since the suffix can only refer to the feminine form Nineveh in Nahum 1:1a. Also, the enemies encountered in the hymn are no longer just enemies from the outside but refer to adversaries inside and outside the community. This is a strong indication for placing this part of the text in the Hellenistic period. Only at this point is the anonymous prophecy identified with the prophet Nahum. Here, at this final stage, the hymn now offers us a lens through which the composite work can be read and utilized at almost any time in history.

Conclusion on the Redactional Process

In conclusion, we find a triple expansion of the original nucleus of the book.

In the oldest edition (Nah 2:2, 4-13; 3:1—4:7*; 3:8-19*) of the book, which can be dated after the fall of Thebes in 663 B.C.E. and before the sack of Nineveh in 612 B.C.E., we simply find an announcement of the immediate destruction of the Assyrian capital at the hands of the invading Babylonian army. It is a striking feature of this prophecy that it does not carry any religious overtones and it has rightly been described by Seybold as "profane prophecy."[24] This prophecy is not yet attached to any named prophet, but simply circulated anonymously as an "oracle concerning Nineveh" (משא נינוה).

After the sack of Nineveh and under the influence of the new Babylonian oppression, a first addition to the book is made in exilic times (Nah 1:11-14; 2:14; 3:5-7*). Now theology is introduced and the fall of the Assyrian Empire begins to be attributed to the intervention of the God of Israel. At the same time, the familiar language of the Near Eastern treaty literature is used—a fact to which we will return below.

After two smaller additions from the Persian period, focusing on the restoration of Israel (Nah 2:1, 3), a final addition is made in Hellenistic times (Nah 1:1b-10). Together with the so-called psalm that shifts the ethnic boundaries of the prophecy, the book is now said to be authored by the otherwise unknown figure of Nahum the Elkoshite and has thus been converted into a classic prophetic writing that attributes the fall of Nineveh to the action of a "jealous and avenging God of Israel."

Anthropological Insights

Probably the most significant progress in the study of stereotypes and ethnicity has been the observation of the relational aspect of both concepts.[25] Therefore, anthropologists have been able to move beyond seeing ethnicity as a biological phenomenon—the use of the rather problematic term "race" can thus be avoided.[26] (However, we should note that recent anthropological research has suggested that the term "race" should be replaced by the term "culture.")[27]

Following these groundbreaking insights we are using the research by the Norwegian anthropologist Thomas Eriksen and are able to offer the following definition of the term *ethnicity*:

Ethnicity is an aspect of social relationship between agents who
consider themselves as culturally distinctive from members of
other groups which whom they have a minimum of regular
interaction.[28]

This definition shows that the boundaries of ethnicity—or an ethnic
group, for that matter—are never static but fluid entities that change
with the adaptation to changes in the "other," i.e., the group that is perceived as an opponent from which one has to distinguish itself.

Further assistance in explaining ethnicity comes from Jonathan
Hall:

The criteria of ethnicity are the definitional set of attributes by
which membership in an ethnic group is ultimately determined.
They are the result of a series of conscious and socially embedded choices, which attach significance to certain criteria from a
universal set while ignoring others.[29]

Ethnicity, therefore, creates an "imagined community," since each
member of an ethnic group will never meet most of his or her fellow
members but will imagine he or she can "know" them all by attributing
to them the same notion of ethnicity and thus expressing community
with them.[30] An ethnic group defines itself by the perceived or imagined
dissimilarities such as history, religion, physical and cultural appearance,[31] language, etc., that seem to exist between itself and others.[32]
Anthropological research has shown that such a notion of ethnicity does
not necessarily need to be connected to a specific physical entity such as
land.[33] Rather, following the proposal put forward by Fredrik Barth,
ethnicity should be seen as a process of self-ascriptive group-belonging
where the members manifest a (changeable) set of signs of cultural difference that function to mark and defend social boundaries and to channel and structure interactions and exchange across those boundaries.[34]
A further point already mentioned in Barth and later developed by
Jonathan Hall is the fact that ethnicity often emerges in the context of
conquest, migration, or the acquisition of resources by one group at the
expense of others.[35]

Ethnicity is furthermore "conceptualized as relationships, not of difference or perceived difference, but of denied or disguised resemblance."[36] This means that ethnic identities tend to emerge during
processes of systematically forgetting most of the shared features or felt
similarities between groups.[37]

If that is so, it is hardly surprising that *stereotypes* figure prominently as part of the discursive character of ethnicity.[38] Basically speaking, stereotypes do represent a cruel way of "doing things with words" (J. L. Austin). Anthropologists have noted that elites encourage the construction of stereotypes; therefore, "stereotypes do serve the interests of power, however, they carry the possibility of subversion and sometimes are used to achieve it."[39]

Stereotypes are an important factor or structuring principle within the ethnic classification—or, in other words, they are used to distinguished between "Us and Them."[40] Of course, the act of stereotyping is by definition reductive and thus serves as a discursive weapon.[41] Michael Herzfeld helpfully comments:

> Stereotypes are both instrument and symbol of hegemony, as they flood the hidden corners of everyday awareness. Like a barium enema, they brightly outline the cultural indigestion of which the national patient so bitterly complains.[42]

The process of stereotyping aims at an interpretation of reality.[43] But since one usually shares stereotypes with others socially proximate to oneself, they also have social functions—in various ways affecting how groups to which one belongs respond to other groups. Therefore, we can structure the phenomenon of stereotyping into five areas:

i. People are ready to characterize large human groups on the basis of a few rather crude attributes;
ii. these stereotypes are very hard to change;
iii. they are learned at a very young age;
iv. they become more pronounced and hostile with a rise in tension between groups; and
v. they are harmful when enunciated in the context of social conflict.[44]

Needless to say that stereotypes can be used in a negative as well as in a positive and self-affirming way.[45]

For our purpose we will use the tripartite concept of ethnicity developed by the British sociologist Simon Harrison, who defines cultural difference as denied resemblance.[46] Surveying fieldwork done on so-called ethnic minorities, he discovers some rather puzzling results. Despite the fact that difference—or felt difference, for that matter—is believed to lie at the heart of ethnicity (and also nationalism in his view), it can be shown "that identities ostensibly 'different' from one another are often remarkably similar."[47] This is to say that most of the groups studied regarded their "ethnicity" as distinctive and pointed to several markers of their distinctiveness (in Harrison's paper to the role of the mother)— "[y]et in sharing this notion they were indistinguishable."[48] For Harrison, this points to the possibility of cultural borrowing and emulation across even the strictest social boundaries. This relational aspect of ethnicity involves a complicated process in which common features are systematically forgotten.[49] This forgetting can lead to grotesque results, such as a fairly recent attempt to rename Turkish coffee Byzantine coffee (καφές βυζαντινό) in some Greek cafés. All this confirms Barth's view that ethnicity is a relational construct and also points to the fact that at the same time "constructs of difference and of shared identity always exist together."[50] Naturally, contrast is part of every group-defining process; however, it only arises if the group feels it necessary— on the basis of resemblance—to differentiate themselves from the others. Therefore, "[w]hat appear as ethnic or national 'differences' are, at another level, more or less elaborate and effortful attempts by groups to forget, deny, or obscure their resemblances."[51]

Harrison then continues to unpack the "notion of cultural difference." His starting point for such an unpacking is Edward Said's observation in 1979 that Europeans very often used the Orient as a negative foil and that "European culture gained in strength and identity by setting itself off against the Orient as a sort of surrogate and even underground self."[52] Along similar veins, Johannes Fabian, in his 1983 study "Time and the Other," has elaborated on the complex processes at work, when (Western) anthropologists study so called "primitive" societies.[53] In contrast to developments in recent cultural anthropology, Harrison does not argue that it is only possible to study a society thoroughly if the observer has always been part of that culture himself or herself.[54] Rather, he uses the (often) negative evaluation of the other, to sketch out "three distinguishable relations to the self."[55] These are, *difference-as-inferiority, difference-as-superiority,* and *difference-as-equality*. Here, difference-as-inferiority is defined as follows:

[T]he cultural Other is made to represent censored and disclaimed attributes of the Self. On the surface, the Other therefore appears essentially alien. But behind this facade or radical alterity lurks a hidden identity between Self and Other, in which the Other represents what Said called "a sort of surrogate and even underground self." . . .[56]

In other words, all those attributes that one is keen to suppress in one's own personality or ethnic group are transferred to the other—this other is in turn, then, labeled negatively. However, the negative attributes are in a way the secret desires or identities of the labeling group. A good test-case for such an evaluation of the other is the scholarly construct of "primitive society":

> The anthropologists took this primitive society as their special subject, but in practice primitive society proved to be their own society (as they understood it) seen in a distorting mirror. For them modern society was defined above all by the territorial state, the monogamous family and private property. Primitive society therefore must have been nomadic, ordered by blood ties, sexually promiscuous and communist.[57]

Such a process naturally involves two-way stereotyping, since every image we create of the other is tied—subconsciously—to a stereotypic image of ourselves.[58] This process in itself is not simply an exercise that serves to valorize one's own self positively. Rather, it has to be seen as ambivalent, incorporating a "double movement," since "the Other represents a kind of screen upon which both the despised and the desired aspects of the Self can be projected, so that the dialectics of sameness and difference is resolved into a kind of difference *in* sameness."[59]

In a second step, Harrison moves beyond this purely negative way of classification. By looking at some forms of nationalism within Australian society, he is able to detect a process that he labels *difference-as-equality*:

> [T]he Other is conceived as essentially similar culturally to the Self, indeed in some respects far too much so. Here, actors define their ethnic or national identities by marking themselves off contrastively from others with whom they are categorized as sharing common features of identity at some more inclusive level.[60]

This form of ethnicity is triggered by the recognition of similarities one shares with the "other." It is necessary to have the perceived other in close proximity, since "[i]t is those who imagine they have most in common...who are most likely to categorize each other as different, as opposites or inversions of one another."[61]

Finally, utilizing insights from the work of Michael Taussig, Harrison develops a third pattern of ethnic group differentiation, which he calls *difference-as-superiority*:

> [P]attern of muted and denied identification with the Other that occurs in the emulation of other, powerful and prestigious, ethnic or national identities. Here, a culturally foreign other is valorized positively rather than negatively, attributed with that superiority Armstrong . . . calls "cultural ascendancy."[62]

Following Taussig's theory he is able to speak of *mimesis*, a process that "involves the attribution of certain kinds of cultural superiority to the Other."[63] This leads to an intense identification with the other so that mimesis can be defined as "an imitation that seeks merger with its model, overcoming the distinction between Self and Other."[64] Within the process, borrowing of certain cultural markers such as language, etc., remains at the margins, if it is employed at all.

In summing up the above insights, we have to note that a notion of ethnicity (and cultural distinctiveness) without a minimum degree of knowledge of or contact with "the Other" is hardly possible. Furthermore, Max Weber's insight that conflict generally triggers ethnicity finds support in current anthropological work: "[G]roups can have strong mimetic attraction to those with whom they are in conflict or whom they oppose in some way, and can imitate them."[65] On the other hand, (ethnic) identity has to be seen as a "scarce resource," in need of protection.[66] Ethnic sentiments do not necessarily remain static and groups are generally able to adopt their expressions of ethnicity to changes in the reference group. This does not have to imply that the stereotypes employed change as well; rather, it is possible to transfer set stereotypes to a new entity. Also, Michael Herzfeld has pointed to the fact that social and cultural segmentation within an ethnic group is possible and indeed often encouraged.[67] If ethnicity can—in a way—be described as a mirroring process, the Self is able to recognize itself by looking in the mirror called the "Other."

Application to the Book of Nahum

In the following we will utilize the above anthropological insights in our work on the book of the prophet Nahum. Our leading interpretative strand will be the theory that a change in the reference group prompts a change in the attitude toward the "Other" that results in a different view of ethnicity. We are aware of the salient problems of an application of recent ethnographic models to ancient texts as well as the fact that the text first and foremost does not tell us any "historical reality" but is rather a document of the historic location(s) of its author(s). However, anthropological discourse has shown that comparative enterprises "emerge as a credible alternative to postmodernist defeatism."[68] In addition to such theoretical considerations, distant comparisons of social conditions seem to replace the more traditional analysis of social structures.[69] Our enterprise has to be seen as such an analysis of the social conditions in which the book of Nahum originated, since the work can be defined as expressions of "symbolic practices by which social groups and categories represent their identities."[70]

Right from the beginning of the oldest part of the book of Nahum we do encounter "the Other," since the work is titled *An oracle concerning Nineveh*. In contrast to later use of the phrase in the Hebrew Bible (Jonah), Nineveh has not yet become the symbol for a metropolis—rather, it is the actual capital of Assyria. Naturally, in a "high context society" (i.e., a society where more meaning is assumed than actually said)[71] this name evokes certain images and we can probably argue that the anonymous author of the book of Nahum aims at describing the relationship between Judah and Assyria as an embodiment of "difference as superiority." This means that the author of the first edition of Nahum is fully aware of the potential powers of Nineveh, while at the same time acknowledging the approaching force of the Babylonian attackers that will eventually topple Assyria. Consider Nahum 2:11:

> What became of the lions' den, the cave of the young lions,
> where the lion goes, and the lion's cubs, with no one to disturb them?
> The lion has torn enough for his whelps and strangled prey for his lionesses; he has filled his caves with prey and his dens with torn flesh.

Since during such a process expressions of cultural superiority are part of the mimetic structure, powerful images are employed to describe Assyria and its concrete embodiment—the city of Nineveh.

In what follows the author of Nahum begins to subvert such a picture of superiority of Nineveh by describing how he imagines the sack of the city at the hand of the Babylonians. Surprisingly, this is done by using fairly general language of conquest:

> A shatterer has come up against you.
> Guard the ramparts; watch the road;
> gird your loins; collect all your strength. (Nah 2:1)

Any appeal to a higher authority is missing and no specific negative labels are found. Even in those passages where the author is reflecting on the state of Nineveh, he does this exclusively by using images of power (lion, harlot) and multitude (merchants, guards, etc.). Despite the absence of any occurrence of Judah, we realize that the picture of the powerful Assyrian capital is used as a sign of cultural difference, marking boundaries. Nineveh is framed between the Egyptian city of Thebes, which Assyria conquered some years earlier, and the immediate sack by the Babylonians.

> Are you better than Thebes that sat by the Nile,
>   her rampart a sea, water her wall? (Nah 3:8)

The conquest of Egypt—once the image of Assyrian power and hegemony—is now used in an ironic way to announce the doom for Nineveh.

By using images of (fallen) power, Judah reflects on her own status while maintaining a sort of "neutrality," which is necessary to avoid any open conflict with the still-existing hegemonic powers. By acknowledging the superiority of Assyria and Babylon, the author of Nahum distances himself from any direct interchange or interaction and carefully avoids getting involved in the fall of the Assyrian capital. For precisely that reason he is able to close his book with the rather general words:

> All who hear news about you clap their hands over you. (Nah 3:19)

A change of the reference group prompts a change in the discourse of ethnicity as well as in the stereotypes employed. Using the terminology of Simon Harrison we can observe that the difference is now perceived as a "difference-as-inferiority." The perception of the Other has changed and one is now careful to focus on one's own status. The inferiority is stressed by introducing a theological dimension and thus appealing to a higher agency—i.e., God—who replaces Babylon as the original oppressor of the oldest edition. Due to the rising tension between the groups of Israel/Judah and the Babylonians, the stereotyping becomes more and more pronounced and hostile:

> From you one has gone out who plots evil against the LORD,
>> one who counsels wickedness.
> Thus says the LORD,
> "Though they are at full strength and many, they will be cut off
>> and pass away.
>> Though I have afflicted you, I will afflict you no more.
> And now I will break off his yoke from you and snap the bonds
>> that bind you." (Nah 1:11-13)

The (hostile) interaction across boundaries that seemed to have been less intensive during the Assyrian domination now deepens due to direct contact in the form of the Babylonian conquest. Due to this contact, the *"knowledge"* of the Other increases with the result that significant signs of the opponent's culture appear in the Self's language—such as formulae from treaties, etc.—and are used to label the Other in a negative way.

Here the language of (Babylonian) power is employed to serve the interest of the God of Israel who deliberately shames the foreign authority and strengthens his own people.

> The LORD has commanded concerning you:
>> "Your name shall be perpetuated no longer;
> from the house of your gods I will cut off the carved image and
>> the cast image.
>> I will make your grave, for you are worthless. (Nah 11:14)

A further aspect worth investigating is the obvious feminization of the Other, as Nahum 3:5-6 indicates:

> I am against you—says the LORD of hosts—
>> and will lift up your skirts over your face;
> and I will let nations look on your nakedness
>> and kingdoms on your shame.

I will throw filth at you and treat you with contempt,
    and make you a spectacle.

This feminization in the form of a subversion of the image of the fascinating and dazzling harlot becomes a stereotype for the shameful behavior of Babylon and thus uses crude attributes to characterize a large human group. Within the context of the ancient Near East such a process is well attested.[72]

In a last step we need to look at the final additions to the prophetic book. It is striking that the negative image of the Other is now even more contrasted with the positive view of the God of Israel and his followers:

A jealous and avenging God is the LORD,
    the LORD is avenging and wrathful;
the LORD takes vengeance on his adversaries
    and rages against his enemies.
The LORD is slow to anger but great in power,
    and the LORD will by no means clear the guilty. (Nah 1:2-3)

The terminology, however, suggests that we have moved beyond political/historical and earthly boundaries. The superiority of YHWH is acknowledged by giving him a certain cosmic dimension that had been missing before. Also, the boundaries seem to become more fluid. The rather general terminology in regard to the characterization of the enemy seems to point to a certain notion of ethnicity that now divides the previously homogeneous ethnic group. Thus, a shift in the difference occurred and one can now speak of difference-as-equality. Ethnicity is now used to solve inner-group conflicts. At this last stage the book of Nahum (now explicitly called *The Book of the Vision of Nahum the Elkoshite*) can be read as an example of what will happen to members outside the ethnic group if they dare to seek the conflict with the "righteous ones"—at this last stage ethnicity is no longer attached to any concrete political entities but rather used as a universal discursive weapon to defend oneself from any outside threats.

Conclusion

We conclude our venture into the question of stereotypes and ethnicity in the book of Nahum by stating that the notions of ethnicity seem to change over time and correspond to different stages in the development of the book. At the same time, the stereotypes employed to characterize the Other remain stable and do not seem to be affected by the change of the reference group. Therefore, it is possible to read the final form of the book of Nahum as an explication of the inner-group conflict outlined in the psalm right at the beginning. Further research has to be done on the question of the social location of the stereotypes employed and on the social status of the ethnic groups who create and use those stereotypes.

CHAPTER SIXTEEN

Maccabees—Symbolic Wars and Age Sets

THE ANTHROPOLOGY OF WAR IN 1 MACCABEES

Mario I. Aguilar

Mario Aguilar explores the theme of symbolism and war within 1 Maccabees by applying anthropological theories of war. War is a central activity in the Maccabean revolt against occupying colonial armies, but it is usually examined in theological terms of God's action on behalf of Israel and in the context of the covenant. Instead, Aguilar argues that models of war provide an excellent theoretical framework to understand the significance of war for social relations within Israel.

War as a biblical theme occurs throughout the Old Testament. Indeed, God's covenant with Israel is set within a symbolic alliance between a particular divine power that is recognized by the keeping of a set of rules regarding kinship, purity, and the sacredness of space, place, and landscape. War is part of such covenant because war as a human activity allows the protection of Israel's fulfilment of such covenant. God protects God's people when they are threatened so that they can keep the covenant and create the necessary conditions for a society based on the principles of that covenant.

It is clear that the study of war in relation to the covenant constitutes an important subject within biblical studies. However, in order to understand such covenant of peace and prosperity one must try to understand the phenomenon of war and warfare that leads eventually to the establishment of peace. Indeed, the covenant as a sacred alliance between God and Israel depends on an ongoing process of defense against enemies and oppressors that challenges and cuts across social organization and political boundaries.

Therefore, within the Old Testament war is both a human and a divine activity, because in order to live in peace Israel needs the protection of God and needs to be able to show strength toward other nations, foreign armies, and their gods. Already within the event of the exodus a group of slaves manages to defeat the armies of Pharaoh that pursue them not by providing an organized army but by a miracle of nature understood within the setting of a divine intervention.

Indeed, the God who has made a covenant with Israel withdraws his military protection when his people forget such covenant. God becomes an enemy warrior who is ready to kill and enslave Israelites.[1] It is within those moments in history that a foreign empire conquers, destroys, and enslaves Israel—for example, the Assyrians, and later the Babylonians. The Temple becomes a symbolic space and a sacred landscape that reminds Israel of the covenant and provides a place where the sacred can dwell and where the priests can mediate a divine covenant that becomes the center of the social, political, and religious life of Israel.

This essay explores aspects of the Maccabean revolt as perceived within the text of the 1 Maccabees by focusing on symbolic aspects of social organization in the text and by exploring some aspects of the contemporary anthropology of war. Thus, this essay argues that by focusing on symbolic aspects of kinship and age-set formation one can understand why it was possible for a family to be so prominent in such historical period. While it has to be recognized that the oppressors appropriated the Temple as sacred landscape with all its ritual meaning, I argue that the subsequent guerrilla warfare came about through symbolic constructions of age grades and age sets. Those systems were already in place for times of conflict and had been implemented in the conquest and settlement within the land. Conditions of peace and prosperity had set them aside due to social changes from a clan tribe-oriented model toward a monarchical paradigm. It was during the Maccabean conflict that they were once again actualized through the strengthening of kinship patterns rather than monarchical ones.

The Materiality of War

Within any study of war and warfare, it is necessary to recognize that the material aspect of such study provides a stronger set of social perspectives that are usually ignored by interpretive and postmodern approaches. Indeed, the avoidance of historical evidence can only lead to a cognitive invention. Thus, the use of models arising out of social anthropology provides the possibility of further understanding of a period within a linear system of historical verification. As Philip Esler notes, "models are heuristic tools, not ontological statements. Accordingly, they are either useful or not, and it is meaningless to ask if they are 'true' or 'false.'"[2] Indeed, language remains a textual expression of a social model that uses words in order to resocialize the materiality of human activity, for example, warfare.[3] However, texts and their materiality remain interwoven so that not only the pillage of war but its commemoration in material culture, including coins, become part of the study of a human and divine war.[4]

Within the anthropology of war it is clear that the materialistic approach has been different from previous ones. Already during the nineteenth century, and indeed throughout the British colonial period, it was assumed that all men were called to war and that war helped create symbolic boundaries of ethnicity and nationhood. Monument and festivals of remembrance expressed the possibility that war was a common human activity and that marching armies helped settle local communities into nations and empires. Thus, human aggression was channelled socially into moments of intense social conflict against those who were classified as enemies. However, after the devastating consequences of World War I, Freud explained the intensity of war by suggesting that wars exist because, first, men are sexually frustrated, and, second, because men have a "death drive."[5] Such Freudian explanation was short-lived and found little support within anthropology. Much later, and within the realm of cultural anthropology, themes related to individual psychology explained war in relational patterns of childhood development and male initiation rites within preindustrial societies.

It is a fact that most anthropologists have to deal with moments of social conflict, tribal warfare, and ethnic wars within their fieldwork in non-Western societies. Within those societies kinship organizes daily life and initiation rituals of manhood create social structures in which men who are initiated together fight together during times of crisis. The social system of war cohorts is not much different from groups of conscripts within contemporary armies or new students at a university; however, it requires a certain system of ordering if it is to function. Within such anthropological concepts of common initiation and related cohorts, men fight not in order to acquire honor but to become adults—

a social understanding common to societies that have compulsory military conscription where men serve in armies in order to mature and as a result they grow socially. Within this model of war activity, a male-only model is used that requires shared male-oriented structures such as patrilocality, patrilineality, and, in some cases, polygyny.

Historicity and Warfare in 1 Maccabees

The Maccabean revolt takes place within a period of conquest by the Seleucid dynasty that extends their empire into Egypt and Israel. The rule of Antiochus IV Epiphanes meant in practice that the privileges of Mosaic law given by the Persian rulers after the exile and by Antiochus III in 198 B.C.E. were abolished. According to such privileges, Mosaic law remained civil law in Israel and therefore it secured Judean ritual practices. In fact, Israel remained a foreign colony within a larger empire ruled by the Seleucid kings with its own legislation based on a separation between Judeans and foreigners. Religious freedom was restored much later with the edict of Antiochus V (1 Macc 6:57-61; 2 Macc 11:22-26).

As the Hellenistic colonizers intensified their unification of what had previously been the Persian Empire, it was common practice for pagans and Judeans sympathetic to the Greeks to stop the practice of circumcision and the keeping of the Mosaic ordinances. The initial attempt to integrate Jerusalem into a Hellenistic empire was aided by the high priest Joshua ("Jason" for the Hellenists) whose appointment had broken the tradition of high priests from priestly families in the absence of an heir to the high priest Onias III. Onias III had gone to Antioch in order to explain to King Seleucus IV that the Judeans did not want to offend the king but could not agree with the building of a gymnasium in the Temple premises at Jerusalem (2 Macc 4:7-10, 19). The persecution against Torah-committed Judeans intensified after the building of Baal Shamem or the Olympian Zeus on the Judean altar of holocausts called in the text "the abomination of desolation" (1 Macc 1:57; Dan 9:27; 11:31). As every town in Judea was obliged to sacrifice to the colonial religion, warfare started.

Mattathias appeared as the main protestor to such pagan practices, and, together with his sons, "tore their garments, put on sackcloth, and observed deep mourning" (1 Macc 2:14). As they moved to the town of Modein, the king's commissioners came to exhort him to abandon the covenant in order to save his life. His response was more than clear as he proceeded to slaughter a Judean who was sacrificing on the pagan altar, all in the presence of the commissioners and the commissioner himself (1 Macc 2:24-25). He tore down the altar and exhorted people to follow him and his sons into the hills.

After more faithful Judeans were slaughtered, Mattathias and his sons decided to organize themselves, with the help of a community of Hasidaeans, and to fight the forces of the king, destroying pagan altars and forcefully circumcising boys throughout the land. On his deathbed Mattathias entrusted the care of Mosaic law to his sons, following the impressive cultural custom of the father's blessing on his descendants.[6]

Thus, 1 Maccabees covers a period of forty years, from the ascension of Antiochus IV Epiphanes (175 B.C.E.) to the death of Simon (134 B.C.E.). While some historical discrepancies occur between 1 and 2 Maccabees and the history of the period written by Josephus, 1 Maccabees is rather accurate in presenting the problem of a Hellenist invasion and an armed response by a single family and their supporters.[7] As I have suggested in a previous paper, the general narrative of a period has become a "production of history" by witnesses located within the same time and space but with different objectives in writing about the Maccabean revolt.[8]

The narrative of 1 Maccabees follows the life of Mattathias and his three sons. All of them became in succession leaders of the resistance movement: (1) Judas Maccabeus (166–160 B.C.E., 1 Macc 3:1—9:22) won battles against Antiochus's armies, reconsecrated the Temple and secured religious freedom; however, he was killed in battle; (2) Jonathan (160–142 B.C.E.) succeeded him, became high priest and secured more territory from the Seleucids (1 Macc 9:23—12:53); he was, however, murdered by a traitor to king Antiochus VI. His brother Simon (142–134 B.C.E.) took over as high priest and was recognized as military governor within a period of prosperity that ended with the assassination of Simon and his two sons (1 Macc 13:1—16:24).

While the intention of Ptolemy and his men had been to kill John Hyrcanus, first of the Hasmonaeans, at that moment stationed in Gezer, he did not succeed. John Hyrcanus continued his reign as high priest (134–104 B.C.E.) and 1 Maccabees concludes with an imitation formula taken from the book of Kings, stating that "The rest of John's acts, the battles he fought and the exploits he performed, the city walls he built, and all his other achievements, are to be found recorded in the Annals

of his pontificate from the day he succeeded his father as high priest"
(1 Macc 16:23-24; JB).

Age-Sets and Models of Age Warfare

War and warfare occur, as in the case of the Maccabean period, when a
society decides to defend itself from socially constructed and symbolically defined outsiders labeled enemies. Indeed, the possibility of the just
war on the part of one society presupposes a moral value of rectitude or
righteousness whereby one society asserts their right to war and military
engagement in order to conquer or to defend territories. Most wars also
presuppose a contestation of landscape, i.e., space that assumes a symbolic meaning of ownership, of ritualized power, or of historical significance. Once those symbolic principles of appropriation, ownership,
and possible attack/defense have been established, society needs to
recruit men in order to fight. Although in most wars men are recruited
from within, it is also possible to pay outsiders to fight on behalf of others, thus providing the recruitment of mercenaries.

As in the case of the Maccabees, the traditional model of recruitment presupposes that men fight and women remain at their homes or
move with their children to a safe place. If this has somehow changed in
modern times, the model of recruitment presupposes a male-oriented
model and a patrilocal sense of locality. Thus, older males command
troops and order recruitment along classificatory categories of inclusion, age, and generational patterns of belonging. In those classificatory
patterns there are groups that have been trained and specifically selected
for war, but when proven insufficient in numbers their leaders quickly
open social inclusion to other males. If biological age assumes a classificatory model where there is a distinctive association between the very
old, the very young, the married, and the unmarried, social categories of
ritual initiation dictate patterns of age that do not run along biological
lines.

The problem of generations and age within the social sciences does
not relate to a biological maturation according to age, but to a social
maturation expressed along patterns of social contestation and warfare.
In preindustrial societies that are socially segmentary rather than centralized, those who are young and aspire to be socially considered as
adults fight enemies in order to prove not their manhood but their adulthood. The case of the Maasai in East Africa is completely pertinent here

because the Maasai were considered during the encounter with the British colonial power fearful fighters who organized themselves in age cohorts similar to the Roman legions and in military formations of a single line very similar to the Roman formations during battle.

Models of age are pertinent to discussions on warfare and Maccabees because it is through social models of a classificatory nature that recruitment for war and warfare itself takes place. There are several models associated with age systems.[9] However, I propose to examine only three of them: (1) the initiation model, (2) the generational model, and, (3) the regimental model.

The three models share some basic characteristics. First, they are male systems that operate a strict kinship descent through male lines, thus connected through patrilocality and patrilineality. Second, they all grant their members particular places within a scale of sociability that operates with mathematical precision, thus it is possible to know the role and social category of every member of a particular age set by knowing the age set name and its year of social formation. However, the systems offer social variations in the numbers and variety of rituals performed, the chronological time of initiation following conceptions of linear or circular time, and the role of those initiated within a particular society organized in different patterns of centralized or semi-centralized organization.

The Initiation Model

Within Maasai as in other groups of pastoralists in East Africa, such as Boorana, Samburu, Rendille, and Somali, the model of initiation followed a model of age. At the time of initiation those considered children changed their sociability into adults by fighting enemies and outsiders and were included into age sets, groups of cohorts that have gone through the same experience of initiation in a particular year. In the case of the Boorana, for example, those who were initiated needed to kill an enemy in order to be considered adults and as a proof of their achievement they brought back his genitals as a sign of their adulthood.[10]

A particular age set was not formed following a particular age pattern but following a chronological pattern related to a certain number of years from their father's initiation. The system resembled entrance into primary school, not with concern for biological age, but for a ritual process of organized classification following their respective father's initiation. A particular age set moved together through a process of social maturation that progressed from boyhood to adulthood, from courtship and marriage to political public life and much later into a life of prayer and ritual actions associated with old age.

Thus, those unmarried men in Maasai and of fighting age (*murran*) did not live with their parents and were not able to have a family of their own and to father children with their name. However, most of them were having biological children while defending Maasai territories through warfare incursions and wars of attack and defense against other groups, including the British. Those who fought well became respected and ritually pure and therefore were able to take positions of leadership in Maasai areas. As a result, the Maasai developed a reputation for having a violent character but also for engaging themselves in ongoing inter-tribal conflicts.[11] In fact, a model of theological thinking supported such intertribal warfare because, according to their creation myth, every cow in the world belonged to Maasai, regardless of social or private ownership, location, or type. Warfare and cattle raiding had a purpose, i.e., the continuity of a cosmological world where Maasai were at the center and they were the only ones who were able to benefit from the deeds, will, and intention of the Creator.

This model is comparable to Maccabees in that young Israelites underwent circumcision as the only physical and symbolic enactment of the covenant between the Lord and Israel. All those uncircumcised were strangers and foreigners and felt under the possible threat of a central-ized religious system of purity located at the center of God's action in the world, a world that was centered on Israel's covenant. Thus, the Mac-cabean revolt suggests a comparative probability of social initiation associated with warfare against enemies and foreigners in order to main-tain clear social and ritual relations despite the interference of a colonial power that did not understand the centrality of the God of Israel located at the Temple.

The Generational Model

I have already suggested that within systems of age there are models in which initiation and adulthood, social maturation and classification do not depend on the age of the individual but on the actual initiation of his father. In the *gada* system of the Oromo, for example, as actualized by the Boorana, male initiates join an age set that could be clearly termed a generation set. Such a generation set includes all those whose fathers were initiated forty years previously, in a system that operated initiation ceremonies only every eight years and where at every genera-tion a new age grade takes over social roles that have been discharged by a group that was initiated eight calendar years before them. Within such an age model every male gets to fulfil particular social obligations related to religion and politics throughout his life.

As in the case of the Maccabees at war with colonial powers, the system allows for a group of cohorts that can replace their fathers in time of need and allows every male to experience political leadership after initiation and religious leadership in old age. Thus, I have already suggested in a previous paper that, within the Old Testament and in African preindustrial societies, genealogies become central in order to know each person's position in the social scale and their social movement upwards within systems based on male descent and social organization.[12] Thus, the blessing of Mattathias toward his sons was not only a moment of symbolic communion, but also a social manifestation of orderly patrilineal descent. Such handing over and individual testament was necessary within a society that needed to know at all times where everybody was located in order to avoid ritual pollution and to continue providing correct classificatory social patterns (1 Macc 2:49-70).

In social terms of a generational model sons took over from their father not in order to restore honor to Israel and their household but because they moved up within a classificatory social model based on age. Within such model their father who had fought previously became part of a system where older age generations prayed and became ritually effective while their sons took over the political leadership. Other sons took over not because of precise kinship ties but because they belonged to different age generation groups that worked with different group alliances and therefore were able to sustain support within warfare and peace from different quarters and from different groups.

The Regimental Model

Another social model based on a social age classification is the regimental model. Within such a regimental system and particularly among peoples of Southern Africa (Zulu, Swasi, Ndebele, Ngoni) social organization and therefore warfare operated along the lines of clans associated by kinship that united their efforts through a close classificatory formation. Those regimental formations, similar to the Roman Legions, worked along close kinship ties and charismatic ability on the part of the clan leaders. In some societies they evolved into the election of a monarch that came from the unequal social position of a clan that became dominant not because of an established pattern but due to success in war against enemies and foreigners.

Within this model the recognized leader arises out of creativity and astuteness in warfare against the enemy in particular situations where numbers of soldiers do not make the difference, either because the enemy has the same number of warriors or because the enemy has a larger number of soldiers. In the case of the Zulu of Southern Africa and their struggle against the British colonial power and the Dutch settlers, the prominent clan (*Dingiswayo*) offered protection to Shaka, a prominent Nguni warrior. In moments of extreme crisis for the Zulu, Shaka made radical changes that created a well-disciplined and well-prepared Zulu army. Thus, Shaka substituted the traditional long spears for shorter ones to be kept during battle, abolished circumcision in order to have able young warriors rather than postsurgery patients, and, divided the Zulu warriors into two factions that would encircle the enemy from the left and from the right during battle.

The Maccabees introduced the same tactics of guerrilla warfare, by attacking different locations of Greek worship, and by spreading fear throughout the land by their creative attacks and physical mobility. While circumcision could not be abolished they relied on ritual adaptation by defending the possibility of keeping the Sabbath holy and fighting enemies at the same time. Their refusal to take part in Hellenistic practices at the gymnasium allowed them not to be discovered because the practices of the Hellenists implied the practice of athletics preceded by offerings to the pagan gods. Within those practices young men followed a special ritual where all participants had to appear naked and those trained at the *ephebum*, place of training for the athletes, were certainly uncircumcised.[13] While circumcision could not be undone, it constituted the material sign of opposition to the Hellenistic colonial power in the same way that other colonial powers expected their subjects to wear clothes, have a moustache, or have particular marks in their bodies as a sign of subordination to their new colonial masters. Thus, the author writes that some "disguised their circumcision, and abandoned the holy covenant, submitting to the heathen rule as willing slaves of impiety" (1 Macc 1:15).

Further Textual Patterns of War in 1 Maccabees

A closer examination of the text of 1 Maccabees suggests that the system of resistance, war, and warfare implemented is male and depends completely on the central parameter of initiation whereby those who resist the Hellenistic movement have been circumcised and therefore initiated into a cultic system of Judaism. Indeed, one of their main concerns is to try to defend such system of initiation and to attack centers of pagan worship that impede proper initiation and ritual continuity.

Nevertheless, the succession of guerrilla warfare depends on the generational model, as the father takes over the leading operations of resistance and immediately at his death one of his sons takes over the leadership and other sons do the same when required. The generational model is fully implemented by an underlined system of patrilineal descent whereby through blessing, exhortation, and testament the father provides a continuity of descent that secures the continuity of the family lineage (1 Macc 2:51-64). However, as a result, not only the continuity of a particular family is secured but also the adherence to the covenant and to warfare as immediate allegiance to such covenant becomes part of the father's remembrance and family honor. Such honor repaired the shame that extended to the whole house of Jacob (1 Macc 1:29) and to the dishonor brought to Jerusalem (1 Macc 1:40).

The context of such warfare was a total ban on possessing books of the law, practicing Mosaic law, and having children circumcised. The penalty was death for those that attempted any of those activities, their household and their helpers, and extended to men and women alike (1 Macc 1:57-64). The family involved included a priest, Mattathias, and his sons John Gaddi, Simon Thassi, Judas Maccabaeus, Eleazar Avaran, and Jonathan Apphus. Their first attempt at resistance included a ritual purification and a protest so that they "tore their garments, put on sackcloth, and observed deep mourning" (1 Macc 2:14). Thus, warfare involved a ritual practice of the generational model, including a collective call to account for their faults in case that God was punishing them for any lack of purity as it had already happened in previous exiles, deportations and attacks by foreigners.

The military model operates through a kinship model of succession so that Simeon is appointed priestly successor while Judas Maccabaeus is named leader of the resistance army (1 Macc 2:65-66). However, Antiochus sent a larger army ahead of his own in order to crush the Maccabean rebellion. Judas prepared for war by offering prayers and imploring compassion and mercy (1 Macc 3:44). This mention of actual prayer is rare within the text, simply because the genre of historical narrative presumes a constant offering of prayers and sacrifices toward the divine imploring God's protection and renewing the covenant through communal and individual prayers that are taken for granted by the author. In fact, the ritual model of prayer sustains, as in most conflicts, the military model and becomes part of it, locating the divine into a multiplicity of gods, each one of them requested to protect and assist a particular army.

Following such practice, the armies of Judas made their way to Mizpah, opposite Jerusalem, "traditionally a place of prayer for Israel" (1 Macc 3:47). There they fasted, wore sackcloth on their bodies and ashes on their heads, and tore their garments. Communal rituals took place as the priestly vestments and the firstfruits were taken out and they acknowledged the Nazirites who had completed the period of their vow. Those who were building their houses, were about to be married, were planting vineyards, or were afraid were allowed to go home. Finally, the army positioned itself south of Emmaus and waited for battle knowing that "whatever be the will of heaven, he will perform it" (1 Macc 3:46-60; 2 Macc 8:16-23).

It is clear that war is a human activity that extends actual social practices and it is guided by the rules of a society that organizes conscription in terms of social and ritual understandings without allowing the weak and those who are not ready to take part. The military model operates only on the principle of non-social contradiction, thus in conjunction with models of initiation and models of generational patterns and larger classifications.

Once Judas's armies were triumphant they completed the cycle of war with prayers, so that "on their return, the Judeans chanted praises to heaven, "For he is good, and his mercy is everlasting" (1 Macc 4:4-25). However, those who escaped the slaughter by the rebel forces regrouped after orders came from Lysias, a noble man in charge of the king's affairs. Once again, Judas prayed for deliverance, in the fashion of Moses and other great leaders of Israel, saying:

> Blessed are you, saviour of Israel, who shattered the might of the Philistine champion by the hand of your servant David, and delivered their camp into the hands of Jonathan son of Saul, and his armour-bearer. Crush this expedition in the same way at the hands of your people Israel; make them ashamed of their forces and their cavalry. Make cowards of them, undermine their confidence in their own strength, and may they reel at their defeat. Overthrow them by the sword of those who love you, and all who acknowledge your name will sing your praises. (1 Macc 4:30-33; JB)

The two armies met at Bethzur, about eighteen kilometers south of Jerusalem on the road to Hebron. Lysias's army finally withdrew after heavy casualties. Then Judas led the rededication of the Temple and the reinstallment of the priesthood together with a festival lasting eight days to annually commemorate the restoration of the Temple, i.e. the Feast of Dedication, Hanukkah, one of the most recent in the Judean calendar (cf. Ex 23:14ff.). Indeed, the period of the Second Temple saw a flourishing individual and communal prayer in Israel (1 Sam 14:1ff.; 17:40ff.).[14]

Conclusions: Symbolic Wars and Warfare

Throughout the Old Testament men were recruited in order to guard Israel from her enemies, who in turn became Yahweh's enemies as well. Within the construction of Israel's history, war served a purpose and holy wars were considered of divine origin because they protected the monarchy, the land, and much later the Temple, where the God of Israel dwelt.

Whereas older men exercised ritual and political power, in most occasions due to conquest and war they gave way to younger men who very quickly established themselves as successful warriors, astute politicians, and religious leaders. This "generational problem" becomes important in order to understand military recruitment and succession within 1 Maccabees, a book in which war becomes the key concept to understand the period, the message and the organization of the Maccabean revolt. Within 1 Maccabees such revolt becomes the adequate process of social initiation and of ritual purification for a group of Israelites that in unusual circumstances do not have the necessary ritual institutions prescribed by the law in order to become adults.

During the Maccabean period the Temple is symbolically changed into a Greek gymnasium, while the oppressors forbid the social practice of circumcision, leaving younger Israelites without the necessary physical means to express their covenant with God. Within those social and historical circumstances war, as an extension of organized military warfare, becomes the social institution that recreates and actualizes the covenant. Martyrdom becomes a path to eternal resurrection, a concept that appears within Israel at the times of the Maccabees and that assures those under the Seleucid persecution, and later under the Roman persecution, that war has a divine resonance while resistance secures the fruits of social and individual salvation.

If the anthropology of war helps to understand some of the social processes that unfolded within the history of the Maccabean revolt and the Hellenist colonial occupation of Israel, such a model of symbolic war could be helpful in understanding other moments of war and colonialism within the Old Testament. Indeed, war and colonialism as themes of divine salvation permeate other Near Eastern civilizations and most processes of religious adaptation and religious wars up to the times of the Roman occupation of Israel. Within that research framework the study of war and prayer within moving armies becomes as important as the study of cultic practices associated with the Temple and it provides new insights for the study of periods of social stability, peace, and proper cultic observances.

CHAPTER SEVENTEEN

Qumran—The Prototypical Teacher in the Qumran Pesharim

A SOCIAL-IDENTITY APPROACH

Jutta Jokiranta

With Jutta Jokiranta's essay we move briefly from the Old Testament to the literature of a specific group within Israel. Jokiranta begins with the observation that considering the fact that the "Teacher of Righteousness" is a well-known character in the reconstructions of the history of the "Qumran community," it is remarkable how few texts mention him. She notes that when the nature of the information about the teacher is studied, one observation stands out: the teacher and the in-group are depicted in very similar ways. This insight allows her to introduce into Qumran studies important notions of individuals who are prototypical for group identity derived from the flourishing branch of social psychology known as social-identity theory.

The title מורה הצדק *(mwrh ḥṣdq)*, "the teacher of righteousness" or "the righteous teacher,"[1] stands out from certain Pesher manuscripts from Qumran. This figure receives more attention in the scriptural commentaries than any other individual member of the community. Consequently, he has played a role in most historical reconstructions of the "Qumran community." Yet the epithet is not frequently found. It occurs in only five of over eight hundred scrolls, and four of these are Pesharim. In its full form it has only about a dozen occurrences,[2] most of which are found in the 4QPsalms Pesher[a] (4QpPs[a]) and in the 1QHabakkuk Pesher (1QpHab).

The purpose of this essay is to look at the *nature* of this scarce material regarding the teacher and to apply insights from the social-scientific theory of prototypes to argue that the teacher of the Pesharim represents an ideal community member, who captures some essential characteristics of group's identity. My purpose is to understand better the outlook of specific Pesharim themselves, not to form a theory of the historical teacher. In the end, the prototypical character of the teacher is looked at in relation to Qumran "social time."

Prototypicality in Social-Identity Approach

Theories of social identity and self-categorization were developed in the 1970s and 1980s by Henri Tajfel and John Turner for the study of group formation and intergroup processes.[3] The social-identity approach, as these theories may be called, is still effectively used and has been tested in social psychology, with some correctives and further developments.[4] Philip Esler has introduced the approach into New Testament scholarship.[5] The approach is here used selectively in order to provide a theoretical basis of prototypes.

Self-categorization theory proceeds from the assumption that people's self-conception reflects their self-categorization, "the cognitive grouping of the self as identical to some class of stimuli in contrast to some other class of stimuli."[6] Self-categories exist on three levels of abstraction: the interpersonal level (personal identity, self as an individual), the intergroup level (social identity, self as a group member), and the interspecies level (self as human being). *Social* categorization is the accentuation of in-group similarities (and out-group similarities) and exaggeration of intergroup differences in order to form a distinct group identity.[7] The salience of a category depends on its relevance to the situation.[8] Social categorization provides a fundamental basis for our social orientation toward others.[9] The focus on social identity causes depersonalization: perceiving oneself and acting as a member of a group rather than as an individual. When group members strive for positive social identity by means of *social comparisons,* in-group bias (favoring one's own group) is likely to occur.[10]

Despite the accentuation of in-group similarities, members within one category vary in their *typicality*: "Members (of a category) do not all share a given set of defining features, but are related through their similarity to a prototype."[11] *A group prototype* is maximally represen-

tative of the shared social identity of the group: it simultaneously max-
imizes intergroup differences and minimizes intragroup differences.[12] It
needs to be stressed that prototype is a fictitious concept; prototypes are
abstract models that best embody a category.[13] The more a group member differs from out-group members and the less he or she differs from
in-group members as regards the dimensions that are thought to be correlated with the categorization, the more that individual will be perceived as prototypical of the group. Thus, prototypicality depends on
both inter- and intragroup comparisons.[14]

According to the social-identity theory of leadership, a leader is a
group member who appears to have the strongest social influence on the
in-group. To be effective, the leader has to be close to the group prototype, that is, the leader best epitomizes the social category of which he
or she is the member.[15] "Leadership is intimately bound up with the
shared concerns of the followers."[16]

Social Memory and the Pesharim

Scriptural quotations play a significant part in understanding Pesher literature. The Pesher formula, adopted from dream interpretation tradition,[17] is designed to introduce identifications of the persons and groups
in the quotation with the persons and groups of the author's reality.[18]

Various group labels are the most evident sign of specific group
identities that are promoted in the Pesharim.[19] The texts are not about
individual piety, nor do they speak of a neutral third party, such as might
be the subject of the scriptural study. The texts—quotations *and* their
interpretations—create a dichotomy between the righteous and the
wicked, and thus call for identification with the right side, the right
group.[20]

On the theological level, group membership is described in terms of
the law and the covenant:[21] the members are those who keep the law
(4QpPs[a] II, 15; 4QFlor IV, 1-3; 1QpHab VIII, 1); they shall have the
covenant blessings (4QpPs[a] III, 1-5). Turning to the law and belonging
to the covenant community seem to be criteria for the in-group membership, but there are other sub-definitions, for example, the self-desig-
nation "the congregation of the poor" in 4QpPs[a], or "the poor" in
1QpHab.[22]

Studies on the teacher usually begin with the Damascus Document
(CD),[23] which is probably an earlier text than the central Pesharim con-

cerning the teacher.[24] Here it suffices to recall the famous passage in CD I, according to which the teacher is an early group leader.[25] In its final form, the Admonition argues in favor of justified particularism, those whom God had chosen for his covenant.[26] The covenant would remain, despite the times of wrath, but its continuation is based on the work of certain individuals who hear God's voice, on God's teachings through the prophets, on revelation of hidden things, and even on hearing the teachings of this document.[27] The message to be conveyed is that God's wrath will come upon that generation too and that a special form of community is necessary in order to avoid the punishment (CD XV, 4-10; XII, 21-22). The teacher's death is mentioned as a point of reference in the B manuscript of the Damascus Document (XX, 1, 14), in a section that probably is a later layer of the Admonition.[28]

The possibility exists that the teacher figure functions differently in different texts, and each Pesher has to be taken on its own. Yet the best-preserved passages concerning the teacher, which are found in the 4QPsalms Pesher[a29] and in the 1QHabakkuk Pesher,[30] can be studied in two groups: the teacher as a persecuted person (4QpPs[a] II, 16-21; IV, 7-10;[31] 1QpHab V, 8-12; IX, 8-12; XI, 3-8), and the privileged teacher (4QpPs[a] I, 25—II, 1; III, 14-17; 1QpHab I, [16]—II, 10; VII, 3-5; VII, [17]—VIII, 2).[32] The following presentation does not enter into detailed connections between quotations and interpretations, but hopes to show the connection that has perhaps not been emphasized so far: the similarities between the portrait of the teacher and of the in-group.

The Persecuted Righteous Teacher

The high degree of prototypicality of the teacher is first of all demonstrated in the *similarity* of the statements about the teacher and the group. As will be seen, they (as a group) are the righteous ones, proven by their faithfulness to the law and their chosen position, on the one hand, and by the wicked acts of the enemies against the righteous, on the other hand. Second, the teacher represents the maximum *difference* to the out-groups, the opponents, who are themselves represented by stereotypical figures, the "liar" (איש הכזב, *ʾyš hkzb*) and the "wicked priest" (הכוהן הרשע, *hkhn hršʿ*). The teacher is portrayed in such a way that he captures the essence of what makes the group distinct from other groups.

That the teacher (priest) is persecuted is shown in 4QpPs[a] II, 16-21. This passage has a very similar structure to II, 13-16: the wicked of the quotation are identified with the opposing group(s) who seek to destroy the community members but fail. In II, 16-21, "the poor and needy" of the quotation (Ps 37:14-15) are identified as "the priest and the men of his council," whereas in II, 13-21, the singular "righteous one" of the quotation (Ps 37:12-13) is surprisingly *not* identified with the teacher but simply "those who observe the law." The picture of the persecuted teacher is very similar to that of the persecuted community members. These two passages claim similar experiences on the part of the group and the individual, here called "priest."

In 4QpPs^a IV, 7-10, the theme of trial of the quotation (Ps 37:32-33) is carried over to the interpretation. The wicked one is identified as the wicked priest. Because of him, the righteous stands in trial but will not be condemned. The group rejoices at the judgment of the wicked (IV, 10-12, 17-22). The victory belongs to the group along with the individual.

In 1QpHab V, 8-12, the citation (Hab 1:13b) reads: "Why do you stare, O traitors, and stay silent, when the wicked swallows up one more righteous than he?"[33] The traitors are identified as the "house of Absalom" and the wicked one as the liar. According to the interpretation, the teacher suffered a setback. A similar setting is pictured *collectively* in X, 6-13: the liar had led many astray and had caused the chosen ones to be derided and insulted.

The passages IX, 8-12 and XI, 3-8 describe the teacher *and his community* in conflict with the wicked priest. The shared fate of the teacher and his group is obvious here: they suffer from the acts of the wicked priest. The injustice of this priest is described in the spirit of the quotations (Hab 2:8b; 2:15), which are themselves stereotypical woes concerning the wicked acts of notorious persons.

It is especially in connection with the "wicked priest" that the teacher can be seen as representing the maximum *difference* vis-à-vis the out-group. The very labels portray the maximum opposites. The teacher's title claims that he was sent by God to give the people a fresh start and to assist it in its search for justice.[34] The wicked priest, on the other hand, corrupted his God-given office. The teacher is the victim, and the wicked priest is the violator.[35] Similarly, the title "liar" expresses distance from the "righteous teacher," or to "the interpreter of knowledge," as will be seen below. However, the liar is depicted as a rival authority who misled people but was not directly violent against the teacher.

In summary, the teacher appears in the Psalms Pesher almost always together with his opponent, either "the liar," or "the wicked priest." He is persecuted and wrongly accused in court, and *similarly*, the group is persecuted, but proven right. In four out of seven occurrences of the Habakkuk Pesher, the teacher appears together with his enemy: either he is persecuted, wrongly accused, or his teaching is rejected (I,[16]—II,10). The teacher in conflict maximally represents the claims and experiences of the in-group. They share the same fate. There is no biographical information concerning the teacher and there are few details about him; he is the teacher in distress.

The Privileged Teacher

The privileged character of the teacher is visible in both the Psalms Pesher and the Habakkuk Pesher. This reflects the in-group's belief in its own chosen status and ownership of revelation.

In 4QpPs[a] I, 25—II, 1 the "interpreter of knowledge" is opposed to the "liar," or rather the "many" that the liar has misled.[36] The opponent is successful in his actions, and the interpreter of knowledge—presumably the same as the teacher figure—is not listened to, which results in the curses of the covenant falling upon those who reject his teaching (similar to CD I, 17). The words "they chose frivolous things" reminds one of CD I, 18, "they sought easy interpretations and chose illusions." Exact similarity of the *statements* about the teacher and the in-group (above) is not found here: no interpretation states directly that the *group's* teaching was the target of disbelief. It might seem that the in-group is not a teacher but a follower of teaching. However, the boundary line between the in- and out-groups runs in relation to the *law*, not following the teacher as such (cf. the next Pesher section II,1-5). Furthermore, the *Pesher form* itself suggests that the group possesses correct interpretations of the scriptures, functioning as a source of revelation, similar to the teacher.

The passage in III, 14-17 suggests that the individual figure has been sent by God to perform his task,[37] and seems to be an elaboration of CD I: God gave the chosen ones a teacher to help them find the right way. Similarly, the group is God's elect. "The congregation/people of his elect" occurs in II, 5; III, 5; IV, 11-12 (reconstruction of "the chosen ones of God" in IV, 14), and either means those who follow the way set out by God's chosen one, or simply those that God has chosen for himself.[38]

In the Habakkuk Pesher, the famous passage in VII, 3-5 asserts that the teacher had special revelation about the secrets of the prophets, and the passage in the beginning (I, 16—I, 10) makes a very similar statement concerning the "priest."[39] This passage gives a very similar picture of the teacher in the Psalms Pesher (he is not listened to) and the beginning of the Damascus Document: God will reveal what will happen to the last generation. In CD I it is not clear if it is the teacher or God who would reveal the fate of the final generation; here it is the teacher. New information provided by the Habakkuk Pesher is that this revelation will be derived from the prophets. Yet it is God who would report these things.

According to 1QpHab VII, 3-5, God had revealed to the teacher all the secrets of the prophets. What were these secrets? The preceding Pesher tells us that the prophet Habakkuk knew what would happen to the last generation but not "completion of the time" (VII, 1-2). This is often read in the sense that Habakkuk knew less than the teacher. Thus, the teacher would have known the fulfillment of time.[40] However, the interpretations that follow in VII, 5-14 clearly state that God's secrets are *more* than what the prophets said—the obvious conclusion from this is that the teacher knew only the secrets of the prophets, but could not master all God's secrets. This is then actually a skilful way of avoiding the reduction of teacher's expertise, even though the group may have moved on and developed its teaching about the end of times.

Nowhere in this Pesher or in other Pesharim do the authors claim that the Pesharim were direct interpretation by the teacher. Rather, they wish to point out the relevance of his teaching and his God-given knowledge to which the Pesher authors and their teaching are definitely faithful.[41]

The teacher's function can be unraveled by analyzing the power involved.[42] The teacher seems to be ascribed at least *referent power* (leader is looked up to and acts as a role model), and *informational power* (leader has a privileged access to information, which he or she uses to persuade others).[43] Referent power appears in the respect enjoyed by the teacher and in the positive nature of his very name. His suffering role may also be admired as a reminder of the suffering servant of God.[44] Informational power is depicted in passages asserting that the teacher was or was not listened to. It is this informational power, use of information *received* from God, rather than expert power, a superior *ability* to gain access to the information, that is present in these passages: the role of God is always mentioned as the source of information and the nature of the information is related to the need to be disciplined in the community in order to avoid judgment.[45]

Finally, the passage in 1QpHab VII, 17—VIII, 2 mentions *faithful-*

ness to the teacher as characteristic of the law-keepers. This passage is similar to other teacher passages to the extent that the adherents of the teacher (this time not the teacher himself) are suffering and they will be saved. But here their distress and faithfulness to the teacher are reasons or motivations for their salvation. This faithfulness, however, is to be seen in its context, deriving from the quotation, "The righteous man will live because of his faithfulness" (Hab 2:4b).[46] The in-group members are "those who observe the law in the house of Judah." Faithfulness to the Torah is the *criterion* of salvation; faithfulness to the teacher is rather a consequence of being among the law-keepers. In other words, group identity is defined by Torah faithfulness, but there are other correlated attributes involved, which are not original criteria of categorization.[47]

Faithfulness to the teacher also appears in the Damascus Document B-manuscript, in the final section of the Admonition (CD XX, 27b-34),[48] which, we believe, helps to understand this role of the teacher:

> But all those who remain steadfast in these judgments, [co]ming and going in accordance to what the Torah says, and listen to the voice of *a/the teacher* (מורה), and confess before God: "*We have sinned and have been wicked, both we and our fathers, walking against the precepts of the covenant; justi[ce] and truth are your judgments against us,*" and who do not raise their hand against his holy precepts and his just judgment[s] and his truthful stipulations, and who are instructed in the first judgments, according to which the men of the unique one/community[49] were judged, and who listen to the voice of *a/the righteous teacher* (מורה צדק), and do not reject the just precepts when they hear them, they shall exult and rejoice and their heart shall be strong, and they shall prevail over all the sons of the world. And God will atone for them, and they shall see his salvation, for they have taken refuge in his holy name.[50]

We cannot study the passage in detail here, but one relevant comparison is to the covenant entry liturgy in 1QS I, 16ff. The confession of sins in 1QS I, 24—II, 1 is very similar to CD XX, 28-30: "*We have acted sinfully, we have [tr]ansgressed, we have [sin]ned, we have been wicked, both we and our fathers before us, walking [. . .] truth and just [. . .] his judgment upon us and upon o[ur] fathers.*" In the light of this parallel, we suggest that listening to the voice of the teacher in CD B comes very close to listening to (and obeying) the teaching of the covenant, as the community possessed it. Rule documents preserve several traces of officials and group members whose task it was to teach and invite people to enter this covenant (1QS I, 21-23; III, 13; V, 9-11, 20-24; VI, 13-15; IX, 21-22; CD XII, 7-16). Actually, CD XX, similar to CD I, preserves the title without the definite article, but this may be due to the poetic form.[51] The title may refer to a special individual and his teaching,[52] but the text does not claim that the law is given exclusively through this individual; rather, it was the necessity of belonging to the covenant community for receiving the right interpretations of the Torah and for constant guidance in them (cf. CD XX, 11-12).[53] It was a necessity to have this guidance from outside. The teacher functioned as a defender of the present regulations: they were the same as in the ancient and perhaps more recent past (cf. CD IV, 6-10).[54] Whoever did not want to submit to the discipline of the community was in danger of slipping out and losing the covenant (the just law and the atonement of sins).

The Teacher in Collective Memory

We may now ask why this figure typifies the group. What is achieved by the image?

A group that bases its teaching on new revelation is vulnerable: it needs to create continuity to the past as well as to argue for the relevance of the new teaching. Social-identity theory has more recently been discussed in connection with time.[55] The sense of continuity is central in social identities: the value and meaning attached to group memberships are often related to one's perception of group origins or past history, even long before the life of existing members. The "possible social identities" are those that the group believes it has had in the past and may have in the future. One link to the past may be outstanding past members of the group; the group creates and maintains its identity by cherishing the memory of its ideal group members.

In the world of the Pesharim, the teacher *could* be past or present. Generally, the teacher-passages require that some time has passed (e.g., 1QpHab IX, 8-12), but outside information is needed in order to place him in the Qumran "social time."[56] If an original part of CD A, the use of the title there suggests that the teacher's appearance in the Pesharim is rather a revival of a *past* prophet-like leader who now serves two functions. First, he provides coherence between the in-group's past and present realities. He represents the idea of particularism that the group needed and needs to stand for: that God has preserved God's covenant in this group (or these groups) only. In the Psalms and the Habakkuk Pesher, the prototypical image of the teacher in conflict makes a statement from the past: all the leaders of the Jerusalem establishment as well as rival authorities were wicked; a distinct community was needed. These conflicts need not be crucial events in the community history; the scripturally loaded descriptions suffice to support the claim. Second, the prototypical picture of the teacher-leader enabled later group members to identify with him and even perceive him as their contemporary. Emphasizing the similar fate of the in-group and the persecuted and afflicted individual served to promote an identity in which all generations could justify setbacks. This picture required the members to reflect on the level of their identification with the group, even in distress,[57] and to modify the in-group prototype in a more flexible direction. Thus, it is a matter of keeping the group together.

Conclusion

I have suggested that in the Psalms Pesher and the Habakkuk Pesher the teacher is portrayed as a prototypical group member *with the traits of bearing distress and attacks by outsiders, of teaching aright (and thus also doing right, keeping the law), and being chosen by God.* The teacher is not portrayed as a unique individual but is rather viewed through the lens of group prototypicality. He represents the in-group and stands opposite to the out-groups. This prototypical image serves a group identity, in which *belonging to the group* is necessary to gain access to God's covenant, and *afflictions* are one part of testing the righteous. This kind of group identity could better survive the threats posed by apostates, by their own minority position, or by political disturbances.

This study also brings the subject of *collective memory* into discussion. The teacher functions as a link with the in-group's past. Even past leaders can be seen to be effective if they are perceived as providing a faithful representation of in-group identity. The Pesharim are not for him, but he is harnessed in the service of the Pesharim. Faithfulness to him can be promoted as faithfulness to the group's foundations.

PART FOUR

Hermeneutics

CHAPTER EIGHTEEN

Biblical Hermeneutics

MARCION'S TRUTH AND
A DEVELOPMENTAL PERSPECTIVE

Douglas E. Oakman

Douglas Oakman proposes that over the past thirty years the social sciences have played an increasingly important role in the study of the Bible. In a manner reminiscent of Marcion's moral appraisal of the deity of the Old Testament, social-scientific criticism confronts biblical theology with a new crisis, especially in the rift that it seems to open up between the biblical world and our own. Nevertheless, incorporating into hermeneutical discussions perspectives from the social sciences on how cultures and religions develop can also suggest persuasive directions for translating meaning across centuries and cultures. Indeed, developmental social-psychology and evolutionary cultural studies may prove surprisingly fruitful for indicating new ways to take seriously the Bible's meaning and the biblical God in the context of an open-ended encounter with global culture in the twenty-first century.

> I expect traditional religious symbolism to be maintained and developed in new directions, but with growing awareness that it is symbolism and that man in the last analysis is responsible for the choice of . . . symbolism. Naturally, continuation of the symbolization characteristic of earlier stages without any reinterpretation is to be expected among many in the modern world, just as it has occurred in every previous period.
>
> —Robert N. Bellah[1]

The "Estranged New World" of the Bible

The tree is known by its fruits. Marcion applied this principle to the Old Testament god. Modern scholars of the effective history of the Bible are beginning to apply it to the book. One no longer concludes that there must be two or more gods; what one does conclude, inevitably, is that holy books can be dangerous—a curse as well as a blessing. The example of Marcion and Harnack reminds us of the urgency of moral (or "ideological") criticism of the Bible. We have to be explicit in our criticism of the Old Testament—and of the New! For the New Testament in its canonical status can be just as dangerous as the Old Testament. There can be "sub-Christian"—or "sub-Jewish"—features in the New Testament as well.[2]

Marcion deserves credit as an early biblical critic and hermeneutical thinker—both for contributing to the proto-New Testament (an early "canon within the canon") and for exercising reasoned moral judgment about biblical theology. His truth, however, as contemplated in this essay, is not the questionable specifics of his theological or canonical proposals. Marcion's truth, chiseled out of the sediment of church history and recast more generally, is the insight that after the moral and cultural critique of social-scientific criticism, not to speak of feminist, postmodern, or postcolonial criticisms, virtually none of the biblical images of deity remains universally influential. They are all now aliens. Even the New Testament "God of love and mercy" depicts a Mediterranean patriarch, whose cultural logic is that of ancient patronage.[3] And there is much internal canonical inconsistency: The God of John's Apocalypse is hardly Universal Love, and the God of Jonah is rather inconsistent with the God of Nahum.

The Bible was formulated within the preindustrial agrarian civilizations of the Middle East.[4] Every biblical understanding of God is situated within the horizon of ancient cultural roles and expectations. Though centuries of biblical interpretation abstracted theology from cultural context, social-scientific criticism has recovered the culturally conditioned meaning of the biblical traditions. While biblical meanings are now understood in much more culturally "incarnate" ways, they seem even more remote and irrelevant to the twenty-first century. Karl Barth's once "strange new world" of the Bible has nearly a century later become the "estranged new world" of the Bible. Brevard Childs's crisis in biblical theology still remains, but canonical approaches offer no real exit.[5] What canon is innocent of ideological interest or cultural conditioning? How can the Bible continue to "mean" for the twenty-first century?

The claim of this essay is that developmental theories from the social sciences can be of help in building new hermeneutical bridges. Though the social sciences alone will not render a biblical image of God universally influential, they must be a vital partner in future conversations about biblical hermeneutics.

Modeling Sociocultural Development

Now, it is certainly true that in some sense each culture is unique—just as each individual, each blade of grass, and each atom in the universe is unique. But how can one ever know this unless one has first compared a given culture with other cultures? What is more, there are degrees of distinctiveness. If a phenomenon were wholly unique, we could not possibly comprehend it. We are able to understand any phenomenon only because it bears some similarities to things we already know.[6]

The construction of cross-cultural models indicates the possibility of meaningful general understandings. Indeed, some today urge that, as human sciences, the social sciences are more hermeneutic than scientific.[7] Though a daunting task, the deployment of social-scientifically informed developmental perspectives in biblical theology must take into account both psychosocial and sociocultural frameworks.[8]

Several social theorists can provide building blocks for suitable developmental models. Heinz Werner's comparative and organismic theory presents human development as the natural result of increasing differentiation integrated through higher control centers. The vivid perceptions of children mix senses and employ physiognomic descriptions; likewise, the cultures of "undeveloped" peoples evince such linguistic characteristics. Eventually, the self becomes distinguishable from the objective world, and maturation entails a process moving from sensori-motor-affective through perceptual to abstract conceptual stages. Different cultures effect these transitions in varying measures.[9]

Emile Durkheim's *The Division of Labor in Society* contrasts "mechanical solidarity" and "organic solidarity."[10] Legal traditions (including ancient and Old Testament law) provide important reference points for developmental assessment. With mechanical solidarity of simple human societies, individuals are "interchangeable" and law is largely punitive; with organic solidarity in complex societies, individuals become interdependent and their relations are governed more by contract law.

Lawrence Kohlberg[11] characterizes moral development in terms of six stages: Action governed by (1) concern for reward and punishment from authorities; (2) self-interest [1–2 preconventional]; (3) achieving goodness as a person; (4) obedience for the good of society as a whole [3–4 conventional]; (5) concern for due process; and (6) concern for equitable justice [5–6 postconventional]. There is movement here from naïve egoism and heteronomous authority to individual freedom within genuine society based upon rational principles.

Finally, Robert N. Bellah proposes a fivefold typology of religious evolution—primitive, archaic, historic, early modern, and modern—each characterized in terms of symbol system, religious action, context of social action, and effects on general social action. Most pertinent to discussion of the biblical cultures are his categories of archaic and historic religion. In archaic symbolization (as seen in Bronze and Early Iron Age religions), deities are more objectively defined within a single world horizon, become the objects of speculative mythologies, and must be dealt with primarily through sacrifice. The archaic world is a two-class social world (elites-peasants), with the elites monopolizing political and religious roles. By contrast, historic symbolization (as seen in Israelite prophets, Greek philosophers, other representatives of Karl Jaspers's Axial Age) depicts a deity or deities within another world of value set over against this world.[12] This symbolic dualism leads to political and moral critique, opening possibilities for historical change. Religious action is oriented to salvation, and the self becomes more defined over against the group. The historic world is now a four-class world (political-military elite, cultural-religious elite, urban low-status groups [merchants, artisans], peasants).

These theorists and perspectives support the following synthetic model of developmental poles within the sociocultural horizon of the biblical periods.[13] Related to biblical theology, these model categories point to the need for developmental assessment of biblical images for God and eventual "interpretive judgment" about the cognitive, moral, and symbolic progress or capacities of various biblical periods and cultures. Only a suggestive sketch is offered here:

Table A: Developmental Model for Biblical Cultures/Periods

	Archaic social organization (Bronze, Early Iron Ages)	Historic social organization (Iron, Jaspers's Axial Age)
Implications for social change	Static orientation	More dynamic orientation
Worldview	One world	Two worlds
Theology	Tribal gods and humans within single world (poly, henotheism), gods reward and punish	God(s) in another world, move toward universal deity (monotheism), dualistic theodicy
Self	Emotive, concrete orientation (perception)	Rational control of emotion, some abstract facilities (conception)
Typical religious personnel	King, priest	Prophet, poet philosopher
Solidarity	Mechanical, two-class	Somewhat more organic, four-class
Religious action	Sacrifice, cult, concern for divine communication and purity	Salvation, concern for group- or self-destiny and eschatology
Morality	Authority and punishment orientation (royal case law), Kohlberg's pre/conventional	Responsibility measured against Covenant or the Good (apodictic law), Kohlberg's post/conventional

Biblical Theology in Developmental Perspective

The discovery of Yahweh was something like the discovery of America; it took several centuries before Israel really began to understand what it had discovered. . . . Israel's response to Yahweh was habitually a response based on imperfect knowledge at best, on misunderstanding and nonrecognition at worst. . . . The one whom Jesus called his father is the Yahweh of the Old Testament. It is here that the totality of the experience becomes vital; for the father is not the Yahweh of any single book or writer of the Old Testament. . . . The theology of the Old Testament has to be a study of the reality of Yahweh.[14]

It is now a standard conception in social-scientific criticism of the Bible that ancient economy and religion were embedded within politics and family as key institutional domains. The ancients were usually dyadic personalities, and collectivism describes the situation better than individualism. These generalities are not in question in this discussion. However, the move from archaic to historic social organization implies that some ancients effectively deployed religious energy in critique of politics and/or family and moved closer to individual selves. Certainly, king, priest, and prophet are well known from the biblical traditions. The emergence of a more complex set of roles and statuses (four-class system) implies more organic than mechanical solidarity. However, morality was most likely to be conventional if not preconventional.

Israel, upon Iron Age appearance, had begun to achieve a historic configuration of symbolization and social organization. Bellah thinks this depended upon the "rationalization of political change."[15] However, there were strong vestiges, "mortgages," of tribal and archaic conceptualization.[16] The world of early Israel was still very much engaged in struggle with fertility deities and mythologies of the ancient Near East. Only with the further rationalizations of the exile does a universalist Yahweh become really thinkable (though never entirely realized: universal law, Isa 42:2b; but nations of unequal value, Isa 43:3).

Ancient cognition was colored heavily by collectivist perceptual modes (gossip, group-think, and political propaganda). Biblical language, moreover, is rich with examples of Werner's physiognomic perception: God, walking (Gen 3:8; Hab 3:6), possessing hands (Ps 95:4-5); nature, singing or clapping (Ps 98:8; Isa 44:23; 55:12); compassion located in the bowels, anger associated with the nose (Ps 78:38). Only a relatively few ancient philosophers managed to reach abstract and conceptual understandings of the world; predictably, these Hellenistic-period philosophical traditions entered into a critical assessment of ancient mythologies and elaborated arguments about physics, metaphysics, and ethics.

Within both Testaments, Israelite and Christian movement struggled between archaic and historic symbolizations of deity, between images of God that enshrine Kohlberg's preconventional (punishment, self-interest) or urges toward postconventional (universal law, hospitality to strangers) moral views, between tribal Tyrant and God of universal mercy and justice. Later, Christologies would also share in this struggle.

It might be claimed that Amos, Second Isaiah, Job, and Jonah mark the high points of Old Testament symbolizations of deity. The first writing prophet conceives of a God whose justice, though still oriented to punishment based upon honor concerns rather than positive delineations of general principle, encompasses and incorporates the surrounding peoples. Deuteronomy and the Deuteronomists, however, seem archaic by comparison. The Second Isaiah envisions a creator God, the holder and wielder of all power and authority. Interestingly, this step toward universal deity involves theodicy problems that are difficult to reconcile with more complex moral conceptions. The emergence of apocalyptic in the postexilic period is the logical result. Job indeed wrestles with the notion of a Deuteronomistic God who hovers over the sinner ready to punish, but Job's wrestling with shame also drives him to seek a more comprehensive notion of God (who has other, or better, things to do than simply account covenant infractions—a possible meaning of Job 40). Jonah's God, as well, marks an interesting move toward empathy and even "love for enemies."

Likewise in the New Testament, the Jesus of Wisdom-Q (Luke 6:35) sees a gracious God at the heart of reality while Deuteronomic-Q is preoccupied with divine vengeance at the coming of the Son of Man (Luke 17:27). Indeed, the God of the Synoptic Apocalypse (Mark 13) or John's Apocalypse seems at a preconventional moral level, while Wisdom-Q expresses the postconventional.

The biblical material mostly does not generate abstract conceptualizations of the world and God, but largely expresses worlds of poetic perception or metaphor. Only texts like Qoheleth, under the impact of foreign culture, engage in more abstract ruminations. Not until the Enoch traditions, Wisdom of Solomon (e.g., chapter 13), Philo, or Paul does this impulse take more complete hold in Israelite tradition. Indeed, in referring to maturity in Christ (Gal 4:7; 1 Cor 13:11-12; Eph 4:13), the Pauline tradition glimpses a deeper movement within the biblical traditions.

The Hermeneutical Task
in Developmental Perspective

The presupposition of every comprehending interpretation is a previous living relationship to the subject, which directly or indirectly finds expression in the text and which guides the direction of the enquiry. Without such a relationship to life in which text and interpreter are bound together, enquiry and comprehension are not possible, and an enquiry is not motivated at all. In saying this we are also saying that every interpretation is necessarily sustained by a certain prior understanding of the subject which lies under discussion or in question.[17]

Marcion recognized the presence in the Bible of differing notions of deity, but did he not have access to the developmental theories of modern social science. Moreover, he could not consider that there were archaic and historic elements intermixed within both Testaments. The social configuration of Christianity and Judaism remained at best historic throughout late antiquity and the Middle Ages. The Protestant Reformation marked a new development, Bellah's early modern type, with simplification of historic dualistic symbolization and heightened focus upon the individual before God. This was based to a degree upon Luther's return to literalism and insistence upon a biblical center in Christ. Lutheranism avoided Marcionism, conservatively retained both "law" and "gospel," and articulated them either dialectically or in the unidirectional "law drives to gospel." However, Lutheranism in either its propositional or experiential forms has not always wrestled with the ideological consequences of these paradoxical views of God (hence, its propensity to conservative ethics). Indeed, based upon its limited social-symbolic repertoire, early Protestantism generally tended toward "characterological rigidity."[18]

Modernity has wrought radical changes and new freedoms, together with profound challenges to traditional (including biblical) religion. Yves Lambert argues that the axial-age religions respond to the modern crisis typically in four distinct ways. They (1) become extinct as relics of the past; (2) undergo adaptation or reinterpretation; (3) adopt a repristinating or fundamentalist stance; or (4) mutate into novel forms (usually with scientist features). In this sense, modernity is a new "axial age" when old things "fade out" and new things "fade in."[19]

Persistent postmodern cultural difficulties highlight important recurring "religiocultural patterns" (RCPs) and the importance of developmental thinking. Indeed, human development generally seems to move between two poles and two broad types of RCPs.[20] Humans survive little on the basis of instinct and adapt through symbolic apparatuses of culture; they always stand somewhere between determinacy and contingency, what is given and volition, nature and culture. These dimensions cannot be separated, but RCPs may focus more on one pole than the other. Humans thus are dependent upon but free relative to their many environments—the largest of which is cosmic. Talcott Parsons gives an account of the human condition as a laminate of inorganic, organic, action, and telic systems:[21]

Table B: Talcott Parsons's Model of the Human Condition

Reproduction (Family) *Means*	Goal attainment (Politics, social system) *End*
Adaptation (Economic system)	Pattern maintenance (Cultural system) *Means*

Adaptation and reproduction have to do with the means of species-survival; goal attainment and pattern maintenance (to some degree) have to do with achievement of group development and progress. As such, especially at the level of the cultural system, these categories are enshrined in a group's mythology through which comes essential identity and notions of ultimate purpose.

These poles—adaptation pressure and arrangements for goal-directed freedom brought about through culture—are recognized in other terms by Henri Bergson in his great discussion of two sources of morality and religion:

> Social life is thus immanent, like a vague ideal, in instinct as well as in intelligence: this ideal finds its most complete expression in the hive or the ant-hill on the one hand, in human societies on the other. Whether human or animal, a society is an organization; it implies a co-ordination and generally also a subordination of elements; it therefore exhibits, whether merely embodied in life or, in addition, specifically formulated, a collection of rules and laws. But in a hive or an ant-hill the individual is riveted to his task by his structure, and the organization is relatively invariable, whereas the human community is variable in form, open to every kind of progress.[22]

Drawing from these general considerations, the following table identifies elements that elucidate the thrust of each polar RCP (along with a prominent pathology of that pole). Human beings ordinarily pass beyond the genetic stage, but realizations of the potentialities and capacities of the secondary stage are limited in actual cultural achievements (as is clear from the biblical traditions). Primary enculturation is never left entirely behind, and is necessary for species survival, but secondary enculturation must also be acquired to adapt to new situations and to direct action in the absence of clear instinctual direction.

Core reality: The tabular analysis recognizes that cultural patterns might be oriented either more closely to the biological-familial sphere and environmental adaptation or to broader cultural horizons beyond the primary reference group.

Core values: These values describe the driving environmental force in the RCP. RCPs formulated on group survival and "genetic culture" will tend to maximize the group's advantages and welfare at the expense of other groups. RCPs formulated within "symbolic culture" will recognize a valid, though relative place for other groups' RCPs.

Theology: Each theological pole is rooted in adaptive-social or symbolic-cultural concerns. Archaizing theology is oriented to social

Table C: General Model of Human Development

RCPs	
(Absolutism) "Genetic culture" Primary socialization	Symbolic culture (Relativism) Secondary socialization[23]
Core reality: Species survival, adaptation Family, economy	Core reality: Goal-directed freedom Culture, politics
Core values: Survival, group-oriented obligation and conformity, identity consolidation	Core values: Openness to change, creative integration of individual and group goals
Theology: Tribal, premodern or archaic	Theology: Universal, historic or modern
Self and personality: Collectivist, self-despising attitudes	Self and personality: Individualist, self-revising attitudes
Religious action: salvation as exclusive group protection and survival, by vicarious sacrifice	Religious action: salvation as realization and redemption of meaningful action, by grace
Cognition: Consistency truth- criterion Ideological indoctrination, group perception	Cognition: Correspondence truth-criterion Search for truth, abstract conception
Solidarity: Mechanical	Solidarity: Organic
Leadership: Formal authority structures Credentials, qualifications	Leadership: Substantive authority Credibility, qualities
Education: Uncritical repristination Apologetics, scholastic sentences "Rationality"[22]	Education: Critical representation Hermeneutics, creative retrieval "Reasonableness"[24]
Morality: Pre/conventional	Morality: Post/conventional
Intergroup dynamics: Intolerant and uncritical disengagement with outsiders Negative reciprocal relations	Intergroup dynamics: Tolerant and critical engagement with outsiders Balanced or generalized reciprocal relations

cohesion and survival; progressive theology is oriented to meaningful individual freedom and responsibility. Biblical theology, though pre-modern, moves away from one pole toward the other pole.

Self and personality: The personality encouraged within the primary group is collectivist, conformist, and submissive; the personality culti-vated within the secondary group is individualist, creative, and exploratory (though not necessarily disrespectful of tradition or the pri-mary group).

Religious action: Familistic value-emphasis points to sacrifice as the highest form of love, and group purity and survival as core objectives; individualist freedom-of-action aims at building culture, struggling against meaninglessness, and a salvation that can only be redemption through grace (reversal of entropy).

Cognition: Truth may express either relative consistency or repre-sentations adequately corresponding to reality (or a mixture). Ideologi-cal truth is truth reduced to group or individual consistency; adequate truth attempts to correspond faithfully to reality even when inconsis-tencies appear within the group's cultural map. Abstract conception is an index of advanced cognitive development (Heinz Werner).

Solidarity: Accords respectively with core reality and values.

Leadership: Leadership in the primary sphere tends to be formal and censorious, backed by group sanctions; leadership in the secondary sphere is interested in the cultivation of substantive authority through assent, rooted in individual and critical thought.

Education: Primary education is constantly under the "gravitational force" of familial or group expectation or tugged toward indoctrination; secondary education proceeds on critical grounds toward greater "truth-adequacy."

Morality and intergroup dynamics: As these various cultural pat-terns play out, group behaviors accord. The primary mode is pre/con-ventional, other groups are treated with suspicion or as religious infidels. Their truths are impugned and their absolutes considered demonic. Conversion is pursued over tolerance and understanding. The secondary mode is post/conventional, the limited perceptions and false absolutes of the primary group as well as the relativity of cultures are recognized.

The model indicates why gender, race, and class become core issues within contemporary religious discussion or modern academy, especially in respect to biblical authority and morality, since these are issues precisely where primary and secondary spheres mesh concretely. Primary culture persists in the face of and even resists secondary RCPs for two main reasons: (1) Primary mythologies are seen as "natural" or rooted in natural order, and (2) primary thinking is reinforced consistency (i.e., "consistency truth" or "rationality" [Warren Nord[25]] constantly enforced by group-reference and group-think).

Secondary culture, dedicated to "correspondence truth," evaluates through rich information sets and multiple frameworks. Secondary RCPs permit critical appraisal of the claims about gender, race, and class thrown up from the primary view. Recovery of women's voices and examination of power relations under patriarchy show breaks in the claim for natural statuses. Homosexual people are discovered to have been present and creative participants all along. Pigmentation is recognized to be no more than skin-deep, and social inequality often the result of power-relations under a veneer of legal justification.

Turning to religion, a conservative type—based in the primary world—has frequently aligned itself with rigid patriarchal role-stereotypes, racist stereotyping, and a conservative politics that enforces social stratification. Even primary religions of the underclasses, though these have held liberating impulses, have not often moved beyond RCPs that promise indefinite transcendence of the situation, or utopia.[26]

Secondary culture discovers the symbolic nature of religion and its power to direct human action. Bellah, for instance, has pondered the correspondence truth of religion in "symbolic realist" terms, in contrast to the history of reductionistic treatments of religion by the social sciences (seen merely as legitimation of political regimes, ideological superstructure, projection).[27] Symbolic realism depicts religion as "the most general mechanism for integrating meaning and motivation in action systems" and "the most general model that [a group] has of itself and its world."[28] All cultures have such compact symbols, serving to relate participants to their most general environment. Werner notes that "primitive people use a single word to express a whole situation or action"; moreover, he says:

The difference between lower and more advanced societies does not consist of the fact that primitive forms of behavior are absent in the latter, but rather that the more primitive the society the greater the homogeneity and the consequent dominance of primitive behavior.[29]

This strong realist position provides a basis for understanding general human truths without reducing cultures to univocal meaning.

Secondary cultural impulses, of course, undergird modern biblical criticism. Lower criticism calls into question any naïve immediacy assumed between modern versions of the Bible and an original "divine word." The facts of text variation and translation, not to mention the messy historical picture of manuscript copying and the politics of Bible translation over centuries, bring some degree of sobriety to discussions about inspiration. Higher criticism incorporates science, history, and now social science into exegetical work. The critical consequences are well known. For instance, science undermines magical thinking and belief in miracles. Historical and cultural judgments come into play— e.g., regarding the historicity of the Markan Passion predictions or Jesus' betrayal by Judas. The Gospels show Jesus as an obedient Mediterranean son ready to do the will of his father. Yet if Jesus predicted his passion (the Markan Passion predictions are adjudged secondary by almost all Gospel scholars) and foreknew that he was going to be arrested in the garden, why then did he need Judas's betrayal? Is there not here information that succumbs to the criteria of both historical and cultural embarrassment—since the betrayal belies the obedience?

Conclusion: Seeking a God of Influence

The adequacy of any ultimate perspective is its ability to transform human experience so that it yields life instead of death. . . . [Tillich's] restless quest for the "dimension of depth" . . . was his great contribution to breaking out of the institutional ghetto and seeing once more, as Augustine did, the figure of Christ in the whole world.[30]

The modeling of human development indeed poses important questions for biblical hermeneutics: Why or how will ancient biblical culture

remain part of modern religious conversation? What biblical understandings about God should endure?

To be sure, genetic options are strongly represented today in conservative, sectarian, or fundamentalist religious groups. In the primary
worldview, the Bible becomes a pattern for building an exclusive society
or culture of the pure. This regression is increasingly evident throughout
global Christianity, even in mainline churches that historically have
founded universities.[31] One is more likely to hear that "we should
relearn all the stories" than that "we should submit our heritage to
searching criticism." Thus, the cultural-linguistic approach of George
Lindbeck seems potentially regressive, perhaps more an expression of
rationality than of reasonableness.[32]

For those willing to live with the Bible after social-scientific criticism, reinterpretation may be the wiser option. If the biblical material is
not simply to become irrelevant, hijacked by fundamentalism, or incorporated into some strange scientistic syncretism, its meaning must be
persuasively translated. A biblical hermeneutic informed by developmental perspectives embraces the secondary paradigm both in terms of
its critically reflective culture and its search for meaningful human direction within the widest possible frame. An authoritarian literalism is ster-
ile insofar as it is incapable of a dialog with the heritage that could
eventuate in a creative development out of it. If the major objective in
reading is a consistent repristination (genetic culture), then one cannot
expect creativity. If the major objective is modeling reality in which
Bible, history, science, and ongoing human experience are part of the
benchmarks for correspondence, then a fruitful discussion is possible.

One must reckon, though, that the gains of secondary enculturation
far outweigh the losses of primary security, if a truer picture of reality is
acquired and richer human options are made available—for surviving
the technological threat to higher culture, participating successfully in a
multiethnic global context without a Sunday School mentality, and
escaping ecological disaster contingent upon religion, economics, and
politics increasingly underwritten by primary cultural concerns.

Developmental perspectives indeed offer a potentially new starting
point for controlled hermeneutical discussion about the Bible and biblical theology. There is the possibility, of course, that the present sketch
leaves pertinent detail out of the picture. However, these ideal-type models—as hopefully useful and incisive simplifications of reality—do have
the virtue of calling attention to possible causes for the persistence of
exclusively primary thinking in ancient or modern religion (rooted in

adaptive survival needs and pressures) and consequent resistance to secondary enculturation (since more complex reality and creative freedom threaten the primary group). As well, developmental models reveal the naïveté of an overconfident age of technology ignorant of broader and deeper human wisdom. The terrors of the present, underwritten by defensive puritanisms and fearful fundamentalisms, make such enriched hermeneutical discussion urgent.

CHAPTER NINETEEN

Interfaith Dialogue

CHALLENGING THE RECEIVED VIEW

Bruce J. Malina

Bruce Malina here assesses a recent Vatican document in the light of a histori-cal understanding enriched with social-scientific perspectives. He argues that a careful reading of this recent document from the Pontifical Biblical Commission indicates that it employs categories and understandings not rooted in the social context of the biblical text. The document presumes a straightforward continu-ity between ancient Israel and contemporary Jewish people, notably by using the (medieval and modern) word "Jew" for ancient Israel, ancient Judean, and otherwise. Similarly with Christian nomenclature. Such attribution of identity, he suggests, is ecumenically convenient but not historically accurate or, ulti-mately, helpful in dealing with the radically different social, religious, and polit-ical contexts of Christians and Jews today.

Social-scientific insights into the context of the Old Testament hold broad and deep implications for today, perhaps nowhere more starkly than in Jewish-Christian dialog. For example, when I looked at the most recent document of the Pontifical Biblical Commission, entitled *The Jewish People and Their Sacred Scriptures in the Christian Bible*, my immediate reaction was chagrin at the fact that the document's authors accepted the "Received View" of speaking about Jewish and Christian relations both today and in antiquity. Of course, not a few professional exegetes working in the area of the Old Testament as well as the New Testament likewise share the Received View. It is these per-spectives and presuppositions that I will consider in this essay in hopes that social-scientific perspectives can inform future efforts at interfaith dialog.

Received View and Meanings in Language

The "Received View" is a label used in the philosophy of science to characterize the prescribed way of asking and answering questions in a given academic discipline.[1] It is the way of understanding things currently in vogue among a large number of practitioners and in the popular mind. The Received View is a powerful and dogmatic orthodoxy, controlling academic departments, key journals, as well as grant- and/or fellowship-bestowing agencies. It dictates the criteria that are to control "convincing" and "unconvincing" contributions to the field. As a label, the term "Received View" connotes a reigning but inadequate or obsolete consensus, and it is in this sense that it has been adopted here.

The Pontifical Biblical Commission document itself consists of an introduction, three major sections, and a conclusion. The introduction and conclusion are of a "pastoral" nature, that is, meant to be relevant to the contemporary situation in one way or another. The whole has a preface by Cardinal Joseph Ratzinger, head of the Vatican Congregation for the Doctrine of the Faith (and now, since April 2005, Pope Benedict XVI), under whose aegis the Pontifical Biblical Commission worked. A list of its main sections appears later in this essay.

According to Donald Senior, a member of the Pontifical Biblical Commission, the major points addressed in the document are the two questions challenging Christians today and noted by Ratzinger in his preface: Can Christians in good conscience still lay claim to the heritage of the Old Testament? And, Does the New Testament itself contribute to hostility toward the Jews?[2]

The document has generally been received quite positively, if with reservations. For example, Senior is quite laudatory, but Roland Murphy underscores the lack of feeling for the Old Testament and modern Jewish biblical scholarship.[3] Amy-Jill Levine points up the lack of reference to traditional Jewish scholarship from which, the document claims, exegetes have much to learn.[4] Ryszard Rubinkiewicz offers a fine overview of the document,[5] while Waldemar Chrostowski notes how the historical ground supporting the document has shifted with the *Nakba* (the "Catastrophe," i.e., the violence accompanying the founding of the modern Jewish state) and ongoing inhumanity against Palestinians.[6]

As the authors of the document themselves state, the purpose of the document is to facilitate Christian–Jewish ecumenical dialogue. Yet the document provides no description or definition of who the Christians and Jews in question are and no clear mention of the focus or subject of the ecumenical dialogue in question. If the dialogue is to be about the Bible, is it to be about the Bible as a book or collection of books (academic) or as sacred scripture (religious: the word of God). What relationship is there between modern Christians and the Christians referred to in the document as authors, hearers, and personages in antiquity? What relationship is there between modern Jews and the Jews referred to in the document as authors, hearers, and personages in antiquity?

Senior (2003) states: "I think it is important to note again that this remarkable document does not pretend to be a detached, religiously neutral assessment of the historical relationship between Judaism and Christianity. It is an official teaching document of the Catholic Church and obviously and clearly represents the faith stance of the church. Its title is significant." And that is where I should like to begin, since the title sets the tone for the (mis)understanding of what is involved in this rather large (200-plus pages in the Editrice Vaticana edition) document.

Briefly put, on the basis of the historical awareness shared by a good number of scholars, the ambiguous title of the document should make one wary. Does the reference to "Jewish People and Their Sacred Scripture" treat of modern Jewish people? Does the "Christian Bible" refer to modern Christians? Are the sacred scriptures of modern Jewish people actually in the Christian Bible? As the document unfolds, the points of contact considered are in fact between first-century Israelites and Jesus-group members. Truth in advertising would have the document's title read: "Ancient Israel and Its Sacred Scriptures in the Modern Jewish and Modern Christian Bible." This perspective, with its historically sensitive switch in categories, radically changes the boundaries of the inquiry.

In fact, the title of the document as well as the labels used in its major headings presume an understanding of the past and of groups in the past that are anachronistic. This anachronism is rooted in the prevailing presuppositions and oversights characteristic of the Received View in this area.[7] Adherents of the Received View systematically ignore the fact that meanings realized in wordings expressed in the sounds of speaking and squiggles of writing always derive from some social system. What in fact did the wordings Israel, *Ioudaios, Hellēn,* or *Christianos* mean in the social systems of antiquity? And what have these wordings come to mean in later centuries and in the contemporary social systems of Euro-Americans? Philology and etymology are about wording not about meaning, hence cannot supply the meanings encoded in these words.

Received View and Reading

Another point ignored by adherents of the Received View is that reading is a social act in which readers always bring in their own experience and understanding of the world based on the social systems into which they have been enculturated.[8] Authors (and speakers) likewise express meanings from the social system into which they have been enculturated. Modern authors who do not take their readership into account are called inconsiderate authors (or speakers or teachers). But what of readers who read the documents of ancient authors who could not possibly have had modern readers and their social systems in view? Without making the effort to understand the social system shared by ancient authors, modern readers are really quite inconsiderate. Their understanding of ancient authors is necessarily anachronistic and ethnocentric. And this is the problem with the Received View. It allows for, even approves of, inconsiderate readings. The document in question is a case in point.

Anachronism accepted in the service of interreligious dialogue becomes a political judgment. That is, it allows for contemporary relevance; but it can hardly serve the demands of honesty, academic or otherwise. The fundamental anachronism in the document is rooted in the typology adopted for classifying modern and ancient groups. To begin with, the labels "Jew/Jewish" and "Christian" are treated as though the meaning of these words has the universal constancy of words like *male* and *female* or *up* and *down*. Universal constants, of course, need no social-system moorings, much like numerals manipulated in abstract mathematics. Obviously, the words in question are the outcome of categorization, serving as labels for categories of social groups.[9] Category use entails the explicit or implicit recognition that some entities share social traits allowing for category membership according to culturally specific criteria. With what categories do groups labeled Christian and/or Jew share category membership? If we put these questions to contemporary, twenty-first-century groups, we can usually discern Jewish and Christian groups, or at least understand the generic significance of how those labels are ascribed. The reason for this is that these labels, like all other words, get their significance from the prevailing social systems. We all know the social systems of our enculturation very well. So we all know the meaning of *Jew* and *Christian* very well from groups in our experience so labeled. The Pontifical Biblical Commission document would have group members so labeled dialogue with each other. Again, one might ask, about what? About the Bible or sacred scripture? Do the groups in question share adequate social constancy and continuity with the ancient groups that the Pontifical Biblical Commission authors called "Jews" and "Christians" to enable a dialogue rooted on a shared (or borrowed) sacred scripture?

The Problem of Retrojecting Labels

The first fundamental problem that the document overlooks is the implication of retrojecting the modern labels "Jew" and "Christian" to previous centuries. To assume that ancient groups dating from two thousand years ago can bear the same labels with the same meanings used for contemporary groups implies a sort of universal constancy and identity. This, in turn, presumes a universally and unaltered stable social system—since words get their meanings from social systems. Given the frequent, often step-level changes experienced by Mediterranean peoples in the social history of groups labeled Jewish and Christian, I submit that there has been no universally constant and stable, historically unaltered social system in the Mediterranean to warrant some universal constant meaning for the group labels in question. To say it in another way, the major problem with this document is that it is very careless in the use of the terms "Jews" and "Christians," implying and asserting a constant identity between first-century Eastern Mediterranean Israelite groups referred to in biblical documents and contemporary groups called "Jews" and "Christians." I perceive this to be a fundamental error.

Of course, the root of this anachronistic perspective is a radical, but undemonstrable, belief in some sort of group identity and persistence over time. This belief is revealed in translation—and translation always involves transition and transformation from one social system to another. Is it correct to call first-century *Ioudaioi* "Jews"? In the contemporary period[10] an increasing number of biblical scholars have called attention to the prevalent ethnocentric and anachronistic reading of the New Testament in general and to the inaccuracy of translating the Greek word *Ioudaios* as "Jew."[11] And a leading Greek-English lexicon has significantly altered its entry on "*Ioudaios*."[12] In a popular article, Reuven Firestone writes:

> It is common knowledge that Christianity is different from the religion of the Old Testament, but some are still unaware that Judaism (sometimes referred to as Rabbinic Judaism, as opposed to the religion or the Judaism practiced during biblical times) is a different religion from that of the Hebrew Bible. What is different about it? Nearly everything: its liturgy, its forms of worship, its codes of laws and its theologies.[13]

This common knowledge is not so common, it seems. Like most historians, professional and nonprofessional, the authors of the Pontifical Biblical Commission overlook these distinctions in their work.

The outcome can only be an anachronistic and ethnocentric historical assessment of the group in question. The Pontifical Biblical Commission would have saved its readers a world of confusion had it attempted to define and/or describe the modern and ancient groups they label "Jew" and "Christian." Since the scholars on this commission share a sense of history, they are fully aware that modern Jews and Christians have perhaps little in common with groups they label "Jews" and "Christians" in antiquity. For the sake of clarity, they might have labeled the group(s) they refer to with the Medieval English word "Jew" as Jew 1, Jew 2, Jew 3, etc., to Jew 21 in terms of the centuries to which they refer. After all the "rabbinization" of some Israelite groups in the fourth century C.E. and the Talmudization of Israelite self-understanding in the fifth and sixth centuries, along with the rise of Zionism and its consequences in Europe and the Middle East in the twentieth century, have all radically reshaped the theology and self-understanding of people who call themselves "Jews." The same holds for Christians. All Christian groups today are rooted in some way in the Council of Nicea (325 C.E.) and Constantine's Christendom. Yet the medieval transformation of Christianity as political and papal religion, the Reformation, the Council of Trent, the proliferation of protesting sects, and the Vatican Councils have all transformed the significance of the term "Christian." Instead of retrojecting modern usages of the words "Jews" and "Christians," the Pontifical Biblical Commission authors might have used the labels that the ancient people of the time used for themselves, considered below, and described them according to their own social system(s).

The first problem then is that the members of the Pontifical Biblical Commission take the terms "Christian" and "Jew" as universal constants, presuming identity between present Christians and Jews and those personages they call Christians and Jews in antiquity. Does such an identity in fact exist? There is something confusing in lumping like features while dismissing differences as though they never existed or have not resulted in rather essential transformations of the entities in question. The Received View mistakenly allows the terms "Jew" and "Christian" to be treated as though they label groups with millennial permanence and continuity.

The Problem of Ancient Labels

A second problem is presented by the document: the members of the Pontifical Biblical Commission do not take the social labels evidenced in antiquity with any seriousness. For example, the Greek word *Ioudaios*, with its *-aios* ending, means of or pertaining to a place called *Ioudaia*, just as *Galilaios* means of or pertaining to a place called *Galilaia*. If Jesus is a Galilean, then persons from Judea are Judeans—not Jews (a medieval English word still in modern use). Calling people from Judea Judeans enables one to understand *Judaismos*, the customs and customary behaviors of people who live in or come from Judea. *Ioudaia*, *Ioudaios,* and *Ioudaismos* are cognate formations that can be well transliterated as Judea, Judean, and Judaism. To read any of these transliterations on the basis of their first syllable "Ju-" is to import meanings from later social systems and thus obfuscate any attempt at a considerate reading. (The English "Jew" is the first syllable of Old English "Judeas" and Middle English "Judeow, Judew").[14]

In other words, by calling Judeans "Jews," a modern person bridges the two thousand-year chasm in time and even deeper chasm in culture that separates modern groups labeled "Jews" from ancient groups labeled "Judeans."

The New Testament documents and their labels are instructive. Notice that in his letters Paul never calls himself a Judean, although he claims Judean birth (Gal 2:15; self-definitions Phil 3:5; 2 Cor 11:22). As a matter of fact, in Paul's letters, the correlative of Judean is Hellene. To be a Hellene was a status label, not a label of regional origin. There was no Hellas in the first century. A Hellene was a person who was cultivated, who spoke a common Hellenic language, practiced some Macedonian or Athenian or, increasingly, Roman customs and behaved in a way that was considered cultivated (Petrochilos). A Hellene might be Roman, Israelite, Egyptian, or whatever. When Paul speaks of Judeans and Hellenes, he is speaking of his fellow Israelites. Israel is Paul's name for his in-group. The correlative of Israel is the (other) peoples (*ta ethnē*). Interestingly, the collocation Judean and (other) peoples (vulgarly "Jew and Gentile") never occurs.

For Paul the world consists of Israel and other peoples, while his Israel consists of Judeans and Hellenes (Rom 3:9; 10:12; 1 Cor 1:24; Gal 3:28). Judeans were Israelites with ties to Judea and its customs. In terms that Philo decried, Judeans were barbarians in Hellene eyes (so too, for example, in Clement of Alexandria, *Stromata* VI, 41, 1: "Just as the kerygma has come now at the right time, so also at the right time the Law and the Prophets were given to the barbarians and philosophy to the Hellenes—to prepare them to hear the kerygma"). Hellenes, on the other hand, also included Israelites who were enculturated and assimilated into Hellenistic ways.

For the author(s) of Matthew, for example, Jesus was concerned solely with the house of Israel (Matt 10:5). In that document, the house of Israel consists of people from Galilee (Galileans), people from Perea (Pereans), and people from Judea (Judeans). Together these groups form the house of Israel. Israel, then, is the in-group name of this people. However, out-groups called Israelites Judeans, regardless of the distinctions Israelites made among themselves. For Romans, Athenians, Alexandrians, Antiochenes, and the like, anyone of the house of Israel was a Judean.[19]

On the other hand, to refer intelligibly to or describe an Israelite to a non-Israelite, even Israelites, notably those living outside Syro-Palestine, must call their fellow in-group members Judeans, the non-Israelite label for Israelites.

It is ignorance of this common labeling practice that leaves many moderns confused. And yet this process of reshaping in-group and out-group labels continues as a common human social phenomenon. For example, in the United States foreigners find U.S. self-description in terms of nationality (ancestral national origin) quite confusing. Yet American citizens have no trouble defining themselves as Irish, Indian, Hispanic, Japanese, African, Italian, and the like. However, should a self-defined Irish American and a self-defined African American find themselves together in London and should a Londoner ask them what is their nationality, both would answer in harmony: American. In-group differences vanish in a new configuration in face of the need for clarity in an intergroup interaction. In the in-group, in the United States, group boundaries are labeled differently by natives than when they are in face of an out-group.

Similarly, I once was present at an Israeli bond rally held in conjunction with the birthday of a rabbi on my faculty. The Israeli salesman did well in Omaha and excused himself for his quick departure from our fair city with the explanation: "I still have lots of Americans to visit." Obviously the Americans he had to visit were American Jews, who, for this Israeli, were simply Americans (although the thirteen million Jews in the United States are numerically inconsequential to count as America).

Such group boundary marking and subsequent labeling are quite important for understanding Paul, the famous "apostle to the Gentiles." Did Paul in fact ever approach Gentiles? Or did he see his task as one among fellow Israelites who lived among Gentiles? In his high-context style of writing and explaining his activity, I believe the latter is the case. Paul was apostle to Israelites living among non-Israelites. He has no message for non-Israelites, who have their own gods and lords (1 Cor 8:5).

These group labels are also useful for discerning the audience of given New Testament documents. For example, Matthew is surely an Israelite document meant for Israelites. Judeans are always Judeans, Galileans are Galileans. The final edict in Matthew is to make disciples of "all nations," that is, of Israelites living among all nations, just like Paul.

Luke, on the other hand, is either writing as a cultivated Hellene or for persons with a Hellene understanding of society, since for him in-group Israelites are Judeans. For example, in his description of Judeans in Jerusalem at Pentecost, Luke classifies Israelite Parthians, Medes, Elamites, Mesopotamians, Cappadocians, Pontians, Asians, Phrygians, Pamphylians, Egyptians, Cyreneans, Cretans, and Arabs as "Judeans." In Acts, there is no passage in which "Hellenes" univocally points to non-Israelite. Luke mentions synagogues of Judeans (Acts 13:5; 14:1; 17:1, 10) as well as of Hellenes (Acts 6:9), and speaks of Judeans and Hellenes as Paul does (Acts 18:4; 9:10, 17; 19:17)

In sum, from the perspective of the members of the house of Israel who described the activities of the God of Israel in the activities and discourses of the Israelite Messiah, Jesus of Nazareth, the map of social groups changes labels depending on where the speaker/writer is located. The following chart illustrates these results:

From an Israelite Perspective When Speaking in Judea, Galilee, or Perea		
With in-group persons	Individually: Judeans, Galileans, Pereans	Collectively: House of Israel
With out-group persons	Individually: Romans, Corinthians, Philippians etc.	Collectively: The People (other than Israel), Gentiles

From an Israelite Perspective When Speaking outside Judea, Galilee, or Perea		
Speaking with fellow Israelites:	About the in-group: general name is Israel, broken down into Judeans (barbarians) and Hellenes (Greeks) or territory names	About the out-group: general name is Gentiles or the people (other than Israel)
Speaking with non-Israelites (Gentiles):	About the in-group: Judeans	About the out-group: specific non-Israelite group names: Romans, Corinthians, etc.

For the out-group, the name for Israelites regardless of provenance was Judean.

It is significant to note that at the time there was in fact no Israelite community that could acquiesce in the title of the one "true Israel." As we see from New Testament authors, the title was still negotiable (arguments in Matthew for true Israel; in Rom 2:28-29 "true Judeans"; Rom 9:6 "true Israel"; Gal 6:16 "Israel of God"; Rev 2:9; 3:9 "true Judeans"). Thus, Jesus groups took the labels "Israel" and "Judean" to themselves. Since all Jesus-group members at the time were Israelites, this early coopting of the generic name "Israel" or "Judean" cannot be labeled "supersessionism." It is important to bear the chronology in mind. The fact is Ben Zakkaism and its organized scribal Pharisaism emerged after the destruction of Jerusalem, when Jesus groups already existed quite independently of Jerusalem. Jesus groups saw themselves as Israel awaiting the theocracy proclaimed by Jesus, while later Ben

Zakkaist groups saw themselves as Israel awaiting the restoration of the Temple. Because Jesus groups were earlier in time and some of their number laid claim to being true Israel, it is historically false to consider Jesus groups as the "younger brother" of "older brother" Ben Zakkaism.[20] Jesus groups were in historical fact older. Both groups sought to coopt Israelite identity, and the Pharisees eventually did so with the rise of Christendom and the rabbinization of non-Jesus group Israelites.

Now if we adopt this set of group labels evidenced in the New Testament, the outline of the Pontifical Biblical Commission document takes on different and more accurate meaning (see chart on p. 294).

Conclusion

The Pontifical Biblical Commission document takes on an explicitly contemporary cast, alluded to by Cardinal Ratzinger and his reference to the *Shoah,* a Hebrew word meaning "catastrophe."[21] In the opening of the document, we read: "Modern times have made Christians more aware of the close fraternal bonds that unite them to the Jewish people. During the second world war (1939–1945), tragic events, or more precisely, abominable crimes subjected the Jewish people to a terrible ordeal that threatened their very existence throughout most of Europe." In fact, the Holocaust and the subsequent establishment of the State of Israel in 1948 have introduced whole new dimensions and context to biblical hermeneutics, as has the Israeli-Palestinian conflict. These contexts make it all the more imperative to recognize and respect the specific social contexts of the biblical texts and the radically different contexts that must inform Jewish-Christian relations today. As the outline indicates, the major part of the commission's document deals with the Israelite Jesus group authors' orientation toward and use of Israel's sacred scripture. This treatment, by and large, is very good. The only problem, again, is the fundamental error of mislabeling the persons in question. Accusations of mislabeling the ancients and denial of their identity with moderns bearing the same label is part of the overall problem indirectly addressed in this document, yet explicitly underscored by Cardinal Ratzinger. With the historical-critical method, "texts from the past could have no meaning other than that intended by the authors in their historical context." To expand the literal meaning of a biblical

document as well as to recover relevance as the Church Fathers did in their interpretation of Israel's sacred scripture, the members of the Pontifical Biblical Commission make reference to a theory of the multidimensional nature of human language. This enables them "to conclude that the Christian hermeneutic of the Old Testament, admittedly very different from that of Judaism, 'corresponds nevertheless to a potentiality of meaning effectively present in the texts' (no. 64)."

Given our understanding of the original social contexts of the biblical text, we must be cautious of attempts to find "potentiality of meaning" never intended in the original sociolinguistic contexts and careful to address our own context with theological language and judgments that are not anachronistic.

CHAPTER TWENTY

Psychology—Moses and Monotheism

THE FUTURE OF FREUD'S ILLUSION

Andrew D. H. Mayes

There has been constant interest in Sigmund Freud's book Moses and Monotheism *since its first publication over seventy years ago. In this essay Andrew Mayes examines its continuing relevance to historical understanding. Much current study is devoted to the significance of the work for the understanding of the cultural-mythological foundations of the Judeo-Christian tradition, or for its insights into the essential nature of Judaism or, indeed, as a covert history of the psychoanalytic movement. It has found little favor, however, as a serious contribution to Old Testament historical scholarship, despite its clear familiarity with Old Testament scholarship contemporary with Freud. Although the detail of Freud's historical proposals cannot withstand criticism, in one area, that of the nature of tradition, Mayes argues that Freud's work deserves scholarly attention.*

Freud's *Moses and Monotheism*

Freud's famous book *Moses and Monotheism* goes back to an unpublished fragment of what was intended to be a historical novel, written in 1934. This was followed by two essays, published in the journal *Imago*. The monograph, beginning with these two essays, finally appeared in 1939.[1] The book reflects these origins. It is marked by repetitions and digressions, and its claimed contribution to its subject, to provide a new understanding based on a psychoanalytic approach to history,[2] does not become clear until its final part.

Moses is argued by Freud not simply to bear an Egyptian name but to have been Egyptian by birth, and by career a high official in the Egyptian royal court. That this royal Egyptian should have taken on the leadership of a culturally inferior group of immigrants is explained by reference to contemporary events of Egyptian history. The reign of the eighteenth-dynasty Pharaoh Akhenaten saw the imposition of the monotheistic worship of Aten. The Aten religion, however, did not appeal to the general populace, and so the short period of Akhenaten's reign, seventeen years, was followed by a violent reaction, a period of turmoil and disorder before stability and traditional religion were restored by Horemhab. It is to that period of turmoil, between 1358 and 1350 B.C.E. that Moses' leadership of his people out of Egypt should be dated.

Moses had been a high official in Akhenaten's Egypt. He transmitted his Egyptian religion to the Jews and led them out of Egypt in order that the values and achievements of Egyptian religious thought should be preserved: his religion that he passed on was the exclusive and intolerant monotheism of Akhenaten. This religion had no mythology or magic, no artistic representation, and was completely silent on Osiris and the realm of the dead. It has remarkable points of contact with Judaism insofar as the latter also is characterized by exclusive monotheism and no belief in an afterlife.

Freud is also clear, however, that there are discrepancies between the nature of Aten and that of Yahweh in the Mosaic period. Aten was a universal god, Yahweh was a volcanic demon; the Aten religion was supposedly mediated by Moses to the Jews in Egypt, the worship of Yahweh was mediated to the Jews by Moses at Kadesh; the worship of Aten involved the rejection of magic, the worship of Yahweh did not exclude serpents as sources of divine healing. The historical resolution to this difficulty runs as follows: The people whom Moses led out of Egypt as followers of the religion of Aten were "just as little able to tolerate such a highly spiritualized religion and find satisfaction of their needs in what it had to offer as had been the Egyptians of the Eighteenth Dynasty," and so they revolted, murdered their leader (Moses), and "threw off the burden of the religion that had been imposed on them."[3] They later formed a union with related tribes at Kadesh. This union represented a compromise between the two groups, in which the followers of the murdered Egyptian Moses adopted the worship of Yahweh, while the

Kadesh group adopted the name Moses for their priest and a wider understanding of the significance of their god. Thus, the Yahweh of the original Kadesh group, who was originally a local volcano god, extended his authority to Egypt and replaced Aten. The Egyptian Moses was never at Kadesh and never knew the name Yahweh, while the Midianite priest who took on the name Moses had never set foot in Egypt and knew nothing of Aten.

This compromise, however, was fully worked out only in the long term. The immediate result of the murder of Moses was that the old strict monotheistic religion of the Egyptian Moses was suppressed; the shadow of his god, whose place had been taken by Yahweh, was preserved, however, and in time became stronger than Yahweh. "No one can doubt that it was only the idea of this other god that enabled the people of Israel to survive all the blows of fate and that kept them alive to our own days."[4] Yahweh had been a rude, narrow-minded local god, violent and bloodthirsty. The only reason for his transformation is that to one part of the people Moses had long ago given another and more spiritual conception of God, "a single deity embracing the whole world, who was not less all-loving than all-powerful, who was averse to all ceremonial and magic and set before men as their highest aim a life in truth and justice."[5] It is this understanding that, in the course of centuries, came to be attached to Yahweh.

This is not to be explained simply as a gradual development in the understanding of Yahweh; the political conditions of the Jews were very unfavorable to a development away from the idea of an exclusive national god to that of ruler of the world.[6] Rather, the transformation of Yahweh into the old Mosaic universal monotheistic god is the return of a repressed tradition. During a long period of latency the old Mosaic religion was handed down by tradition. To the transmission of this tradition not only the Levites but also the succession of the prophets especially contributed.[7] Yet the idea of an old tradition being transmitted by teachers, eventually to gain acceptance in the mass of the people, is inadequate in itself to explain the strength and power with which the old Mosaic religion eventually won over the hearts and minds of the Jewish people, to be "preserved by them as a precious possession." "A tradition that was based only on communication could not lead to the compulsive character that attaches to religious phenomena."[8]

It is a psychoanalytic contribution that provides the explanation for the transformative power of the repressed religion of Moses. Just as very early traumatic experiences of the individual may be repressed and, after a long latency period, may manifest themselves as neurotic symptoms, so also traumatic experiences in the history of the group may be repressed, and later manifest themselves in neurotic symptoms. The pattern typical of the history of the individual—early trauma, repression, latency, outbreak of neurosis and partial return of the repressed[9]—is true also of the history of the group. The murder of Moses was a traumatic event; the memory of it, together with the monotheistic religion of Moses, was repressed, but, after a long latency period, returned with force to take over the life and thought of the Jewish people. Moreover, this issue of the origin of Jewish monotheism belongs within a much wider psychoanalytic context: "When Moses brought the people the idea of a single god, it was not a novelty but signified the revival of an experience in the primaeval ages of the human family which had long vanished from men's conscious memory."[10]

Moses' murder by his followers is a repetition of the primal event, which formed part of the archaic heritage.[11] The murder of the father in the primal horde is part of the archaic heritage of mankind, in which civilization and religion are rooted; the murder of Moses is its repetition. The fact that it represented a repetition of the primal event ensured the transformative significance of Moses and his teaching. Only in terms of a return of the repressed memory of such an event can the obsessive commitment of the Jews to Mosaic monotheism be adequately understood. This commitment represented a renunciation of instinct; with its aniconic and anti-magical features inherited from Egypt, it represented a triumph of spirituality over the senses. Prophetic denunciation reinforced the sense of guilt for the original crime, so providing the motivation for the constantly increasing instinctual renunciation through which the Jews attained "ethical heights which had remained inaccessible to the other peoples of antiquity."[12]

Freud and His Motives

Freud[13] was well aware of the fact that his book would offend nearly everyone: devout Jews, because it denied the Jewish ancestry of Moses and ascribed the origins of Jewish monotheism to Egypt; the Catholic church, because of the argument that what we find in Judaism and Christianity is a repetition of that primordial event, the murder of the primal father by his sons, which lies at the root of religion and civilization; biblical scholars, because he seemed to play fast and loose with the biblical text, choosing those bits that favored a preconceived theory and rejecting others. What Freud seemed to be doing here was not simply

attempting to show how a psychoanalytic approach could make a positive contribution to history but rather almost the reverse of that, using
history in order to try to add further significance and legitimacy to the
psychoanalytic movement. Akhenaten, Moses, and Israelite monotheism are used in order to show the universal validity of the insights into
the nature of the human mind that psychoanalysis claimed to have
demonstrated.[14]

Yet, whatever he may have consciously intended, what Freud actually achieved in the book was something of enduring and comprehensive
significance. His book can be read as his final contribution to the development of a comprehensive cultural myth that deals with how things
really are in Judeo-Christian civilization; it can be read as an attempt to
provide an account of the essence of Judaism with which he himself
could identify; it can be read as a kind of covert history of psychoanalysis in which Moses stands for Freud himself. The degree to which Freud
himself was aware of what he was doing is not open to any easy answer,
but there are more than incidental indications of the possibility that he
was using the form of an account of Moses and monotheistic religion to
achieve a range of objectives. His constant, and historically inappropriate, use of the terms "Jew(s)" and "Jewish" is an immediate indication
of this.[15] What this implies is that it is valid, in the sense of being true to
Freud, to interpret his work in terms other than the purely historical, to
see in his book the working out of an understanding of the fundamental nature of the reality in which he lived, on a variety of levels.

With his presentation of the historically unverifiable murder of
Moses as a repetition of the murder of the primal father, and of the
Christian story as a further very disguised form of the same event, Freud
was developing a psychoanalytic understanding of Western civilization
in terms of what has been called its master narrative. Throughout his so-
called "cultural books"[16] Freud was developing his view that the evolution of society and of civilization can be understood by analogy with the
maturation of the individual human life. In both instances the sequence
of early trauma, defense, latency, outbreak of neurosis, and partial
return of the repressed, characterize development. In *Moses and
Monotheism*, from this perspective, the Egyptian origin of Moses and
his transmission of monotheistic belief to his followers is not the central
thesis;[17] rather, it is the presentation of Judeo-Christian civilization in
terms of the primal-horde theory.[18] This is a cultural myth, a paradigmatic tale, a story that provides a classic account of meaning precisely
because it echoes the sensed experience of individual human life. The

historical accuracy of the myth is not the issue. Its essential attribute is that it illuminates and informs contemporary life and experience. As with the psychoanalysis of the individual, so the psychoanalysis of culture has retrieved the distorted fragments of repressed experience and expressed them in a narrative account whose power to convince derives from its meaningful coherence.[19]

Freud himself may have believed that the primal horde and primal murder were historical data of human social development, but there is room to doubt that such a view is essential to his argument. For what Freud effectively does in *Moses and Monotheism* is to recreate the Judeo-Christian myth in an alternative form, providing "a sort of stripped-down generic version of the myth that allows us to see its contours and dynamics clearly,"[20] and a version with which, indeed, the sort of secularized Jew that Freud represents could live. Thus Freud's achievement can be understood as that of discovering the basic mythic pattern that informs Judeo-Christian civilization, and, indeed, since that mythic pattern is but a variant and recapitulation of the myth of the primal horde, it is in the end a mythic pattern that informs human civilization in general.

Freud clearly also had concerns much closer to home in this final work. A preface he wrote to the Hebrew translation of *Totem and Taboo* indicates as much, for here Freud says that he is "completely estranged from the religion of his fathers as well as from every other religion," and yet he "never repudiated his people," and "feels that he is in his essential nature a Jew." If asked what then is left to him that is Jewish, he says that his reply would be "A very great deal, and *probably its very essence*."[21] It is with this that Freud is concerned in *Moses and Monotheism*: the nature of religious tradition, the essence of Jewishness, and, indeed, his own Jewishness.

Ignoring everything to do with religious rituals, festivals, and ceremonies, Freud characterizes monotheism as a harsh, rigorous, spiritual faith, demanding a life characterized by truth and justice, which could not be tolerated by the post-Akhenaten generation in Egypt that reverted to its customary polytheistic practice. Even Moses' first followers rejected it and murdered their leader. Yet it was in Israel that the monotheistic religion became latent, eventually to reemerge with the power to change the god Yahweh into the Mosaic God, and to reestablish itself as the defining tradition of Judaism. In the description of this tradition Freud's thinking is characterized by the contrast between intellectuality or spirituality on the one hand, and the senses or sensuality on

the other. The prohibition of images is particularly important: it signified "a triumph of spirituality over the senses" (of *Geistigkeit* over
Sinnlichkeit), and it was this spirituality that came to define Judaism.[22]
Freud strongly identifies with the spiritual, ethical, and intellectual
power of the Jewish tradition inspired by Moses, the power that both
defines Jewishness and empowers its survival.

Freud believed not only that the Jewish tradition represented an
advance in spirituality (*Fortschritt in der Geistigkeit*), carrying an ethical imperative to live a life of truth and justice, but also that psychoanalysis is a further development in that process. His own discovery of
psychoanalysis is thus continuous with the tradition that goes back to
Moses.[23] It is consistent with this that he saw himself as a Moses-like figure. Freud explicitly makes the connection between himself and Moses
in a letter to Carl Jung: "If I am Moses then you are Joshua and will take
possession of the promised land of psychiatry, which I shall only be able
to glimpse from afar,"[24] but it is that identification that lies behind his
obsession with Michelangelo's statue of Moses from his first encounter
with it in 1901, and his obsession with his final book from 1934
onwards. Freud's biographer, Peter Gay, has written,

> A Founder murdered by followers unable to raise themselves to
> his level but inheriting the consequences of their crime and even-
> tually reforming under the pressure of their memories—no fan-
> tasy could be more congenial to Freud. . . . he saw himself as the
> creator of a subversive psychology who was now near the end
> of a long, embattled career that had been steadily obstructed by
> abusive enemies and craven deserters. . . . The idea that there
> were those who wanted to murder him was . . . only too famil-
> iar to him.[25]

There is sufficient in Freud's account of the rise of monotheism that
resonates with his experience of the development of psychoanalysis for
the conclusion to be drawn that in *Moses and Monotheism* Freud is
writing something that is quasi-autobiographical. To illustrate the
inevitability, indeed the necessity, for a new idea such as monotheism to
meet with opposition and struggle before it finally prevails, he proposes
an analogy: "Let us take, for instance, the history of a new scientific
theory, such as Darwin's theory of evolution [for which we may substitute the Freudian theory of psychoanalysis]. At first it met with embit-
tered rejection and was violently disputed for decades; but it took no
longer than a generation for it to be recognized as a great step forward

towards truth."[26] In *Moses and Monotheism* Freud is clearly projecting onto Moses and his followers his concerns and convictions about his own life's work and its cultural significance.

Freud and the Historian

Even given all that has been said above on his motives, it is clear that Freud did have a historical interest. In a 1936 letter to Ernest Jones[27] he gives as a reason for his reluctance to publish that "I lack historical verification for my construction." It is appropriate then to approach the work also from that perspective. Again, it would be wrong to reject the work on the grounds of the tentative and highly controversial nature of psychoanalysis. As Gay has noted,[28] "It may be . . . that some of Freud's theories may require careful reexamination, serious modification, perhaps even replacement. But his general model of the mind . . . remains a solid, indeed indispensable, contribution to our knowledge of the human mind." If this is so then psychoanalysis must be directly relevant and of basic significance for all those human science disciplines that focus on human nature active in culture.

It should be noted in passing that Freud's view of the Old Testament and early Israelite origins fits in significant respects with the best of German-language Old Testament scholarship of his time. So, the Pentateuchal documents J and E are held to go back to a common source that may have been either oral or written; the exodus and Sinai traditions are regarded as originally separate; Moses is not an original figure in all the Pentateuchal traditions in which he is now to be found; the "Israel" referred to in the Merneptah Stele is not necessarily the group that came out of Egypt in the exodus.[29] These are incidental points, however, and in the main illustrate Freud's indebtedness to Old Testament scholarship rather than any contribution that he made or may continue to make to it. For any possible ongoing significance of Freud for biblical scholarship we must look elsewhere.

In addition to any merit that the model of "advance in spirituality" may continue to have for our understanding of the significance of monotheistic religion, Freud's chief contribution is a general one which has not yet been adequately assimilated into historical scholarship in general or Old Testament scholarship in particular. That contribution relates to our understanding of the nature and dynamics of tradition. While it is true that in recent years it has been increasingly acknowl-

edged that tradition, whether written or oral, is more than the mechanical transmission of material from the past, that it is subject to acciden-
tal change and deliberate manipulation in the context of the changing
interests of the group or community,[30] it is to Freud that the impulse
must be traced to try to understand the dynamics of the processes
involved. Tradition cannot be adequately accounted for by reference to
external, conscious mental processes (such as storytelling, rituals, and
ceremonies); rather, it is something which is *inherited* by the group in the
form of memory traces of the past that are collectively transmitted and
subject to unconscious distortion in that process.

As far as Mosaic monotheism is concerned, Freud refers at different
points to the Levites, as those who transmitted the Mosaic tradition, to
the prophets, as a succession of men who "were enthralled by the great
and mighty tradition which had grown up little by little in obscurity,"[31]
but these are at most external agencies and cannot account for the
power of the tradition eventually to prevail. It is now that Freud introduces the analogy of the psychology of an individual. Just as a person
involved in an accident may not experience the symptoms of it for some
time, so there is a long period after the break from the religion of Moses
during which there is no trace of it in the Jewish people. What is true of
the individual is true also of the group, of the Jewish people, who in turn
replicate and repeat the experience of humanity. Early experience of a
traumatic kind is repressed, but eventually, when the strength of the
need for repression is diminished, it reappears in changed form. It is
repression, through the period of latency, which accounts for the
strength and forcefulness of the return of that which has been
repressed.[32]

What creates the bridge between individual and mass psychology,
and so allows for the application to the group of the psychoanalytic
approach developed in the treatment of the individual, is that the memory traces lodged in the individual mind are not restricted to actual experiences of the individual but include also "things that were innately
present in him at his birth, elements with a phylogenetic origin—an
archaic heritage." This archaic heritage, transmitted through the generations, includes not only certain dispositions (such as reactive tendencies
to certain stimuli), but also "subject matter—memory traces of the experience of earlier generations,"[33] experiences that are not those of the
individual. Thus, we can speak of the psychology of the mass and not
simply that of the individual. In the case of Judaism the archaic heritage
repressed in the group is not only the traumatic murder of Moses but
also the content of his religious teaching.

Freud's view that the individual harbors in the unconscious memory traces of the experiences of former generations is based on the recognition that an adequate theory of biological evolution should explain such psychological phenomena as the Oedipus complex. Whether or not this implies that Freud adhered at this point to a "discredited Lamarckism,"[34] it is clear that the analogous application of Freudian concepts, developed in the context of individual psychoanalysis, to the understanding of cultural phenomena is increasingly recognized as legitimate and productive.[35] As Robert A. Paul has argued, "The challenge in psychological anthropology is to understand how cultural symbols, social institutions, and individual actors interact to produce the various observed phenomena . . . to show how cultural symbol systems and individual psychodynamic constellations form and inform one another in a dialectical, mutually constitutive process."[36] One may thus speak of repression and the return of the repressed in both an individual and a cultural context. Moreover, just as on the individual level, so on the cultural, repression involves distortion and displacement. Displacement functions "to reduce the intensity of the passions bursting to express themselves, and then to transform them."[37] This is a familiar aspect of the analysis of individual psychosis but, as will be indicated below, finds a clear analogy also on the level of cultural memory and repression. Freud's extension of the findings of individual psychology to the understanding of culture may at least to this extent be followed, and has fundamental implications for our understanding of the dynamics of tradition.

Conclusion

Let us return to a major theme in Freud's book, in the light of what has been said about tradition, and of what is now better understood of Israelite origins and of Egyptian history than was available to Freud: the theory that Israelite monotheism is derived from the cult of the Aten in the time of Akhenaten, in whose court the Egyptian Moses served. The Egyptian origin of Moses as a figure of the Egyptian court in this time is still argued,[38] but there is little that can be said in support of this apart from the not unimportant fact of the Egyptian origin of the name Moses itself.[39] That the founder of Israel should bear an Egyptian name reflects a positive attitude toward Egypt as the putative place of origin of Israel, which appears also in the Joseph story, but little in the way of historical knowledge can be derived from this. Freud emphasized the similarity of the Egyptian and Israelite monotheisms, but the significant differences should also be given attention. In particular, the ethical dimension of Israelite monotheism and its related concern with the relationship between God and people, rather than God and the king, distinguish biblical monotheism from that of Egypt.[40]

But even apart from these points, it is likely that the Freudian picture can no longer serve as anything like an adequate heuristic model within which we can set whatever scraps of more or less satisfactory historical knowledge we possess. The highly literary structure of the exodus story, the clear signs of a strongly formative secondary impact on it of the Passover festival, the fact that archaeological results point to a strong continuity from Late Bronze Age to Iron Age Palestine, indicating the Canaanite roots of what was eventually to emerge as Israel,[41] all point to the exodus story as an ideological construct with a highly elusive historical foundation, so creating a significant break between Egypt and Israelite origins.

As far as Egyptian history is concerned, Akhenaten's revolution introduced a counter-religion alien to traditional Egyptian culture, and was later perceived to have reduced the land to a state of divine absence, darkness, and disease. The record of this period, however, was suppressed from official Egyptian history. This, as Jan Assmann especially has demonstrated, led to the dislocation of the memory of it, the externalization of what was an internal conflict, and its projection on to the foreign Hyksos who had earlier invaded and subjugated the land. It is this conflation of the memory of the religious revolution of Akhenaten with the tradition of the Hyksos that is reflected in the much-later accounts of Hecataeus and Manetho. The resulting Egyptian tradition of foreign invasion, religious suppression, and subsequent expulsion of foreigners from the country then came to be transferred to the Jews in the classical sources.[42] As far as history is concerned, the only documented event lying behind the Egyptian tradition, forming a background also to the biblical story of the exodus, is the Hyksos control of Egypt and their expulsion, especially by the Pharaoh Ahmose at the beginning of the eighteenth dynasty. It is the tradition of this event that has undergone independent development in the Egyptian context, where it was conflated with memories of Akhenaten's religious revolution, and in the Canaanite context whence it was inherited by the Hebrews.[43]

This is a very complex situation. The result of these considerations, however, is this: that the tradition of the defeat and expulsion of the Hyksos had originally nothing to do with religious confrontation, that this dimension of it, which appears already in the Ramesside period[44] and in a much-developed form in the later classical writers, was the result of the transfer to the Hyksos episode of the traumatic memories of Akhenaten's religious revolution. It was not in the form of a religious conflict that the Hyksos tradition was first transmitted in either the Egyptian or the Canaanite context. The historical basis and framework, therefore, for seeing any connection between the religious innovation of Akhenaten and the early religion of Israel disappears. While there was movement between Egypt and Palestine, and indeed an expulsion of the Hyksos from Egypt to Palestine, this had no connection with religious confrontation in general or with Akhenaten's religious revolution in particular.

That, however, does not exhaust the possibilities for retrieving something of significance from Freud for the question of the origins of Israelite monotheism. Whatever the difficulties in establishing any historical connection, it is still the case that there is an important structural parallel between the monotheism of Egypt and that of Israel: in neither case is monotheism simply a natural development out of polytheism. Indeed, monotheism must be understood as a revolutionary rejection of polytheism.[45] Such movements certainly have antecedents, but the element of discontinuity that is involved is of great significance. In Egypt the Aten was known and worshiped in a polytheistic framework before Akhenaten's revolution. This revolution rejected polytheism, and especially the worship of Amun. In Israel Yahweh was known and worshiped in a polytheistic context before the monotheistic revolution.[46] Throughout the monarchic period in Israel various El deities, Baal, Asherah, and the Queen of Heaven were worshiped alongside Yahweh. The ninth-century prophetic revolution in Israel rejected the worship of Baal, and, insofar as it asserted the truth of the worship of Yahweh alone, rejected polytheism in general. As Akhenaten's confrontation with Amun introduced a monotheistic distinction between true and false religion in Egypt, so in Israel Elijah's confrontation with Baal introduced a monotheistic distinction between true and false religion in Israel. It may be that it is not until the exile that a universalism, carrying with it an idea of absolute uniqueness, became characteristic of Yahweh, parallel to the presentation of Aten as the first principle of creation,[47] but the significance of the revolutionary achievement of the ninth-century prophets should not be underestimated: exclusiveness and uniqueness in this context are closely related. It was first in the historical and social crises of the ninth-century B.C.E. in the Northern Kingdom that the prophetic demand for the exclusive worship of Yahweh appears.[48] This remained a minority movement throughout the preexilic period, a movement sustained by ongoing social and historical crises, and reflected in prophetic denunciations and occasional, temporary reform movements, while in general preexilic Israel remained polytheistic.

It is here that Freud's and Assmann's understanding of tradition, and especially religious tradition, becomes relevant. As with Akhenaten's revolution and its aftermath, as with the supposed murder of Moses, so with the prophetic revolution and its suppression in the Northern Kingdom there was violent religious confrontation, murderous violence all the more traumatic for being rooted in issues of internal identity. In the case of Akhenaten, as Assmann has demonstrated, there is a displacement of the memory of this religious confrontation, so that it came in tradition to be associated with the earlier Hyksos subjugation of the Egyptians. In Israel the same sort of displacement took place in relation to the religious confrontation of the ninth-century prophets with the Omride dynasty, and indeed ultimately a displacement onto the same event. In both cases, violent internal religious dissent is externalized and projected onto foreigners. The internal religious conflict of the Amarna period was projected back onto the external Hyksos oppressors; the religious confrontation of the Omride period was externalized and projected back onto Egyptian oppressors through being related to Israel's tradition of origins in Egypt, a tradition that itself is rooted in the expulsion of the Hyksos.

It is now that the Hyksos-Canaanite tradition of Egyptian origins, inherited by Israel, came to be transformed into a tradition of deliverance in the context of religious confrontation.[49] The religious demand of the prophetic revolution had been socially repressed, sporadically reemerging in the preaching of the eighth- and seventh-century prophets and occasional reform movements. It was the destruction of the state in 586 B.C.E., and the disappearance of the state apparatus of religion and government, with the consequent shift of the religious focus to the individual, that stimulated the return of the repressed tradition of the exclusiveness of Yahweh. Its new association with the exodus brought the theme of religious confrontation into the exodus tradition so identifying Israel from its exodus origins as the people of Yahweh, and, by setting this confrontation on the world stage, ensured the transformation of Yahweh into a unique focus of monotheistic worship.

Notes

Notes to Chapter One

1. See Elliott 1995a (1993); Esler 1987: 6–12, 1995b, 2000; Malina 1986a and 2001 (1981, 1993); Horrell 1999 and 2000; and Holmberg 2004.

2. I have set out a brief outline of the central argument concerning Weber in Esler 2004.

3. See Elliott 1995 (1993): 48.

4. For the history and interpretive approach of the Context Group, see Esler 2004.

5. Comte 1970; for a succinct discussion of positivism, see Wacquant 1993.

6. See Winch 1976 (1958) and Taylor 1977.

7. See Worsley 1970: 57–58.

8. Parsons 1964: 10.

9. Swingewood 1991: 142.

10. Parsons 1964: 9.

11. Ibid.

12. From Weber 1964 (1947): 88.

13. Swingewood 1991: 143.

14. Weber 1964 (1947): 107–108. The parenthetic comment is added.

15. Parsons at Weber 1964 (1947): 108 (emphasis added).

16. Weber 1964 (1947): 88.

17. Ibid., 120.

18. Ibid., 110: "Theoretical analysis in the field of sociology is possibly only in terms of such pure types."

19. Weber 1968a (1880, 1949): 90 (emphasis original).

20. On the relationship of types and models, see Esler 1987: 6–9.

21. So McKinney 1966: 3. For a discussion of types within the methodology of the social sciences, see Esler 1987: 6–9

22. Parsons 1964: 13–15.

23. Swingewood 1991: 147.

24. Weber 1964 (1947): 107–108.

25. See Triandis 1990 (just one of numerous works in this area).

26. Weber 1964 (1947): 109.

27. See Weber's *The Protestant Ethic and the Rise of Capitalism*, first published in article form in 1904–05 (Swingewood 1991: 150).

28. Meeks 1983: 5.

29. Meeks's citation of Weber here was to his 1922 work *Grundriss der Sozialökonomic: Wirtschaft und Gesellschaft*, in the 1947 edition and translation by A. M. Henderson and Talcott Parsons, *The Theory of Social and Economic Organization*, at p. 98.

30. Weber 1964 (1947): "In this case the correspondence between the theoretical interpretation of motivation and its empirical verification is entirely satisfactory and the cases are numerous enough so that verification can be considered established."

31. Meeks 1983: 5–6.

32. See Geertz 1973a: 3–30. He derived the expression "thick description" from the Oxford philosopher Gilbert Ryle.

33. Elliott 1985; Malina 1985.

34. Although Malina 2001 (1981, 1993) was a notable omission from her bibliography.

35. She had expressed herself on the "postivist" versus "interpretivist" distinction a few years earlier (Garrett 1989: 33–35).

36. Garrett 1992: 90.

37. I have elsewhere subjected Garrett's views to a detailed critique in relation to recent anthropological discussion and will not repeat my full response here; see Esler 1995b.

38. See Garrett 1992: 92–93.

39. Descola 1992. She herself had made a virtually identical point three years earlier: "Insistence on taking account of the particularity of a people's culture is what makes cross-cultural comparison and generalization so difficult from the interpretive viewpoint" (Garrett 1989: 34).

40. Garrett 1989.

41. Esler 1995b: 7.

42. Elliott 1981: 9 (at that time Elliott spoke of "sociological" rather than "social-scientific" exegesis).

43. See Esler 1987: 6.

44. Elliott 1981: 9. For the same point, see Elliott 1995a (1993): 14 (and the Appendix).

45. Although even here, why some work should not be allowed to be more theoretical, with fuller applications to the data to be left to others, escapes me: *In domo Patris mei mansiones multae sunt.*

Notes to Chapter Two

1. See Rogerson 1978; Lang 1985; Clements 1989; Mayes 1989; Overholt 1996; Carter and Meyers 1996; Chalcraft 1997.

2. Evans-Pritchard 1951: 27ff.

3. Worth mentioning is the joke concerning the chief of a tribe who says to a postmodernist anthropologist who for some time has been doing fieldwork among them, "We're sick of talking about you; let's talk about us."

4. W. R. Smith 1885.

5. His second and third series of Burnett lectures (delivered in 1890 and 1891) remained surprisingly undiscovered and unpublished, until his handwrit-

ten version was found in the Cambridge library by John Day on 3 October 1991—see J. Day 1995—and have now been published (W. R. Smith 1995). For the broad-ranging papers presented at a conference held in Aberdeen in 1994 to mark the centennial of his death, see Johnstone 1995.

6. On W. R. Smith, see Rogerson 1995.

7. See the discussion by Rogerson 1978: 24–27.

8. W. R. Smith 1956 [1889]: 226–227; also see 236–243.

9. See Carter 1996: 14; Meyers 1995: 78.

10. In the totemic stage a group considered itself "to be physically akin to some natural kind of animate or inanimate things, most generally to some kind of animal"; see W. R. Smith 1956 [1889]: 124. Also see Stocking 1995b.

11. See Rogerson 1995: 74–93.

12. Ibid., 93.

13. On Wellhausen see Smend 1989: 99–113.

14. Ibid., 107.

15. See Smend 1995: 226–242 for a thorough treatment of the relationship of the two men.

16. Rogerson 1995: 84.

17. Smend 1995: 238.

18. Rogerson 1995: 98–101.

19. Rogerson 1984: 276.

20. See Stocking 1995c.

21. Rogerson 1978: 51–52.

22. Frazer 1918.

23. Mayes 1989.

24. Tönnies 1955 [1887].

25. Mayes 1989: 7.

26. See Wallis 1912, 1935, and 1942; Mendenhall 1973 and 1976a; Brueggemann 1979; P. D. Hanson 1979; Dietrich 1979; and Herion 1981 and 1986.

27. Mayes 1989: 15-17.

28. Swingewood 1991: 98-99.

29. Durkheim 1976 [1915]: 423.

30. Mayes 1989: 34.

31. Swingewood 1991: 125.

32. See Parsons 1937 and 1951.

33. See Malina 1982: 233–234 for a good description of structural-functionalism. Also see Mayes 1989: 27–35. For anthropological assessments of structural-functionalism, see Layton 1997: 27–97 and Barnard 2000: 61–79.

34. Causse 1937.

35. See Mayes 1989: 78–87 and Kimbrough 1978.

36. For a new critical edition of some of his most important works, see Kippenberg 2005 and Otto 2005.

37. Parsons 1964: 24.

38. Weber 1968b.

39. Weber 1952.

40. For the difficulties attached to referring to ancient Israelites as "Jews" and to designating their *ethnic* identity as captured by the word for a religion, "Judaism," see Esler 2003a: 40–76.

41. For Weber's understanding of Judaism, see Otto 2001. The writings on Weber of David Chalcraft, a sociologist interested in working with biblical texts, are worthy of attention (Chalcraft 2001 and 2002, and Chalcraft and Harrington 2001).

42. See Alt 1966 and Noth 1960; discussed by Mayes 1989: 49–53.

43. Only in passing we will refer to Julian Pitt-Rivers who provides an excellent anthropological reading of the book of Genesis and other Old Testament stories as well as a critique of E. Leach's approach to stories of the Bible (see Pitt-Rivers 1977: 126–71).

44. Douglas herself says "grid and group gives you a method for sorting out the dramatis personae of any social situation" (Gosden 2004: 280).

45. On Douglas in general see Barnard 2000: 152–6.

46. "The object of this study is to open a place for a new reading of the book of Numbers. Trying to apply the practice of anthropology to Numbers produces several surprises . . ." (Douglas 1993: 21).

47. Cf. Sawyer 1996.

48. Douglas 2004: 13.

49. Leach and Aycock 1983: 21–22, cf. also Leach's introductory remarks: "None of the essays in this volume could have been written if they had not been preceded by Lévi-Strauss' two seminal essays, 'The Structural Study of Myth' and 'The Story of Asdiwal', but the discrepancies between the methodology developed here and that employed by Lévi-Strauss are numerous and fundamental" (1).

50. Leach 1976 [1985]: 136–50.

51. Ibid., 140–1.

52. Leach 1969.

53. Ibid.

54. W. R. Smith 1956 [1889]: 18.

55. R. A. Segal 1998: 17.

56. W. R. Smith 1956 [1889]: 17–18 [= R. A. Segal 1998: 28].

57. Durkheim 1976 [1915]; van Gennep 1960; Radcliffe-Brown 1952; Geertz 1973a.

58. Douglas 1996.

59. V. Turner 1967: 19.

60. On ritual and biblical studies see the contributions by F. H. Gorman and B. C. Alexander in McVann 1995: 13–36, 209–225.

61. See also Bowie 2000: 153–157; cf. Herzfeld 2001: 257–262.

62. Rappaport 1999: 24 defines ritual as "the performance of more or less invariant sequences of formal acts and utterances not entirely encoded by the performers"; see also p. 33 where he states that "unless there is a performance there is no ritual."

63. Cf. the rich evidence for biblical festivals and sacrifices in Bourdieu 1977: 132–139; this repetition is also tied to a certain formality of rituals: "Formality, i.e. adherence to form, is an obvious aspect of all rituals. It is often, but not always, through the perception of their formal characteristics that we recognize events as rituals, or designate them as such. Behavior in ritual tends to be punctilious and repetitive. . . . Rituals are performed in specified contexts, that is, they are regularly repeated at times established by clock, calendar . . . and often they occur in special places as well" (Rappaport 1999: 33).

64. "Ritus, als Mitteilung, ist eine Art Sprache; so ist es selbstverständlich, daß das leistungsfähigste Kommunikationssystem des Menschen dazu in Beziehung tritt, die objektbezogene Wortsprache. . . . Zweifellos gehen daher, seit es Sprache gibt, Riten mit Sprache zusammen," Burkert 1997: 39 [= R. A. Segal 1998: 341–342].

65. Jackson 1998: 24, 26; Bowie 2000: 161–176; the three stages of a *rite de passage* (separation—transition—incorporation/reaggregation or preliminal—liminal—postliminal) according to van Gennep are well known, have often been discussed and are used frequently in biblical studies (see most recently Olyan 2004) so that we can neglect further discussion.

66. Janzen 2004: 14.

67. "In a ritual, the world as lived and the world as imagined, fused under the agency of a single set of symbolic forms, turn out to be the same world" (Geertz 1973b: 112).

68. One must, however, note that many religious rituals seem to function along these lines: "In religious belief and practice a group's ethos is rendered intellectually reasonable by being shown to represent a way of life, ideally adapted to the actual state of affairs the world view describes, while the world view is rendered emotionally convincing by being presented as an image of an actual state of affairs peculiarly well-arranged to accommodate such a way of life" (Geertz 1973b: 89–90).

69. See Janzen 2004 who regards sacrifice as simply being one of many ritual available to ancient Israel.

70. Olyan 2004: 4.

71. Douglas 1996; Burkert 1997 [1972]: 39 also notes the limiting effect of language.

72. Janzen 2004: 55.

73. Olyan 1998, 2000, and 2004.

74. Janzen 2004.

75. McVann 1995.

76. See Brueggemann 1980: 443.

77. Boer 2002a: 1 (with obvious hagiographic tendencies).

78. Frick 2002: 18.

79. Gottwald 1999: xxvi.

80. Ibid.

81. How far one can actually label Gottwald's work social-scientific criticism remains open, since he himself prefers the term 'social history', but a social history "set in a strong social theoretical framework" (Gottwald 1999: xxix).

82. "The coalescing Yahwists were astonishingly diverse ethnically and culturally, but they had common social and political experiences and were forging together a common life of mutual defense and self-development" (Gottwald 1979: 215).

83. See Wilson 1975 for formative material and Elliott 1981 and Esler 1987 for applications of sectarian theory.

84. See Chaney 1989 (Eighth-century B.C.E. prophecy); Hanson and Oakman 1998 (Roman Palestine).

85. Lenski 1980.

86. See Chaney 1983 and 1989.

87. See Coote and Whitelam 1987.

88. See Overholt 1982 and 1986.

89. Overholt 1974 and 1986.

90. Overholt 1982 and 1989.

91. See R. R. Wilson 1979 and 1980.

92. Carroll 1979.

93. Ibid., 215.

94. See Grabbe 2000 and 2001.

95. See Nissinen 2003 for texts from Mari, Neo-Assyria, and other sites, including the ostraca from Lachish referring to (Yahwist) prophets; also see Parpola 1997 for a fine edition of the Neo-Assyrian materials, with introductory essays and notes.

96. Grabbe 2000: 14; also see remarks to similar effect in Grabbe 2001. For further reflections on the comparative method in this area, see Barstad 2000.

97. S. Roberts 1979: 17; cf. Bennett 2002: 12–21.

98. Otto 2002.

99. Otto 1994 and Barton 2002.

100. Fitzpatrick-McKinley 1999.

101. Otto 1998b: 107.

102. Patrick 1984; Otto 2002: 1–91.

103. Crüsemann 1992 [1996].

104. Otto 2002.

105. Bennett 2002.

106. Hagedorn 2004.

107. Willis 2001.

108. Otto 1998a: 128–146 with a plea for a diachronic analysis of the legal material; Matthews 1998: 97–112, and especially C. B. Anderson 2004.

109. Pressler 1993.

110. See Bloch-Smith 2003.

Notes to Chapter Three

1. There is no reason to assume that pre-Iron-Age Israel was not a settled Israel. For references for the Merneptah Stele see the essay by Andrew Mayes in this volume (chapter 20), n. 29, below.

2. The Iron I settlement of the highland falls under Wilbur Zelinsky's "doctrine of effective first settlement": "whenever an empty territory undergoes settlement, or an earlier population is dislodged by invaders, the specific characteristics of the first group able to effect a viable, self-perpetuating society are of crucial significance for the later social and cultural geography of the area"; Zelinsky 1992 [1973]: 13.

3. Lakoff 1996: 4–7.

4. E.g., Halpern 1991, 1996b; McCarter 1988.

5. Eickelman 1981: 85–90, reprinted and later incorporated into successive editions of Eickelman 2001, which, however, changes the heading to "Constructed Meanings" and transfers the opening discussion of ideology to the end of the chapter (2001: 135–137). The current best account of Near Eastern tribalism that I am aware of is Shryock 1997: 11–37.

6. R. R. Wilson 1977.

7. Matthews 1978; Anbar 1991; Whiting 1995: 1238–1241.

8. Eickelman 1981: 88; 2001: 116–117.

9. McNutt is aware of this issue and treats it briefly; 1999: 164–165.

10. Lewis 1968.

11. *American Heritage Dictionary of the English Language*, 4th ed. (Boston: Houghton Mifflin, 2000), *s.v.* The names of the tribes of Israel did not all represent eponyms; some apparently referred to geographical features.

12. Lehmann 2003: 136–146.

13. This fluidity has been recognized in theory in biblical studies for at least a generation: cf., e.g., R. R. Wilson 1977; Gottwald 1979; Meyers 1983a: 47–48.

14. Hütteroth and Abdulfattah 1977: 49; Musil 1928; Lancaster 1981. In other cases clan designations might be more persistent: Batatu 1999: 22–29.

15. Hirsch 1906: 253; Sparks 2003.

16. Zevit 2001: 622–624, with several paragraphs of examples, including a few ethnographic parallels of the kind first applied to ancient Israel, as Zevit notes, by Winckler in 1895.

17. Sykes 2003: 163–182.

18. Lancaster 1981: 151–152. Martin likes Rogerson's criticism of this view (Martin 1989: 98–99), but the evidence for it is overwhelming.

19. Bates and Rassam 1983: 259–263.

20. Halpern 1991: 49. Cf. Faust 2000: 29.

21. Schloen 2001: 152–153; Zevit 2001: 613–614.

22. Zevit 2001: 614, n. 7. At Mari, "as we have learned more about tribes, the terminology of linkage between Amorites and Israel has proved slippery. They seem to share etymology but not application: for example Amorite *ga'um/gâyum* ('clan') seems closest *not* to Hebrew *gôy* but to *mišpaḥâ*, whereas Hebrew *gôy* parallels Amorite *ummatum* and not *ga'um*"; Sasson 1998: 104–105.

23. In her discussion of Greek tribes, Morgan uses the phrase "localizing ethnos" as an equivalent for "tribe"; Morgan 2003: 6–7, 12–15.

24. Halpern 1991: 54. For the *ḥamula*, cf. A. Cohen 1965, Eickelman 1981: 108–109. Faust proposes that this intermediate group, which could also go by the designation *mišpāḥâ*, might often have constituted an entire village corporation or a sector thereof: 2000: 29–32.

25. Gottwald 1979: 257–284.

26. Schloen 2001:152.

27. Cf. Boehm 1984.

28. E.g., Barth 1969a; Noll 2001: 165–166.

29. For the Hebrew scriptures, contra Noll 2001: 165.

30. An example of the practice of communal reservation of grazing territory among tribal pastoralists, in this case for agrarian Syria, is described in Shoup 1990.

31. Halpern 2001: 414–415. Halpern regards Joseph as an invention of the Davidic united monarchy (417).

32. As Meyers 1983a shows, the association of tribes with territories as described in Joshua and Judges was far from novel or arbitrary.

33. For a recent treatment of the relationship between early political forms and landscape, see A. T. Smith 2003.

34. Eickelman 1981: 88; cf. Meeker 1979: 9–47.

35. Khazanov 1994 [1984]: 152, cited also by Cross 1998: 70, n. 58; cf. especially Rowton 1976.

36. Eickelman 1981: 158. McInerney traces the modern elaboration of this idea to Barth (1969a), while recognizing that it had already played a significant role as far back as Herodotus; McInerney 2001: 57–59.

37. Quoted from a 1988 work by McInerney 2001: 61.

38. Knauf-Belleri 1995: 108.

39. Ibid., 108–111. Knauf-Belleri of course here shares the view that "state" should be used of more powerful monarchies but not of less powerful ones.

40. McNutt 1999: 83.

41. Bates and Rassam 1983: 258. For an exemplary contemporary account of state-tribe relations, see Dresch 1989. Although states vary in their power to regulate and coerce within a given sphere, the *structure* of state-tribe interaction rarely changes in step with such variation. It is for this reason among others that

comparisons with modern tribal societies remain illuminating for the biblical period.

42. For Greece, see Ferguson 1991; J. M. Hall 1997.

43. Schloen 2001: 69–73, 113–115. For an overview of numerous instances of the influence of state relations on tribal formation among Arabs in the pre-Islamic period, see Hoyland 2001: 16–83.

44 Khoury and Kostiner 1990.

45 There is a growing awareness of such fallacies: see, e.g., Noll 2001: 140–164. That a monarchy ruled patrimonially does not require that the ruling house and its subjects shared a single political identity.

46 Cf. J. M. Hall 1997: 19.

47 Exceptions include Gottwald 1979; Lemche 1985; and McNutt 1999.

48 Frankel (1994): 29–30. On the other hand, Frankel shares the view of many that the archaeology of Tel Dan does correspond to the report of its settlement by an Israelite tribe from the southern hills as described in Judges 18, given its wide range of Iron I highland, Tyrian, and Philistine ware, and he is even inclined to join the minority who follow Yadin's view that the small village remains above the thirteenth-century destruction layer at Hazor represent an Israelite settlement; 1994: 30–32.

49 Petter 2003; cf. Routledge 2000: 63–65.

50 The origin, meaning, and use of ʿibrî remain profoundly uncertain. Its derivation from the term habiru/ʿapîru widely attested in Bronze Age sources is now highly doubtful. Its rare appearances in the Hebrew scriptures tell us little. That it was a synonym for "Israelite," as it is universally used in historic Jewish and modern parlance, is improbable.

51 "Tribes appear to have existed more as a set of ordered names that provided a range of potential identities for various groups at different times than as a base for sustained collective action, although coalitions of various sections and rural local communities with the 'tribes' frequently occurred. When these coalitions did occur, it was not necessarily along lines of lineal descent" (Eickelman 2001: 132). Cf. Eickelman 1981: 95–96.

52 Eickelman 1981: 88; 2001: 117.

53 LaBianca 2003: 119.

54 Ibid.

55 Durand 1992; for the political background of the early Israel highland settlement, see Coote 1990.

56 See J. M. Hall 1997: 17–19 for the pros and cons of the so-called instrumentalist and primordialist views.

57 Sachs 2004. Also: "The late Egyptian diplomat Tahseen Bashir once famously described the countries of the Arab Middle East as 'tribes with flags,' suggesting that citizenship and nationhood were concepts that had not yet supplanted tribal loyalties."

58 Bienkowski and Van der Steen 2001.

59 Such attenuation in no way precludes the likely continuation of tribalism in Palestine, in erstwhile "Israelite" parts as well as elsewhere.

60 Views differ widely as to how long an original Israelite tribal structure
lasted.

Notes to Chapter Four

1. The idea of "conjugal union" comes from Lowenthal 1987: 139–148.

2. Service in the royal court is not, as we usually imagine, an opportunity
to "get ahead" in a job with "inside work, no heavy lifting." Instead, it is the
occasion for becoming part of another man's house and giving up the possibility of establishing a "house" of one's own.

3. These projects may also include pioneering new lands, undertaking
risky occupations, or even serving as terrorists.

4. Bastien 1985: 21; Moral 1961: 42.

5. Lowenthal 1987: 494.

6. Ibid.

7. Ibid.

8. Ibid.

9. Moral 1961: 50.

10. G. E. Simpson 1942: 661.

11. Lowenthal 1987: 180.

12. G. E. Simpson 1942: 655–656.

13. Moral 1961: 23.

14. G. E. Simpson 1942: 663.

15. Ibid., 668.

16. Bijoux 1990: 46.

17. Ibid., 82.

18. Lowenthal 1987: 497.

19. Moral 1961: 50.

20. Locher 1977: 5.

21. Moral 1961: 63–64.

22. Meyers 1991: 41; Gottwald 1979: 248, 285–292.

23. Stager 1985: 17–18.

24. Meyers 1978; Meyers 1983b.

25. Abu-Lughod 1993.

26. See especially Meyers 1991: 50.

27. Compare the situation of the "widow," who likewise has no tie to the
household of her deceased husband (Leeb 2002).

28. Steinberg 1993: 16.

Notes to Chapter Five

1. See Mauss and Hubert 1898; Burkert 1997 [1972]; Durant 1985; Valeri 1985, 1994; Grottanelli 1988, 1999; Detienne and Vernant 1982; De Surgy 1988; Destro 2001.

2. Eilberg-Schwartz 1990; Malina 1996a, 2001; Cardellini 2001; Gruenwald 2001.

3. Destro and Pesce 2002c.

4. Destro 2001; Destro and Pesce 2002c.

5. Identifying rituals and distinguishing one from another does not always imply an absolute separation of one act from another: "Relative contrastive distinctions (rather than absolute distinctions) help to distinguish between certain kinds of social activity" (Tambiah 1985: 125). A rite of sacrifice may belong to a chain or paradigmatic set of relative contrastive actions.

6. Bascom 1980.

7. Kalinowski 2003.

8. Divination in its different forms has the purpose of identifying the causes of events. It necessarily presupposes that it be followed by a series of rituals, among which prayer and exorcism. A ritual practice can be defined as exorcistic when it has as its purpose the neutralisation of an evil power. Exorcistic practices may include both the use of talismans and recourse to sacrificial rites.

9. Douglas 1999: 110.

10. Kaufmann 1960; Knohl 1995, 1996.

11. See Cardellini 2001: 44–457.

12. Milgrom 1991: 887.

13. Ibid.

14. Ibid., 887–888.

15. The blood has an essential ritual function. The sacrificial rite is therefore not merely symbolic in meaning (against Milgrom 1991: 888).

16. B. A. Levine 1989: 99.

17. See Bettini 1991.

18. See Milgrom 1991: 841–842.

19. "The person need no longer remain outside his tent, but can now enter it . . . for he no longer contaminates sancta by overhang, only by touch" (Milgrom 1991: 844). Even after the ritual bathing, a degree of impurity remains in the body, otherwise there could not be the need for further purification rites. Jenson (1992: 169–170) observes that "It is probably anachronistic to say that different grades of purity are indicated," in that such conceptions are mentioned explicitly only in the *Mishnah* (*Negaim* 14:2-3), "but the context appears to imply some kind of intensification or completeness of purification."

20. We assume the rite of the seventh day to be an autonomous phase of the ritual process and not a part of the rite of the eighth day (against Milgrom 1991: 844).

21. B. A. Levine 1989: 85.

22. See ibid., 46.

23. Milgrom 1991: 852. This is underlined also by the fact that only in this case the *tenufah* is performed with the whole animal and by the fact that the animal for the *ašam* cannot be substituted by other animals.

24. B. A. Levine 1989: 88. The three sacrifices *ašam*, *ḥaṭṭaʾt*, and *ʿolah* present divinatory functions (the animals are previously presented before the entrance of the Tent and, more important, the rite of elevation takes place during the *ašam* sacrifice), and exorcistic functions (the blood of the *ašam* and the oil of the offering are put onto the body of the former leper, and the blood from the three sacrifices is also used to purify the sacred places of the sanctuary).

25. B. A. Levine 1989: 74.

Notes to Chapter Six

1. Elliott 1995a [1993]: 63. See also Carney 1975: 12.

2. Chapter 5 in Sahlins 1972.

3. Ibid., 188.

4. Ibid., 194.

5. Carney (1973: 64) recognized, even before Sahlins's influence had grown, that the setting of the Graeco-Roman world with its patronage and clientage involved an adaptation of the simpler categories of exchange presented by Sahlins.

6. Stegemann and Stegemann 1995: 43.

7. Saller 1989: 57.

8. Meeks 1983.

9. Lebra 1975: 551; Boissevain 1974.

10. Sahlins 1972: 205–209.

11. These limitations of Sahlins's model are apparently missed by Hans van Wees (1998) who attempts to define reciprocity in a manner useful to classicists. Van Wees adds to the problems, however, when he repeatedly casts reciprocity as a *sentiment* as opposed to *a model* (van Wees 1998: 19, 20, 35). This is most apparent in the trouble he has with negative reciprocity (since it does not presuppose friendliness, altruism, or grace).

12. Stegemann and Stegemann 1995: 43. Since the Stegemanns' negative reciprocity does not differ from that of Gouldner (1960) or Sahlins (1972), it will not be treated here.

13. Helpful discussions with Philip Esler pushed me to reconsider the appropriateness of the common titles.

14. See Elliott 2002.

15. Hanson and Oakman 1998: 31–43.

16. Gary Stansell's excellent work on the gift would be improved only, in

my opinion, by a greater clarity in distinguishing between gifts in the technical sense and gifts in the general sense (anything that is exchanged). The latter definition allows him to conflate the reciprocity of gift and patronage exchanges. See, for instance, Stansell, 1999, 2002.

17. Van Wees's (1998: 41) insistence that market exchange and reciprocity are diametrically opposed is another sign of his sentimentalization of reciprocity. Nonetheless, he correctly identifies that market or commercial exchanges do not "establish relations of power." For fascinating examples of the socializing benefits of markets, see Davis 1996.

18. For some discussion of how social status *can* influence the attractiveness of some commodity exchanges see Bell 1991a. Nonetheless, he does not argue that status changes the value of commodities, but simply that the personal element cannot always be completely extricated even from commodity or market transactions.

19. Stegemann and Stegemann 1999: 36.

20. This, of course, becomes complicated by the Graeco-Roman practice of referring to clients as "friends," but between people whose relationship (and status) was clearly unequal, this term was an idiom that reflected a social practice and it was not understood as a literal description of equality. See Gold 1987: 134; Saller 1989: 57; and Strauss 1986: 22–23. Cf. Konstan 1995, who argues that, even in Roman society, "friend" might very well mean what it says, and not stand euphemistically for "client."

21. Wolf 1966: 16.

22. Eisenstadt and Roniger 1980; Saller 1989; Saller 1982; and Wallace-Hadrill 1989.

23. See for instance Stegemann and Stegemann, 1999: 39, where only patronage and clientage but not benefaction is listed under "general exchange" (they also list the teacher-disciple relationship, but this relationship clearly works along the lines of patronal exchange—teaching and salvation in exchange for loyalty and imitation).

24. Joubert 2001; Joubert 2000; and Batten 2004.

25. For other ways to describe the relationship between patronage and benefaction, see Crook 2004: 59–66.

26. The rules and expectations of patronage and clientage are so well known and thoroughly explained elsewhere, that in the following pages I shall assume that knowledge. Summaries of scholarship and of the institution can be found in Crook 2004.

27. Mendenhall 1955: 25.

28. On the fruitfulness of the motif exegetically and theologically, see Muilenburg 1965b: 97; Hillers 1969; Olyan 1996; and see especially the influential work of Eichrodt 1957. For a fine history of the debate concerning the date and provenance of the covenant motif, see Oden 1987.

29. Also, beginning with ancient Near Eastern treaties to derive the structure of covenantal exchange indicates that the category of covenantal exchange is not a theological category. For a sample of suzerain-vassal treaties, see the vassal treaty of Esarhaddon with Ramataya, city ruler of Urakazabanu, in Pritchard 1969: 534–541.

30 This level of formality is reflected throughout Liverani 1990: 180–196.

31. Mendenhall 1955: 30.

32. Mendenhall and Herion 1992: 1180.

33. Korosec 1931 cited in Mendenhall 1955: 32, with no further citation given there.

34. It is, of course, possible for covenants to have occurred between equals (especially in the form of parity, or non-aggression, treaties); what I have in mind here, then, are the more common forms of the *vassal* treaty.

35. Eisenstadt and Roniger 1980: 50.

36. Lemche 1995.

37. With Glueck 1967.

38. Crook 2004.

39. Lemche 1995: 122: "publicly expressed by both parties in the form of a vow," and "bound together by mutual oaths." See also Lemche 1996. In this article he also believes that "The bond between patron and client is a personal one, the client *having sworn* allegiance to the patron and the patron *having sworn* to protect his client" (p. 111, emphasis added). I think that Lemche's observations concerning the personalization and vertical hierarchy of the Israelite transition into statehood are fine; it may be, however, that he would be better off to describe it as something other than a "patronage society." Since that term is so culturally specific, it does not lend itself to the broader and more general application he desires.

40. Olivier 1996.

41. Ibid., 295–296.

42. Ibid., 296.

43. Vineyard leases were typical covenants—they laid out in detail stipulations, namely, what work was required of the lessees and the lessor, what lessees would gain from their work, dates produce was to be delivered and the amount, and they detailed the consequences and ramifications of breaking the contract (often in the form of fines), or failing to care for the plants and soil or destroying both purposely, and failing to give over the required amount of produce. See for instance *PRyl* IV 583 (170 B.C.E.); *POxy* IV 729 (137 B.C.E.); *BGU* IV 1122 (13 B.C.E.); *PKoln* III 144 (152 B.C.E.); *POxy* IV 707 (136 C.E.). See also the treatment of these and other vineyard leases in Kloppenborg 2000.

44. Olivier 1996: 301.

45. Simkins 1999. Hobbs's (1997) critical note was very brief, and probably meant as a conversation starter, not a sustained argument.

46. Simkins 1999: 128.

47. Stevenson 1992.

48. Fensham 1974. The same observation holds for other examples of "father" terminology Simkins points out: 2 Kgs 2:12 (but note the three oaths Elisha swears to Elijah at 1 Kgs 2:2, 4, 6); 2 Kgs 5:13.

49. See also the covenant formed between Abraham and Abimelech for the explicit connection drawn between "swearing" and making a covenant in Gen 21:22-30.

50. Hobbs 1997: 501.

Notes to Chapter Seven

1. Gowan 1987; Malina 1987.

2. Weber 1976 [1908]: 134–146; Silver 1983.

3. Levy 1964.

4. Isa 60:5, 11; 61:6; 66:12; further cf. 10:14; 45:14. Blenkinsopp (2003: 13) thinks Adam Smith got the title for his book, *An Inquiry into the Nature and Causes of the Wealth of Nations* from Isaiah 60:5. But the expression "wealth of nations" "had some currency before Adam Smith in the title of his famous work, but its history is obscure" (*OED* 20: 42).

5. Eisenstadt and Roniger 1984; Malina 1998: 2–32; 1993: 90–116; Elliott 1995b: 144–156.

6. Simkins 1999: 128.

7. Neyrey 1993: 122–127; Malina 1993: 90–116; Foster 1965: 293–315.

8. Neyrey and Rohrbaugh 2001: 467–468.

9. Hanson and Oakman 1998: 111; Neyrey and Rohrbaugh 2001: 467–468.

10. Pitt-Rivers 1968; Malina 1993: 28–62; Moxnes 1996: 19–41; Neyrey 1998: 14ff.

11. Root שׁוּל, שִׁיל (*šwl, šyl*)(II.) conveys the notion of power and ability, which have their tangible expression in acquiring wealth; Gen 34:29; Num 31:9; Deut 8:17-18; 33:11; Isa 8:4; 10:14; 30:6 (//אוצרתם [*ṣrtm*]"treasures"); 60:5 (//המון [*hmwn*]"abundance"); 60:11; 61:6; Jer. 15:13; 17:3 (//אוצרותך [*ṣrwtk*] "treasures"); Ezek 26:12 (//רכלתך [*rkltk*]"merchandise"); Job 5:5; 15:29 (// אשר [*šr*]"to be rich"); etc.

12. Young 1962: 818.

13. *OED* 20: 42. Modern economists speak of "national wealth" as well as "household wealth"—assets and liabilities that have a current market value and that are directly or indirectly marketable; "household wealth" indicates those assets over which the family or individual has control.

14. Mill 1909: 8–10.

15. Streeten 1964: 755.

16. *Harper's Bible Dictionary.*

17. Lenski 1966: 229.

18. Heilbroner 1962: 27, cited in Lenski 1966: 229.

19. Heilbroner 1985: 45.

20. Malina 1987: 359.

21. Heilbroner 1985: 45.

22. Carney 1975: 181.

23. Kautsky 1982: 211.

24. Heilbronner 1985: 57–58.

25. Assuming that Abraham is presented as a chief, cross-cultural studies of chiefs in Africa may illuminate certain aspects of the Abraham narrative. For example, not only is cattle the "chief's main source of wealth"; he is the richest man in his tribe because of all the goods and services he receives, the wealth being a significant part of his power (Shapera 1963: 104–108).

26. Abraham is in economic need (famine) and is powerless in comparison to the Pharaoh. The story perfectly illustrates what Simkins (1999: 127) says about "Patronage in Israel": "Patronage is a system of social relations that are rooted in an unequal distribution of power and goods and expressed socially through a generalized exchange of different types of resources. The structure of these relations is hierarchical. Patrons are those who have access to goods and centers of power, whereas clients are in need of such access."

27. Is Abraham "pimping" in order to be paid and retained? Gunkel speaks of oriental "procurers"; or is it that Abraham and Sarah could not otherwise remain alive (thus Westermann 1981: 191)?

28. Cf. Malina : "Lying and deception are or can be honorable and legitimate. To lie in order to deceive an outsider, one who has no right to the truth, is honorable. On the other hand to be called a liar by anyone is a great public dishonor. Thus to deceive by making something ambiguous or to lie to a person is to deprive the other of respect . . . and to humiliate him" (1981: 36). Again, the irony is thick: Abraham affronts a patron who could humiliate him or kill him; but the link to his patron involves an element of kinship. Hence Abraham's deception undermines "family" as well as goes against the loyalty required of a client. This heightens all the more the motif of Abraham's gaining of wealth, in this case as a trickster.

29. Westermann 1981: 192.

30. On the nature of the gift-giving in this story, see Stansell (1999): 79–80.

31. The structure of the various traditions is complicated; the redaction is postexilic (thus Westermann 1981).

32. בלעדי "not at all" (BDB), an emphatic rejection of the gift and the implied subordination of client status.

33. Gottwald 1992: 83.

34. Hanson and Oakman 1998: 41.

35. Finley 1956: 65.

36. Cf. 1 Sam 22:2 and Hanson (2002): 284.

37. DeVaux 1961: 255, "This is how fighting men made themselves rich, for there was no other way." According to Carney (1975: 252), ". . . wealth was

generally accumulated by robbery, the earliest labour-saving device, rather by increasing one's productivity. Plunder from war generally constituted the base on which important elite families were founded."

38. Gottwald 2001: 92.

39. Gottwald 1992: 84. On the structures of government and "state" under David in Hebron and later in Jerusalem, see Schäfer-Lichtenberger (1996: 100, 104), who finds in Hebron no "contributory system," but income from booty (2 Sam 3:22); in Jerusalem the operations indicate an economic surplus; income is from gifts, booty, tributes, crown estate, forced labor and services.

40. Myers 1962: 401.

41. See Gottwald 2001: 93 on extraction of surplus from farmers and taxes on merchants.

42. Carney 1975: 252, following Lenski.

43. Fritz 1996: 188.

44. Long 1984.

45. Gottwald 1992: 84.

46. Tomoo Ishida, "Solomon," in *ABD* 6: 108; Gottwald 2001: 93.

47. Similarly Noth 1968: 224; RSV translates "retinue."

48. 1 Kgs 10:11-12 is a later insertion that interrupts the Sheba story. It intensifies, however, the motif: "The fleet of Hiram brought gold from Ophir. . . ."

49. Gottwald 1992: 84.

50. Von Rad 1965: 296.

51. Muilenberg 1965a: 702.

52. E.g, Duhm 1892, Muilenberg 1965a.

53. Some critics find in vv. 5-7 or 3-7 later insertions.

54. Blenkinsopp 2003: 226.

55. Blenkinsopp, 2003: 304.

56. True, in the dream-theophany of Solomon, Yahweh promises riches and honor, but this is in response to a prayer and has to do only with the glory of the king himself (1 Kgs 3:13).

57. Cf. Gen 39:21 and Westermann 1981: 420.

Notes to Chapter Eight

1. Quinn 1998.

2. Joseph Smith History of 1832 (Vogel 1996: 1:28).

3. Variety of sources (Vogel 1996: 1:146, 169–170, 181, 207).

4. Joseph Smith History of 1839 (Vogel 1996: 1:60–61).

5. Joseph Smith History of 1832 (Vogel 1996: 1:28).

6. Orson Pratt account, c. 1839 (Vogel 1996: 1:146–147).

7. Brodie 1971: 16, 21.

8. J. L. Brooke 1994: 150.

9. Vogel 1996: 1:27–28, 146; Orson Pratt account, 1840 (Vogel 1996: 1:150); Oliver Cowdery letter to W. W. Phelps, Dec. 1834 (Vogel 1998: 2:424–425).

10. Vogel 1996: 1:70.

11. Vogel 2002: 4:378–381.

12. Vogel 2002: 4:382–386.

13. Vogel 2002: 4:414–417.

14. Brodie 1971: 170.

15. Interviews with John A. Clark, 1827 & 1828 (Vogel 1998: 2:267).

16. Joseph Smith History of 1832 (Vogel 1996: 1:30); Truman Coe account, 1836 (Vogel 1996: 1:47); interviews with John A. Clark, 1827 & 1828 (Vogel 1998: 2:266).

17. Charles Anthon letter to E. D. Howe, 17 Feb. 1834 (Vogel 2002: 4:378).

18. Martin Harris interview with *Rochester Gem*, c. June 1829 (Vogel 1998: 2:273).

19. Martin Harris in an interview with Joel Tiffany, 1859 (Vogel 1998: 2:305) gave the only measurement available, a total width of eight inches.

20. Cf. Quinn 1998: 169.

21. David Whitmer interview with Eri B. Mullin, 1874 (Vogel 2003: 5.15), though it is not clear when Whitmer would have had the opportunity to observe Smith directly when he translated with the "spectacles."

22. David Whitmer interview with the Omaha *Herald*, 10 Oct. 1886 (Vogel 2003: 5:179).

23. Martin Harris interview with Edward Stevenson, 1870 (Vogel 1998: 2:321).

24. Truman Coe account, 1836 (Vogel 1996: 1:47); Emma Smith Bidamon interview with Joseph Smith III, Feb. 1879 (Vogel 1996: 1:539); Martin Harris interview with John A. Clark, 1827 & 1828 (Vogel 1998: 2:268); Martin Harris interview with Edward Stevenson, 1870 (Vogel 1998: 2:324); David Whitmer, *Address to All Believers in Christ*, 1887 (Vogel 2003: 5:196).

25. Joseph Smith History of 1832 (Vogel 1996: 1:31); Joseph Smith History of 1839 (Vogel 1996: 1:73); Lucy Smith History of 1845 & 1853 (Vogel 1996: 1.370–371).

26. Lucy Smith History of 1845 & 1853 (Vogel 1996: 1:370–371).

27. Emma Smith Bidamon letter to Emma Pilgrim, 27 March 1870 (Vogel 1996: 1:532); Martin Harris interview with Edward Stevenson, 1870 (Vogel 1998: 2:320); David Whitmer interview with *Omaha Herald*, 10 Oct. 1886 (Vogel 2003: 5:179); cf. Quinn 1998: 171.

28. Martin Harris interview with William Pilkington, 1874-1875 (Vogel 1998: 2:354).

29. Martin Harris interview with Simon Smith, 5 July 1875 (Vogel 1998: 2:380, 382, 384).

30. Joseph Smith interview with Peter Bauder, Oct. 1830 (Vogel 1996: 1:17) and Martin Harris letter to H. B. Emerson, Jan. 1871 (Vogel 1998: 2:339). Another version is that they were reburied where they were found: Sidney Rigdon account, c. 1836 (Vogel 1996: 1:50), Nancy Towell account, Oct. 1831 (Vogel 1996: 1:204), and William Smith interview with James Murdock, 18 April 1841 (Vogel 1996: 1:479).

31. Statement of Peter Ingersoll, 2 Dec. 1833 (Vogel 1998: 2:43–44).

32. Lucy Smith History of 1845 & 1853 (Vogel 1996: 1:296).

33. Interview of Emma Smith Bidamon by Joseph Smith III, Feb. 1879 (Vogel 1996: 1:539). The quotation is taken from the interviewer's notes; the published version (Vogel 1996: 1:541) is worded slightly differently, though not differing in actual content.

34. Martin Harris interview with Anthony Metcalf, c. 1873–1874 (Vogel 1998: 2:346; Reuben P. Harmon statement, c. 1885 (Vogel 1998: 2:385).

35. Martin Harris interviews with John A. Clark, 1827 & 1828 (Vogel 1998: 2:270; also 2:291, 325).

36. Letter to Anthony Metcalf, 2 April 1887 (Vogel 2003: 5:193; cf. 5:169–170).

37. Court statement, c. 1838-48 (Vogel 1998: 2:486).

38. Vogel 2000: 3:464-72.

39. John Whitmer testimony, 1839 (Vogel 2003: 5:241). Vogel's introduction to the testimony notes, "it seem to imply that while Whitmer's handling of the plaes (perhaps in a box or through a covering) was physical, his seeing the plates was visionary."

40. Letter to Lyman E. Johnson, 15 April 1838 (Vogel 1998: 2:290–291).

41. Vogel 2000: 3:333.

42. Vogel 1998: 2:292–293.

43. Quinn 1998: 43–44.

44. David Whitmer interview with the Chicago *Times*, 14 Oct. 1881 (Vogel 2003: 5:85–86); J. L. Traughber letter to *Saints' Herald*, 13 Oct. 1879 (Vogel 2003: 5:58–59). Cf. Vogel 1996: 1:52; Quinn 1998: 174.

45. David Whitmer, *An Address to All Believers in Christ* (Vogel 2003: 5:199–200).

46. Quinn 1998: 244–45.

47. The information received by Smith via his seer stones looks more like prophetic messages than the apparent yes-no answers of the biblical ephod and Urim/Thummim. We cannot be certain that they gave only yes-no answers, but most of the few examples we have are consistent with this interpretation.

48. Grabbe 1995: 139–141.

49. David Whitmer implied that Smith's revelations came through the seer stone until he gave it up in 1830 (Vogel 2003: 5:198–204). He seemed to say directly that this particular revelation (no. 8 in the present edition of *Doctrine and Covenants*) was through the seer stone (Vogel 2003: 5:207).

50. See, e.g., R. R. Wilson 1980: 28–32, 42–60, 66–68.

51. Twain 1961: 83.

52. For example, the prophecies against Egypt in Ezekiel 29–30 do not fit any historical data that we have or are likely to find.

53. David Whitmer, *An Address to All Believers in Christ* (Vogel 2003: 5:198–199).

Notes to Chapter Nine

1. Grabbe 2001: 13.

2. Lewis 2003: 23. Generally anthropologists do not use the word *ecstasy* and instead prefer the word *trance* to refer to a type of behavior (Carter 1996: 408). I shall be using the terms "trance," "possession," and "ecstasy" interchangeably even though some make a distinction between them.

3. Lewis 2003: 23

4. Lindblom engages in an extensive excursus on the nature of ecstasy in ancient Israel (1962: 35).

5. Carter 1996: 5.

6. Van Gennep 1960: 52; Berquist 2002: 33–34.

7. Neyrey 1991: 333–387.

8. Burton 2000: 43.

9. Synnott 1994: 248 (italics mine).

10. Bourdieu 1984.

11. Bourdieu 1984; Shilling 1993: 127; Keenan 2001: 32.

12. R. R. Wilson 1996: 412–422.

13. Bourdieu 1984: 190.

14. Bourdieu 1984; Keenan 2001: 32.

15. Baker 1998: 221.

16. Lewis 2003: 23.

17. Ibid., 27–31; 58–59; 90–113.

18. Ibid., 25

19. Ibid., 69.

20. The notion of male dominance in sexually stratified societies does not mean that women are left powerless (Meyers 1988: 40–41).

21. Lewis 2003: 74.

22. As Meyers has correctly pointed out, the term patriarchy is a diffuse and value-laden term and if applied must recognize its fluid and local character (1988: 37).

23. Inhorn 1996: 1.

24. Ibid.

25. Ibid., 58.

26. Ibid., 59

27. Ibid.

28. Ibid.

29. Ibid.

30. Ibid.

31. Ibid., 6; Meyers 1988: 37–45.

32. Mbuwayesango 1997: 28.

33. Lewis 2003: 74, 75.

34. Ibid., 77

35. Plato, *Timaeus* 91c. Translated by Jowett.

36. King 1994: 102–114.

37. Num 27:1-11 addresses the question of inheritor in a patrimonial and patrilineal system.

38. Phaedra's *aidos* (shame) keeps her from conduct that would harm her good name and disgrace her husband (Halleran 1995: 44).

39. I do not wish to equate ideology with reality, but whether this text records the actual words of Sarai is irrelevant to this paper (Meyers 1988: 13). My interest lies in how the text functions rhetorically in its literary context.

40. Brayford 1999: 170.

41. Ibid.

42. Inhorn 1996: 6.

43. Translation of Speiser 1964: 116.

44. Schneider 1971: 18.

45. Lewis 2003: 34–39.

46. Lewis 2003: 77.

47. Lewis 2003: 63.

48. Lewis 2003: 26–27.

Notes to Chapter Ten

1. See, e.g., Coote 1981; Mays 1976; Sweeney 1996; Yee 1987.

2. See, e.g., Cross 1973: 274–289; Knoppers 1993, 1994; Nelson 1981; Sweeney 2001.

3. Coote 1981.

4. Chaney 1986, 1989, 1993, 1999, 2004.

5. See the works cited in Chaney 2004: 102, n. 12.

6. See Chaney 1999: 110–111, and the works there cited.

7. See Chaney 2004: 104, and the works there cited.

8. See ibid., 105, and the works there cited.

9. See Andersen and Freedman 2000: 539–560; Ben Zvi 2000: 155–165; McKane 1998: 193–206; Runions 2001: 169–172; and the works they cite.

10. Mays 1976: 148–149; McKane 1998: 203–206; Wolff 1990: 186, 197–198; see White 1997.

11. C. L. Miller 1996: 331–340.

12. See, e.g., L. C. Allen 1976: 375; Mays 1976: 143, 146; McKane 1998: 193, 205; 1993: 162; Wolff 1990: 185, 191; and the works they cite.

13. BDB: 641a; *HALOT*, 2: 693b.

14. See McKane 1998: 193–194, and Runions 2001: 169–170, for citation of earlier scholars who variously follow Wellhausen or propose even less felicitous "solutions."

15. Wellhausen 1963: 148.

16. BDB: 417–118; *HALOT*, 2: 557–558.

17. A majority of commentators identifies "the city" as Jerusalem. For a partial list, along with citation and critique of a minority opinion that Samaria is involved, see Ben Zvi 2000: 158, 162–164.

18. See, e.g., Pope 1973: 72; somewhat differently, but to the same effect, Habel 1985: 182–183.

19. For a summary of scholars choosing each option, see McKane 1998:194–195.

20. Chaney 1999:110–111.

21. Scott 1976: 71; cited partially by Hillers 1984: 82.

22. Cited in Scott 1976: 71.

23. Chaney 1999: 112–116.

24. Ehrman 1973: 103–105; Cathcart and Jeppesen 1987: 110–115; McKane 1998: 196–198.

25. GKC 144d.

26. Pope 1972: 178–179; Loretz 1977.

Notes to Chapter Eleven

1. P. E. Wilson 1997: 220.

2. Eslinger 1981: 269.

3. Beside the commentaries on Deuteronomy (Tigay 1996 is especially instructive on rabbinic interpretation), see the studies of Eslinger 1981; Schrager 1986–87; and P. E. Wilson 1997.

4. See, e.g., Dhorme 1923; Paul and Rabinowitz 1971; Pope 1992; Schorch 2000.

5. See Benveniste 1939; Bonfante 1939; McCartney 1950; Balharek 1958; Hoffner 1966; Opelt 1966; Veenker 1999-2000; Griffen 1985; Pope 1992; S. Paul 2002.

6. Enright 1985; Griffen 1985; Allan and Burridge 1991; Hughes 1991.

7. R. Burchfield in Enright 1985: 13.

8. Griffen 1985: 32.

9. Allan and Burridge 1991: 26, 221.

10. Ibid., 11, 221.

11. See Opelt 1966; Adams 1982; Griffen 1985; Pope 1992.

12. R. A. Adams in Enright 1985: 48, 51.

13. Allan and Burridge 1991: 52-152, representative of most studies.

14. Ibid., 228.

15. E.g., Pope 1992; Schorch 2000.

16. Allan and Burridge 1991: 222. For ancient examples see the studies listed above in notes 4 and 5.

17. So also Opelt 1966: 946–947; Griffen 1985.

18. See Hoffner 1966; Opelt 1966; Pope 1992; Schorch 2000; S. Paul 2002.

19. This is noted in all discussions of euphemism, ancient and modern.

20. The association with shame is echoed in the translations of Jerome (*verenda*), Luther (*Scham*), Bible de Jerusalem (*parties honteuses*), and La Sacra Bibbia (*vergogne*)..

21. Milgrom 2000: 1534 (ad 18:6).

22. On the "feet" euphemism, see S. H. Smith 1990; Pope 1992.

23. On the heel euphemism, see S. H. Smith 1990.

24. On the thigh and thigh-socket euphemism, see Dhorme 1923: 202–203; Brueggemann 1962; Pope 1962, 1992; Koch 1980; Malul 1985. Gen 32:24-32 should be included here; see Smith 1990 and Eilberg-Schwartz 1994: 152–158.

25. See Pope 1992: 721.

26. See S. Paul 2002: 497–498.

27. On the "hand" euphemism, see Delcor 1967; van der Woude 1975; Botterweck 1982: 494; Pope 1992: 720-721; S. Paul 2002: 490–491. On כף see Eslinger 1981: 273–274; S. H. Smith 1990: 466–469; Walsh 2004: 53–55.

28. See Gen 2:25; 1 Sam 20:30; 2 Sam 6:20; Isa 47:3; Jer 13:26; Lam 1:8-9; Ezek 16:36-37; 23:10; Nah 3:5; Mic 1:11; cf. also 1 Cor 12:23-24; Phil 3:19; Rev 3:18; 16:15.

29. Γύμνωσις, Gen 9:22, 23.

30. Αἰσχύνη (Isa 47:3; Ezek 16:36, 38; 22:10, 18, 29) and ἀσχημοσύνη (Exod 20:26; 28:38 [42]; Lev 18:6, 7).

31. This is illustrated in the studies listed in notes 4 and 5 above; for the euphemisms see pp. 168–69 above. For the Latin sexual vocabulary and euphemisms see Adams 1982.

32. As also in Akkadian (*bāštu[m]*, deriving from *bâšum*, "feel shame;" cf. also Schorch 2000: 144. For בשׁת designating genitals in the Talmud, see *y. Yeb.* 7.7b.

33. Lev 18:6-19; 20:17-21; 1 Sam 20:30; Lam 1:8; Ezek 15:7, 8; 16:37; 23:10, 29.

34. Gen 9:23-24; Exod 32:25; Lev 20:17; 1 Sam 20:30; Isa 20:4; Ezek 16:7, 22, 39; Mic 1:11.

35. For this reason the phallus and testicles were considered a powerful apotropaic (τὸ βάσκανον) against the Evil Eye and related dangers; see Elliott 1988.

36. For example, 2 Sam 6:20; Isa 3:17; Jer 13:26; Lam 1:8, 9; Ezek 16:36, 37; 23:10, 18, 29; Hos 2:9, 10.

37. Translation according to Roth 1997: 156–157.

38. *Woman* rather than wife, *crushing* rather than seizing of *one* testicle rather than genitals as a whole, amputation of *fingers* rather than of entire hand, infection or crushing of *second* testicle in a two-pronged attack, and the *gouging out* of *two* anatomical parts of the woman—possibly her eyes?

39. For examples of amputation as punishment in other law codes see Nielsen 1995: 234.

40. Milgrom 2000: 1537 underlines this sacrosanct nature; see also S. H. Smith 1990: 468, n. 17.

41. Mayes 1979: 328.

42. Eilberg-Schwartz 1994: 156–157.

43. The pioneering study of shame and honor in the biblical world by Malina (2001: 27–57) is indispensable on this subject.

44. Bechtel 1991, following Daube 1969, offers an informative and relevant discussion of shame as a sanction of social control in biblical Israel.

45. P. E. Wilson 1997.

46. Personal communication, September 14, 2004.

47. For shame as the central issue see also Carmichael 1974: 234, Patrick 1985: 138; and Nielsen 1995: 232, 233.

48. See above, pp. 168–69, and n. 27. The euphemism occurs also in a Ugaritic text (CAT 1.23) where El's phallus is referred to as his "hand" as well as his "rod" and "love-staff" (Eilberg-Schwartz 1994: 107–110, citing the translation of Pope 1955: 38–39).

49. So, e.g., Blenkinsopp 1968: 117, citing a parallel in Assyrian law (ANET 181).

50. Eslinger 1981: 273.

51. Carmichael 1974: 234.

52. P. E. Wilson 1997: 232–235.

53. Walsh 2004: 55–56.

54. On the laying hold of the penis/genitals in the oath-taking process see Gen 24:1-9; 47:29-31; and 31:25-53; Pope 1962; Speiser 1964; Koch 1980; Malul 1985.

55. This material was contained in the larger version of this paper delivered at the St. Andrews conference and will be published separately under the title "No Tweaking of the Twins: More on the Euphemistic History of Deut 25:11-12."

56. Also discussed extensively in the forthcoming essay mentioned in n. 55.

Notes to Chapter Twelve

1. Marcus 1986.
2. Römer 1998.
3. Weems 1988: 54; Tapp 1989: 158.

4. Fuchs 1993.

5. Tapp 1989: 171.

6. Bal 1989c: 23.

7. Exum 1989b.

8. Bodoff 2000: 254.

9. Fuchs 1993: 116.

10. Landes 1991b: 5.

11. Weems 1988: 55.

12. Trible 1984: 96-7.

13. Thompson 2001: 100.

14. Hamlin 1990: 108.

15. Bodoff 2000: 252.

16. Bal 1989b: 213.

17. Marcus 1986: 54.

18. O'Connor 1990: 140.

19. Humphreys 1989: 87.

20. Weems 1988: 56.

21. V. Turner 1967: 93–111; Douglas 1966: 94–97; van Gennep 1960: passim.

22. V. Turner 1969: 10.

23. Myerhoff 1982: 113, 129; Mead 1973: 89–91; Crocker 1973: 49.

24. Turner 1980: 151–152.

25. Gilmore 1982: 191; Pitt-Rivers 1977: 1–3.

26. Pitt-Rivers 1977: 3.

27. Peristiany and Pitt-Rivers 1992b: 2.

28. Cartledge 1992: 15.

29. Ibid., 12.

30. Berlinerblau 1996.

31. Cartledge 1992: 12, Berlinerblau 1996: 30.

32. Kish (1 Sam 9:1) is a "man of wealth." David (1 Sam 16:18) is a "man of valor." Jeroboam (1 Kgs 11:28) is "very able." Boaz (Ru 2:1) is a "prominent rich man." And the woman of Proverbs 31 is a "good wife"! (NRSV).

33. Already this is recognized as a ritual of disinheritance by Mendelsohn 1954: 116–119.

34. Willis 1997: 33–43.

35. Abou-Zeid 1966.

36. Boling 1975: 208; Setel 1992: 31.

37. Tsevat 1974: 340–343; Wenham 1972: 326–348; Keukens 1983: 41–42; Bal 1988: 46–48; Day 1989b: 59; Schmitt 1992: 853–854; Steinberg 1999: 126–127.

38. Steinberg 1999: 127; Exum 1993b: 141; Niditch 1997: 116; Exum 1993a: 39.

39. Ackerman 1998: 264.

40. Exum 1993a: 35.

Notes to Chapter Thirteen

1. See Esler 1994 and Elliott 1995a [1993].

2. Exum 1992: 13.

3. Esler 1998b (Saul), 2001, 2002 (Judith).

4. For a classic composition historical approach, see Rost 1982 [1926]: 57–62. For a provocative and recent attempt to discover history beneath the account of the Ammonite War in 2 Samuel 10–12, see Halpern 2001: 345–353.

5. See McCarter 1984: 4–8. We are now witnessing, it is worth noting, a resistance to "pan-Deuteronomism," that is, the tendency to see the work of Deuteronomistic editing across vast sweeps of the Old Testament—see Schearing and McKenzie 1999.

6. See Malina 2001.

7. Bourdieu 1966 and Malina 2001: 32–36.

8. See Lemche 1995, 1996; Hobbs 1997 and Simkins 1999.

9. See Lemche 1995 and Hobbs 1997 expressing the same view in relation to covenants and treaties. On *ḥesed*, see Clark 1993.

10. See Moxnes 1991 for a theory- and data-rich discussion of patron-broker-client in relation to Luke 7:2-10.

11. Malina 1996d: 146.

12. Malina 1988; reprinted in Malina 1996d: 143–175.

13. A. A. Anderson 1989: 145–146.

14. McCarter 1984: 288.

15. Fokkelman 1981: 41–96: at one point he speaks of David's reaction being discharged only gradually, but this is the lull before the storm of 12:26-31 (1981: 45). The real problem is that David does not react as a king should until the very end, when Joab forces him to it.

16. On the reciprocal dimension of *ḥesed*, see Clark 1993. The LXX translates *ḥesed* as *eleos*.

17. The text does not tell us precisely how, but since Saul had previously inflicted a major defeat on Nahash (1 Samuel 11), Nahash may have offered David assistance on the principle of "my enemy's enemy is my friend." For a similar view, see Hertzberg 1964: 303.

18. Perhaps they had private motives, just as Joab killed Abner (2 Sam 3:27) not because of the threat he represented to David but to avenge Abner's murder of his brother Asahel (2 Sam 2:22-23). Yet within the narrative logic of 2 Samuel a basis for their suspicions (even if unfounded) exists in the fact that two of David's opponents, Abner and Ishbaal, had been murdered (2 Sam 3:22-23 and 4:1-12), even though he disavowed responsibility for their deaths. Note Hertzberg's comment: "The unnatural deaths of Abner and Ishbaal will certainly not have gone unnoticed round about" (1964: 303).

19. Note the helpful remarks about the challenge and response dimensions to 2 Sam 10:1-6 in Stansell 1992: 109–110.

20. MT; in the LXX they lose all their beards.

21. So Gordon 1986: 250.

22. In 2 Sam. 10:6 the Septuagint translates precisely in line with the explanation here: "And the sons of Ammon saw that the people of David had been put to shame" (ὁ λαὸς Δαυίδ κατῃσχύνθησαν, *ho laos Dauid katēischynthē-san*). It must be noted, however, that at 1 Sam. 13:3-4 LXX there are considerable differences from the Masoretic text. Now Saul does not proclaim the victory, but says throughout the land "[t]he slaves [i. e., the Philistines] have despised us" (1 Sam 10:3). In the next verse the Septuagint follows up on this theme by including the sentence: "Israel has been put to shame (ἠσχύνθησαν, *ēschynthēsan*) before the foreigners." While in the Hebrew version it is the Philistines who have been shamed, this change makes sense as a reflection of the different point made in the previous verse and still retains the honor/shame dimension of the social dynamic in play between Israel and the Philistines. In the case of Absalom, the Septuagint is closer to the Masoretic text, since it reads: "All Israel will hear that you have dishonored (κατῄσχυναι, *katēischynai*) your father" (2 Sam. 16:21).

23. Ackroyd 1977: 100.

24. Other witnesses reading "kings" include the LXX, Old Latin, Targum, and the Vulgate.

25. Ackroyd 1977: 100. Gordon also misses the criticism of David present in the text (1986: 252), since in offering 2 Sam 10:7-14 as an occasion when David did stay behind in Jerusalem, he fails to notice how greatly David's personal presence was demanded then as well.

26. As revealed by 1 Sam 11:6.

27. Hertzberg raises this possibility (1964: 309)

28. Hertzberg 1964: 310.

29. So Barton 1998: 26.

30. Ackroyd 1977: 102.

31. "The word of the LORD" occurs in the Masoretic text; the versions have "the LORD."

32. The phrase "enemies of" is often omitted in translations, yet it occurs in all the ancient witnesses and there the piel can have a causative sense (so Hertzberg 1964: 315).

Notes to Chapter Fourteen

1. Kazin 1976: 256–258.

2. See the history of the Context Group in Esler 2004.

3. Pilch 2004a. I draw upon the models and details in this book to analyze

and interpret Ezekiel 1–3. For an analysis of Ezekiel 8–11, see Pilch 2002a. Relative to the Synoptic Gospels, see Pilch 2000b.

4. In his discussion of prophecy and ecstasy, R. R. Wilson 1979: 321–337 encouraged the judicious use of anthropology in future studies of the Hebrew prophets. In this article, he summarized key anthropological insights about spirit possession (ecstasy) and then applied these insights to his analysis of the Hebrew words for prophet and to prophesy. It is a praiseworthy pioneering effort, which my own research and publications on altered states of consciousness have extended still further in the Bible.

5. Blenkinsopp 1990: 1.

6. Block 1997: 78.

7. Hals 1989: 9–25.

8. Habel 1965: 297–323.

9. Habel 1965: 313 begins the Introductory Word at v. 29, which must be an error since there are only twenty-eight verses in Ezekiel 1. Others have divided the final verse into 28a and 28b, which we insert into Habel's outline. This is most likely what he himself intended.

10. For these perspectives I draw on the research reported and applied in Pilch 2004, the most complete analysis of altered states of consciousness (ASCs) that I have published thus far.

11. Habel 1965: 310. He makes a similar comment with regard to Gideon on p. 298.

12. Ibid., 317.

13. Ibid., 313, see also 310.

14. Block 1997: 79 at this point clearly draws with approval upon Habel who says the same thing.

15. Blenkinsopp 1990: 20.

16. Pilch 2004: 181–182. Even psychiatrists admit that "trance capacity is inherent in an individual. The operator merely provides an appropriate occasion for the subject to explore his or her own trance capacity if he or she wishes it" (Spiegel and Spiegel 2004: 9).

17. Ibid.

18. Pilch 2004b.

19. Block 1997: 84.

20. Pilch 2004a: 5, 74, 141, but especially 148–149 which discusses the language(s) in which the visionary can hear the message.

21. Zimmerli 1979: 117–118.

22. J. J. M. Roberts 1971: 244–251.

23. Ibid., 245.

24. Lindblom 1962: 58.

25. Web site: http://www.ritualbodypostures.com.

26. J. J. M. Roberts 1971: 251.

27. For an extreme view, see Broome 1946: 272–292.

28. Block 1997: 90.

29. Pilch 2004a: 20

30. Malina and Pilch 2000: 85; Malina 1995: 99.

31. Malina 1995: 97.

32. Blenkinsopp 1990: 18.

33. Ibid., 19.

34. Block 1997:111 notes that the phrase "and he said to me" (וַיֹּאמֶר אֵלַי, *wy'mr 'ly*) interprets visions in Ezek 9:9; 11:2; 37:11; 41:4; 42:13; 43:7, 18; 46:20, 24; 47:6.

35. Blenkinsopp 1990: 20.

36. Pilch 2004a: 86, but see also 152.

37. Blenkinsopp 1990: 24

38. Pilch 1998: 58.

39. Carley 1974: 23 says, "sensations of taste within visionary experiences are reported in other literature," but does not cite sources.

40. Pilch 2004a: 16–17.

41. Block 1997: 125.

42. Pilch 2004a: 181.

43. Habel 1965: 313.

44. Brownlee 1986: 36. Missing the ASC entirely is the NAB rendition: "The spirit which had lifted me up seized me, and I went off spiritually stirred, while the hand of the LORD rested heavily upon me."

45. According to Ezra 2:59 and 8:17, the diaspora Israelites had settled in Telmela, Telharsha, Cherub, Addan, Immer, and Casiphia. Ezekiel alone mentions Tel-abib. His call vision very likely took place at a place away from the village.

46. Block 1997: 50 identifies the spirit as an "agent of conveyance" six times in Ezekiel (Ezek 3:12, 14; 8:3; 11:24; 37:1; 43:5). Indeed, he prefers the word *wind* (see p. 133), which would blow him around like a scrap of paper.

47. Pilch 2004a: 67.

48. Blenkinsopp 1990: 28.

49. Block 1997: 138.

50. Malina 2001: 60-67; Pilch 1999a: 169–170.

51. Zimmerli 1979: 142-144.

52. See Broome 1965, revived in recent years by others but not gaining wide support. See Block 1997: 154, n. 23.

53. Block 1997: 155 offers a solid critical evaluation of E. F. Davis 1989 who interprets it as a symbol of the fundamentally textual nature of Ezekiel's career.

54. Blenkinsopp 1990: 32.

55. Habel 1965: 321–322: Introductory word: Gen 24:34-36; Commission: Gen 24:37-38; Objection: Gen 24:39; Reassurance (angel of the LORD be with you): Gen 24:40-41; Sign: Gen 24:42-48.

56. Pilch 2004a: 75–76.

Notes to Chapter Fifteen

1. "The stranger and enemy we've seen him in the mirror"; translation according to E. Keeley/P. Sherrard, *George Seferis: Collected Poems*, rev. ed. (Princeton: Princeton University Press, 1995), 6.

2. Ewald 1868 II: 75, cf. Ewald 1868 I: 74.80.

3. On the role of Nineveh in the Bible, see Dietrich 2002: 115–131.

4. Nogalski 1993: 100.

5. The literature on the psalm is legion; cf. Seybold 1989: 71–85; Floyd 1994: 421–437; Sweeney 1992: 354–377.

6. Different is Sweeney 1992: 354–377, who wants to date the psalm to the seventh century B.C.E. since he opts for the literary unity of the book.

7. LXX reads τοὺς ἐπηγειρόμενους, i.e., a participle of the root קום. Driver 1935: 300–301 eliminates the mappik to read "resistance," from the Arabic *maqama*.

8. Seybold 1989: 35–53.

9. Thus most recently Levin 2003: 43.

10. Against J. J. M. Roberts 1991: 56f.

11. Of course, the three masculine imperatives can be understood as *infinitiva absoluta* that are used like an imperative feminine (JM §123u)—the problematic change in person would thus be avoided; however, since the oldest layer of Nahum is able to use a feminine imperative to address the city of Nineveh (cf. Nah 3:14 [מי מצור שׁאבי־לך חזקי מבצריך]) one should probably opt for different addressees here.

12. Cf. the map in Stronach 1997: 321.

13. Vuilleumier and Keller 1990: 130: "Nahoum parle en prophète et en poète, non en géographe."

14. The Hebrew נא (Jer 46:25; Ezek 30:14–16) is always rendered "Alexandria" in the *Tg.* Prophets (cf. Cathcart/Gordon 1989: 140).

15. Against Machinist 1997: 181 n. 10 who regards the book as "a report and exultation over this [i.e., the fall of Nineveh] event as having already occured."

16. On the verbal form see GK §52q.

17. Cf. Watson 1995: 54.

18. Cf. Cathcart 1973: 62; for a different view, see J. J. M. Roberts 1991: 53 who wants to regard the suffix as referring to Judah.

19. Spronk 1997: 56.

20. VTE 435–36.472.484; cf. VTE 525.538–39.543; Sefire I C 24–25; Sefire II A 4–5; KAI 13:7–8; 14:8–10.11–12; 225:9–11; 226: 10; 228: 13–14; Bukan line 3.

21. There are many proposals for the emendation of כי קלות, cf. the detailed discussion in Cathcart 1996: 145–146; since all the versions support the Masoretic text, we will maintain the reading provided.

22. On the formula הנני אליך see Humbert 1933: 101–108.

23. Compare לא עוד in Nah 1:12.14; עבר in Nah 1:12; כרת in Nah 1:14.

24. Seybold 1989: 17–18.

25. Cf. Barth 1969b: 16; Eriksen 1993: 11; Harrison 2003: 343; J. M. Hall 1997: 19–33.

26. Herzfeld 2001: 11 remarks rather sarcastically: "Ethnicity, too, has achieved a new ubiquity. The concept itself has come in for a good deal of deconstruction, but it dies hard."

27. Todorov 1993: 156–157; Wikan 1999: 57–64 and Wikan 2002, see also the critical view of Wikan's approach in Grillo 2003: 169–170.

28. Eriksen 1993: 12.

29. J. M. Hall 1997: 20–21.

30. Anderson 1991: 6.

31. J. M. Hall 2002: 9 (following Horowitz 1975: 119–121) has rightly stressed that "[b]iological features, language, religion or cultural traits may appear to be highly visible markers of identification but they do not ultimately define the ethnic group. They are, instead, secondary *indicia* . . . or 'surface pointers.'"

32. Harrison 2003: 343. Thus already Weber 1922 [1972]: 237 [1968: 389]: "We shall call 'ethnic groups' those human groups that entertain a subjective belief in their common descent because of similarities of physical type or of customs or both, or because of memories of colonization and migration; this belief must be important for the propagation of group formation; conversely, it does not matter whether or nor an objective blood relation exists."

33. "Ethnic groups are not merely or necesarily based on the occupation of exclusive territories" (Barth 1969b: 15).

34. Barth 1969b: 18–20 followed by Harrison 2003: 343–361; for a first application of Barth's view on ethnicity to texts from the Hebrew Bible, see Esler 2003b: 413–426 and to recent developments with biblical archaeology, cf. Brett 2003: 400–412 and Bloch-Smith 2003: 401–425.

35. Barth 1969b: 21; J. M. Hall 2002: 10 (cf. J. M. Hall 1997: 32) but see already Weber 1922: [1972] 20–21 [1968: 43].

36. Harrison 2003: 345.

37. Ibid.

38. On the question of ethnicity as a discursive construct, see J. M. Hall 1997: 111–42 and 2002: 19.

39. Herzfeld 1997: 158. Cf. Chock 1987: 351: "stereotypes' metaphor-likeness draws attention to larger, ususally hegemonizing, discourses and the socio-cultural contexts of use and understanding that are essential to their production of meaning."

40. Eriksen 1993: 13.

41. Herzfeld 1997: 157.

42. Herzfeld 1995: 222.

43. Here, anthropologists have to be careful not to subject themselves to stereotypes that exist about the society/culture they study; on the problem see Gefou-Madianou 1993: 160–181; Herzfeld 1984: 439–454; Herzfeld 2002a: 139–170.

44. Hogg and Abrams 1988: 67.

45. Herzfeld 2003: 302–304.

46. "[P]rocesses of ethnic opposition and boundary-formation may be accompanied by inflated perceptions, not only of dissimilarity, but also of resemblance" (Harrison 1999: 239).

47. Harrison 2003: 344.

48. Ibid.

49. Probably the best example for such a systematic forgetting is the Greek attitude to much of its Turkish heritage: "As Rethemniots in particular became increasingly bourgeois and with growing fastidiousness sought to put a conceptual and social barrier between themselves and the animal-stealing swashbucklers of the hinterland hill villages, they identified agnatic kinship as a mark of Cain—of a violence originating, so they came to assume, in the deleterious effects of Turkish culture and controllable only through the policing powers of the state" (Herzfeld 2004: 171, see also Herzfeld 1991: 125–127, 227–227).

50. Harrison 2003: 345.

51. Ibid.

52. Said 1979: 3.

53. "Among the historical conditions under which our discipline emerged and which affected its growth and differentiataion were the rise of capitalism and its colonialist-imperialist expansion into the very society which became the target of our inquiries" (Fabian 1983: 143–144).

54. For such an approach (to modern Greece) see Panourgia 1995 and Yalouri 2001.

55. Harrison 2003: 346.

56. Ibid., 357.

57. Kuper 1988: 5; see also Stocking 1987: 187–237.

58. "[S]tereotyped and essentialist representations of the cultural Other are linked inextricably to similarly distorted, tendentious, and simplified representations of the cultural self" (Harrison 2003: 346).

59. Sax 1998: 294, taken up by Harrison 2003: 347.

60. Harrison 2003: 357.

61. Ibid., 349.

62. Ibid., 357.

63. Ibid., 350.

64. Ibid.

65. Ibid., 356.

66. Harrison 1999: 240.

67. Herzfeld 2003: 292–296.

68. Munck 2002: 15.

69. Cf., for example, the recent ventures of M. Herzfeld towards a comparsion of Greek and Thai responses to the so-called phenomenon of "crypto-colonialism" (Herzfeld 2002b: 899–926). On the social-scientific technique of distant comparison generally, see Esler 1987: 9–12.

70. Harrison 1999: 240.

71. See E. T. Hall 1976.

72. Cf. the passages given in Hillers 1964: 58–59.

Notes to Chapter Sixteen

1. Longman III and Reid 1995.

2. Esler 1995b: 4.

3. Hobbs 1995.

4. See Esler 1995c: 249-254, featuring specially commissioned drawings of most of the images on the Flavians' *Judaea Capta* coinage.

5. See G. D. Pearle, "At Reason's Edge: Freud's Death Drive and the Enigma of Human Destructivenes," diss., Pacifica Graduate Institute, 1998.

6. See Aguilar 2002 for an African interpretation of this custom.

7. See Dancy 1954: 7.

8. Aguilar 2000.

9. Bernardi 1985.

10. Baxter 1979: 69.

11. Jacobs 1979.

12. Aguilar 2002.

13. Pearlman 1973: 31.

14. Cf. Fischel 1948: 42 n.. 30.

Notes to Chapter Seventeen

1. Also מורה הצדקה, *mwrh hṣdqh* (1QpHab II, 2); מורה צדק, *mwrh ṣdq* (CD I, 11; XX, 32).

2. Lim 2002: 75. The texts are the Damascus Document (CD), Micah Pesher (1QpMic), Habakkuk Pesher (1QpHab), and two Pesharim on Psalms (4QpPsa, 4QpPsb). See further details below. In addition, the noun מורה (*mwrh*) occurs in 4QpHosb frag. 5-6 2; 4QpIsac frag. 21 6; 4QMidrEschat[b] XII, [13-14] (= 4Q177); 11QMelch frag. 1,2i,3i,4 II,5; CD XX, 1,14 (/מורה יורה היחיד [*mwrh/ywrh hyḥyd*] cf. יוריהם in III, 8); XX, 28 (מורה [*mwrh*]); 4Q381 frag. 1 1; and 4Q172 frag. 7 1.

3. E.g., Tajfel 1978; J. C. Turner 1985; Hogg and Abrams 1988. See the relationship between the two theories and research history in Hogg and McGarty 1990.

4. Abrams and Hogg 1990; Worchel, Morales et al. 1998.

5. Esler 1998a; Esler 2000a; Esler 2003a.

6. Oakes, Haslam et al. 1998: 76.

7. Tajfel 1978: 31 defined social identity as "the individual's knowledge that he belongs to certain social groups together with some emotional and value significance to him of group membership."

8. The meta-contrast principle predicts the relevant level of comparison, Oakes, Haslam et al. 1998: 78.

9. Oakes, Haslam et al. 1998: 80.

10. In some circumstances, out-group favoritism is more likely to occur (e.g., when the in-group is clearly of lower status to the relevant out-group). Some prerequisites for the in-group bias to occur are salience of group identity, competitive context, and higher or equal status with the relevant out-groups; Hinkle and Brown 1990; Brown 2000: 322–333.

11. Oakes, Haslam et al. 1998: 75.

12. Marques, Páez, and Abrams 1998: 127. Prototypes have been seen to function as criteria for category membership, but rather than simple determinants of categorization, they should be seen as context-dependent outcome of the categorization process, Oakes, Haslam, et al. 1998: 85–91; Smith and Zarate 1990.

13. Oakes, Haslam et al. 1998: 75–76. Esler has employed the concept in the perception of Abraham in Romans (2003a: 171–194).

14. Abrams and Hogg 1990; Oakes, Haslam, et al. 1998: 80. Furthermore, prototypical images are not fixed but depend on judgments in different comparative *contexts;* Oakes, Haslam, et al. 1998: 80–83, 87.

15. Hogg 2001; Hogg, Martin, et al. 2003; Haslam 2004: 45–48. Group prototype is a dynamic concept: the prototype both *defines* and *is defined by* the the group.

16. Haslam 2004: 45.

17. פשר הדבר על‎ ,פשרו על‎ (*pšrw ʿl, pšr hdbr ʿl*) and the like. In the Hebrew Bible, the Book of Daniel and Genesis 40–41 use this or a similar formula when introducing interpretations of dreams and visions. See discussion of the Pesher genre and the meaning of the term in Horgan 1979: 230–237, 252–259; Brooke 1979/81.

18. Pesharim are full of idiomatic scriptural terminology, as has been shown by Brooke 1991, 1994. Historical identifications require a careful study of the scriptural and other allusions; see also Callaway 1988: 140–171.

19. For the in-group: the men of truth, the chosen of God, the congregation of his elect, the congregation of the poor, the poor, his holy people, those who do his will; see the table by Lim 2002: 41–42.

20. This does not mean that there could not be variation in depicting one side or the other; there is. For example, in the Habakkuk Pesher, the Kittim (Romans) are evil but not directly opposing the community members. Within the text, they function as the background to which the wickedness of the other out-groups is paralleled.

21. Similar to CD III, 12-16; XV, 12; 1QS I, 7, 16-17. We can assume that there is both continuity and discontinuity in the way the Psalms Pesher and the Habakkuk Pesher present the group identity in relation to rule texts.

22. It must be borne in mind that the Pesharim are dependent on the scriptural exegesis, and many of their self-designations are indebted to scriptural texts and other exegetical traditions; for the "poor," cf., e.g., 1QM XI; 1QH XIII.

23. See the text of CD and literature in Broshi 1992.

24. The oldest manuscript 4Q266 is written in a semi-cursive Hasmonean hand and comes from the first half of the first century B.C.E. It preserves parallel material of almost all the columns of CD A, plus material that is not part of CD A (J. M. Baumgarten 1996). On internal grounds, the document has been dated closer to 100 B.C.E., Knibb 1994: 150. For the Pesharim, see below.

25. Davies 1983: 199–200 suggests that the "teacher" in CD I, 11 is part of "Qumranic recension" of the work. In contrast, Boyce 1990 regards it as original, but the time references in CD I are probably later additions. If an original part of the Admonition, the teacher appears as one, albeit central, individual whom God had raised in order to preserve a holy remnant. Another individual figure is "the staff," "the interpreter of law" (CD VI, 7,9), which is often identified with the teacher. These titles are woven into the question of eschatological expectations in the document; we follow J. J. Collins's view that CD VI, 10-11 "until there arises one that teaches righteousness in the latter times (יורה הצדק באחרית הימים, ywrh ḥṣdq bʾḥryt hymym)" expresses expectation of yet a future prophet or priest; J. J. Collins 1995: 102–126.

26. Similar to Davies 1983: 53–54, 66, 71: "One of the central themes of CD as a whole is the presentation of the remnant group as the Israel with whom God is presently dealing. The rest of 'Israel' has been and is rejected, subject to covenant vengeance of God." Similarly, A. I. Baumgarten 2000: 9; Grossman 2002: 112. Note that the Laws, including both halakhah and communal legislation, are a substantial part of the document; the Admonition is rather an introduction to the Laws; see Hempel 1998.

27. Cf. "communal authority" by Grossman 2002: 33. It is not, however, based on the excellence of these people but on the fact that God keeps up his covenant (CD VIII, 14-18). The covenant is one that you enter; people are not born into it.

28. See Knibb 1994: 157. The traitors are in CD B more emphatically those who have turned to the covenant but *then* stray away (CD XIX, 16-17; 31-35; XX, 1-2, 8-9).

29. Original publication by Allegro 1968, but see also Strugnell 1970 and Horgan 1979.

30. Burrows 1950; Brownlee 1979. Both Pesharim are written in Herodian script and are dated to the turn of the era, give or take a generation, cf. Lim 2002: 21–22, but they are probably not autographs; Horgan 1979: 3–4. Internal evidence suggests the dating before the coming of the Romans in 63 B.C.E.

31. The names "interpreter of knowledge" (I, 25—II, 1), "priest" (II, 16-21), and "righteous" (IV, 7-10) most likely refer to the same figure (so also Stegemann 1967: 204, n. 43), and are here included in the analysis. The Psalms Pesher connects the "teacher" and the "priest" in line III,15. For the "righteous," compare 1QpHab I, 12-13; V, 8-12. The name "interpreter of knowledge" probably derives from the Hodayot, e.g., 1QH X, 13 (previously II, 13); that it refers to the teacher is suggested by teacher's wisdom and revelation (1QpHab VII, 4-5).

32. The "righteous teacher" occurs also in 4QpPsa III, 17-29; IV, 26-27; 1QpHab I, 12-13; 4QpPsb frag. 1 4; frag 2 [1], and 1QpMic frag, 10, 3-7, but these are too fragmentary to make any further conclusions.

33. See Lim 1997: 98–104 for the textual change in the citation.

34. Lim 2002: 74–75 conveniently summarizes the scriptural context of the teacher's title (cf. Joel 2:23; Hos 10:12; Isa 30:20-21).

35. The question of whether the title "wicked priest" denote one or several individuals is not that central here, unless we think that the title "righteous teacher" can also mean several different persons; see Schiffman 1994: 117. The theory of "wicked priests" as several high priests was suggested by van der Woude 1982.

36. The term מזמות (*mzmwt*) of the quotation (and the root זמם [*zmm*]) and the noun דעת (*zᶜt*) are used closely to each other in the Hebrew Bible (Prov. 1:4; 5:2; 8:12). The writer may have been led by this connection and by the use of the term מזמות (*mzmwt*) in 1QH, and found מליץ דעת (*mlyṣ dᶜt*) a proper term here (in contrast to suggestion of a word play by Horgan 1979: 247).

37. Rather than claiming that he is *the* founder of the group, this passage may claim that although being persecuted, the teacher has received his mandate from God.

38. In Qumran Hebrew, the suffix in בחירו (*bḥyrw*) can be either singular, "his chosen one," as in biblical Hebrew, or plural, "his chosen ones," see Qimron 1986: 33. In 1QpHab V, 4; IX, 12, the likelier interpretation is plural, as it is referred to in plural (but for the opposite view: see Brooke 1997: 624). A clear plural form is found, e.g. in 1QpMic 10, 7. Even the singular word can be understood collectively, cf. Isa 43:20, Carmignac, Cothenet, et al. 1963: 120 n. 4. The Damascus Document refers to the election of a remnant, even individually by name (e.g., II, 7, 11).

39. The passage possibly depicts several groups here, distinct either temporally or in location; cf. Horgan 1979: 24.

40. It has been suggested that the teacher calculated the time of the end, which then proved wrong; Steudel 1993: 235–236; A. I. Baumgarten 1997: 178–180.

41. It is possible, however, that the teachings of the teacher are *thought* to be preserved by the group (note the *yiqtol* in I,7) and that the group is to continue in this tradition (VII, 6-8). Those who do not join the group or those who leave it reject the in-group's teaching as well.

42. Raven 1993 analyses six types of power. A leader may use different types of power at different times.

43. Yet, consistent with social-identity theory of leadership, prototypical leaders do not need to exercise power to be influential. They embody the norms of the group and are influential because of attraction due to their high prototypicality; Hogg 2001: 194. Here the question is not what the teacher did in order to gain his position but how he is perceived to act.

44. Cf. the so-called "Teacher Hymns" (1QHa X-XVI), which many scholars ascribe to the teacher, see Puech 2000. They portray an individual who is the target of scoff and slander but whom God has set "a banner for the elect ones of righteousness, and interpreter of knowledge of secret wonders" (X, 13). J. J. Collins 2000 discusses the nature of the servant ideology in these hymns. Even if not written by the teacher, it seems possible, as Davies 1987: 87–105 has proposed, that the members *viewed* these hymns as written by the teacher and were inspired by them in their Pesher interpretations.

45. E.g., 4QpPsa I, 25—II,5.

46. This citation has not been preserved in 1QpHab, but is probably to be reconstructed according to MT in the end of column VII.

47. Cf. Tajfel 1981: 150.

48. This final section is usually regarded as belonging to a late layer of the Admonition, see Knibb 1994: 156.

49. Qimron 1992: 49 reads הישיד (hyhyd) as היחד (hyhd).

50. Cf. translation and poetic nature of the section by Boyce 1990.

51. Lim 2002: 75.

52. Cf. also parallel of CD XX, 31-32 in 1QS IX, 9-11: the teacher is not mentioned as a decisive determinant of the right rules. However, J. J. Collins 1995: 113 sees a correspondence between 1QS IX, 9-11 and CD VI, 8-11, and interprets "first precepts" to mean those ascribed by the interpreter of the law, which he identifies with the teacher.

53. Although fragmentary, the occurrence of the title in Micah Pesher (frag. 10, 3-7) is significant, since the usual term in 1QS but not in the Pesharim, המתנדבים (hmtndbym) "those who volunteer," is here connected with the teacher: "[Interpreted, this concerns] the tea[ch]er of righteousness, who is the one [. . .]w, and to a[l]l those who volunteer to be added to the chosen ones [of God]." For the arrangement of the fragments we follow Horgan 1979: 55–57, The texts, 10.

54. Boyce 1990: 627 makes a distinction between the Mosaic law and the sectarian law in the passage, but 4Q266 frag. 11 shows how integral was the view of the Mosaic law and its exact interpretation. Furthermore, that passage mentions only the community officials, not the teacher.

55. Cinnirella 1998. See also Esler 2003a: 22–24, 172–180.

56. "Social time" is here related to the possible social identities; it marks the events and beliefs that the group depicted central to its existence; cf. Esler 2003a: 23–24.

57. Not all the members needed to be similarly persecuted than the teacher even though they themselves claimed to have received the time of affliction.

Notes to Chapter Eighteen

1. Bellah, "Religious Evolution," 1991: 42–43.

2. Räisänen 1997: 79. Concerning Marcion of Pontus, see Harnack 1990; Jonas 1963: 137–146; or Frend 1984: 212–218.

3. Thoroughly discussed in Malina 1996b and Neyrey 2004.

4. Rohrbaugh 1978; Malina 1991; and Bossman 1993 give perceptive formulations of the cultural problem.

5. Childs 1970; see Sheppard 1998 and Barr 1999. Stuhlmacher's "hermeneutics of consent" (1977: 38–39, 87) still does not grasp the depth of the problem; neither does Brueggemann's rhetorical strategy (1997).

6. Kaplan and Manners 1972: 5.

7. Regarding the "hermeneutical turn" in social science, see Grondin: 1994: 110; Skinner 1985: 37–38; Craffert 1994.

8. Crain 1992; Eichrodt and most twentieth-century biblical theologies rejected developmental approaches; the argument here is closer to Eissfeldt's historical approach: Barr 1999: 24; Hasel 1972: 1–47.

9. Werner 1948; Werner and Kaplan 1963.

10. Durkheim 1984 [1893].

11. Kohlberg 1981.

12. Jaspers 1953; Bellah, "Religious Evolution," 1991: 22.

13. This and following models are understood as ideal typical.

14. McKenzie 1974: 26, 28–29.

15. Bellah, "Religious Evolution," 1991: 31.

16. Eilberg-Schwartz 1990 is particularly helpful.

17. Bultmann 1955: 252.

18. Bellah, "Religious Evolution," 1991: 44.

19. Analyses of Lambert 1999 and Armstrong 2000 depend upon Jaspers 1953.

20. Parsons (1978) refers to the organic and action systems; Bergson (1977) to group and human morality or "static" and "dynamic" religion. These are other terms for the two poles I have in mind.

21. Parsons 1978: 361; R. Collins 1988: 58.

22. Bergson 1977: 27–28; compare Reventlow (1992: 488) on biblical eschatology/nationalism or Galtung's (1997–98) distinction between "hard" and "soft" religion.

23. The term "genetic" culture derives from Geertz 1973: 93–94; "primary" and "secondary" socialization are discussed by Berger and Luckmann 1966: 129–147.

24. Nord (1995: 180) distinguishes between rationality and reasonableness as follows: ". . . the attempt to be reasonable is inevitably less a matter of being rigorously logical than of being deliberative; it requires that we be open to new patterns of meaning; and it will not yield certainty so much as insight and, perhaps, a measure of plausibility. *Rationality*, as I shall use the term, is a matter of following rules, of being logical, within a system of accepted truths; *reasonableness* requires self-critical questioning of a system's most basic assumptions and an openness to alternative ways of making sense of the world."

25. Nord 1995.

26. Cone 1972: 95.

27. Bellah ("Between Religion and Social Science," 1991: 237–259, esp. 251) is inspired by Augustine's intellectual search for faith (or faithful search for understanding: *credo ut intelligam*) and Paul Tillich's notions of the depth dimension of experience and religion at the heart of culture.

28. Bellah, "Sociology of Religion," 1991: 12, 16.

29. Werner 1948: 271 and 277.

30. Bellah, "Between Religion and Social Science," 1991: 245, 255.

31. Jenkins 2002.

32. Lindbeck 1984; Esler (1995a: 16–18 and 1998a: 26) stresses Lindbeck's importance in relation to an "intercultural approach."

Notes to Chapter Nineteen

1. Malina 1986b.

2. Senior 2003.

3. Murphy 2002.

4. A.-J. Levine 2003

5. Rubinkiewicz 2003.

6. Chrostowski 2003

7. See Crick 1982.

8. See Malina 1996c.

9. Malina and Neyrey 1988.

10. See Bowersock 1988.

11. See, for example, Cohen 1999; Elliott 2000; Esler 1998a: 3–5 and 2003a: 40–76, R. J. Miller 1992; Horsley 1994; Koester 1994; Malina and Rohrbaugh (1992 and 1998); Pilch 1999b; Von Wahlde 2000; a notable opposing voice: Grelot 1995.

12. Danker 2000.

13. Prof. Reuven Firestone in *The Jewish Journal of Greater Los Angeles*, December 14, 2001.

14. See Kuhn and Reidy 1968 and Simpson and Weiner 1989.

15. See Arnaiz-Villena et al. 2001.

16. See Brook 1999.

17. See Sharif 1983.

18. Stephen Magagnini, "DNA Helps Unscramble the Puzzles of Ancestry," *Sacramento Bee*, August 3, 2003, http://www.sacbee.com.

19. See Malina and Rohrbaugh 1992, 1998.

20. See John Paul II, *L'Osservatore Romano*, April 13, 1986.

21. See Finkelstein 2000.

Notes to Chapter Twenty

1. On the writing and publication history see Freud 1939: 3–5.

2. Ibid., 10.

3. Freud (1939: 36–37, 47) here appealed to the suggestion of Ernst Sellin that Hosea preserved the tradition of Moses' having met a violent end in a popular rebellion.

4. Freud 1939: 50–51.

5. Ibid., 50.

6. Ibid., 65.

7. Ibid., 39, 51.

8. Ibid., 85, 101.

9. Ibid., 80.

10. Ibid., 129.

11. Ibid., 101.

12. Ibid., 134.

13. Ibid., 7, 54–58, 103–104.

14. Freud was anticipated in his discussion of Akhenaten by his pupil Karl Abraham. The latter's work is, strangely, unacknowledged by Freud. See Abraham 1955. The main purpose of Abraham's paper is to show that Akhenaten's character and actions reflect his strong oedipal attachment to his mother. Abraham also claims, however, just as Freud in his later work, that Akhenaten's religion of the Aten is the precursor to Moses' monotheism, and indeed also suggests that this was connected with Syrian cults mediated to Egypt by Akhenaten's mother, Tiy. For the oedipal character of Akhenaten cf. also Velikovsky 1960, who believes that the classical myth of Oedipus is in fact rooted in historical events and personalities of the Egyptian eighteenth dynasty. For criticism of Freud's arbitrary use of the Bible, cf., e.g., Ricoeur 1970: 245–246.

15. Cf. also Freud 1939: 105, 123, where Freud states that his concern is to understand the ability of the Jewish people to survive in the face of misfortune.

16. Cf. R. A. Paul 1991: 267. These works include Freud 1913, 1921, 1930, and 1939.

17. Why did Freud hold to the Egyptian nationality of Moses, involving as it did the rather tortuous treatment of Otto Rank's study of the myth of the birth

of the hero? The answer lies in part in Freud's self-identification with Moses and his longing for assimilation into the Gentile world. The latter wish is reflected in one of Freud's dreams (see Freud 1900: 194), where Rome appears as "the Promised land seen from afar." Freud is in the same relation to Rome as Moses to the land of Israel. See also Breger 2000: 361.

18. R. A. Paul 1991: 281, concludes that "Freud arrived at the construct of the primal crime not from reading Robertson Smith and Darwin, but by performing upon the central Christian ritual, the Eucharist or Mass, the same sort of analysis and reconstruction of early events he would have carried out had the same constellation of ideas and actions been presented to him as the fantasy or ceremony of an individual obsessional patient."

19. Cf. Frankland 2000: 184–185.

20. R. A. Paul 1996: 17.

21. Quoted in Bernstein 1998: 1.

22. Freud 1939: 111–115; cf. Bernstein 1998: 30–35. The translation of *Geistigkeit* as "spirituality" is to be preferred to the Standard Edition translation by James Strachey as "intellectuality," without prejudice to Freud's declared atheism. See the translation by Jones (Freud 1939a: 142–147). For a general critique of the Strachey translation, cf. Bettelheim 1989.

23. Cf. Bernstein 1998: 83.

24. McGuire 1974: 196–197; cf. Gay 1988: 604–605.

25. Gay 1988: 608.

26. Freud 1939: 66. For an excellent account of the complex relationship of Freud to Moses, cf. Frankland 2000: 220–231. For a psychoanalytic account of Freud's *Moses and Monotheism,* which sees reflected in it Freud's relationship with his father and the Jewish tradition, cf. Robert 1976: 133–167.

27. Paskausas 1995: 751.

28. Gay 1995: xxiv.

29. Freud 1939: 40, 61. The Merneptah Stele, mainly concerned to celebrate the defeat of the Libyans by that nineteenth-dynasty pharaoh, concludes by praising the pharaoh for his victory over all Egypt's neighbors, including Israel: "Israel is laid waste; his seed is no longer." For the translated text see, for example, W. K. Simpson 2003: 356–360; discussion in Yurco 1997: 27–55.

30. The literature on the subject of tradition and ideology is, of course, extensive. Immediately relevant is van Henten and Houtepen 2001.

31. Freud 1939: 51.

32. Ibid., 94-5.

33. Ibid., 98, 99.

34. This refers to the theory, associated with the French naturalist Jean Baptiste Lamarck, that experiences of former generations are somehow "encoded" within the genetic inheritance of individual members of a group; see the discussion in Yerushalmi 1991: 30–33, and Bernstein 1998: 52–64.

35. This is particularly the case in relation to understanding the trauma of

the holocaust; see the brief discussion and bibliography in Bernstein 1998: 131 n. 10. Traumatic events in the history of any people, as, for example, the nineteenth-century famine in Ireland, would be susceptible to similar analysis.

36. R. A. Paul 1996: 3–4, 5.

37. Gay 1988: 115. Cf. Freud 1939: 167–168, 266–267.

38. Cf. Knauf 1988: 97–149; de Moor 1990: 136–138.

39. Cf. Assmann 1997: 150, but against taking Moses as an Egyptian name, cf. Kitchen 2003: 296–297.

40. Cf. Assmann 1997: 168–207. Assmann also points to the difference between Egyptian and Israelite beliefs about creation: in Egyptian monotheism creation is ongoing, in Israelite belief creation is a past event.

41. For a recent survey of the archaeological evidence, indicating Israel's Canaanite origins in the Late Bronze-Iron I transition, see Dever 2003.

42. See Assmann 1997: 29–44; Schäfer 1997: 163; and especially Gruen 1998: 41–72. Gruen provides a subtle and persuasive account of the background and development of an Egyptian tradition, appropriated by Egyptian diaspora Jews, and subsequently appearing especially in Hecataeus and Manetho.

43. If I understand Assmann 1997: 40–41 correctly, his argument is that the biblical and Egyptian stories are inversions of each other: in the Old Testament the Egyptians are the oppressors, idolators, and magicians, while in the Egyptian version the Asiatics (eventually to be identified with the Jews) are the impure and the sacrilegious, but both accounts are parallel expressions of "the experience of counter-religion." It should be noted, however, the Egyptian version of the tradition presupposes the dislocated transfer to the Hyksos of the Amarna experience, by which time the "Canaanite" Hyksos tradition had already begun its independent development. It was only at a much later stage (see below) that a "counter-religion" dimension was projected on to it. The older Hyksos tradition in the Canaanite/Israelite environment was simply a tradition of origins, taken over by Israel perhaps as a "charter myth" (for which, cf. van der Toorn 2001: 113–127). For reminiscences of the Hyksos occupation of Egypt and their later expulsion as lying behind the biblical exodus tradition, cf. also Redford 1992: 408–422. On the biblical and classical accounts of the exodus as parallel traditions among which the biblical tradition has no claim to priority, cf. also Davies 2001: 108–128. Nearly all Hyksos names have been decoded as west Semitic. Their frequency also in Palestine suggests that a number of rulers of southern Palestine were vassals to the Hyksos fifteenth-dynasty kings. The Hyksos were first defeated in a revolt led by a new family that came to power in Thebes. The chief records relate to Kamose, the last king of the seventeenth dynasty, and Ahmose, his successor and founder of the eighteenth dynasty. The latter destroyed the Hyksos capital Avaris, and pursued them to Sharuhen in the southern coastal plain of Palestine which, in the course of three campaigns, he also destroyed. For a discussion, see Redford 1992: 127–129 and Bietak 2001.

44. Cf. Assmann 1997: 28–29, referring to the fragmentary tale of the quarrel of Apophis and Sekenenre, in which Apophis, the Hyksos king, practiced monolatry and disputed the power of Amon-Re to protect Sekenenre; for the tale, cf. W. K. Simpson 2003: 69–71.

45. Cf. Theissen 1984: 64–65; Assmann 1997: 7.

46. For this cf. Theissen 1984: 51–81.

47. On Aten as first principle, cf. J. P. Allen 1989: 89–101.

48. On the "Yahweh-alone movement" see especially M. Smith 1987 and Lang 1983. See also Keel 1980.

49. I would associate with this transformation the point that the Pentateuch, which is now dominated by a tradition of Israelite origins in Mesopotamia rather than in Egypt still preserves traces of an older attitude to Egypt and Israelite origins there that was much more positive; on this see especially Greifenhagen 2002. On the exodus tradition as having been originally a "charter myth" rather than a deliverance tradition, cf. above, n. 27.

Bibliography

Abel, P. Felix Marie (1949). *Les livres des Maccabées*. Paris: Librairie Lecoffre, J. Gabalda et Cie, Editeurs.

Abraham, Karl (1955). "Amenhotep IV: A Psycho-Analytical Contribution towards the Understanding of his Personality and of the Monotheistic Cult of Aton." *Clinical Papers and Essays on Psycho-Analysis*. London: Hogarth.

Abrams, D. and M. A. Hogg (1990a). "An Introduction to the Social Identity Approach." In Abrams and Hogg 1990b: 1–9.

———, eds. (1990b). *Social Identity Theory: Constructive and Critical Advances*. New York: Harvester Wheatsheaf.

Abu-Lughod, Lila (1993). *Writing Women's Worlds: Bedouin Stories*. Berkeley: University of California Press.

Abu-Zeid, Ahmed (1966). "Honour and Shame among the Bedouins of Egypt." In Peristiany 1966: 243–259.

Ackerman, Susan (1998). *Warrior, Dancer, Seductress, Queen: Women in Judges and Biblical Israel*. ABRL. New York: Doubleday.

Ackroyd, Peter R. (1977). *The Second Book of Samuel*. CRC. Cambridge, UK: Cambridge University Press.

Adams, J. N. (1982). *The Latin Sexual Vocabulary*. Baltimore: Johns Hopkins University Press.

Aguilar, Mario I. (2000). "Rethinking the Judean Past: Questions of History and a Social Archaeology of Memory in the First Book of the Maccabees." *BTB* 30 (2): 58–67.

——— (2002). "Time, Communion and Ancestry in African Biblical Interpretation: A Contextual Note on 1 Maccabees 2:49-70." *BTB* 32 (3): 129–144.

——— and Louise Lawrence, eds. (2004). *Anthropology and Biblical Studies: Avenues of Research*. Leiden: Deo Publishing.

Allan, Keith, and Kate Burridge (1991). *Euphemism and Dysphemism Language Used as Shield and Weapon*. New York: Oxford University Press.

Allegro, John Marco (1968). *Qumran Cave 4 Volume I*. Oxford: Oxford University Press.

Allen, James P. (1989). "The Natural Philosophy of Akhenaten." In

Religion and Philosophy in Ancient Egypt, YES 3: 89–101. New Haven: Yale University Press.

Allen, Leslie C. (1976). *The Books of Joel, Obadiah, Jonah, and Micah*. NICOT. Grand Rapids, Mich.: Wm. B. Eerdmans.

Alt, Albrecht (1966). *Essays on Old Testament History and Religion*. Oxford: Blackwell.

Anbar, Moshe (1991). *Les tribus amurrites de Mari*. Freiburg: Universitätsverlag/Göttingen: Vandenhoeck & Ruprecht.

Andersen, Francis I., and David Noel Freedman (2000). *Micah: A New Translation with Introduction and Commentary*. AB 24E. New York: Doubleday.

Anderson, A. A. (1989). *2 Samuel*. WBC 11. Dallas: Word Books.

Anderson, Benedict (1991). *Imagined Communities: Reflections on the Origin and Spread of Nationalism*. Revised edition. London/New York: Verso.

Anderson, Cheryl B. (2004). *Women, Ideology, and Violence: Critical Theory and the Construction of Gender in the Book of the Covenant and the Deuteronomic Law*. JSOTSup 394. London and New York: T&T Clark.

Armstrong, Karen (2000). *The Battle for God: A History of Fundamentalism*. San Francisco: HarperSanFrancisco.

Arnaiz-Villena, Antonio, and Nagah Elaiwa, Carlos Silvera, Ahmed Rostom, Juan Moscoso, Eduardo Gómez-Casado, Luis Allende, Pilar Varela, Jorge Martínez-Laso (2001). "The Origin of Palestinians and Their Genetic Relatedness with Other Mediterranean Populations." *Human Immunology* 62: 889–900.

Assmann, Jan (1997). *Moses the Egyptian*. Cambridge, Mass.: Harvard University Press.

Attridge, Harold W. (1976). *The Interpretation of Biblical History in the* Antiquitates Judaicae *of Flavius Josephus*. HDR 7. Missoula: Scholars Press.

Avigad, Nahman (1953). "Another *bat le-melekh* Inscription." *IEJ* 3:121–122.

Baker, Cynthia M. (1998). "Ordering the House: On the Domestication of Jewish Bodies." In Wyke 1997.

Bal, Mieke (1988). *Death and Dissymmetry: The Politics of Coherence in the Book of Judges*. Chicago: University of Chicago.

———, ed. (1989a). *Anti-Covenant: Counter-Reading Women's Lives in the Hebrew Bible*. Bible and Literature Series 22. Sheffield: Almond Press.

——— (1989b). "Between Altar and Wandering Rock: Toward a Feminist Philology." In Bal 1989a: 211–231.

——— (1989c). "Introduction." In Bal 1989a: 11–24.

Balharek, G. (1958). Euphêmia, euphêmismos *in der Antike und neuzeitlicher Gebrauch des Terminus Euphemismus.* Unpublished doctoral dissertation, Heidelberg University.

Barnard, Alan (2000). *History and Theory in Anthropology.* Cambridge, UK: Cambridge University Press.

Barr, James (1999). *The Concept of Biblical Theology: An Old Testament Perspective.* Minneapolis: Fortress Press.

Barstad, Hans (2000). "Comparare necesse est? Ancient Israelite and Ancient Near Eastern Prophecy in a Comparative Perspective." In Nissinen 2000: 1–11.

Barth, Fredrik (1969a). *Ethnic Groups and Boundaries: The Social Organization of Cultural Difference.* Boston: Little, Brown.

——— (1969b). "Introduction." In Barth 1969a: 9–38.

Barton, John (1998). *Ethics and the Old Testament: The 1997 Diocese of British Columbia John Albert Hall Lectures at the Centre for Studies in Religion and Society in the University of Victoria.* London: SCM Press.

——— (2001). *Joel and Obadiah.* OTL. Louisville: Westminster John Knox.

——— (2002). *Ethics and the Old Testament.* Second edition. London: SCM Press.

Bascom, William (1980). *Sixteen Cowries: Yoruba Divination from Africa to the New World.* Bloomington and Indianapolis: Indiana University Press.

Bastien, Rémy (1985). *Le paysan haïtien et sa famille: Vallée de Marbial.* Paris: Editions Karthala.

Batatu, Hanna (1999). *Syria's Peasantry, the Descendants of Its Lesser Rural Notables, and Their Politics.* Princeton: Princeton University Press.

Bates, Daniel, and Amal Rassam (1983). *Peoples and Cultures of the Middle East.* Englewood Cliffs, N.J.: Prentice-Hall.

Batten, Alicia (2004). "God in the Letter of James: Patron or Benefactor?" *NTS* 50: 257–272.

Baumgarten, Albert I. (1997). *The Flourishing of Jewish Sects in the Maccabean Era: An Interpretation.* JSJSup 55. Leiden: Brill.

——— (2000). "The Perception of the Past in the Damascus Document." In Joseph M. Baumgarten, Esther G. Chazon, and Avital Pinnick. eds., *The Damascus Document: A Centennial of Discovery: Proceedings of the Third International Symposium of the Orion Center for the Study of the Dead Sea Scrolls and Associated Literature, 4–8 February, 1998.* STDJ 34: 1–15. Leiden: Brill.

Baumgarten, Joseph M. (1996). *Qumran Cave 4 XIII: The Damascus Document (4Q266–4Q273).* Oxford: Clarendon Press.

Baxter, P. T. W. (1978). "Boran Age-Sets and Generation-Sets: *Gada*, a Puzzle or a Maze?" In Baxter and Almagor 1978: 151–182.

—— (1979). "Boran Age-Sets and Warfare." In Fukui and Turton 1979: 69–95.

——, and Uri Almagor, eds. (1978). *Age, Generation and Time: Some Features of East African Organisations.* London: C. Hurst.

Bechtel, Lyn M. (1991). "Shame as a Sanction of Social Control in Biblical Israel: Juridical, Political and Social Shaming." *JSOT* 49: 47–76.

Becking, Bob (1995). "Divine Wrath and the Conceptual Coherence of the Book of Nahum." *SJOT* 9: 277–296.

Bell, Catherine (1992). *Ritual Theory, Ritual Practice.* Oxford: Oxford University Press.

Bell, Duran (1991a). "Modes of Exchange: Gift and Commodity." *Journal of Socio-Economics* 16: 96–124.

—— (1991b). "Reciprocity as a Generating Process in Social Relations." *Journal of Quantitative Anthropology* 3: 251–260.

Bellah, Robert N. (1991). *Beyond Belief: Essays on Religion in a Post-Traditional World.* Berkeley: University of California Press.

Bendor, Shunya (1996). *The Social Structure of Ancient Israel: The Institution of the Family* (Beit 'Ab) *from the Settlement to the End of the Family.* Jerusalem: Simor.

Bennett, Harold V. (2002). *Injustice Made Legal: Deuteronomic Law and the Plight of Widows, Strangers, and Orphans in Ancient Israel.* The Bible in Its World series. Grand Rapids, Mich.: Wm. B. Eerdmans.

Benveniste, E. (1939). "Euphemismes anciens et modernes." In *Mélanges Ch. Bally,* 116–122. Geneva.

Ben Zvi, Ehud. (2000). *Micah.* FOTL 21B. Grand Rapids, Mich.: Wm. B. Eerdmans.

Berger, Peter L. (1969). *The Sacred Canopy: Elements of a Sociological Theory of Religion.* New York: Anchor.

——, and Thomas Luckmann (1966 [1967]). *The Social Construction of Reality: A Treatise in the Sociology of Knowledge.* London: Pelican [Garden City, N.Y.: Doubleday].

Bergson, Henri (1977). *The Two Sources of Morality and Religion.* Notre Dame, Ind.: University of Notre Dame Press.

Berlinerblau, Jacques (1996). *The Vow and the 'Popular Religious Groups' of Ancient Israel: A Philological and Socological Inquiry.* JSOTSup 210. Sheffield: Sheffield Academic Press.

Bernardi, Bernardo (1985). *Age Class Systems: Social Institutions and Polities Based on Age.* CSSCA 57. Cambridge, U.K.: Cambridge University Press.

Bernstein, Richard J. (1998). *Freud and the Legacy of Moses.* CSRCT 4. Cambridge, U.K.: Cambridge University Press.

Berquist, Jon L. (2002). *Controlling Corporeality: The Body and the Household in Ancient Israel.* Piscataway, N.J.: Rutgers University Press.

Bettelheim, Bruno (1989). *Freud and Man's Soul.* London: Penguin.

Bettini, Maurizio, ed. (1991). *La maschera, il doppio e il ritratto.* Bari: Laterza.

Bienkowski, Piotr, and Eveline van der Steen (2001). "Tribes, Trade, and Towns: A New Framework for the Late Iron Age in Southern Jordan and the Negev." *BASOR* 323: 21–47.

Bietak, M. (2001) "Hyksos." In Donald B. Redford, ed., *Oxford Encyclopedia of Ancient Egypt.* Vol. 2: 136–143. Oxford: Oxford University Press.

Bijoux, Legrand (1990). *Coup d'oeil sur la famille haïtienne.* Port-au-Prince, Haïti: Editions des Antilles.

Blenkinsopp, Joseph (1968). "Deuteronomy." In Raymond E. Brown, Joseph A. Fitzmyer, and Roland E. Murphy, eds., *The Jerome Biblical Commentary,* 101–122. Englewood Cliffs, N. J.: Prentice-Hall.

——— (1990). *Ezekiel.* Int. Louisville: John Knox Press.

——— (2003). *Isaiah 56–66.* AB 19B. New York: Doubleday.

Bloch-Smith, Elizabeth (2003). "Israelite Ethnicity in Iron I: Archaeology Preserves What Is Remembered and What Is Forgotten in Israel's History." *JBL* 122: 401–425.

Block, Daniel I. (1997). *The Book of Ezekiel: Chapters 1–24.* NICOT. Grand Rapids, Mich. and Cambridge, U.K.: Wm. B. Eerdmans.

Bodoff, Lippman (2000). "The Tragedy of Jephthah." *JBQ* 28 (4): 251–255.

Boehm, Christopher (1984). *Blood Revenge: The Enactment and Management of Conflict in Montenegro and Other Tribal Societies.* Philadelphia: University of Pennsylvania.

Boer, Roland (2002a). "Introduction: On Re-Reading *The Tribes of Yahweh.*" In Boer 2002b: 1–9.

————, ed. (2002b). *Tracking* The Tribes of Yahweh: *On the Trail of a Classic*. JSOTSup 351. London: Continuum.

Bohannan, Paul (1997). "Ethnography and Comparison in Legal Anthropology." In Laura Nader, ed., *Law in Culture and Society*, 401–418. Second edition. Berkeley: University of California Press.

Boissevain, Jeremy (1974). *Friends of Friends: Networks, Manipulators, and Coalitions*. New York: St. Martin's Press.

Boling, Robert G. (1975). *Judges: Introduction, Translation and Commentary*. AB 6A. Garden City, N.Y.: Doubleday.

Bonfante, G. (1939). "Étude sur le tabou dans les langues indoeuropéennes." In *Mélanges Ch. Bally*, 195–207. Geneva.

Bossman, David (1993). "Canon and Culture: A Call for Biblical Theology in Context." *BTB* 23 (1): 4–13.

Botterweck, G. Johannes (1982). "*Yd.*" *TWAT* 3: 486–512.

Bourdieu, Pierre (1966). "The Sentiment of Honour in Kabyle Society." In Peristiany 1966: 191–241.

———— (1977). *Outline of a Theory of Practice*. CSSCA 16. Cambridge, U.K.: Cambridge University Press.

———— (1984). *Distinction*. Cambridge, Mass.: Harvard University Press.

Bourguignon, Erika (1973). *Altered States of Consciousness, and Social Change*. Columbus: Ohio State University Press.

———— (1976). *Possession*. San Francisco: Chandler and Sharp.

Bowersock, Glen W. (1988). "Palestine, Ancient History and Modern Politics." In Edward Said and Christopher Hitchens, eds., *Blaming the Victim: Spurious Scholarship and the Palestinian Question*, 181–191. London/New York: Verso.

Bowie, Fiona (2000). *The Anthropology of Religion: An Introduction*. Oxford: Blackwell.

Boyce, Mark (1990). "The Poetry of the Damascus Document and Its Bearing on the Origin of the Qumran Sect." *RdQ* 14 (56): 615–628.

Brayford, Susan A. (1999). "To Shame or not to Shame: Sexuality in the Mediterranean Diaspora." *Semeia* 87: 163–176.

Breger, Louis (2000). *Freud: Darkness in the Midst of Vision*. New York: Wiley.

Brenner, Athalya, ed. (1993). *A Feminist Companion to Judges*. Feminist Companion to the Bible 4. Sheffield: JSOT Press.

Brett, Mark G. (2003). "Israel's Indigenous Origins: Cultural Hybridity and the Formation of Israelite Ethnicity." *BibInt* 11: 400–412.

Brodie, Fawn M. (1971). *No Man Knows My History: The Life of*

Joseph Smith the Mormon Prophet. Second edition, revised and enlarged. New York: Random House.

Brook, Kevin Alan (1999). *The Jews of Khazaria.* Northvale, N.J.: Jason Aronson.

Brooke, George J. (1979/81). "Qumran Pesher: Towards the Redefinition of a Genre." *RdQ* 10: 483–503.

——— (1991). "The Kittim in the Qumran Pesharim." In Loveday Alexander, ed., *Images of Empire,* 135–159. Sheffield: Sheffield Academic Press.

——— (1994). "The Pesharim and the Origins of the Dead Sea Scrolls." In Michael O. Wise, Norman Golb, John J. Collins, and Dennis G. Pardee, eds., *Methods of Investigation of the Dead Sea Scrolls and the Khirbet Qumran Site: Present Realities and Future Prospects,* 339–353. New York: The New York Academy of Sciences.

——— (1997). "Isaiah in the Pesharim and Other Qumran Texts" In Craig C. Broyles and Craig A. Evans, eds., *Writing and Reading the Scroll of Isaiah: Studies of an Interpretive Tradition,* VTSup 70: 609–632. Leiden: Brill,

Brooke, John L. (1994). *The Refiner's Fire: The Making of Mormon Cosmology, 1644–1844.* Cambridge, U.K.: Cambridge University Press.

Broome, Edwin C. (1946). "Ezekiel's Abnormal Personality." *JBL* 65: 272–292.

Broshi, Magen, ed. (1992). *The Damascus Document Reconsidered.* Jerusalem: The Israel Exploration Society.

Brown, Rupert (2000). *Group Processes: Dynamics within and between Groups.* Oxford: Blackwell.

Brownlee, William H. (1979). *The Midrash Pesher of Habakkuk.* Missoula, Mont.: Scholars Press.

Brueggemann, Walter (1962). "Thigh." *IDB* 4: 630.

——— (1979). "Trajectories in Old Testament Literature and the Sociology of Ancient Israel." *JBL* 98: 161–185.

——— (1980). "*The Tribes of Yahweh*: An Essay Review." *JAAR* 48: 441–451.

——— (1997). *Theology of the Old Testament: Testimony, Dispute, Advocacy.* Minneapolis: Fortress Press.

Budd, Philip J. (1996). *Leviticus.* NCB. Grand Rapids, Mich.: Wm. B. Eerdmans.

Bultmann, Rudolf. (1955). "The Problem of Hermeneutics." In *Essays, Philosophical and Theological,* 234–261. London: SCM Press.

Burkert, Walter (1997 [1972]). *Homo Necans: Interpretation alt-griechischer Opferriten und Mythen* [ET: *Homo Necans: The Anthropology of Ancient Greek Sacrificial Ritual and Myth*]. Second edition. Berlin and New York: de Gruyter.

Burrows, Millar (1950). *The Dead Sea Scrolls of St. Mark's Monastery*, Vol. I: *Isaiah Manuscript and the Habakkuk Commentary*. New Haven: ASOR.

Burton, John W. (2000). *Culture and the Human Body*. Long Grove, Ill.: Waveland Press.

Caillé, Alain (1998). *Il terzo Paradigma: Antropologia filosofica del dono*. Torino: Bollati Boringhieri.

Callaway, Mary (1986). *Sing, O Barren One: Study in Comparative Midrash*. SBLDS. Atlanta: Scholars Press.

Callaway, Phillip R. (1988). *The History of the Qumran Community: An Investigation*. JSOTSup 3. Sheffield: JSOT Press.

Campbell, Anthony F. (2003). *I Samuel*. FOTL 7. Grand Rapids, Mich.: Wm. B. Eerdmans.

Cardellini, Innocenzo (2001). *I sacrifici dell'antica alleanza: Tipologie, Rituali, Celebrazioni*. Cinisello Balsamo: San Paolo.

Carley, Keith W. (1974). *The Book of the Prophet Ezekiel*. CBC. Cambridge, U.K.: Cambridge University Press.

Carmichael, Calum (1974). *The Laws of Deuteronomy*. Ithaca, N.Y.: Cornell University Press, 1974.

Carmignac, Jean, Édouard Cothenet, et al. (1963). *Les Textes de Qumran: Traduits et annotés*. Paris.

Carney, T. F. (1973). *The Economies of Antiquity*. Lawrence, Kans.: Coronado Press.

——— (1975). *The Shape of the Past: Models and Antiquity*. Lawrence, Kans.: Coronado Press, 1975.

Carroll, Robert P. (1979). *When Prophecy Failed: Cognitive Dissonance in the Prophetic Traditions of the Old Testament*. New York: Seabury.

——— (1992). "Israel, History of (Post-Monarchic Period)." In David Noel Freedman, ed., *ABD* 3: 567–576. New York: Doubleday.

———, and M. Daniel, eds. (2000). *Rethinking Contexts, Rereading Texts: Contributions from the Social Sciences to Biblical Interpretation*. JSOTSup 299. Sheffield: Sheffield Academic Press.

Carter, Charles E. (1996). "A Discipline in Transition: The Contributions of the Social Sciences to the Study of the Hebrew Bible." In Carter and Meyers 1996: 3–36.

———, and Carol L. Meyers, eds. (1996). *Community, Identity, and*

Ideology: Social Science Approaches to the Hebrew Bible. SBTS 6. Winona Lake, Ind.: Eisenbrauns.

Cartledge, Tony W. (1992). *Vows in the Hebrew Bible and the Ancient Near East.* JSOTSup 147. Sheffield: Sheffield Academic.

Cathcart, Kevin J. (1973). *Nahum in the Light of Northwest Semitic.* BibOr 26. Rome: Pontifical Biblical Institute.

——— (1996). "Curses in Old Aramaic Inscriptions." In Kevin J. Cathcart and Michael Maher, eds., *Targumic and Cognate Studies in Honour of Martin McNamara,* JSOTSup 230: 140–152. Sheffield: Sheffield Academic Press.

———, and Robert P. Gordon (1989). *The Targum of the Minor Prophets.* The Aramaic Bible 14. Edinburgh: T&T Clark.

———, and Knud Jeppesen (1987). "More Suggestions on Mic 6,14." *SJOT* 1: 110–115.

Causse, Antonin (1937). *Du groupe ethnique à la communauté religieuse: le problème sociologique de la religion d'Israel.* Études d'histoire et de philosophie religieuses 33. Paris: Felix Alcan.

Chalcraft, David J., ed. (1997). *Social Scientific Old Testament Criticism: A Sheffield Reader.* Biblical Seminary Series 47. Sheffield: JSOT Press.

——— (2001). "The Lamentable Chain of Misunderstanding: Weber's Debate with H. Karl Fischer," *Max Weber Studies* 2:1: 65–80.

——— (2002). "Max Weber on the Watchtower." In C. Rowland and J. Barton, eds., *Apocalyptic in History and Tradition.* Sheffield: Sheffield, 253–270.

——— (2004). "Comparative Sociology on Israel: Herbert Spencer's Contribution." In L. Lawrence and M. Aquilar, *Anthropology and Biblical Studies.* Leiden: Deo, chap. 1.

———, ed. (2006, forthcoming). *Sectarianism in Early Judaism.* London: Equinox.

Chalcraft, D. J., and Austin Harrington, eds. (2001). *The Protestant Ethic Debate.* Liverpool: Liverpool University Press.

Chaney, Marvin L. (1983). "Ancient Palestinian Peasant Movements and the Formation of Premonarchic Israel." In David Noel Freedman and David Frank Graf, eds., *Palestine in Transition: The Emergence of Ancient Israel,* 39–90. Sheffield: Almond Press in association with ASOR.

——— (1986). "Systemic Study of the Israelite Monarchy." *Semeia* 37: 53–76.

——— (1989). "Bitter Bounty: The Dynamics of Political Economy Critiqued by the Eight-Century Prophets." In Robert L. Stivers, ed.,

Reformed Faith and Economics, 15–30. Lanham, Md.: University Press of America.

———— (1993). "Bitter Bounty: The Dynamics of Political Economy Critiqued by the Eighth-Century Prophets." In Norman K. Gottwald and Richard A. Horsley, eds., *The Bible and Liberation: Political and Social Hermeneutics*, 250–263. Maryknoll, N.Y.: Orbis.

———— (1999). "Whose Sour Grapes? The Addressees of Isaiah 5:1-7 in the Light of Political Economy." *Semeia* 87: 105–122.

———— (2004). "Accusing Whom of What? Hosea's Rhetoric of Promiscuity." In Holly E. Hearon, ed., *Distant Voices Drawing Near: Essays in Honor of Antoinette Clark Wire*, 97–115. Collegeville, Minn.: Liturgical Press.

Chertok, Shlomo (2000). "Mothers, Sons and Heroic Infertility; A Study of the Function of Barrenness in the Bible." *Le'ela* 50: 21–27.

Childs, Brevard S. (1970). *Biblical Theology in Crisis*. Philadelphia: Westminster Press.

Chock, Phyllis P. (1987). "The Irony of Stereotypes: Toward an Anthropology of Ethnicity." *Cultural Anthropology* 2: 347–368.

Chrostowski, Waldemar (2003). "Dokument Papieskiej Komisji Biblijnej 'Naród żydowski I jego Święte Pisma w Biblii chrześcijańskiej.' XIII Sympozjum Teologiczne 'Kościół a Żydzi I Judaizm,' Warszawa, 22 V 2002." *Collectanea Theologica* 73 (2): 5–12.

Cinnirella, Marco (1998). "Exploring Temporal Aspects of Social Identity: The Concept of Possible Social Identities." *European Journal of Social Psychology* 28 (2): 227–248.

Clark, Gordon R. (1993). *The Word Hesed in the Hebrew Bible*. JSOT-Sup 157. Sheffield: Sheffield University Press.

Clements, Ronald E. (1975). *Prophecy and Tradition*. Oxford: Blackwell.

————, ed. (1989). *The World of Ancient Israel: Sociological, Anthropological and Political Perspectives*. Cambridge, U.K.: Cambridge University Press.

Cohen, Abner (1965). *Arab Border-Villages in Israel: A Study of Continuity and Change in Social Organization*. Manchester: Manchester University Press.

Cohen, Shaye J. D. (1999). *The Beginnings of Jewishness: Boundaries, Varieties, Uncertainties*. Berkeley: University of California Press.

Collins, John J. (1995). *The Scepter and the Star: The Messiahs of the Dead Sea Scrolls and Other Ancient Literature*. New York: Doubleday.

———— (2000). "Teacher and Servant." *RHPR* 80 (1): 37–50.

Collins, Randall (1988). *Theoretical Sociology*. San Diego: Harcourt Brace Jovanovich.

Comte, Auguste (1970). *Introduction to Positive Philosophy*. Edited, with an introduction and revised by Frederick Ferré. Indianapolis: Bobbs-Merrill.

Cone, James (1972). *The Spirituals and the Blues: An Interpretation*. New York: Seabury Press.

Cook, Stephen L., and Sara C. Winter, eds. (1999). *On the Way to Nineveh: Studies in Honor of George M. Landes*. ASOR Book 4. Atlanta: Scholars.

Coote, Robert B. (1981). *Amos among the Prophets: Composition and Theology*. Philadelphia: Fortress Press.

——— (1990). *Early Israel: A New Horizon*. Minneapolis: Fortress Press.

——— and Keith W. Whitelam (1987). *The Emergence of Early Israel in Historical Perspective*. The Social World of Biblical Antiquity Series 5. Sheffield: Almond.

Craffert, Pieter F. (1994). "Taking Stock of the Emic-etic Distinction in Social-scientific Interpretations of the New Testament." *Neotestamentica* 28 (2): 1–21.

Craigie, Peter C. (2002 [1978]). *The Problem of War in the Old Testament*. Eugene, Ore.: Wipf and Stock.

Crain, William (1992). *Theories of Development: Concepts and Applications*. Third edition. Englewood Cliffs, N.J.: Prentice-Hall.

Crick, Malcolm (1982). "Anthropology of Knowledge." *Annual Review of Anthropology* 11: 287–313.

Crocker, Christopher (1973). "Ritual and the Development of Social Structure: Liminality and Inversion." In Shaughnessy 1973: 47–86.

Crook, Zeba (2004). *Reconceptualising Conversion: Patronage, Loyalty, and Conversion in the Religions of the Ancient Mediterranean*. Berlin: W. de Gruyter.

Cross, Frank Moore. (1973). *Canaanite Myth and Hebrew Epic: Essays in the History of The Religion of Israel*. Cambridge, Mass.: Harvard University Press.

——— (1998). "Reuben, the Firstborn of Jacob: Sacral Traditions and Early Israelite Tradition." In *From Epic to Canon: History and Literature in Ancient Israel*, 53–70. Baltimore: Johns Hopkins University Press.

Crüsemann, Frank (1992 [1996]). *Die Tora: Theologie und Sozialgeschichte des alttestamentlichen Gesetzes*, Munich: Chr. Kaiser [ET: *The Torah: Theology, and Social History of Old Testament Law* (Minneapolis: Fortress Press)].

Cryer, Frederick H. (1994). *Divination in Ancient Israel and its Near Eastern Environment*. JSOTSup 142. Sheffield: Sheffield Academic Press.

Culley, Robert C. and Thomas W. Overholt, eds. (1982). *Anthropological Perspectives on Old Testament Prophecy*. *Semeia* 21. Atlanta: Scholars Press.

Dancy, John C. (1954). *A Commentary on I Maccabees*. Oxford: Basil Blackwell.

Danker, Frederick W., ed. (2000). *A Greek-English Lexicon of the New Testament and Other Early Christian Literature by Walter Bauer*. Third revised edition. Chicago: University of Chicago Press.

Daube, David (1947). *Studies in Biblical Law*. Cambridge, U.K.: Cambridge University Press.

—— (1969). "The Culture of Deuteronomy." *Orita* 3: 27–52.

Davidson, Robert (1989). "Covenant Ideology in Ancient Israel." In Clements 1989: 323–347. Cambridge, U.K.: Cambridge University Press.

Davies, Philip R. (1983). *The Damascus Covenant: An Interpretation of the "Damascus Document."* JSOTSup 25. Sheffield: JSOT Press.

—— (1987). *Behind the Essenes: History and Ideology in the Dead Sea Scrolls*. BJS 94. Atlanta: Scholars Press.

—— (2001). "Judaeans in Egypt. Hebrew and Greek Stories." In Lester L. Grabbe, ed., *Did Moses Speak Attic?* JSOTSup 317: 108–128. Sheffield: Sheffield Academic Press.

Davis, Ellen F. (1989*). Swallowing the Scroll: Textuality and the Dynamics of Discourse in Ezekiel's Prophecy*. JSOTSup 78. Sheffield: The Almond Press.

Davis, John (1996). "An Anthropologist's View of Exchange." *Social Anthropology* 4: 213–226.

Day, John (1995). "William Robertson Smith's Hitherto Unpublished Second and Third Series Burnett Lectures on the Religion of the Semites." In Johnstone 1995: 190–202.

Day, Peggy L. (1989a). *Gender and Difference in Ancient Israel*. Minneapolis: Fortress.

—— (1989b). "From the Child Is Born the Woman: The Story of Jephthah's Daughter." In Day 1989a: 58–74.

Delcor, Mathias (1967). "Two Special Meanings of the Word *yād* in Biblical Hebrew." *JSS* 12: 230–234.

Descola, Philippe (1992). "Societies of Nature and the Nature of Society." In Adam Kuper, ed., *Conceptualizing Society*, 107–126. London and New York: Routledge.

Destro, Adriana (2001). "Il dispositivo sacrificale: Strumento della morte e della vita." *Annali di Storia dell'Esegesi* 18: 9–46.

———, and Mauro Pesce (1992). "Il rito ebraico di Kippur: Il sangue nel tempio, il peccato nel deserto." In G. Galli, ed., *Interpretazione e Perdono*, 47–73. Genova: Marietti.

——— (2002a). "Forgiveness of Sins without a Victim: Jesus and the Levitical Jubilee." In Albert I. Baumgarten, ed., *Sacrifice in Religious Experience*, Numen Book Series 93: 151–173. Brill: Leiden.

——— (2002b). "I corpi sacrificali: smembramento e rimembramento. I presupposti culturali di Rom 13,1-2." In L. Padovese, ed., *Atti del VII simposio di Tarso su Paolo Apostolo (Turchia: la chiesa e la sua storia)*, 85–113. Roma: Istituto Francescano di Spiritualità, Pontificio Ateneo Antoniano.

——— (2002c). "Between Family and Temple. Jesus and Sacrifices." *HTS* 58: 472–501.

——— (2004). "Repentance as Forgiveness, and the Role of Sacrifices in Jesus." In Adriana Destro and Mauro Pesce, eds. *Ritual and Ethics: Patterns of Repentance*. Paris-Louvain: Peeters: 29–54.

De Surgy, Albert (1988). *De l'universalité d'une forme africaine de sacrifice*. Paris: Ed. du CNRS.

Detienne, Marcel, and Jean-Pierre Vernant (1982). *La cucina del sacrificio in terra greca*. Torino: Boringhieri.

Dever, William G. (2003). *Who Were the Early Israelites and Where Did They Come From?* Grand Rapids, Mich.: Wm. B. Eerdmans.

Dhorme, P. (1923). "L'emploi métaphorique des noms de parties du corps en Hébreu et en Accadien." *RB* 32: 202–203.

Dietrich, Walter (1979). *Israel und Kanaan: Vom Ringen zweier Gesellschaftssysteme*. SBS 94. Stuttgart: Verlag Katholisches Bibelwerk.

——— (2002). "Ninive in der Bibel." In O. Loretz, K.A. Metzler, and H. Schaudig, eds., *Ex Mesopotamia et Syria Lux. FS Manfried Dietrich*, AOAT 28: 115–131. Münster: Ugarit Verlag.

Dorival, Gilles (2001). "Le sacrifice dans la traduction grecque de la Septante." *Annali di Storia dell'Esegesi* 18: 61–79.

Douglas, Mary (1963). *The Lele of the Kasai*. London: International African Institute.

——— (1966). *Purity and Danger: An Analysis of Concepts of Pollution and Taboo*. London: Routledge & Kegan Paul.

——— (1975). *Implicit Meanings: Essays in Anthropology*. London: Routledge & Kegan Paul.

—— (1993). *In the Wilderness: The Doctrine of Defilement in the Book of Numbers*. JSOTSup 158. Sheffield: Sheffield Academic Press.

—— (1996). *Natural Symbols: Explorations in Cosmology*. Second edition. London: Routledge.

—— (1999). *Leviticus as Literature*. Oxford: Oxford University Press.

—— (2004). *Jacob's Tears: The Priestly Work of Reconciliation*. Oxford: Oxford University Press.

Dresch, Paul (1989). *Tribes, Government, and History in Yemen*. New York: Oxford University Press.

Driver, Godfrey R. (1935). "Studies in the Vocabulary of the Old Testament VIII." *JThSt* 36: 293–301.

Duhm, Bernhard (1892). *Das Buch Jesaia*. Fifth edition 1968. Göttingen: Vandenhoeck & Ruprecht.

Durand, Jean-Marie (1992). "Unité et diversités au Proche-Orient à l'époque amorrite." In D. Charpin and F. Joannès, eds., *La circulation des biens, des personnes et des idées dans le Proche-Orient ancien* (Actes de la XXXVIIIème Rencontre Assyriologique Internationale, Paris, 8–10 juillet 1991), 97–128. Paris: Editions Recherche sur les Civilisations.

Durant, J. L. (1985). "Sacrifier, partager, répartir." *L'Uomo* 9: 53–62.

Durkheim, Emile (1976 [1915]). *The Elementary Forms of the Religious Life*. English translation by J. W. Swain. London: George Allen & Unwin.

—— (1984 [1893]). *The Division of Labor in Society*. Translated by George Simpson, with an introduction by Lewis Coser. New York: The Free Press.

Dutcher-Walls, Patricia (2002). "The Circumscription of the King: Deuteronomy 17:16-17 in its Ancient Social Context." *JBL* 121 (4): 601–616.

Eichrodt, Walter (1957). *Theologie des Alten Testaments*. Stuttgart: Klotz Verlag.

Eickelman, Dale F. (1981). *The Middle East: An Anthropological Approach*. Englewood Cliffs, N.J.: Prentice-Hall.

—— (2001). *The Middle East and Central Asia: An Anthropological Approach*. Fourth edition. Englewood Cliffs, N.J.: Prentice-Hall.

Eilberg-Schwartz, Howard (1990). *The Savage in Judaism: An Anthropology of Israelite Religion and Ancient Judaism*. Bloomington and Indianapolis: Indiana University Press.

——— (1994). *God's Phallus and Other Problems for Men and Monotheism*. Boston: Beacon, 1994.

Eisenstadt, S. N., and Luis Roniger (1980). "Patron-Client Relations as a Model of Structuring Social Exchange." *CSSH* 22: 42–77.

——— (1984). *Patrons, Clients and Friends: Interpersonal Relations and the Structure of Trust in Society*. Themes in the Social Sciences. Cambridge, U.K.: Cambridge University Press.

Elazar, Daniel J. (1995). *Covenant and Polity in Biblical Israel: Biblical Foundations and Jewish Expressions*. Covenant Tradition in Politics, vol. 1. London: Transaction Publishers.

Elliott, John H. (1981). *A Home for the Homeless: A Sociological Exegesis of 1 Peter, Its Situation and Strategy*. Philadelphia: Fortress Press.

——— (1985). Review of Wayne A. Meeks, *The First Urban Christians*, in *RSR* 11: 329–385.

——— (1987). "Patronage and Clientism in Early Christian Society: A Short Reading Guide." *Forum* 3: 39–48.

——— (1988). "The Fear of the Leer: The Evil Eye from the Bible to Li'l Abner." *Forum* 4 (4): 42–71.

——— (1995a [1993]). *Social-Scientific Criticism of the New Testament: An Introduction*. London: SPCK [*What Is Social-Scientific Criticism?* Guides to Biblical Scholarship. Minneapolis: Fortress Press].

——— (1995b). "Patronage and Clientage." In Richard Rohrbaugh, ed., *The Social Sciences and the New Testament*, 144–158. Peabody, Mass.: Hendrickson.

——— (2000). *I Peter: A New Translation with Introduction and Commentary*. AB 37B. New York: Doubleday.

——— (2002). "Jesus Was Not an Egalitarian: A Critique of an Anachronistic and Idealist Theory." *BTB* 32: 75–91.

Enright, D. J., ed. (1985). *Fair of Speech: The Uses of Euphemism*. Oxford: Oxford University Press.

Ensminger, Jean, ed. (2002). *Theory in Economic Anthropology*. Walnut Creek, Calif.: AltaMira.

Eriksen, Thomas Hylland (1993). *Ethnicity and Nationalism: Anthropological Perspectives*. Anthropology, Culture and Society. London: Pluto.

——— (2001). "Some Current Priorities for Ethnicity Studies." *Ethnicities* 1: 17–19.

Esler, Philip F. (1987). *Community and Gospel in Luke-Acts: The Social and Political Motivations of Lucan Theology*. SNTSMS 57. Cambridge, U.K.: Cambridge University Press.

—— (1994). *The First Christians in Their Social Worlds: Social-Scientific Approaches to New Testament Interpretation*. London and New York: Routledge.

——, ed. (1995a). *Modelling Early Christianity: Social-Scientific Studies of the New Testament in Its Context*. London and New York: Routledge.

—— (1995b). "Introduction: Models, Context and Kerygma in New Testament Interpretation." In Esler 1995a: 1–20.

—— (1995c). "God's Honour and Rome's Triumph: Responses to the Fall of Jerusalem in 70 CE in Three Jewish Apocalypses." In Esler 1995a: 239–258.

—— (1998a). *Galatians*. New Testament Readings. London: Routledge.

—— (1998b). "The Madness of Saul: A Cultural Reading of 1 Samuel 8–31." In J. Cheryl Exum and Stephen D. Moore, eds., *Biblical Studies/Cultural Studies,* Gender, Culture, Theory 7: 220–262. Sheffield: Sheffield Academic Press.

—— (2000a). "Jesus and the Reduction of Intergroup Conflict: The Parable of the Good Samaritan in the Light of Social Identity Theory." *BibInt* 325–327.

—— (2000b). "Models in New Testament Interpretation: A Reply to David Horrell." *JSNT* 78: 107–113 (A reply to David G. Horrell's "Models and Methods in Social Scientific Interpretation: A Response to Philip Esler," in the same issue of this journal).

—— (2001). "'By the Hand of a Woman': Culture, Story and Theology in the Book of Judith." In John J. Pilch, ed., *Social Scientific Models for Interpreting the Bible: Essays by the Context Group in Honor of Bruce J. Malina*, Biblical Interpretation Series 53: 64–101. Leiden: Brill.

—— (2002). "Ludic History in the Book of Judith: The Reinvention of Israelite Identity?" *BibInt* 10: 107–143.

—— (2003a). *Conflict and Identity in Romans: The Social Setting of Paul's Letter*. Minneapolis: Fortress Press.

—— (2003b). "Ezra-Nehemiah as a Narrative of (Re-Invented) Israelite Identity." *BibInt* 11: 413–426.

—— (2004). "The Context Group Project: An Autobiographical Account." In Aguilar and Lawrence 2004: 46–61.

—— (2005). *New Testament Theology: Communion and Community*. Minneapolis: Fortress Press.

Eslinger, Lyle (1981). "The Case of the Immodest Lady Wrestler in Deuteronomy XXV 11-12." *VT* 31: 269–281.

Evans-Pritchard, Edward E. (1951). *Social Anthropology*. London: Cohen & West.

Ewald, H. (1868). *Die Propheten des Alten Bundes*. 3 vols. 2d ed. Göttingen: Vandenhoeck & Ruprecht.

Exum, J. Cheryl, ed. (1989a). *Signs and Wonders: Biblical Texts in Literary Focus*. Semeia Studies. Atlanta: Scholars Press.

—— (1989b). "The Tragic Vision and Biblical Narrative: The Case of Jephthah." In Exum 1989a: 59–83.

—— (1992). *Tragedy and Biblical Narrative: Arrows of the Almighty*. Cambridge, U.K.: Cambridge University Press.

—— (1993a). *Fragmented Women: Feminist (Sub)Versions of Biblical Narratives*. Valley Forge, Pa.: Trinity Press International.

—— (1993b). "On Judges 11." In Brenner 1993: 131–144.

Fabian, Johannes (1983). *Time and the Other: How Anthropology Makes Its Object*. New York: Columbia University Press.

Fager, Jeffrey A. (1993). *Land Tenure and the Biblical Jubilee: Uncovering Hebrew Ethics through the Sociology of Knowledge*. JSOTSup 155. Sheffield: Sheffield Academic Press.

Faust, Avraham (2000). "The Rural Community in Ancient Israel during Iron Age II." *BASOR* 317: 17–39.

Fensham, F. Charles (1974). "Father and Son as Terminology for Treaty and Covenant." In Hans Goedicke, ed., *Near Eastern Studies in Honor of William Foxwell Albright*, 121–135. London and Baltimore: Johns Hopkins University Press.

Ferguson, R. Brian, ed. (1984). *Warfare, Culture, and Environment*. London: Academic Press.

——, and Neil L. Whitehead, eds. (1992). *War in the Tribal Zone: Expanding States and Indigenous Warfare*. Santa Fe: School of American Research.

Ferguson, Yale H. (1991). "Chiefdoms to City-States: The Greek Experience." In Timothy Earle, ed., *Chiefdoms: Power, Economy, and Ideology*, 169–192. New York: Cambridge University Press.

Fiensy, David A. (1991). *The Social History of Palestine in the Herodian Period: The Land Is Mine*. Studies in the Bible and Early Christianity 20. Lewiston, N.Y.: Edwin Mellen Press.

Finkelstein, Norman G. (2000). *The Holocaust Industry: Reflection on the Exploitation of Jewish Suffering*. London/New York: Verso.

Finley, Moses I. (1956). *The World of Odysseus*. London: Chatto and Windus.

Fischel, H. A. (1948). *The First Book of the Maccabees.* New York: Schocken Books.

Fitzpatrick-McKinley, Anne (1999). *The Transformation of Torah from Scribal Advice to Law.* JSOTSup 287. Sheffield: Academic Press.

Floyd, Michael H. (1994). "The Chimerical Acrostic of Nahum 1:2–10." *JBL* 113: 421–437.

Fokkelman, J. P. (1981). *Narrative Art and Poetry in the Books of Samuel: A Full Interpretation Based on Stylistic and Structural Analyses. Volume 1: King David (II Sam. 9–20 & I Kings 1–2).* Assen: Van Gorcum.

Forbes, Christopher (1997). *Prophecy and Inspired Speech in Early Christianity and its Hellenistic Environment.* Peabody, Mass.: Hendrickson.

Foster, George (1965). "Peasant Society and the Image of Limited Good." *American Anthropologist* 67: 293–315.

Frankel, Rafael (1994). "Upper Galilee in the Late Bronze-Iron I Transition." In Israel Finkelstein and Nadav Na'aman, eds., *From Nomadism to Monarchy: Archaeological and Historical Aspects of Early Israel*, 18–34. Jerusalem: Israel Exploration Society/Washington: Biblical Archaeology Society.

Frankland, Graham (2000). *Freud's Literary Culture.* Cambridge, U.K.: Cambridge University Press.

Frazer, James George (1918). *Folk-Lore in the Old Testament: Studies in Comparative Religion.* Legend and Law. London: Macmillan.

Frend, W. H. C. (1984). *The Rise of Christianity.* Philadelphia: Fortress Press.

Freud, Sigmund (1900). *The Interpretation of Dreams* (Standard Edition, vol. IV). London: Hogarth.

—— (1913). *Totem and Taboo* (Standard Edition, vol. 13). London: Hogarth.

—— (1921). *Group Psychology and the Analysis of the Ego* (Standard Edition, vol. 18). London: Hogarth.

—— (1930). *Civilization and Its Discontents* (Standard Edition, vol. 21). London: Hogarth.

—— (1939). *Moses and Monotheism* (Standard Edition, vol. 23). London: Hogarth.

—— (1939a). *Moses and Monotheism.* Trans. Katherine Jones. London: Hogarth.

Frick, Frank S. (1986). "Social Science Methods and Theories of Significance for the Study of the Israelite Monarchy: A Critical Review Essay." *Semeia* 37: 9–52.

——— (2002). "Norman Gottwald's *The Tribes of Yahweh* in the Context of 'Second-Wave' Social-Scientific Biblical Criticism." In Boer 2002a: 17–34.

Fritz, Volkmar (1996). "Monarchy and Re-urbanization: A New Look at Solomon's Kingdom." In Volkmar Fritz and Philip R. Davies, *The Origins of the Ancient Israelite States*, JSOTSup 228: 187–195. Sheffield: Sheffield Academic Press.

Fuchs, Esther (1993). "Marginalization, Ambiguity, Silencing: The Story of Jephthah's Daughter." In Brenner 1993: 116–130.

Fukui, Katsuyoshi, and David Turton, eds. (1979). *Warfare among East African Herders*. Senri Ethnological Studies 2. Osaka: National Museum of Ethnology.

Gager, John G. (1975). *Kingdom and Community*. Englewood Cliffs, N.J.: Prentice-Hall.

Galtung, Johan (1997–98). "Religions, Hard and Soft." *Cross Currents* 47 (4): 437–450.

Garrett, Susan (1989). *The Demise of the Devil: Magic and the Demonic in Luke's Writings*. Minneapolis: Fortress Press.

——— (1992). "Sociology of Early Christianity." *ABD* 6: 89–99.

Gay, Peter (1988). *Freud: A Life for Our Time*. New York: Norton.

——— (1995). *The Freud Reader*. London: Vintage.

Geertz, Clifford (1973a). *The Interpretation of Cultures*. New York: Basic Books.

——— (1973b). "Religion as a Cultural System." In Geertz 1973b: 87–125.

Gefou-Madianou, Dimitra (1993). "Mirroring Ourselves through Western Texts: The Limits of an Indiginous Anthropology." In Henk Driessen, ed., *The Politics of Ethnographic Reading and Writing: Confrontation of Western and Indigenous Views*. Nijmegen Studies in Development and Cultural Change 13: 160–181. Saarbrücken: Breitenbach.

Gennep, Arnold van (1960). *The Rites of Passage*. Chicago: University of Chicago Press.

Gilmore, David D. (1982). "Anthropology of the Mediterranean Area." *Annual Review of Anthropology* 11: 175–205.

Ginzburg, Carlo (1991). *Ecstasies: The Deciphering of the Witches' Sabbath*. Trans. Raymond Rosenthal. New York: Penguin Books.

Gluckman, Max (1966). *Custom and Conflict in Africa*. Oxford: Basil Blackwell.

Glueck, Nelson (1967). *Hesed in the Bible*. Cincinnati: Hebrew Union.

Gold, Barbara K. (1987). *Literary Patronage in Greece and Rome*. Chapel Hill and London: University of North Carolina Press.

Goodman, Felicitas D. (1988). *Ecstasy, Ritual and Alternate Reality*. Bloomington: Indiana University Press.

Gordon, Robert P. (1986). *1 & 2 Samuel: A Commentary*. Library of Biblical Interpretation. Exeter: The Paternoster Press.

Gorman, Frank H., Jr. (1990). *The Ideology of Ritual: Space, Time and Status in the Priestly Theology*. JSOTSup 91. Sheffield: Sheffield Academic Press.

Gosden, Chris (2004). "Grid and Group: An Interview with Mary Douglas." *Journal of Social Archaeology* 4: 275–287.

Gottwald, Norman K. (1979). *The Tribes of Yahweh: A Sociology of the Religion of Liberated Israel 1250–1050 B.C.E.* Maryknoll, N.Y.: Orbis.

———, ed. (1986). *Social-Scientific Criticism of the Hebrew Bible and Its Social World: The Israelite Monarchy*. Semeia 37. Decatur, Ga.: Scholars Press.

——— (1975). "Domain Assumptions and Societal Models in the Study of Pre-Monarchic Israel." In *Congress Volume Edinburgh 1974*, VTSup 28: 89–100. Leiden: Brill. Reprinted in Carter and Meyers 1996: 170–181.

——— (1985). *The Hebrew Bible: A Socio-Literary Introduction*. Philadelphia: Fortress Press.

——— (1992). "Sociology of Ancient Israel." *ABD* 6:79–89.

——— (1993). "Method and Hypothesis in Reconstructing the Social History of Early Israel." *ErIs* 24 [Abraham Malamat Volume]: *77–*82.

——— (1999). "Preface to the Reprint." In Norman K. Gottwald, *The Tribes of Yahweh: A Sociology of the Religion of Liberated Israel 1250–1050 B.C.E.* Reprint edition. The Biblical Seminar 66: xxvi–xlx. Sheffield: Sheffield Academic Press,.

——— (2001). *The Politics of Ancient Israel*. Library of Ancient Israel. Louisville: Westminster John Knox.

——— (2002). "Responses to the Contributors." In Boer 2002a: 172–185.

Gouldner, Alvin W. (1960). "The Norm of Reciprocity: A Preliminary Statement." *American Sociological Review* 25: 161–178.

Gowan, Donald E. (1987). "Wealth and Poverty in the Old Testament." *Interpretation* 41 (4): 341–353.

Grabbe, Lester L. (1995). *Priests, Prophets, Diviners, Sages: A Socio-*

historical Study of Religious Specialists in Ancient Israel. Valley Forge, Pa.: Trinity Press International.

—— (2000). "Ancient Near Eastern Prophecy from an Anthropological Perspective." In Nissinen 2000: 13–32.

—— (2001). "Sup-Urbs or only Hyp-Urbs? Prophets and Populations in Ancient Israel and Socio-Historical Method." In Grabbe and Haak 2001: 95–123.

——, and Robert D. Haak, eds. (2001). *'Every City Shall Be Forsaken': Urbanism and Prophecy in Ancient Israel and the Near East*. JSOTSup 330. Sheffield: Sheffield Academic Press.

Greifenhagen, F. V. (2002). *Egypt on the Pentateuch's Ideological Map*. JSOTSup 361. Sheffield: Sheffield Academic Press.

Grelot, Pierre (1995). *Les Juifs dans l'Évangile selon Jean: enquête historique et réflexion théologique*. Cahiers de la Revue Biblique 34. Paris: Gabalda.

Griffen, Jasper (1985). "Euphemisms in Greece and Rome." In Enright 1985: 32–43.

Grillo, Ralph D. (2003). "Cultural Essentialism and Cultural anxiety." *Anthropology Theory* 3: 157–173.

Grondin, Jean (1994). *Introduction to Philosophical Hermeneutics*. Foreword by Hans-Georg Gadamer. Yale Studies in Hermeneutics. New Haven and London: Yale University Press.

Grossman, Maxine L. (2002). *Reading for History in the Damascus Document: A Methodological Study*. STDJ 45. Leiden: Brill.

Grottanelli, Cristiano (1988). "Aspetti del sacrificio nel mondo greco e nella Bibbia ebraica." In Cristiano Grottanelli, and Nicola Franco Parise, eds. *Sacrificio e società nel mondo antico*. Bari: Laterza: 123–162.

—— (1998). "Gli errori di Saul." In Cristiano Grottanelli, *Sette storie bibliche*, 207–262. Brescia: Paideia.

—— (1999). *Il sacrificio*. Bari: Laterza.

Gruen, Erich (1998). *Heritage and Hellenism*. Berkeley: University of California Press.

Gruenwald, Ithamar (2001). "Sacrifices in Biblical Literature and Ritual Theory." *The Review of Rabbinic Judaism* 4.

Gunkel, Hermann (1996 [1901]). *Genesis*. Mercer Library of Biblical Studies. Trans. Mark Biddle. Macon: Mercer University Press.

Habel, Norman (1965). "The Form and Significance of the Call Narratives." *ZAW* 77: 297–323.

—— (1985). *The Book of Job: A Commentary*. OTL. Philadelphia: Westminster.

Hagedorn, Anselm C. (2000). "Guarding the Parents' Honour—
Deuteronomy 21.18-21." *JSOT* 88: 101–121.

——— (2004). *Between Moses and Plato: Individual and Society in
Deuteronomy and Ancient Greek Law*. FRLANT 204. Göttingen:
Vandenhoeck & Ruprecht.

Halfpenny, Peter (1982). *Positivism and Sociology: Explaining Social
Life*. London: Allen & Unwin.

Hall, Edward T. (1976). *The Silent Language*. Second edition. New
York: Doubleday.

Hall, Jonathan M. (1997). *Ethnic Identity in Greek Antiquity*. New
York: Cambridge University Press.

——— (2002) *Hellenicity: Between Ethnicity and Culture*. Chicago:
University of Chicago Press.

Halleran, Michael R. (1995). *The Plays of Euripides: Hippolytus*.
Warminster, England: Aris & Phillips Ltd.

Halpern, Baruch (1991). "Jerusalem and the Lineages in the Seventh
Century BCE: Kinship and the Rise of Individual Moral Liability." In
Baruch Halpern and Deborah W. Hobson, eds., *Law and Ideology
in Monarchic Israel*, JSOTSup 124: 11–107. Sheffield: Sheffield
Academic Press.

——— (1996). "Sybil, or the Two Nations? Archaism, Kinship, Alienation, and the Elite Redefinition of Traditional Culture in Judah in
the 8th–7th Centuries B.C.E." In Jerrold S. Cooper and Glenn M.
Schwartz, eds., *The Study of the Ancient Near East in the Twenty-
First Century: The William Foxwell Albright Centennial Conference*, 291–338. Winona Lake, Ind.: Eisenbrauns.

——— (2001). *David's Secret Demons: Messiah, Murderer, Traitor,
King*. Grand Rapids, Mich., and Cambridge, U.K.: Wm. B. Eerdmans.

Hals, Ronald L. (1989). *Ezekiel*. FOTL 19. Grand Rapids, Mich.: Wm.
B. Eerdmans.

Hamlin, E. John (1990). *At Risk in the Promised Land: A Commentary
on the Book of Judges*. ITC. Grand Rapids, Mich.: Wm. B. Eerdmans.

Hanson, K. C. (2002). "Jesus and the Social Bandits." In Wolfgang
Stegemann, Bruce J. Malina, Gerd Theissen, eds., *The Social Setting
of Jesus and the Gospels*, 283–300. Minneapolis: Fortress Press.

———, and Douglas E. Oakman (1998). *Palestine in the Time of Jesus:
Social Structures and Social Conflicts*. Minneapolis: Fortress Press.

Hanson, Paul D. (1979). *The Dawn of Apocalyptic: The Historical and*

Sociological Roots of Jewish Apocalyptic Eschatology. Revised edition. Philadelphia: Fortress Press.

Harnack, Adolf von (1990). *Marcion: The Gospel of the Alien God*. Durham, N.C.: Labyrinth Press.

Harrison, Simon (1993). *The Mask of War: Violence, Ritual and the Self in Melanesia*. Manchester and New York: Manchester University Press.

—— (1996). "War, Warfare." In Alan Barnard and Jonathan Spencer, eds., *Encyclopedia of Social and Cultural Anthropology*, 561–562. London and New York: Routledge.

—— (1999). "Identity as a Scarce Resource." *Social Anthropology* 7: 239–251.

—— (2003). "Cultural Difference as Denied Resemblance: Reconsidering Nationalism and Ethnicity." *CSSH* 45: 343–361.

Hasel, Gerhard F. (1972). *Old Testament Theology: Basic Issues in the Current Debate*. Grand Rapids, Mich.: Wm. B. Eerdmans.

Haslam, S. Alexander (2004). *Psychology in Organizations: The Social Identity Approach*. London: SAGE Publications.

Heilbroner, Robert L. (1962). *The Making of Economic Society*. Englewood Cliffs, N.J.: Prentice-Hall.

—— (1985). *The Nature and Logic of Capitalism*. New York: Norton & Co.

Hempel, Charlotte (1998). *The Laws of the Damascus Document: Sources, Tradition and Redaction*. STDJ 29. Leiden: Brill.

Henten, Jan Willem van, and Anton Houtepen, eds. (2001). *Religious Identity and the Invention of Tradition*. Assen: van Gorcum.

Herion, Gary A. (1981). "The Role of Historical Narrative in Biblical Thought: The Tendencies Underlying Old Testament Historiography." *JSOT* 21: 25–37.

—— (1986). "The Impact of Modern and Social Science Assumptions on the Reconstruction of Israelite History." *JSOT* 34: 3–33.

Herter, Hans (1978). "Genitalien." *RAC* 10: cols. 1–52.

Hertzberg, Hans Wilhelm (1964). *I & II Samuel: A Commentary*. OTL. London: SCM Press.

Herzfeld, Michael (1980). "On the Ethnography of 'Prejudice' in an Exclusive Community." *Ethnic Groups* 2: 283–305.

—— (1984). "The Horns of the Mediterraneanist Dilemma." *American Ethnologist* 11: 439–454.

—— (1991). *A Place in History: Social and Monumental Time in a Cretan Town*. Princeton Modern Greek Studies. Princeton: Princeton University Press.

—— (1995). "Les enjeux du sang: la production officielle des stéréo-types dans les Balkans. Les cas de la Grèce." *Anthropologie et Sociétés* 19: 37–51.

—— (1997). *Cultural Intimacy: Social Poetics in the Nation State.* New York and London: Routledge.

—— (2001). *Anthropology: Theoretical Practice in Culture and Society.* Oxford: Blackwell.

—— (2002a). "The European Self: Rethinking an Attitude." In Anthony Pagden, ed., *The Idea of Europe: From Antiquity to the European Union,* 139–170. Cambridge, U.K.: Cambridge University Press.

—— (2002b). "The Absent Presence: Discourse of Crypto-Colonialism." *South Atlantic Quarterly* 101: 899–926.

—— (2003). "Localism and the Logic of Nationalistic Folklore: Cretan Reflections." *CSSH* 45: 281–310.

—— (2004). *The Body Impolitic: Artisans and Artifice in the Global Hierarchy of Value.* Chicago: University of Chicago Press.

Hillers, Delbert R. (1964). *Treaty-Curses and the Old Testament Prophets.* BibOr 16. Rome: Pontifical Biblical Institute.

—— (1969). *Covenant: The History of a Biblical Idea.* Baltimore: Johns Hopkins University Press.

—— (1984). *Micah.* Hermeneia. Philadelphia: Fortress Press.

Hinkle, Steve, and Rupert Brown (1990). "Intergroup Comparisons and Social Identity: Some Links and Lacunae." In Abrams and Hogg 1990: 48–70.

Hirsch, Emil G. (1906). "The Twelve Tribes." In *The Jewish Encyclopedia* 12: 253–254. New York: Funk and Wagnalls.

Hobbs, T. Raymond (1995). "The Language of Warfare in the New Testament." In Esler 1995a: 259–273.

—— (1997). "Reflections on Honor, Shame, and Covenant Relations." *JBL* 116: 501–503.

Hoffner, Harry A., Jr. (1966). "Symbols for Masculinity and Femininity: Their Use in Ancient Near Eastern Sympathetic Magic Rituals." *JBL* 85: 326–334.

Hofstede, Geert (1980). *Culture's Consequences: International Differences in Work-Related Values.* Beverly Hills: Sage Publications.

Hogg, M. A. (2001). "A Social Identity Theory of Leadership." *Personality and Social Psychology Review* 5: 184–200.

——, and D. Abrams (1988). *Social Identifications: A Social Psychology of Intergroup Relations and Group Processes.* London and New York: Routledge.

————, R. Martin, et al. (2003). "Leader-Member Relations and Social Identity." In D. V. Knippenberg and M. A. Hogg, eds., *Leadership and Power: Identity Processes in Groups and Organizations*, 18–33. London: SAGE Publications.

————, and C. McGarty (1990). "Self-Categorization and Social Identity." In Abrams and Hogg 1990: 10–27.

Holm, Nils G., ed. (1982). *Religious Ecstasy*. Sweden: Almqvist & Wiksell International.

Holmberg, Bengt (2004). "The Method of Historical Reconstruction in the Scholarly 'Recovery' of Corinthian Christianity." In Edward Adams and David G. Horrell, eds., *Christianity at Corinth: The Quest for the Pauline Church*, 255–271. Louisville and London: Westminster John Knox.

Hölscher, Gustav (1914). *Die Propheten: Untersuchungen zur Religionsgeschichte Israels*. Leipsig: J. C. Hinrichs.

Horgan, Maurya P. (1979). *Pesharim: Qumran Interpretations of Biblical Books*. Washington, D.C.: The Catholic Biblical Association of America.

Horowitz, Donald L. (1975). "Ethnic Identity." In Nathan Glazer and Daniel P. Moynihan, eds., *Ethnicity: Theory and Experience*, 111–140. Cambridge, Mass.: Harvard University Press.

Horrell, David (1999). "Introduction: Social-Scientific Interpretation of the New Testament." In David Horrell, ed., *Social-Scientific Approaches to New Testament Interpretation*, 3–27. Edinburgh: T&T Clark.

———— (2000). "Models and Methods in Social Scientific Interpretation: A Response to Philip Esler." *JSNT* 78: 83–105.

Horsley, Richard A. (1994). "The Death of Jesus." In Bruce Chilton and Craig A. Evans, eds., *Studying The Historical Jesus: Evaluations of the State of Current Research*, 395–422. Leiden: Brill.

Hoyland, Robert G. (2001). *Arabia and the Arabs: From the Bronze Age to the Coming of Islam*. New York: Routledge.

Hughes, Geoffrey (1991). *Swearing: A Social History of Foul Language, Oaths and Profanity in English*. Oxford: Blackwell.

Humbert, P. (1933). "Die Herausführungsformel 'hinnenî êlêkâ.'" *ZAW* 51: 101–108.

Humphreys, W. Lee (1989). "The Story of Jephthah and the Tragic Vision: A Response to J. Cheryl Exum." In Exum 1989a: 85–96.

Hütteroth, Wolf-Dieter, and Kamal Abdulfattah (1977). *Historical Geography of Palestine, Transjordan and Southern Syria in the Late 16th Century*. Erlangen: Fränkische Geographische Gesellschaft.

Inge, Charles (1941). "Post-Scriptum." *PEQ* 73: 106–109.

Inhorn, Marcia Claire (1996). *Infertility and Patriarchy: The Cultural Politics of Gender and Family Life in Egypt*. Philadelphia: University of Pennsylvania Press.

———, and Frank Van Balen, eds. (2002). *Infertility around the Globe: New Thinking on Childlessness, Gender, Reproductive Technologies*. Berkeley: University of California Press.

Jackson, Michael (1998). *Minima Ethnographica: Intersubjectivity and the Anthropological Project*. Chicago: University of Chicago Press.

Jacobs, Alan H. (1979). "Maasai Inter-Tribal Relations: Belligerent Herdsmen or Peaceble Pastoralists." In Fukui and Turton 1979: 33–52.

Janowski, Bernd, and Michael Welker, eds. (2000). *Opfer. Theologische und kulturelle Kontexte*. Frankfurt a. M.: Surkamp.

Janzen, David (2002). *Witch-hunts, Purity and Social Boundaries: The Expulsion of the Foreign Women in Ezra 9–10*. JSOTSup 350. London: Sheffield Academic Press.

——— (2004). *The Social Meanings of Sacrifice in the Hebrew Bible: A Study of Four Writings*. BZAW 334. Berlin and New York: W. de Gruyter.

Jaspers, Karl (1953). *The Origin and Goal of History*. New Haven and London: Yale University Press.

Jenkins, Philip (2002). *The Next Christendom: The Coming of Global Christianity*. New York: Oxford University Press.

Jenson, Philip P. (1992). *Graded Holiness: A Key to the Priestly Conception of the World*. JSOTSup 106. Sheffield: Sheffield Academic Press.

Jobling, David, Peggy L. Day, and Gerald T. Sheppard, eds. (1991). *The Bible and the Politics of Exegesis: Essays in Honor of Norman K. Gottwald on His Sixty-Sixth Bbirthday*. Cleveland: The Pilgrim Press.

Johnstone, William, ed. (1995). *William Roberston Smith: Essays in Reassessment*. JSOTSup 189. Sheffield: Sheffield Academic Press.

Jonas, Hans (1963). *The Gnostic Religion: The Message of the Alien god and the Beginnings of Christianity*. Second edition, revised. Boston: Beacon Press.

Joubert, Stephan (2000). *Paul as Benefactor*. Tübingen: Mohr/Siebeck.

——— (2001). "Coming to Terms with a Neglected Aspect of Ancient Mediterranean Reciprocity." In *Social Scientific Models for Interpreting the Bible*, ed. J. J. Pilch. Leiden: Brill.

Kalinowski, Marc, ed. (2003). *Divination et société dans la Chine médiévale: Étude des manuscrits de Dunhuang de la Bibliothèque nationale de France et de la British Library*. Paris: Bibliothèque nationale de France.

Kallai, Zecharia (1976). "Tribes, Territories of." In Keith Crim, ed., *IDB*, Supplementary Vol. 5: 920–923. Nashville: Abingdon.

Kang, Sa-Moon (1989). *Divine War in the Old Testament and in the Ancient Near East*. Berlin and New York: Walter de Gruyter.

Kaplan, David, and Robert A. Manners (1972). *Culture Theory*. Foundations of Modern Anthropology Series. Englewood Cliffs, N.J.: Prentice-Hall.

Kaufmann, Yechezkel (1960). *The Religion of Israel: From Its Beginnings to the Babylonian Exile*. Chicago: University of Chicago Press.

Kautsky, John H. (1982). *The Politics of Aristocratic Empires*. Chapel Hill: University of North Carolina Press.

Kazin, Alfred, ed. (1976). *The Portable Blake*. New York: Penguin Books.

Keel, Othmar (1980). *Monotheismus im alten Israel und seiner Umwelt*. Fribourg: Verlag Schweizerisches Katholisches Bibelwerk.

Keenan, W. J. F. (2001). *Dressed to Impress: Looking the Part*. New York: Berg.

Keukens, Karlheinz H. (1982). "Richter 11,37f: Rite de Passage und Übersetzungsprobleme." *BN 19*: 41–42.

Khazanov, Anatoly M. (1994 [1984]). *Nomads and the Outside World*. Second edition. Madison: University of Wisconsin.

Khoury, Philip S., and Joseph Kostiner, eds. (1990). *Tribes and State Formation in the Middle East*. Berkeley: University of California.

Kimbrough, S. T. (1978). *Israelite Religion in Sociological Perspective: The Work of Antonin Causse*. Studies in Oriental Religions 4. Wiesbaden: Harrassowitz.

King, Helen (1994). "Producing Women: Hippocratic Gynaecology." In Leonie J. Archer, Susan Fischler, and Maria Wyke, eds., *Women In Ancient Societies*, 102–114. New York: Routledge.

Kippenberg, H. G., ed. (2005). *Max Weber. Wirtschaft und Gesellschaft. Die Wirtschaft und die gesellschaftlichen Ordnungen und Mächte*. Nachlaß Teilband 2. *Religiös Gemeinschaften*. Max Weber Studienausgabe I/22,2. Tübingen: Mohr Siebeck.

Kitchen, Kenneth (2003). *The Reliability of the Old Testament*. Grand Rapids, Mich.: Wm. B. Eerdmans.

Kloppenborg, John S. (2000). "Isaiah 5:1-7, The Parable of the Tenants

and Vineyard Leases on Papyrus." In S. G. Wilson and M. Des-
jardins, eds., *Text and Artifact in the Religions of Mediterranean
Antiquity*, 111–134. Waterloo: Wilfred Laurier University Press.

—— (2002). "Egyptian Viticultural Practices and the Citation of Isa
5:1-7 in Mark 12:1-9." *NovT* 44: 134–159.

Knauf, Ernst Axel (1988). *Midian. Untersuchungen zur Geschichte
Palästinas und Nordarabiens am Ende des 2. Jt. v. Chr.* Wiesbaden:
Harrassowitz.

Knauf-Belleri, Ernst Axel (1995). "Edom: The Social and Economic History." In Diana Vikander Edelman, ed., *You Shall Not Abhor an
Edomite for He Is Your Brother: Edom and Seir in History and Tradition*. Archaeology and Biblical Studies 3: 93–117. Atlanta: Scholars Press.

Knibb, Michael A. (1994). "The Place of the Damascus Document." In
Michael O. Wise, Norman Golb, John J. Collins, and Dennis G.
Pardee, eds., *Methods of Investigation of the Dead Sea Scrolls and
the Khirbet Qumran Site: Present Realities and Future Prospects*,
149–162. New York: The New York Academy of Science.

Knight, Douglas A., ed. (1983). *Julius Wellhausen and His Prolegomena
to the History of Israel. Semeia* 25. Chico, Calif.: Scholars Press.

Knohl, Israel (1995). *The Sanctuary of Silence*. Minneapolis: Fortress
Press.

—— (1996). "Between Voice and Silence: The Relationship between
Prayer and Temple Cult." *JBL* 115: 17–30.

Knoppers, Gary N. (1993). *Two Nations under God: The Deuterono-
mistic History of Solomon and the Dual Monarchies*. Vol. 1: *The
Reign of Solomon and the Rise of Jeroboam*. HSM 52. Atlanta:
Scholars Press.

—— (1994). *Two Nations under God: The Deuteronomistic History
of Solomon and the Dual Monarchies*. Vol. 2: *The Reign of Jeroboam, the Fall of Israel, and the Reign of Josiah*. HSM 53. Atlanta:
Scholars Press.

Koch, Klaus (1980). "*paḥad jiṣḥaq*—eine Gottesbezeichnung?" In
Rainer Albertz, et al., eds. *Werden und Wirken des Alten Testa-
ments,* Claus Westermann FS, 107ff. Göttingen: Vandenhoeck &
Ruprecht; Neukirchen-Vluyn: Neukirchner.

Koester, Helmut (1994). "The Historical Jesus and the Historical Situation of the Quest: An Epilogue." In Bruce Chilton and Craig A.
Evans, eds., *Studying The Historical Jesus: Evaluations of the State
of Current Research*, 535–545. Leiden: Brill.

Kohlberg, Lawrence (1981). *The Philosophy of Moral Development Moral Stages and the Idea of Justice*. San Francisco: Harper & Row.

Konstan, David (1995). "Patrons and Friends." *Classical Philology* 90: 328–342.

Kuhn, Sherman, and John Reidy, eds. (1968). *Middle English Dictionary*. Ann Arbor: University of Michigan Press.

Kuper, Adam (1988). *The Invention of Primitive Society: Transformations of an Illusion*. London and New York: Routledge.

LaBianca, Øystein S. (2003). "Subsistence Pastoralism." In Suzanne Richards, ed., *Near Eastern Archaeology: A Reader*, 116–123. Winona Lake, Ind.: Eisenbrauns.

Lakoff, George (1996). *Moral Politics: What Conservatives Know That Liberals Don't*. Chicago: University of Chicago Press.

Lambert, Yves. (1999). "Religion in Modernity as a New Axial Age: Secularization or New Religious Forms?" *Sociology of Religion* 60 (3): 301–333.

Lancaster, William (1981). *The Rwala Bedouin Today*. New York: Cambridge University Press.

Landes, Daniel, ed. (1991a). *Confronting Omnicide: Jewish Reflections on Weapons of Mass Destruction*. Northvale, N.J.: Jason Aronson.

——— (1991b). "A Vow of Death." In Landes 1991a: 5–11.

Lang, Bernhard (1983). *Monotheism and the Prophetic Minority: An Essay in Biblical History and Sociology*. SWBA 1. Sheffield: Almond Press.

———, ed. (1985). *Anthropological Approaches to the Old Testament*. Issues in Religion and Theology 8. Philadelphia and London: Fortress Press and SPCK.

Layton, Robert (1997). *An Introduction to Theory in Anthropology*. Cambridge, U.K.: Cambridge University Press.

Leach, Edmund R. (1969). "The Legitimacy of Solomon." In Edmund R. Leach, *Genesis as Myth and Other Essays*, 25–83. London: Jonathan Cape.

——— (1976 [1985]). "The Logic of Sacrifice." In Lang 1985: 136–150.

———, and D. Alan Aycock (1983). *Structuralist Interpretations of Biblical Myth*. Cambridge, U.K.: Cambridge University Press.

Lebra, Takie S. (1975). "An Alternative Approach to Reciprocity." *American Anthropologist* 77: 550–565.

Leeb, Carolyn S. (2002). "The Widow: Homeless and Post-Menopausal." *BTB* 32: 160–162.

Lehmann, Gunnar (2003). "The United Monarchy in the Countryside: Jerusalem, Judah, and the Shephelah during the Tenth Century B.C.E." In Andrew G. Vaughn and Anne E. Killebrew, eds., *Jerusalem in Bible and Archaeology: The First Temple Period*, SBLSS 18: 117–162. Atlanta: Scholars Press.

Lemche, Niels Peter (1985). *Early Israel: Anthropological and Historical Studies on the Israelite Society Before the Monarchy*. VTS 37. Leiden: Brill.

—— (1990). "On the Use of 'System Theory,' 'Macro Theories,' and 'Evolutionistic Thinking' in Modern Old Testament Research and Biblical Archaeology." *SJOT* 2: 73–88.

—— (1995). "Kings and Clients: On Loyalty between the Ruler and the Ruled in Ancient 'Israel.'" In Douglas A. McKnight, ed., *Ethics and Politics in the Hebrew Bible. Semeia* 66: 119–132. Atlanta: Scholars Press.

—— (1996). "From Patronage Society to Patronage Society." In Volkmar Fritz and Philip R. Davies, eds., *The Origins of the Ancient Israelite States*, JSOTSup 228: 106–120. Sheffield: Sheffield Academic Press.

Lenski, Gerhard E. (1966). *Power and Privilege: A Theory of Social Stratification*. Chapel Hill: University of North Carolina Press.

—— (1980). Review of Norman K. Gottwald's *The Tribes of Yahweh*. *RSR* 6: 275–278.

——, and Lenski, Jean (1987). *Human Societies: An Introduction to Macrosociology*. Fifth edition. New York: McGraw Hill. (See Nolan 1999 for latest edition.)

Levin, Christoph (2003). *Das Alte Testament*. Second edition. Munich: C. H. Beck Wissen.

Levine, Amy-Jill (2003). "Roland Murphy, The Pontifical Biblical Commission, Jews, and the Bible." *BTB* 33: 104–113.

Levine, Baruch A. (1989). *Leviticus Wyqr'*. The JPS Torah Commentary. Philadelphia: The Jewish Publication Society.

Levy, Jean-Philippe (1964). *The Economic Life of the Ancient World*. Chicago: University of Chicago Press.

Lewis, I. M. (1968). "Tribal Society." In David L. Sils, ed., *International Encyclopedia of the Social Sciences*, 16: 146–151. New York: Macmillan and The Free Press.

—— (2003). *Ecstasy in Religion: A Study of Shamanism and Spirit Possession*. London and New York: Routledge.

Lim, Timothy H. (1997). *Holy Scripture in the Qumran Commentaries and Pauline Letters*. Oxford: Clarendon Press.

——— (2002). *Pesharim*. Companion to the Qumran Scrolls 3. London: Sheffield Academic Press.

Lind, Millard C. (1970). "The Concept of Political Power in Ancient Israel." *Annual of the Swedish Theological Society* 7: 4–24.

Lindbeck, George A. (1984). *The Nature of Doctrine: Religion and Theology in a Postliberal Age*. Philadelphia: Westminster.

Lindblom, Johannes (1962). *Prophecy in Ancient Israel*. Philadelphia: Fortress Press.

Liverani, Mario (1990). *Prestige and Interest: International Relations in the Near East ca. 1600–1100 B.C.* Padova: Sargon.

Locher, Uli (1977). *Rural-Urban Migration and the Alleged Demise of the Extended Family: The Haitian Case in Comparative Perspective.* Working Papers—Centre for Developing Area Studies, McGill University. Montreal: Centre for Developing-Area Studies, McGill University.

Long, Burke O. (1984). *1 Kings*. FOTL 9. Grand Rapids, Mich.: Wm. B. Eerdmans.

Longman III, Tremper, and Daniel G. Reid (1995). *God Is a Warrior*. Grand Rapids, Mich.: Zondervan.

Loretz, Oswald (1977). "Hebräisch *tjrwš* und *jrš* in Mi 6,15 und Hi 20,15." *UF* 9: 353–354.

Lowenthal, Ira P. (1987). *"Marriage Is 20, Children Are 21": The Cultural Construction of Conjugality and the Family in Rural Haiti.* Unpublished dissertation, Johns Hopkins University, Baltimore, Md.

MacCormack, G. (1976). "Reciprocity." *Man* n.s. 11: 89–103.

Machinist, Peter (1997). "The Fall of Assyria in Comparative Perspective." In Simo Parpola and Robert M. Whiting, eds., *Assyria 1995: Proceedings of the 10th Anniversary Symposium of the Neo-Assyrian Text Corpus Project, Helsinki, September 7–11, 1995*, 179–195. Winona Lake, Ind.: Eisenbrauns.

Maine, Henry S. (1986 [1861]). *Ancient Law: Its Connection with the Early History of Society and its Relation to Modern Ideas*. Reprint edition. Tuscon: University of Arizona Press.

Malina, Bruce J. (1982). "The Social Sciences and Biblical Interpretation." *Interpretation* 37: 229–242.

——— (1985). Review of Wayne A. Meeks, *The First Urban Christians*. *JBL* 104: 346–349.

——— (1986a). *Christians Origins and Cultural Anthropology*: Atlanta: John Knox Press.

——— (1986b). "The Received View and What It Cannot Do: III John and Hospitality." In John H. Elliott, ed., *Social-Scientific Criticism of the New Testament and Its Social World. Semeia* 35: 171–194.

—— (1987). "Wealth and Poverty in the New Testament and Its World." *Interpretation* 41 (4): 364–367.

—— (1988). "Patron and Client: The Analogy behind Synoptic Theology." *Forum* 4 (1): 2–32.

—— (1991). "Interpretation: Reading, Abduction, Metaphor." In Jobling, Day, and Shepperd 1991: 253–266.

—— (1993 [1981, 2001]). *The New Testament World: Insights from Cultural Anthropology.* Second edition. Atlanta: John Knox Press.

—— (1995). *On the Genre and Message of Revelation: Star Visions and Sky Journeys.* Peabody, Mass.: Hendrickson.

—— (1996a). "Mediterranean Sacrifice: Dimensions of Domestic and Political Religion." *BTB* 26: 26–44.

—— (1996b). "Patron and Client: The Analogy behind Synoptic Theology." In Malina 1996d: 143–175.

—— (1996c). "Reading Theory Perspectives," In Malina 1996d: 3–31.

—— (1996d). *The Social World of Jesus and the Gospels.* London and New York: Routledge.

—— (1998). "Patronage." In John J. Pilch and Bruce J. Malina, eds., *Handbook of Biblical Social Values,* 151–158. Revised edition. Peabody, Mass.: Hendrickson.

—— (2000). "Three Theses for a More Adequate Reading of the New Testament." In Michael G. Lawler and Gail S. Risch, eds., *Practical Theology: Perspectives from the Plains,* 33–60. Omaha: Creighton University Press.

—— (2001 [1981, 1993]). *The New Testament World: Insights from Cultural Anthropology.* Third revised and expanded edition. Louisville: Westminster John Knox.

—— (2002). "We and They in Paul's Letter to the Romans." *HTS* 58: 608–631.

——, and Jerome H. Neyrey (1988). *Calling Jesus Names: The Social Value of Labels in Matthew.* Sonoma, Calif.: Polebridge Press.

——, and John J. Pilch (2000). *A Social-Science Commentary on the Book of Revelation.* Minneapolis: Fortress Press.

——, and Richard L. Rohrbaugh (1992). *A Social-Science Commentary on the Synoptic Gospels.* Minneapolis: Fortress Press.

——, and Richard L. Rohrbaugh (1998). *A Social-Science Commentary on the Gospel of John.* Minneapolis: Fortress Press.

Malul, Meir (1985). "More on Paḥad Yiṣḥāq (Genesis XXXI 42, 53) and the Oath by the Thigh." *VT* 35: 192–200.

Marcus, David (1986). *Jephthah and His Vow*. Lubbock: Texas Tech University Press.

Marques, José M., Darío Páez, and Dominic Abrams (1998). "Social Identity and Intragroup Differentiation as Subjective Social Control." In Worchel, Morales, Páez, and Deschamps 1998: 124–141.

Martin, James D. (1989). "Israel as a Tribal Society." In Clements 1989: 95–117.

Matthews, Victor Harold (1978). *Pastoral Nomadism in the Mari Kingdom (ca. 1830–1760 BC)*. Cambridge, U.K.: ASOR.

——— (1998). "Honor and Shame in Gender-Related Legal Situations in the Hebrew Bible." In Matthews, Levinson, and Frymer-Kensky 1998: 97–112.

———, and Don C. Benjamin (1993). *The Social World of Ancient Israel 1250–587 BCE*. Peabody, Mass.: Hendrickson.

———, Bernard M. Levinson, and Tikva Frymer-Kensky (1998). *Gender and Law in the Hebrew Bible and the Ancient Near East*. JSOTSup 262. Sheffield: Sheffield Academic Press.

Mauss, Marcel (1923–24). "Essai sur la don." *Année sociologique* 1: 30–186.

———, and Henri Hubert (1899). "Essai sur la nature et la fonction du sacrifice." *L'Année sociologique* 2: 29–138.

Mayes, Andrew D. H. (1979). *Deuteronomy*. NCB. Grand Rapids, Mich.: Wm. B. Eerdmans.

——— (1989). *The Old Testament in Sociological Perspective*. London: Marshall Pickering.

Mays, James Luther (1976). *Micah: A Commentary*. OTL. Philadelphia: Westminster.

Mbuwayesango, Dora Rudo (1997). "Childlessness and Woman-to-Woman Relationships in Genesis and in African Patriarchal Society: Sarah and Hagar from a Zimbabwean Woman's Perspective (Gen 16:1-16; 21:8-21)." *Semeia* 78: 27–36.

McCarter, Kyle P. (1980). *I Samuel*. AB 8. Garden City, N.Y.: Doubleday.

——— (1984). *II Samuel*. AB 9. Garden City, N.Y.: Doubleday.

——— (1988). "The Historical Abraham." *Interpretation* 42: 341–352.

McCarthy, Dennis J. (1972). "Berît and Covenant in the Deuteronomistic History." In *Studies in the Religion of Ancient Israel*, VTSup 23: 65–85. Leiden: Brill.

———— (1978). *Treaty and Covenant*. Rome: Pontifical Biblical Institute.

McGuire, William, ed. (1974). *The Freud/Jung Letters*. Princeton: Princeton University Press.

McInerney, Jeremy (2001). "Ethnos and Ethnicity in Early Greece." In Irad Malkin, ed. *Ancient Perceptions of Greek Ethnicity*, 51–73. Cambridge, Mass.: Harvard University Press.

McKane, William (1998). *Micah: Introduction and Commentary*. Edinburgh: T&T Clark.

McKenzie, John L. (1974). *A Theology of the Old Testament*. Garden City, N.Y.: Doubleday.

McKinney, John C. (1966). *Constructive Typology and Social Theory*. New York: Meredith.

McNutt, Paula M. (1999). *Reconstructing the Society of Ancient Israel*. Louisville: Westminster John Knox.

McVann, Mark, ed. (1995). *Transformations, Passages, and Processes: Ritual Approaches to Biblical Texts*. *Semeia* 67. Atlanta: Society of Biblical Literature.

Mead, Margaret (1973). "Ritual and Social Crisis." In Shaughnessy 1973: 87–101.

Meeker, Michael E. (1979). *Literature and Violence in North Arabia*. New York: Cambridge University Press.

Meeks, Wayne (1972). "The Man from Heaven in Johannine Sectarianism." *JBL* 91: 44–72.

———— (1983) *The First Urban Christians: The Social World of the Apostle Paul*. New Haven and London: Yale University Press.

———— (2005). "Why Study the New Testament?" Presidential Address to the Meeting of the Society of New Testament Studies, Barcelona, 4th August 2004. *NTS* 51: 155–170.

————, and Robert Wilken (1978). *Jews and Christians in Antioch in the First Four Centuries of the Common Era*. Missoula, Mont.: Scholars Press.

Mendelsohn, Isaac (1954). "The Disinheritance of Jephthah in the Light of Paragraph 27 of the Lipit-Ishtar Code." *IEJ* 4 (2): 116–119.

Mendenhall, George E. (1955). *Law and Covenant in Israelite and the Ancient Near East*. Pittsburgh: The Presbyterian Board of Colportage.

———— (1962). "The Hebrew Conquest of Canaan." *BA* 25: 66–87.

———— (1973). *The Tenth Generation: The Origins of the Biblical Tradition*. Baltimore: Johns Hopkins University Press.

———— (1976a). "Social Organization in Early Israel." In Frank Moore

Cross, Werner E. Lemke, and Patrick D. Miller, eds., *Magnalia Dei: The Mighty Acts of God: Essays on the Bible and Archaeology in Memory of G. Ernest Wright*, 132–151. New York: Doubleday.

——— (1976b). "Tribe." In Keith Crim, ed., *IDB*, Supplementary Vol. 5: 919–920. Nashville: Abingdon.

———, and Gary A. Herion (1992). "Covenant." In David Noel Freedman, ed., *ABD* 1: 1179–1202. New York: Doubleday.

Meyers, Carol (1978). "The Roots of Restriction: Women in Early Israel." *BA* 41: 91–103.

——— (1983a). "Of Seasons and Soldiers: A Topological Appraisal of the Premonarchic Tribes of Galilee." *BASOR* 252: 47–59.

——— (1983b). "Procreation, Production, and Protection: Male-Female Balance in Early Israel." *JAAR* 51: 569–593.

——— (1988). *Discovering Eve: Ancient Israelite Women in Context*. New York: Oxford University Press.

——— (1991). "To Her Mother's House: Considering a Counterpart to the Israelite *Bêt ʾab*." In Jobling, Day, and Sheppard 1991: 39–52.

——— (1995). "An Ethnoarchaeological Analysis of Hannah's Sacrifice." In Wright, Freedman, and Hurvitz 1995: 77–91.

Milgrom, Jacob (1991). *Leviticus 1–16: A New Translation with Introduction and Commentary*. AB 3. New York: Doubleday.

——— (2000). *Leviticus 17–22*. AB 3A. New York: Doubleday.

Mill, John Stuart (1909). *Principles of Political Economy*. London: Longmans, Green.

Miller, Cynthia L. (1996). *The Representation of Speech in Biblical Hebrew Narrative*. HSM 55. Atlanta: Scholars Press.

Miller, Robert J., ed. (1992). *The Complete Gospels: Annotated Scholars Version*. Sonoma, Calif.: Polebridge Press.

Mittmann, Siegfried. (1992). "'Königliches bat' und 'tēt-Symbol'. Mit einem Beitrag zu Micha 1,14b und 1 Chronik 4,21-23." *ZDPV* 107: 59–76.

Montgomery, J. A. (1939). "Hebrew *Ḥesed* and Greek *Charis*." *HTR* 32: 97–102.

Moor, Johannes C. de (1990). *The Rise of Yahwism: The Roots of Israelite Monotheism*. Louvain: Leuven University Press.

Moral, Paul (1961). *Le Paysan Haïtien*. Paris: Maisonneuve et Larose.

Morgan, Catherine (2003). *Early Greek States Beyond the Polis*. New York: Routledge.

Mott, Stephen C. (1996). "Wealth." In *HarperCollins Bible Dictionary*, 1202–1203. New York: Harper.

Moxnes, Halvor (1988). *The Economy of the Kingdom: Social Conflict and Economic Relations in Luke's Gospel*. OBT. Philadelphia: Fortress Press.

—— (1991). "Patron-Client Relations and the New Community in Luke-Acts." In Neyrey 1991: 241–68.

—— (1996). "Honor and Shame." In Richard Rohrbaugh, ed., *The Social Sciences and New Testament Interpretation*, 19–40. Peabody, Mass.: Hendrickson.

Muilenberg, James (1965a). "Isaiah 40–66." *IB* 5: 381–773.

—— (1965b). "The Office of the Prophet in Ancient Israel." In J. P. Hyatt, ed., *The Bible in Modern Scholarship*, 74–97. Nashville: Abingdon.

Munck, V. C. de (2002). "Contemporary Issues and Challenges for Comparativists: An Appraisal." *Anthropological Theory* 2: 5–19.

Murphy, Roland E. (2002). "The Biblical Commission, the Jews, and Scriptures." *BTB* 32: 145–149.

Musil, Alois (1928). *The Manners and Customs of the Rwala Bedouins*. New York: Czech Academy of Sciences and Arts/Charles R. Crane.

Myerhoff, Barbara (1982). "Rites of Passage: Process and Paradox." In Turner 1982: 109–135.

Myers, Jacob M. (1962). "Solomon." *IDB*, vol. K–Z: 401–408.

Narotzky, Susana (1997). *New Directions in Economic Anthropology*. London: Pluto Press.

Naveh, Joseph (1992). "The Numbers of *Bat* in the Arad Ostraca." *IEJ* 42: 52–54.

Nelson, Richard D. (1981). *The Double Redaction of the Deuteronomistic History*. JSOTSup 18. Sheffield: JSOT Press.

Newsom, Carol A., and Sharon H. Ringe, eds. (1992). *The Women's Bible Commentary*. Louisville: Westminster John Knox.

Neyrey, Jerome H. (1991). *The Social World of Luke-Acts: Models for Interpretation*. Peabody, Mass.: Hendrickson.

—— (1993). "Limited Good." In John J. Pilch and Bruce J. Malina, eds., *Handbook of Biblical Social Values*, 122–126. Updated edition 1998. Peabody, Mass.: Hendrickson.

—— (1998). *Honor and Shame in the Gospel of Matthew*. Louisville: Westminster John Knox.

—— (2004). *Render to God: New Testament Understandings of the Divine*. Minneapolis: Fortress Press.

Niditch, Susan (1997). *Ancient Israelite Religion*. Oxford and New York: Oxford University Press.

Nielsen, Edward (1995). *Deuteronomium*. HAT I/6. Tübingen: Mohr (Siebeck).

Nissinen, Martti, ed. (2000). *Prophecy in Its Ancient Near Eastern Context: Mesopotamian, Biblical, and Arabian Perspectives*. SBLSS 13: 1–11. Atlanta: Society of Biblical Literature.

——— ed., with contributions from C. L. Seow and Robert K. Ritner (2003). *Prophets and Prophecy in the Ancient Near East*. Writings from the Ancient World. Atlanta: Society of Biblical Literature.

Nogalski, J. D. (1993). *Redactional Processes in the Book of the Twelve*. BZAW 218. Berlin/New York: W. de Gruyter.

Nolan, Patrick, and Gerhard Lenski (1999). *Human Societies: An Introduction to Macrosociology*. Eighth edition. New York: McGraw-Hill.

Noll, Kurt L. (2001). *Canaan and Israel in Antiquity: An Introduction*. BS 83. New York: Sheffield Academic Press.

Nord, Warren A. (1995). *Religion and American Education: Rethinking a National Dilemma*. Chapel Hill: University of North Carolina Press.

Noth, Martin (1960) *The History of Israel*. Edinburgh: T&T Clark.

——— (1968). *Könige 1*. *BK* 9/1. Neukirchen: Neukirchener Verlag.

Oakes, P., S. A. Haslam, et al. (1998). "The Role of Prototypicality in Group Influence and Cohesion: Contextual Variation in the Graded Structure of Social Categories." In Worchel, Morales, Páez, and Deschamps 1998: 75–92.

Oakman, Douglas (1996). "The Ancient Economy." In Richard Rohrbaugh, ed., *The Social Sciences and the New Testament*, 126–143. Peabody, Mass.: Hendrickson.

——— (2004). "The Promise of Lutheran Biblical Studies." *Currents in Theology and Mission* 31 (1): 40–52.

O'Connor, Michael (1990). "Judges." In *NJBC* 132–144.

Oden, Robert A. (1987). "The Place of Covenant in the Religion of Israel." In Patrick D. Miller, Paul D. Hanson, and S. Dean McBride, eds., *Ancient Israelite Religion: Essays in Honor of Frank Moore Cross*, 429–447. Philadelphia: Fortress Press.

Olivier, H. (1996). "God as Friendly Patron: Reflections on Isaiah 5:1-7." *In die Skriflig* 30: 293–303.

Olyan, Saul M. (1996). "Honor, Shame, and Covenant Relations in Ancient Israel and Its Environment." *JBL* 115: 201–218.

——— (1998). "What Do Shaving Rites Accomplish and What Do They Signal in Biblical in Biblical Ritual Contexts?" *JBL* 117: 611–622.

———— (2000). *Rites and Rank: Hierarchy in Biblical Representation of Cult*. Princeton: Princeton University Press.

———— (2004). *Biblical Mourning: Ritual and Social Dimensions*. Oxford and New York: Oxford University Press.

Opelt, Ilona (1966). "Euphemismus." *RAC* 6: cols. 947–964.

Otto, Eckart (1994). *Theologische Ethik des Alten Testaments*. ThW 3.2. Stuttgart: Kohlhammer.

———— (1998a). "False Weights in the Scales of Biblical Justice? Different Views of Women from Patriarchal Hierarchy to Religious Equality in the Book of Deuteronomy." In Matthews, Levinson, and Frymer-Kensky 1998: 128–146.

———— (1998b). "'Um Gerechtigkeit im Land sichtbar werden zu lassen . . .': Zur Vermittlung von Recht und Gerechtigkeit im Alten Orient, in der Hebräischen Bibel und in der Moderne." In J. Mehlhausen, ed., *Recht, Macht, Gerechtigkeit*, Gütersloh, VWGTh 14: 107–145. Gütersloh: Gütersloher Verlagshaus.

———— (2001). "Die Tora in Max Webers Studien zum Antiken Judentum. Grundlagen für einen religions- und rechtshistorischen Neuansatz in der Interpretation des biblischen Rechts," *Zeitschrift für Altorientalische und Biblische Rechtsgeschichte* 7: 1–188.

———— (2002). *Gottes Recht als Menschenrecht: Rechts- und literaturhistorische Studien zum Deuteronomium*. BZAR 2. Wiesbaden: Harrassowitz.

————, ed. (2005). *Die Wirtschaftsethik der Weltreligionen: Das antike Judentum. Schriften und Reden 1911–1920. Max Weber-Gesamtausgabe I/21,1*. Tübingen: Mohr (Siebeck).

Outhwaite, William, and Tom Bottomore, eds. (1993). *The Blackwell Dictionary of Twentieth Century Thought*. Oxford: Blackwell.

Overholt, Thomas W. (1974). "The Ghost Dance of 1890 and the Nature of the Prophetic Process." *Ethnohistory* 21: 37–63.

———— (1982). "Prophecy: The Problem of Cross-Cultural Comparison." In Culley and Overholt 1981: 55–78.

———— (1986). *Prophecy in Cross-Cultural Perspective: A Sourcebook for Biblical Researchers*. SBLSBS 17. Atlanta: Scholars Press.

———— (1989). *Channels of Prophecy: The Social Dynamics of Prophetic Activity*. Minneapolis: Fortress Press.

———— (1996). *Cultural Anthropology and the Old Testament*. Guides to Biblical Scholarship. Minneapolis: Fortress Press.

Panourgia, Neni (1995). *Fragments of Death, Fables of Identity: An Athenian Anthropology*. New Directions in Anthropological Writing. Madison: University of Wisconsin Press.

Parker, Robert (1983). *Miasma: Pollution and Purification in Early Greek Religion*. Oxford: Clarendon Press.

Parpola, Simo (1997). *Assyrian Prophecies*. State Archives of Assyria. Volume 9. Helsinki: Helskinki University Press.

Parsons, Talcott (1937). *The Structure of Social Action*. New York: McGraw-Hill.

—— (1951). *The Social System*. Glencoe, Ill./London: Free Press/Routledge & Kegan Paul.

—— (1964). "II. Weber's Methodology of Social Science." In Weber 1964: 8–29.

—— (1978). "A Paradigm of the Human Condition." In *Action Theory and the Human Condition*, 352–433. New York and London: The Free Press.

Paskausas, R. Andrew, ed. (1995). *The Complete Correspondence of Sigmund Freud and Ernest Jones 1908–1939*. Cambridge, Mass.: Harvard University Press.

Patrick, Dale (1985). *Old Testament Law: An Introduction*. London: SCM Press/Atlanta: John Knox.

Paul, Robert A. (1991). "Freud's Anthropology: A Reading of the 'Cultural Books.'" In Jerome Neu, ed., *The Cambridge Companion to Sigmund Freud*, 267–286. Cambridge, U.K.: Cambridge University Press.

—— (1996). *Moses and Civilization: The Meaning behind Freud's Myth*. New Haven: Yale University Press.

Paul, Shalom M. (2002). "The Shared Legacy of Sexual Metaphors and Euphemisms in Mesopotamian and Biblical Literature." In Simo Parpola and Robert M. Whiting, eds., *Sex and Gender in the Ancient Near East: Proceedings of the 47th Rencontre Assyriologique Internationale, Helsinki, July 2–6, 2001*. Part II: 489–498. Helsinki: The Neo-Assyrian Text Corpus Project.

——, and Louis Isaac Rabinowitz (1971). "Euphemism and Dysphemism." *Encyclopedia Judaica* 6: 959–960.

Pearlman, Moshe. 1973. *The Maccabees*. London: Weindenfeld and Nicolson,

Peristiany, J. G., ed. (1966). *Honour and Shame: The Values of Mediterranean Society*. The Nature of Human Societies Series. Chicago: University of Chicago Press.

——, and Julian Pitt-Rivers, eds. (1992a). *Honor and Grace in Anthropology*. CSSCA 76. New York: Cambridge University Press.

—— (1992b). "Introduction." In Peristiany and Pitt-Rivers 1992a: 1–17.

Pesce, Mauro (2001). "Gesù e il sacrificio ebraico." *Annali di Storia dell'Esegesi* 18: 129–168.

Péter-Contesse, Rene (1993). *Lévitique 1–16*. Genève: Labor et Fides.

Petrochilos, Nicholas K. (1974). *Roman Attitudes to the Greeks*. Athens: Kovanis.

Petter, Thomas David (2003). "Shifting Ethnic Identities in Iron I Northern Moab: A Summary of Possible Evidence." Paper delivered at SBL, Atlanta, November 24, 2003; summary in *Abstracts 2003*, 119–120.

Pilch, John J. (1995–1997). *The Cultural World of Jesus Sunday by Sunday*. Three volumes. Collegeville, Minn.: The Liturgical Press.

——— (1998). "Appearances of the Risen Jesus in Cultural Context: Experiences of Alternate Reality." *BTB* 28: 52–60.

——— (1999a). *The Cultural Dictionary of the Bible*. Collegeville, Minn.: The Liturgical Press.

——— (1999b). "Jews and Christians." In Pilch 1999a: 98–104.

——— (2002a). "The Nose and Altered States of Consciousness: Tascodrugites and Ezekiel." *HTS* 58: 708–720.

——— (2002b). "Altered States of Consciousness in the Synoptics." In Wolfgang Stegemann, Bruce J. Malina, and Gerd Theissen, eds., *The Social Setting of Jesus and the Gospels*, 103–115. Minneapolis: Fortress Press.

——— (2004a). *Visions and Healing in Acts of the Apostles: How the Early Believers Experienced God*. Collegeville, Minn.: The Liturgical Press.

——— (2004b). "A Window into the Biblical World: Heaven in the Bible." *The Bible Today* 42 (4): 241–245.

Pitt-Rivers, Julian (1977). *The Fate of Shechem or The Politics of Sex: Essays in the Anthropology of the Mediterranean*. Cambridge Studies and Papers in Social Anthropology 19. Cambridge, U.K.: Cambridge University Press.

Polanyi, Karl (1944). *The Great Transformation*. New York: Rinehart.

Pongratz-Leisten, Beate (2001). "The Other and the Enemy in the Mesopotamian Conception of the World." In Robert M. Whiting, ed., *Melammu Symposia II*, 195–231. Helsinki.

Pope, Marvin H. (1955). *El in the Ugaritic Texts*. VTSup 2. Leiden: Brill.

——— (1962). "Oaths." *IDB* 3: 575–577.

——— (1972). "A Divine Banquet at Ugarit." In James M. Efird, ed., *The Use of the Old Testament in the New and Other Essays: Studies in Honor of William Franklin Stinespring,* 170–203. Durham, N.C.: Duke University Press.

—— (1973). *Job: Introduction, Translation, and Notes.* Third edition. AB 15. Garden City, N.Y.: Doubleday.

—— (1976). "Rainbow." *IDBSup* 725–726.

—— (1977). *Song of Songs.* AB 7C. Garden City, N.Y.: Doubleday.

—— (1992). "Bible, Euphemism and Dysphemism in the." *ABD* 1: 720–725.

Pressler, Carolyn (1993). *The View of Women Found in the Deuteronomic Family Laws.* BZAW 216. Berlin: W. de Gruyter.

Preuss, J. Samuel (1987). *Explaining Religion.* New Haven: Yale University Press.

Price, Sally (1978). "Reciprocity and Social Distance." *Ethnology* 17: 339–350.

Pritchard, James B. (1969). *Ancient Near Eastern Texts Relating to the Old Testament.* Princeton: Princeton University Press.

Puech, È. (2000). "Hodayot." In Lawrence H. Schiffman and James C. VanderKam, eds., *Encyclopedia of the Dead Sea Scrolls,* 1: 365–369. Oxford: Oxford University Press.

Qimron, Elisha (1986). *The Hebrew of the Dead Sea Scrolls.* HSS 29. Atlanta: Scholars Press.

—— (1992). "The Text of CDC." In Magen Broshi, ed., *The Damascus Document Reconsidered,* 9–49. Jerusalem: The Israel Exploration Society.

Quinn, D. Michael (1998). *Early Mormonism and the Magic World View.* Revised and enlarged edition. Salt Lake City: Signature Books.

Rad, Gerhard von (1965). *Old Testament Theology,* vol. 2. Trans. David M. G. Stalker. London: SCM Press.

Radcliffe-Brown, Alfred R. (1952). *Structure and Function in Primitive Society: Essays and Addresses.* London: Free Press.

Räisänen, Heikki (1997). "Attacking the Book, Not the People: Marcion and the Jewish Roots of Christianity." In *Marcion, Muhammad and the Mahatma: Exegetical Perspectives on the Encounter of Cultures and Faiths,* The Edward Cadbury Lectures at the University of Birmingham 1995–96: 64–80. London: SCM Press.

Rappaport, Roy A. (1999). *Ritual and Religion in the Making of Humanity.* CSSCA 110. Cambridge, U.K.: Cambridge University Press.

Raven, B. H. (1993). "The Bases of Social Power: Origins and Recent Developments." *Journal of Social Issues* 49: 227–251.

Redford, Donald B. (1992). *Egypt, Canaan, and Israel in Ancient Times.* Princeton: Princeton University Press.

Reventlow, Henning Graf (1992). "Theology (Biblical), History of." In *ABD* 6: 483–505. New York: Doubleday.

Reviv, Hanoch (1979). "The Strucure of Society." In Abraham Malamat, ed., *Kingship and the Ideology of the State,* 125–146. Jerusalem: Masada Press.

Ricoeur, Paul (1970). *Freud and Philosophy.* New Haven: Yale University Press.

Robert, Marthe (1976). *From Oedipus to Moses: Freud's Jewish Identity.* New York: Doubleday.

Roberts, J. J. M. (1971). "The Hand of Yahweh." *VT* 21: 244–251.

——— (1991). *Nahum, Habakkuk, and Zephaniah.* OTL. Louisville: Westminster John Knox.

Roberts, Simon (1979). *Order and Dispute: An Introduction to Legal Anthropology.* Harmondsworth: Penguin.

Rogerson, John W. (1970). "Structural Anthropology and the Old Testament." *BSOAS* 33: 490–500.

——— (1978). *Anthropology and the Old Testament.* Oxford: Basil Blackwell.

——— (1984). *Old Testament Criticism in the Nineteenth Century: England and Germany.* London: SPCK.

——— (1992). "Anthropology and the Old Testament." *ABD* 1: 258–262.

——— (1995). *The Bible and Criticism in Victorian Britain: Profiles of F. D. Maurice and W. Roberston Smith.* JSOTSup 201. Sheffield: Sheffield Academic Press.

Rohrbaugh, Richard L. (1978). *The Biblical Interpreter: An Agrarian Bible in an Industrial Age.* Philadelphia: Fortress Press.

Römer, Thomas C. (1998). "Why Would the Deuteronomists Tell about the Sacrifice of Jephthah's Daughter?" *JSOT* 77: 27–38.

Rost, Leonhard (1982 [1926]). *The Succession to the Throne of David* [ET of *Die Überlieferung von der Thronnachfolge Davids*, trans. Michael D. Rutter and David M. Gunn]. Historical Texts and Interpreters in Biblical Scholarship 1. Sheffield: The Almond Press.

Roth, Martha T. (1997). *Law Collections from Mesopotamia and Asia Minor.* SBL Writings from the Ancient World. Atlanta: Scholars Press.

Routledge, Bruce (2000). "Seeing through the Walls: Interpreting Iron Age I Architecture at Khirbat al-Mudayna al-'Aliya." *BASOR* 319: 37-70.

Rowton, Michael B. (1976). "Dimorphic Structure and the Tribal Elite." In *Al-Bahit: Festschrift Joseph Henninger, Studia Instituti Anthropos* 28: 219–257.

Rubinkiewicz, Ryszard, "Główne linie dokumentu Papieskiej Komisji Biblijnej 'Naród żydowski I jego Święte Pisma w Biblii chrześcijańskiej.'" *Collectanea Theologica* 73/1 (2003): 9–18.

Runions, Erin (2001). *Changing Subjects: Gender, Nation and Future in Micah*. Playing the Texts 7. London: Sheffield Academic Press.

Sachs, Susan (2004). "In Iraq's Next Act, Tribes May Play the Lead Role." *New York Times*, June 6, "Week in Review," 14.

Sahlins, Marshall (1972). *Stone Age Economics*. Chicago: Aldine-Atherton Inc.

Said, E. W. (1979). *Orientalism: Western Conceptions of the Orient*. London: Penguin.

Saller, Richard (1989). (1982). *Personal Patronage under the Early Empire*. New York: Cambridge University Press.

———— "Patronage and Friendship in Early Imperial Rome: Drawing the Distinction." In A. Wallace-Hadrill, ed., *Patronage in Ancient Society*, 49–62. London: Routledge.

Sasson, Jack (1998). "About 'Mari and the Bible.'" *Revue d'Assyriologie* 92: 97–123.

Sawyer, John F. A., ed. (1996). *Reading Leviticus: A Conversation with Mary Douglas*. JSOTSup 227. Sheffield: Sheffield Academic Press.

Sax, William S. (1998). "The Hall of Mirrors: Orientalism, Anthropology, and the Other." *American Anthropologist* 100: 292–301.

Schäfer, Peter (1997). *Judeophobia*. Cambridge, Mass.: Harvard University Press.

Schäfer-Lichtenberger, Christa (1996). "Sociological and Biblical Views of the Early State." In Volkmar Fritz and Philip R. Davies, *The Origins of the Ancient Israelite States*, JSOTSup 228: 78–105. Sheffield: Sheffield Academic Press.

Schearing, Linda S., and Steven L. McKenzie, eds. (1999). *Three Elusive Deuteronomists: The Phenomenon of Pan-Deuteronomism*. JSOTSup 268. Sheffield: Sheffield Academic Press.

Schiffman, Lawrence H. (1994). *Reclaiming the Dead Sea Scrolls: The History of Judaism, the Background of Christianity, the Lost Library of Qumran*. Philadelphia: The Jewish Publication Society.

Schloen, J. David (2001). *The House of the Father as Fact and Symbol: Patrimonialism in Ugarit and the Ancient Near East*. Winona Lake, Ind.: Eisenbrauns.

Schmitt, John (1992). "Virgin." In *ABD* 6: 853–854.

Schneider, Jane (1971). "Of Vigilance and Virgins: Honor and Shame and Access to Resources in Mediterranean Societies." *Ethnology* 9: 1–24.

Schorch, Stefan (2000). *Euphemismen in der Hebräischen Bibel.* Orientalia Biblica et Christiana 12. Wiesbaden: Harrassowitz.

Schrager, M. (1986–87). "A Unique Biblical Law." *Dor-le-Dor* 15: 190–194.

Scott, James C. (1976). *The Moral Economy of the Peasant: Rebellion and Subsistence In Southeast Asia.* New Haven: Yale University Press.

Segal, Alan F. (2004). *Life After Death: A History of the Afterlife in Western Religion.* New York: Doubleday.

Segal, Robert A., ed. (1998). *The Myth and Ritual Theory: An Introduction.* Oxford: Blackwell.

Senior, Donald (2003). "Rome Has Spoken: A New Catholic Approach to Judaism." *Commonweal* (January 31, 2003) 130: 20–23.

Setel, Drorah O'Donnell (1992). "Exodus." In Newsom and Ringe 1992: 26–35.

Seters, John van (1968). "The Problem of Childlessness in Near Eastern Law and the Patriarchs of Israel." *JBL* 87: 401–408.

Seybold, Klaus (1989). *Profane Prophetie: Studien zum Buch Nahum.* SBS 135. Stuttgart: Katholisches Bibelwerk.

——— (1989a). "Vormasoretische Randnotizen in Nahum 1." *ZAW* 101: 71–85.

Shapera, Issac (1963). *Government and Politics in Tribal Societies.* London: C. A. Watts & Co. Ltd.

Sharif, Regina (1983). *Non-Jewish Zionism: Its Roots in Western History.* London: Zed Press.

Shaughnessy, James D., ed. (1973). *The Roots of Ritual.* Grand Rapids, Mich.: Wm. B. Eerdmans.

Shaw, Charles S. (1993). *The Speeches of Micah: A Rhetorical-Historical Analysis.* JSOTSup 145. Sheffield: JSOT Press.

Sheppard, Gerald T. (1998). "Childs, Brevard." In Donald K. McKim, ed., *Historical Handbook of Major Biblical Interpreters,* 575–584. Downers Grove, Ill.: InterVarsity Press.

Shilling, Chris. (1993). *The Body and Social Theory.* London: Sage Publications.

Shoup, John (1990). "Middle Eastern Sheep Pastoralism and the Hima System." In John G. Galaty and Douglas L. Johnson, eds., *The*

World of Pastoralism: Herding Systems in Comparative Perspective, 195–215. New York: The Guilford Press.

Shryock, Andrew (1997). *Nationalism and the Genealogical Imagination: Oral History and Textual Authority in Tribal Jordan*. Berkeley: University of California Press.

Silver, Morris (1983). *Prophets and Markets: The Political Economy of Ancient Israel*. The Hague: Nijhoff.

Simkins, Ronald A. (1999). "Patronage and the Political Economy of Monarchic Israel." In Ronald A. Simkins and Stephen L. Cook, eds., *The Social World of the Hebrew Bible: Twenty-Five Years of the Social Sciences in the Academy. Semeia* 87: 123–244.

Simpson, George Eaton (1942). "Sexual and Familial Institutions in Northern Haiti." *American Anthropologist* 44: 655–674.

Simpson, J. A., and E. S. C. Weiner, eds. (1989) *The Oxford English Dictionary*. Second edition. Oxford: Clarendon Press.

Simpson, William Kelly, ed. (2003). *The Literature of Ancient Egypt*. New Haven: Yale University Press.

Skinner, Quentin, ed. (1985). *The Return of Grand Theory in the Human Sciences*. Cambridge, U.K.: Cambridge University Press.

Smend, Rudolf (1989). "Julius Wellhausen," in Rudolf Smend, *Deutsche Alttestamentler in drei Jahrhunderten*, 99–113. Göttingen: Vandenhoeck & Ruprecht.

——— (1995). "William Robertson Smith and Julius Wellhausen." In Johnstone 1995: 226–242.

Smith, Adam T. (2003). *The Political Landscape: Constellations of Authority in Early Complex Polities*. Berkeley: University of California Press.

Smith, E. R., and M. A. Zarate (1990). "Exemplar and Prototype Use in Social Categorization." *Social Cognition* 8 (1): 243–262.

Smith, Morton (1987). *Palestinian Parties and Politics that Shaped the Old Testament*. Second edition. London: SCM Press.

Smith, S. H. (1990). "'Heel' and 'Thigh': The Concept of Sexuality in the Jacob-Esau Narratives." *VT* 40: 464–473.

Smith, Wilfred Cantwell (1980). "The True Meaning of Scripture: An Empirical Historian's Nonreductionist Interpretation of the Qur'an." *International Journal of Middle Eastern Studies* 11: 487–505.

Smith, William Robertson (1885). *Kinship and Marriage in Early Arabia*. Cambridge, U.K.: Cambridge University Press.

——— (1956 [1889]). *Lectures on the Religion of the Semites: The Fundamental Institutions*. Second edition. New York: Meridian Books.

—— (1995) *The Religion of the Semites: Lectures on the Religion of the Semites (Second and Third Series) by William Robertson Smith*. Edited by John Day. JSOTSup Series 183. Sheffield: Sheffield Academic Press.

Solomon, Norman (1984). "Political Implications of the Belief in Revelation." *HeyJ* 25: 129–141.

Sparks, Kent (2003). "Genesis 49 and the Tribal List Tradition in Ancient Israel." *ZAW* 115: 327–347.

Speiser, Ephraim A. (1964). *Genesis*. AB 1: Garden City, N.Y.: Doubleday.

Spiegel, Herbert, M.D., and David Spiegel, M.D. (2004). *Trance and Treatment: Clinical Uses of Hypnosis*. Washington, D.C., and London, England: American Psychiatric Publishing.

Spronk, Klaas (1997). *Nahum*. HCOT. Kampen: Kok Pharos.

Stager, Lawrence E. (1985). "The Archaeology of the Family in Ancient Israel." *BASOR* 260: 1–35.

Stannard, David E. (1992). *American Holocaust: Columbus and the Conquest of the New World*. New York: Oxford University Press.

Stansell, Gary (1992). "Honor and Shame in the David Narratives." In Frank Crüsemann, Christof Hardmeier, and Rainer Kessler, eds., *Was ist der Mensch . . . ?: Beiträge zur Anthropologie des Alten Testaments*, 94–114. Munich: Chr. Kaiser.

—— (1994 [96]). "Honor and Shame in the David Narratives." *Semeia* 68: 55–79.

—— (1999). "The Gift in Ancient Israel." *Semeia* 87: 65–90.

—— (2002). "Gifts, Tributes, and Offerings." In Wolfgang Stegemann, Bruce J. Malina, and Gerd Theissen, eds., *The Social Setting of Jesus and the Gospels*, 349–364. Minneapolis: Fortress Press.

Stegemann, Ekkehard W., and Wolfgang Stegemann (1995). *Urchristliche Sozialgeschichte: Die Anfänge im Judentum und die Christusgemeinden in der mediterranen Welt*. Stuttgart: Verlag W. Kohlhammer.

—— (1999). *The Jesus Movement: A Social History of Its First Century*. Trans. O. C. Dean Jr. Minneapolis: Fortress Press.

Stegemann, Hartmut (1967). "Weitere Stücke von 4QpPsalm37, von 4QPatriarchal Blessings und Hinweis auf eine unedierte Handschrift aus Höhle 4Q mit Exzerpten aus dem Deuteronomium." *RdQ* 6: 193–227.

Steinberg, Naomi (1993). *Kinship and Marriage in Genesis: A Household Economics Perspective*. Minneapolis: Fortress Press

—— (1999). "The Problem of Human Sacrifice in War: An Analysis of Judges 11." In Cook and Winter 1999: 114–135.

Steudel, Annette (1993). "אחרית הימים in the Texts from Qumran." *RdQ* 16: 225–246.

Stevenson, T. R. (1992). "The Ideal Benefactor and the Father Analogy in Greek and Roman Thought." *Classical Quarterly* 42: 421–436.

Stocking, George W. (1987). *Victorian Anthropology*. New York: Free Press.

—— (1995a). *After Tylor: British Social Anthropology 1888–1951*. Madison: University of Wisconsin Press.

—— (1995b). "William Robertson Smith and the Merry Sacrificial Feast of Totemism." In Stocking 1995a: 63–83.

—— (1995c). "James Frazer and The Golden Bough: From Magic to Religion to Science." In Stocking 1995a: 126–151.

Storace, Patricia (1996). *Dinner with Persephone: Travels in Greece*. New York: Vintage.

Strauss, Barry S. (1986). *Athens after the Peloponnesian War: Class, Faction, and Policy, 403–386 BC*. London: Croom Helm.

Streeten, Paul (1964). "Wealth." In Julius Gould and William L. Kolb, eds., *A Dictionary of the Social Sciences*, 755–756. New York: Free Press.

Stronach, D. (1997). "Notes on the Fall of Ninive." In Somi Parpola and Robert M. Whiting, eds., *Assyria 1995: Proceedings of the 10th Anniversary Symposium of the Neo-Assyrian Text Corpus Project, Helsinki, September 7–11, 1995, 307–324*. Winona Lake, Ind.: Eisenbrauns.

Strugnell, John (1970). "Notes en marge du volume V des 'Discoveries in the Judaean Desert of Jordan.'" *RdQ* 7: 163–276.

Stuhlmacher, Peter (1977). *Historical Criticism and Theological Interpretation of Scripture: Toward a Hermeutics of Consent*. Philadelphia: Fortress Press.

Sweeney, Marvin A. (1992). "Concerning the Structure and Generic Character of the Book of Nahum." *ZAW* 104: 354–377.

—— (1996). *Isaiah 1–39, with an Introduction to Prophetic Literature*. FOTL 16. Grand Rapids, Mich.: Wm. B. Eerdmans.

—— (2001). *King Josiah of Judah: The Lost Messiah of Israel*. Oxford: Oxford University Press.

Swingewood, Alan (1991). *A Short History of Sociological Thought*. Second edition. London: Macmillan.

Sykes, Bryan (2003). *Adam's Curse: A Future without Men*. New York: Norton.

Synnott, Anthony (1994). *The Body Social: Symbolism, Self and Society*. London and New York: Routledge.

Tajfel, Henri (1978). *Differentiation between Social Groups: Studies in the Social Psychology of Intergroup Relations*. London: Academic Press.

—— (1981). "Social Stereotypes and Social Groups." In John C. Turner and Howard Giles, eds., *Intergroup Behavior*, 144–167. Oxford: Basil Blackwell.

Talmon, Shemeryahu (1979). "Kingship and the Ideology of the State." In Abraham Malamat, ed., *The Age of the Monarchies: Culture and Society*, 3–26. Jerusalem: Masada Press.

Tambiah, Stanley J. (1985). *Culture, Thought, and Social Action*. Cambridge, Mass.: Harvard University Press.

Tapp, Anne Michele (1989). "An Ideology of Expendability: Virgin Daughter Sacrifice." In Bal 1989a: 157–174.

Taves, Ann (1999). *Fits, Trances, and Visions: Experiencing Religion and Explaining Experience from Wesley to James*. Princeton: Princeton University Press.

Taylor, Charles (1977). "Interpretation and the Sciences of Man." In Fred Dallmayr and Thomas McCarthy, eds., *Understanding and Social Inquiry*, 101–131. Notre Dame, Ind.: University of Notre Dame Press.

Theissen, Gerd (1978). *The First Followers of Jesus*. London: SCM.

—— (1984). *Biblical Faith: An Evolutionary Approach*. London: SCM Press.

Thompson, John L. (2001). *Writing the Wrongs: Women of the Old Testament among Biblical Commentators from Philo through the Reformation*. New York: Oxford University Press.

Tigay, Jeffrey H. (1996). *Deuteronomy*. JPS Torah Commentary. Philadelphia: Jewish Publication Society.

Todorov, T. (1993). *On Human Diversity: Antionalism, Racism and Exoticism in French Thought*. Cambridge, Mass.: Harvard University Press.

Tönnies, Ferdinand (1955 [1887]). *Community and Association*. Translation of *Gemeinschaft und Gesellschaft* (1887) and supplementation by Charles P. Loomis. London: Routledge.

Toorn, Karl van der (2001). "The Exodus as Charter Myth." In Jan Willem van Henten and Anton Houtepen, eds., *Religious Identity and the Invention of Tradition*, 113–127. Assen: van Gorcum.

Triandis, Harry C. (1990). "Cross-Cultural Studies of Individualism and

Collectivism." In Richard A. Dienstbier and John J. Berman, eds., *Nebraska Symposium on Motivation 37: 41–133: Cross Cultural Perspectives.* Lincoln and London: University of Nebraska Press.

Trible, Phyllis (1984). *Texts of Terror: Literary-Feminist Readings of Biblical Narratives.* OBT. Philadelphia: Fortress Press.

Tsevat, Matitiahu (1974). *"betûlâ," "betûlîm." TDOT* 1: 340–343.

Turner, John C. (1985). "Social Categorization and the Self-Concept: A Social-Cognitive Theory of Group Behavior." In E. J. Lawler, ed., *Advances in Group Processes: Theory and Research,* 2. Greenwich, Ct.: JAI Press.

Turner, Victor (1967). *The Forest of Symbols: Aspects of Ndembu Ritual.* Ithaca, N.Y., and London: Cornell University Press.

—— (1969). *The Ritual Process: Structure and Anti-Structure.* Chicago: Aldine Publishing Company.

—— (1980). "Social Dramas and Stories about Them." *Critical Inquiry* 7: 141–168.

——, ed. (1982). *Celebration: Studies in Festivity and Ritual.* Washington, D.C.: Smithsonian Institution Press.

Twain, Mark (1961). *Roughing It.* With an Introduction by Rodman W. Paul. Sixth printing. New York: Holt, Rinehart and Winston.

Valeri, Valerio (1985). *Kingship and Sacrifice: Ritual and Society in Ancient Hawaii.* Chicago and London: University of Chicago Press.

—— (1994). "Wild Victims: Hunting as Sacrifice and Sacrifice as Hunting in Huaulu." *History of Religions* 24: 101–131.

Vaux, Roland de (1962). *Ancient Israel: Its Life and Institutions.* Trans. John McHugh. New York: McGraw-Hill.

Veenker, Ronald. A. (1999–2000). "Forbidden Fruit: Ancient Near Eastern Sexual Metaphors." *HUCA* 70–71: 57–73.

Velikovsky, Immanuel (1960). *Oedipus and Akhenaten: Myth and History.* London: Sidgwick and Jackson.

Vogel, Dan, ed. (1996–2003). *Early Mormon Documents,* volumes 1–5. Salt Lake City: Signature Books.

Vuilleumier, René, and Carl-Albert Keller (1990). *Michée, Nahoum, Habacuc, Sophonie.* CAT Xib. Second edition. Geneva: Labor et Fides.

Wacquant, Loïc J. D. (1993). "Positivism." In Outhwaite and Bottomore 1993: 495–498.

Wahlde, U. C. von (2000). "'The Jews' in the Gospel of John." *ETL* 76: 30–55.

Wallace-Hadrill, Andrew, ed. (1989). *Patronage in Ancient Society.* London: Routledge.

Wallis, Louis (1912). *The Sociological Study of the Bible*. Chicago: University of Chicago Press.

—— (1935). *God and the Social Context*. Chicago: University of Chicago Press.

—— (1942). *The Bible Is Human*. New York: Columbia University Press.

Walsh, Jerome T. (2004). "'You Shall Cut Off Her . . . Palm'? A Reexamination of Deuteronomy 25:11-12." *JSS* 49: 47–58.

Watson, Wilfred G. E. (1995). *Classical Hebrew Poetry: A Guide to its Techniques*. JSOTSup 26. Second edition. Sheffield: Sheffield Academic Press.

Watts, James W. (1999). *Reading Law: The Rhetorical Shaping of the Pentateuch*. BS 59. Sheffield: Sheffield Academic Press.

Weber, Max (1922 [1972]). *Wirtschaft und Gesellschaft. Grundriss der verstehenden Soziologie*. Fifth edition. Tübingen [ET: Guenther Roth and Claus Wittich, eds., *Economy and Society*, vol. 1 (New York: Bedminister Press, 1968)].

—— (1952 [1917–1919]). *Ancient Judaism*. Translated and edited by E. Shils and H. A. Finch. New York: Free Press.

—— (1964 [1947]). *The Theory of Social and Economic Organization*. Translation of *Grundriss der Sozialökonomic: Wirtschaft und Gesellschaft* (1922) by A. M. Henderson and Talcott Parsons, edited by Talcott Parsons. New York and London: The Free Press and Collier Macmillan Publishers.

—— (1968a [1880, 1949]). *The Methodology of the Social Sciences*. Translated and edited by E. A. Shils and H. A. Finch. New York: The Free Press.

—— (1968b [1916, 1951]). *The Religion of China: Confucianism and Taoism*. Translated and edited by Hans H. Gerth. New York: Free Press.

—— (1976 [1908]). *The Agrarian Sociology of Ancient Civilizations*. Translated by R. I. Frank. London: NLB.

Weems, Renita J. (1988). *Just a Sister Away: A Womanist Vision of Women's Relationships in the Bible*. San Diego, Calif.: LuraMedia.

Wees, Hans van (1998). "The Law of Gratitude: Reciprocity in Anthropological Theory." In Christopher Gill, Norman Postlethwaite, and Richard Seaford, eds., *Reciprocity in Ancient Greece*, 13–49. Oxford: Oxford University Press.

Weinfeld, Moshe (1973). "Covenant Terminology in the Ancient Near East and Its Influence on the West." *JAOS* 93: 190–199.

—— (1975). "Berit—Covenant vs. Obligation." *Biblica* 56: 120–128.

—— (1977). "Covenant." In *TDOT* 2:253–279.

Wellhausen, Julius (1963). *Die kleinen Propheten übersetzt und erklärt.* Third edition. Berlin: de Gruyter.

Wenham, Gordon J. (1972). "Betulah, 'A Girl of Marriageable Age.'" *VT* 22: 326–48.

Werner, Heinz (1948). *Comparative Psychology of Mental Development.* Revised edition. New York: International Universities Press.

——, and Bernard Kaplan (1963). *Symbol Formation: An Organismic-Developmental Approach to Language and the Expression of Thought.* New York: John Wiley & Sons.

Westermann, Claus (1969). *Isaiah 40–66: A Commentary.* Trans. David M. G. Stalker Philadelphia: Westminster.

—— (1981). *Genesis 12–36.* CC. Trans. John J. Scullion. Minneapolis: Fortress Press.

White, Marsha C. (1997). *The Elijah Legends and Jehu's Coup.* BJS 311. Atlanta: Scholars Press.

Whitelam, Keith (1996). *The Invention of Ancient Israel: The Silencing of Palestinian History.* London: Routledge.

Whiting, Robert M. (1995). "Amorite Tribes and Nations of Second-Millennium Western Asia." In Jack M. Sasson, ed., *Civilizations of the Ancient Near East*, vol. 2: 1231–1242. New York: Scribner.

Wikan, Unni (1999). "Culture: A New Concept of Race," *Social Anthropology* 7: 57–64.

—— (2002). *Generous Betrayal: Politics of Culture in the New Europe.* Chicago: University of Chicago Press.

Willis, Timothy M. (1997). "The Nature of Jephthah's Authority." *CBQ* 59: 33–43.

—— (2001). *The Elders of the City. A Study of the Elders-Laws in Deuteronomy.* SBLMS 55. Atlanta: Society of Biblical Literature.

Wilson, Bryan (1975). *Magic and the Millennium.* St Albans: Paladin.

Wilson, P. Eddy (1997). "Deuteronomy XXV 11-12—One for the Books." *VT* 47: 220–235.

Wilson, Robert R. (1977). *Genealogy and History in the Biblical World.* New Haven: Yale University Press.

—— (1979). "Prophecy and Ecstasy: A Reexamination." *JBL* 98: 321–337. Reprinted in Culley and Overholt 1996: 404–422.

—— (1980). *Prophecy and Society in Ancient Israel.* Philadelphia: Fortress Press.

—— (1984). *Sociological Approaches to the Old Testament*. Guides to Biblical Scholarship. Philadelphia: Fortress Press.

—— (1996). "Prophecy and Ecstasy: A Reexamination." In Carter and Meyers 1996: 404–422.

Winch, Peter (1976 [1958]). *The Idea of a Social Science and Its Relation to Philosophy*. London: Routledge & Kegan Paul.

Wolf, Eric R. (1966). "Kinship, Friendship, and Patron-Client Relations in Complex Societies." In Michael Banton, ed., *The Social Anthropology of Complex Societies*, 1–22. New York: Tavistock Publications.

Wolff, Hans Walter (1990). *Micah: A Commentary*. CC. Trans. Gary Stansell. Minneapolis: Augsburg.

Worchel, Stephen, J. Franscisco Morales, Dario Páez, and Jean-Claude Deschamps, eds. (1998). *Social Identity: International Perspectives*. London: SAGE Publications.

Worsley, Peter (1970). "Sociology as a Discipline." In Peter Worsley et al., eds., *Introducing Sociology*, 19–68. Harmondsworth: Penguin.

Woude, A. S. van der (1975). "יד *jad* Hand." *THAT* 1: 667–674.

—— (1982). "Wicked Priest or Wicked Priests? Reflections on the Identification of the Wicked Priest in the Habakkuk Commentary." *JJS* 23: 349–359.

Wright, David P., David Noel Freedman, and Avi Hurvitz, eds. (1995). *Pomegranates and Golden Bells: Studies in Biblical, Jewish, and Near Eastern Ritual, Law, and Literature in Honor of Jacob Milgrom*. Winona Lake, Ind.: Eisenbrauns.

Wyke, Maria, ed. (1997). *Parchments of Gender: Deciphering the Bodies of Antiquity*. Oxford: Clarendon Press.

Yalouri, Eleana (2001). *The Acropolis: Global Fame, Local Claim*. Oxford and New York: Berg.

Yee, Gale E. (1987). *Composition and Tradition in the Book of Hosea: A Redaction Critical Investigation*. SBLDS 102. Atlanta: Scholars Press.

Yerushalmi, Yosef Hayim (1991). *Freud's Moses*. New Haven: Yale University Press.

Young, Franklin W. (1962). "Wealth." In IDB 4: 818–819.

Yurco, Frank J. (1997). "Merneptah's Canaanite Campaign and Israelite Origins." In Ernest S. Frerichs, and Leonard H. Lesko, eds., *Exodus: The Egyptian Evidence*, 27–55. Winona Lake, Ind.: Eisenbrauns.

Zelinsky, Wilbur (1992 [1973]). *The Cultural Geography of the United States*. Revised edition. Englewood Cliffs, N.J.: Prentice-Hall.

Zevit, Ziony (2001). *The Religions of Ancient Israel: A Synthesis of Parallactic Approaches*. New York: Continuum.

Zimmerli, Walther (1979). *Ezekiel 1*. Hermeneia. Trans. Ronald E. Clements. Philadelphia: Fortress Press.

Indexes

Ancient Sources

Names